KU-273-302

Brad Stone is senior executive editor of global technology at *Bloomberg News* and the author of the international bestseller *The Everything Store: Jeff Bezos and the Age of Amazon*, and *The Upstarts: Uber, Airbnb, and the Battle for the New Silicon Valley*. He has covered Silicon Valley for more than twenty years and lives in the San Francisco Bay area.

Praise for *Amazon Unbound*

'There are really only a handful of writers who can craft a page-turning narrative about the most transformative business ideas. Brad Stone is one. In this book, he gives us his second must-read account of how the world's most important company and technology titan captured not only global retail, but Washington, Hollywood, outer space and your brain.' **Rana Foroohar, author of *Makers and Takers* and *Don't Be Evil***

'In this vivid, anecdote-filled page-turner of a book, Stone goes deep inside a company with colossal power... With rare access to Amazon executives, readers are taken inside Amazon meetings, see up close Jeff Bezos's brilliance but also his belligerence, understand the trade-off between impressive efficiency versus the perils of market dominance, and get an up-to-the-moment appreciation of why government is now awake to the monopoly dangers posed by digital giants.' **Ken Auletta, author of *Googled***

ALSO BY BRAD STONE

The Upstarts
The Everything Store
Gearheads

Amazon Unbound

JEFF BEZOS *and the* INVENTION
of a GLOBAL EMPIRE

Brad Stone

SIMON &
SCHUSTER

London · New York · Sydney · Toronto · New Delhi

First published in the United States by Simon & Schuster Inc., 2021
First published in Great Britain by Simon & Schuster UK Ltd, 2021
This edition published in Great Britain by Simon & Schuster UK Ltd, 2022

1 3 5 7 9 10 8 6 4 2

Simon & Schuster UK Ltd
1st Floor
222 Gray's Inn Road
London WC1X 8HB

www.simonandschuster.co.uk
www.simonandschuster.com.au
www.simonandschuster.co.in

Simon & Schuster Australia, Sydney
Simon & Schuster India, New Delhi

A CIP catalogue record for this book
is available from the British Library

Paperback ISBN: 978-1-3985-0099-0
eBook ISBN: 978-1-3985-0098-3

Interior design by Paul Dippolito

Printed in the UK by CPI Group (UK) Ltd, Croydon, CR0 4YY

To my father, Robert Stone

Contents

"His genius was not in inventing; rather, it was in inventing a system of invention. Dozens of researchers and engineers and developmental tinkerers labored beneath Edison in a carefully constructed hierarchical organization that he founded and oversaw."

—Graham Moore, *The Last Days of Night: A Novel*

"It has always seemed strange to me.... The things we admire in men—kindness and generosity, openness, honesty, understanding, and feeling—are the concomitants of failure in our system. And those traits we detest—sharpness, greed, acquisitiveness, meanness, egotism, and self-interest—are the traits of success. And while men admire the quality of the first, they love the produce of the second."

—John Steinbeck, *Cannery Row*

Amazon
Unbound

Introduction

I t was the kind of large indoor gathering that would soon feel anachronistic, like an ancient custom from a lost civilization. On a Sunday night in November 2019, one month before Covid-19 first appeared in Wuhan, China, kicking off the worst pandemic in modern history, luminaries from the worlds of politics, media, business, and the arts gathered at the Smithsonian's National Portrait Gallery in Washington, D.C. Michelle Obama, Hillary Clinton, Nancy Pelosi, and hundreds of other guests packed the museum courtyard for an invitation-only, black-tie affair. They were there to celebrate the addition of six new portraits to the gallery's permanent collection, honoring iconic Americans such as *Hamilton* creator Lin-Manuel Miranda, and *Vogue* editor Anna Wintour, as well as the richest person in the world: Amazon founder and CEO, Jeff Bezos.

Bezos's lifelike portrait by the photorealistic painter Robert McCurdy depicted him against a stark white background, wearing a crisp white shirt, silver tie, and the severe gaze that had flustered Amazon employees over the last twenty-five years. In his speech that night, accepting the Portrait of a Nation Prize for commitment to "service, creativity, individuality, insight, and ingenuity," Bezos thanked his large coterie of family and colleagues in the audience and struck a characteristic note of public humility.

"My life is based on a large series of mistakes," he said, after an eloquent introduction from his oldest son, nineteen-year-old Preston. "I'm kind of famous for it in the business realm. How many people here have a Fire Phone?" The crowd guffawed and was silent—Amazon's 2014 smartphone had infamously bombed. "Yeah, no, none of you do. Thanks," he said to laughs.

"Every interesting thing I've ever done, every important thing I've ever done, every beneficial thing I've ever done, has been through a cascade of experiments and mistakes and failures," Bezos continued. "I'm covered in scar tissues as a result of this." He recalled selecting McCurdy from binders of artists provided by the museum, and said he was looking for "someone who would paint me hyper-realistically, with every flaw, every imperfection, every piece of scar tissue that I have."

The audience responded to Bezos's speech with a rapturous standing ovation. It was that kind of evening. The band Earth, Wind & Fire played, guests drank and danced, and the comedian James Corden presented an award to Wintour while impersonating her in a blond wig, black sunglasses, and fur-lined coat. "Ask Jeff Bezos to get me a coffee!" he vamped. The well-heeled crowd roared in delight.

Outside that prosperous gathering though, the feelings toward Amazon and its CEO in the midst of the company's twenty-sixth year were far more complicated. Amazon was booming, but its name was stained. Wherever there was applause, there was also discordant criticism. Amazon was admired and even beloved by customers while its secretive intentions were often mistrusted, and the towering net worth of its founder, set against the plight of its blue-collar workforce in company warehouses, provoked unsettling questions about the asymmetric distribution of money and power. Amazon was no longer just an inspiring business story but a referendum on society, and on the responsibilities that large companies have toward their employees, their communities, and the sanctity of our fragile planet.

Bezos had attempted to address that latter concern by conceiving the Climate Pledge, a promise that Amazon would be carbon neutral by 2040, ten years before the most ambitious goals set by the Paris climate accords. Critics were hammering Amazon to follow other companies and reveal its carbon footprint—its contribution to the harmful gasses that were rapidly warming the globe. Its sustainability division had labored for years to create more efficient standards for its buildings and to cut down on wasteful packaging materials. But it wasn't enough to simply publicize their work and follow other companies by releasing a carbon impact report. Bezos insisted that Amazon approach the issue creatively, so that it might be viewed as a leader and its millions of customers around the world could still feel good about visiting the site and clicking the buttons labeled "Buy Now."

No concrete way existed to achieve this goal, particularly in the face of Amazon's growing armada of pollution-spewing airplanes, trucks, and delivery vans. Nevertheless, Bezos wanted to unveil the pledge and invite other companies to sign it with a grand gesture. One idea actively discussed inside the company was for him to announce the initiative with a video that he would personally record from one of the polar ice caps. Employees in Amazon's sustainability and public relations departments actually spent a few days contemplating how to pull off that nightmarishly complex and carbon-intensive feat, until they mercifully gave up the notion. Bezos would do it in the far more accessible and warmer confines of the National Press Club in Washington, D.C.

On the morning of September 19, 2019, two months before the gala at the Smithsonian, a few dozen members of the press gathered for a rare audience with Amazon's CEO. Bezos sat on a small stage with Christiana Figueres, former executive secretary of the United Nations Framework Convention on Climate Change. "Predictions made by climate scientists just five years ago are turning out to be wrong," he began. "The Antarctic ice sheets are melting 70 percent faster than predicted five years ago. Oceans are warming 40 percent faster." To help meet its new goals, he continued, Amazon would move to power its operations with 100 percent renewable energy. It would start by placing an order for one hundred thousand electric vans from the Plymouth, Michigan–based startup that Amazon had helped fund, Rivian Automotive.

In the Q&A session that followed, a reporter asked Bezos about a group of workers who had banded together under the mantle "Amazon Employees for Climate Justice." They were demanding, among other things, that the company withdraw financial support for climate-denying politicians and break its cloud computing contracts with fossil fuel companies. "I think it's totally understandable," said Bezos of the group's concerns, while noting that he didn't agree with all of their demands. "We don't want this to be the tragedy of the commons. We all have to work together on this." A few months later, in the midst of the Covid-19 pandemic, Amazon would fire two of the group's organizers.

I was in the audience that day as well, and raised my hand to ask Bezos the last question of the morning: Was he confident that humanity could move quickly enough to escape the direst scenarios for a warming planet? "I'm congenitally optimistic," he replied, fixing me with the laser-eyed stare that the artist Robert McCurdy so faithfully captured. "I really do believe when ingenuity gets involved, when invention gets involved, when people get determined, when passion comes out, when they make strong goals—you can invent your way out of any box. That's what we humans need to do right now. I believe we're going to do it. I'm sure we're going to do it."

His answer suggested total faith in the underlying virtues of technology, and in the ability of the cleverest, most determined innovators to navigate out of any jam. At least in that moment, he seemed like the *same old Jeff*, and not at all the billionaire who founded and operated a business that, depending on your perspective, was either propelling the world into an exciting future or helping to blot out the nurturing sun of fair competition and free enterprise itself.

Today, Amazon sells nearly everything and delivers its packages promptly, powers much of the internet in its data centers, streams television shows and movies to our homes, and sells a popular line of voice-activated speakers. But nearly three decades ago, it was just an idea, circulating on the fortieth floor of a midtown Manhattan skyscraper. In case you're not familiar with that foundational piece of internet lore, the story went like this:

Vowing upon the age of thirty to risk the entrepreneurial path, Jeffrey Preston Bezos quit his high-paying job at the esteemed Wall Street hedge fund D. E. Shaw to start a seemingly modest business: an online bookstore. With his twenty-four-year-old wife, MacKenzie, he flew from New York City to Fort Worth, took his family's '88 Chevy Blazer out of storage, and asked her to drive northwest while he sat in the passenger's seat, tapping financial projections into a spreadsheet on his laptop. It was 1994, the paleolithic year of the internet.

He set up his startup in the enclosed garage of a three-bedroom ranch house in an eastern Seattle suburb, with an old iron potbellied stove at its center, and fashioned the first two desks himself out of sixty-dollar wooden doors from Home Depot. He called the company Cadabra Inc., then wavered and considered the names Bookmall.com, Aard.com, and Relentless.com, before finally deducing that the Earth's largest river could represent its biggest selection of books—Amazon.com.

He financed the startup himself at first, along with a $245,000 investment from his devoted parents, Jackie and Mike. When the website went live in '95, Amazon immediately got caught up in a dawning mania for a novel technology called the World Wide Web. There was 30, 40, 50 percent growth in orders each week, undermining any attempts at careful planning and pushing that earliest batch of eclectic recruits into such a frenetic pace that they would later share a palpable sense of amnesia about those early times. The first potential investors mostly balked, distrustful of the internet and this geeky, self-assured young man from the East Coast with a crazy, barking laugh. But in 1996, Silicon Valley venture capitalists got ahold of the startup, and the abundance of money flipped a switch in the brain of the budding CEO, sparking a bullish fervor of wild ambitions and fever dreams of domination.

The first company-wide motto was "Get Big Fast." Amazon's rapid expansion, during what became known as the dot-com boom in the late 1990s, was epic. Bezos hired new executives, opened new warehouses, staged a well-publicized IPO in 1997, and fought off a desperate lawsuit from his first rival, the bookseller Barnes & Noble. He thought the Amazon brand could be malleable, like Richard Branson's Virgin, so he dove headlong into new product categories and started selling CDs, DVDs, toys, and electronics. "We are going to take this thing to the moon," he told then fellow Seattle CEO Howard Schultz of Starbucks.

Bezos wanted to set his own metrics for success, without interference from impatient outsiders, so he encoded his operating philosophy in his first letter to shareholders, vowing a focus not on immediate financial returns or on satisfying the myopic demands of Wall Street, but on increasing cash flow and growing market share to generate value over the long term for loyal shareholders. "This is Day 1 for the Internet and, if we execute well, for Amazon.com," he wrote, coining the sacred phrase "Day 1" that inside Amazon would come to represent the need for constant invention, fast decision-making, and the eager embrace of broader technology trends. Investors signed on for the ride, bidding the stock price to unimaginable heights. The CEO became a millionaire and a celebrity, landing on the cover of *Time* magazine as "Person of the Year" in 1999, at the twilight of the century, his balding head peeking goofily out of a cardboard box filled with colored Styrofoam peanuts.

But behind the scenes, things were a mess. Amazon's profligate investments in other dot-com startups were souring, a host of acquisitions hadn't worked, and many of the early hires, from traditional retailers like Walmart, looked askance at the sprawling chaos and fled. The first warehouses were so overwhelmed by orders over the Christmas holidays that employees from Seattle had to leave their desks every December, roll up their sleeves, and work on the front lines, packing and wrapping gifts while doubling up in economy hotel rooms.

Over the next two years, the company bled money and almost died during the period known as the dot-com bust. A financial paper dubbed the company "Amazon.bomb"—declaring that "Investors Are Beginning to Realize This Storybook Stock Has Problems"—and it stuck. Bezos was widely ridiculed and in 2001 was even frivolously investigated by the SEC for insider trading. One analyst generated frequent headlines by repeatedly predicting that the company was about to run out of money. By then, Amazon had moved into a 1930s-era art deco VA hospital that sat on a hill facing downtown Seattle. When the Nisqually earthquake struck the Pacific Northwest in February 2001, bricks and mortar rained down in what seemed like an ominous prophecy. Bezos and his employees survived by diving under their thick door desks.

Amazon's stock sank into the single digits, ruining dreams of quick fortune. The thirty-seven-year-old Bezos scrawled "I am not my stock price!" on a whiteboard in his office and doubled down on giveaways to customers, like rapid delivery of the latest Harry Potter novel on the day of publication.

Employees were scared, but Bezos seemed to have ice in his veins. Through some well-timed debt offerings and a last-minute $100 million infusion from the online service AOL in the summer of 2001, the company raised enough money to cover its obligations and evade the fate that befell most other dot-coms. When Amazon finally cut enough costs to notch a quarter of profitability in the spring of 2003, the grudge-holding CEO hid an acronym, *milliravi*, in an earnings press release, an inside joke ridiculing the analyst who had predicted Amazon's demise.

The company had survived, but there was little about it that seemed special. The rival online store eBay had a far larger selection of products for sale. The discount physical retailer Walmart had lower prices. The growing search engine Google was attracting the world's best engineers and siphoning away online shoppers to its eponymous website, then charging Amazon to place advertisements within search results to lure them back.

What followed was one of the most remarkable turnarounds in business history. After failing to match eBay's success with online auctions, Bezos opened the site to third-party sellers and allowed them to list their wares alongside Amazon's own products and let customers decide who to buy from. Then he had an epiphany, recognizing the flywheel, or virtuous cycle, that was powering his business. By adding outside vendors and additional selection to Amazon.com, the company drew in new shoppers and earned commissions on those sales, which it could use to lower prices or subsidize faster delivery. That in turn drew in more shoppers and attracted more sellers—and the process repeated itself. Invest in any part of the loop, Bezos reasoned, and this cycle would accelerate.

Bezos also hired an executive named Jeff Wilke from the aerospace and automotive giant AlliedSignal. Wilke was a lot like Bezos: precocious, ambitious, and focused on satisfying customers over just about everything else, including the feelings of his employees. Together they redesigned the warehouses, christening them "fulfillment centers" or FCs, and rewrote their logistics software from scratch. The ability to efficiently and predictably fulfill customer orders allowed Amazon to resume expansion into new product categories, like jewelry and apparel—and eventually, to introduce the enticing $79-a-year two-day shipping guarantee, Amazon Prime.

With another like-minded deputy, Andy Jassy, Bezos also expanded in an even more surprising direction. Contemplating the way his own engineers worked, and the expertise the company had developed in building a stable computing infrastructure that could withstand enormous seasonal spikes in traffic, he conceived of a new business called Amazon Web Services. The idea was that Amazon would sell raw computing power to other organizations, who could access it online and use it to economically run their own operations.

The business plan was barely understandable to many of Amazon's own employees and board members. But the forty-year-old Bezos believed in it, micromanaging the project and sending extraordinarily detailed recommendations and goals to AWS team leaders, often late at night. "This has to scale to infinity with no planned downtime," he told the beleaguered engineers working on the project. "Infinity!"

At the same time, Bezos was shocked by Apple's rapid ascendance in music sales with its iPod music player and iTunes store. Concerned about a similar incursion into books, he initiated a secret project to create Amazon's own digital book reader, the Kindle. Colleagues thought it was crazy for the perennially money-losing Amazon to make gadgets. "I absolutely know it's hard, but we'll learn how to do it," Bezos told them.

He put another deputy, Steve Kessel, in charge and asked him to drop his responsibilities running Amazon's original bookselling business and to "proceed as if your goal is to put everyone selling physical books out of a job." The resulting skirmishes with traditional publishers over the terms for the new e-book market spanned years and generated charges that Amazon was engaging in predatory conduct. Paradoxically, it also resulted in an antitrust case against five large book publishers and Apple, alleging they had illegally conspired to fix digital prices for e-books above the Kindle's $9.99 standard.

The confluence of those three initiatives—in the fulfillment centers, and with AWS and the Kindle—vaulted Amazon back into the graces of Wall Street. In 2008, Amazon surpassed eBay in market capitalization and was beginning to be mentioned in the same breath as Google, Apple, and a new Silicon Valley upstart, Facebook. Bezos then used every bit of leverage at his disposal to outduel Walmart and acquire two emerging online rivals: the shoe-retailer Zappos and a seller of consumable goods called Quidsi, which owned the popular website Diapers.com. Antitrust authorities approved those deals quickly—decisions that would later be regarded skeptically in light of Amazon's growing dominance.

It turned out that there was more depth than anyone had suspected to the increasingly fit CEO with the now clean-shaven head. He was a ravenous reader, leading senior executives in discussion of books like Clayton Christensen's *The Innovator's Dilemma*, and he had an utter aversion to doing anything conventionally. Employees were instructed to model his fourteen leadership principles, such as customer obsession, high bar for talent, and frugality, and they were trained to consider them daily when making decisions about things like new hires, promotions, and even trivial changes to products.

PowerPoint presentations, with their litany of bullet points and incomplete thoughts, were banned inside the company despite being popular in the rest of corporate America. Instead, all meetings started with almost meditative readings of data-rich, six-page documents, called "narratives." The act of business building at Amazon was an editorial process, with papers subject to numerous revisions, debate over the meaning of individual words, and meticulous consideration by company leaders, most of all from Bezos himself. Meanwhile, working groups inside Amazon were broken into small versatile units, called two-pizza teams (because they were small enough to be fed with two pizzas), and were ordered to move quickly, often in competition with one another.

This unusual and decentralized corporate culture hammered into employees that there was no trade-off between speed and accuracy. They were supposed to move fast and *never* break things. Goals, accountability, and deadlines were pushed down into the organization, while metrics were fed upward, via weekly and quarterly business reports and biannual companywide reviews, called OP1 (for operating plan, in the late summer) and OP2 (after the holidays). The performance of each team was evaluated by Bezos's hallowed leadership council of like-minded math whizzes: the S-team (for senior team). Sitting atop it all was Bezos himself, who would home in on promising new projects, or on fixing teams whose results were disappointing, with the same focus and exacting standards that he had brought to Amazon's earliest days. He took nothing for granted, including Amazon's increasing success.

His blasts of annoyance, directed at employees who failed to meet those standards, were legendary inside the company. "Why are you wasting my life?" he'd ask, scoffing at disappointing underlings. Or he leveled them with "I'm sorry, did I take my stupid pills today?" While the brutal leadership style and distinct culture was enervating to many employees, it was also proving unmistakably effective. In the spring of 2011, Amazon was valued at $80 billion. Buoyed by the rise of his stock holdings, the forty-seven-year-old Bezos was the thirtieth richest person in the world, with an $18.1 billion net worth.

That outsized success started to draw attention. State legislatures recognized that the growing flood of tax-free sales over the internet was depleting their coffers, and they passed legislation requiring on-line retailers to pay sales taxes, closing a loophole that had been cre-ated before the internet age for mail-order companies. Bezos was prepared to fight to protect a significant price advantage over offline rivals, and even backed a California ballot initiative to undo a new state law that would force online retailers to collect sales tax. But in the middle of the fight, he changed course; sales tax avoidance had tied the company in knots, requiring it to limit where it opened fa-cilities and even where employees could travel. By agreeing to collect sales tax, Bezos surrendered his prized advantage. Instead, he took the longer view, making it possible for Amazon to open up offices and fulfillment centers in more populous states, much closer to its cus-tomers, laying the groundwork for one of the largest expansions in business history.

Amazon was sprawling out in every direction, both online and back home. It moved from a scattered collection of offices around Se-attle to nearly a dozen buildings in a developing office district by the freshwater Lake Union, north of downtown. In early 2012, anonymous fliers taped around South Lake Union found a derogatory name for the growing cadre of employees spreading out over the area with their identifiable badges: "Am-holes." It presaged a growing unease between the company and its left-leaning, blue-collar hometown.

While he had triumphed against enormous odds, Jeff Bezos preferred those negative articles, like the old "Amazon.bomb" cover story in *Barron's*, to be posted on his office walls, so that he and his colleagues would remain frightened and motivated. "It's still Day 1!" he dutifully reminded his employees and investors in the shareholder letter published that spring. After all, there was so much more to do to augment the nearly endless selection of physical and digital goods on the virtual shelves of the everything store.

———

I published a book by that title in October 2013, right into the grip of the world's growing fascination with Amazon. It was an attempt to explain a classic modern business story—how the impresario of online books had fought off near ruin and upended not only retail but digital media and enterprise computing.

There were generally positive reviews and a few infamous negative ones. "I wanted to like this book," wrote MacKenzie Bezos in a one-star brickbat posted to Amazon.com. She alleged factual inaccuracies, a "lopsided and misleading portrait of the people and culture at Amazon," and criticized my characterization of Bezos's disciples, who channeled his maxims and leadership style, as "Jeff Bots." Later, I also learned that Bezos was upset with how I had handled tracking down his biological father, the now-deceased Ted Jorgensen, a man who had left his family when Bezos was a toddler and did not know what had become of his son until I visited him forty-five years later.

At the time I thought I had written the comprehensive book on Amazon's rise. But then a strange thing happened. In 2014, Amazon released the first Echo, a voice-activated speaker running the virtual assistant Alexa. The product was a hit, and over the next five years the company sold more than a hundred million devices, initiating a new wave of voice-connected computing and eliminating the odor of Amazon's previous failure in consumer gadgets, the Fire Phone. Amazon was moving from its customers' doorsteps to their living rooms, with access to their broad range of requests and questions, and potentially their most intimate conversations.

At around the same time, Amazon's AWS division expanded its line of database services to lure large enterprises and government agencies into that ethereal future of enterprise computing known as "the cloud." Amazon reported AWS's financial results for the first time in the spring of 2015, shocking investors with its profitability and growth, only to generate another round of feverish enthusiasm for Amazon's stock.

A few years later, Amazon opened its first prototype Amazon Go physical retail store in Seattle, using artificial intelligence and computer vision so customers could walk out of the store and be automatically charged rather than checking out with a human cashier. The company also expanded geographically, pushing into India, Mexico, and other countries, at massive expense and in direct competition with the largest company in the world by sales: Walmart. Meanwhile, its investments in Hollywood, via Amazon Studios, yielded critical hits like *Transparent*, *The Marvelous Mrs. Maisel*, and *Jack Ryan*, along with a few notorious bombs, like Woody Allen's *Crisis in Six Scenes*. It put Amazon right behind Netflix in the race to redefine home entertainment for a new age.

While all this was unfolding, Amazon was also reinvigorating its older businesses. Amazon Marketplace, where independent sellers hawked their wares on Amazon.com, exploded with a surge of low-priced products (including counterfeits and knockoffs) manufactured in China. In 2015, the total value of the products sold on the marketplace surpassed the value of the units that Amazon sold itself on its own site. Amazon acquired the organic supermarket chain Whole Foods Market in 2017, saving the iconic American grocer from an unwelcome incursion by activist investors, and boosting its own ineffectual efforts to crack the food business.

Amazon also remade its delivery operations, lessening its reliance on partners like UPS with its own network of sortation centers, drivers, and cargo aircraft branded with the Amazon Prime logo. And it revived its advertising business, embedding ads in its search results just as Google had pioneered a decade before to Amazon's annoyance, generating a profitable new revenue line for the company.

The Amazon that I had written about was worth nearly $120 billion at the end of 2012. The company's market capitalization touched a trillion dollars for the first time in the fall of 2018—eight times more valuable in less than six years—and returned to surpass that threshold, apparently for good, in early 2020. My Amazon had under 150,000 employees. By the end of 2020, it had an astounding 1.3 million employees. I was writing about the Kindle company, but this was now the Alexa company. Also, the cloud company. And a Hollywood studio. And a video game maker, robotics manufacturer, grocery store owner—and on and on.

While Amazon seduced investors and customers, it also moved to the center of an acrimonious political struggle that had the potential to redefine free market capitalism. Its vocal critics believed that such brazen accumulation of wealth and power had a significant cost, exacerbating income inequality and stacking the odds against workers and locally owned businesses.

"Today's big tech companies have too much power—too much power over our economy, our society, and our democracy," wrote Senator Elizabeth Warren at the debut of her unsuccessful bid for the White House in 2019. "Amazon crushes small companies by copying the goods they sell on the Amazon Marketplace and then selling its own branded version." She urged that Jeff Bezos's meticulous creation be forced to spin off Zappos and Whole Foods Market and be stamped into smaller parts.

———

As Amazon changed, so too did Bezos undergo his own startling transformation.

In the company's early years, he usually sported pleated khakis and navy-blue button-down shirts and rode his two-wheel Segway scooter around the office, his laugh ricocheting off the walls. He lived with his wife and four children in the opulent waterfront suburb of Medina, Washington, outside Seattle, and fiercely guarded their privacy. Despite his budding wealth, he appeared to have little interest in collecting assets like vintage sports cars or expensive paintings won at exclusive auctions. He was not, by any means, an aficionado of luxury yachts. Only his private jet seemed to kindle his overt enthusiasm, because avoiding public air travel saved him a resource that money couldn't buy: time.

But by the late 2010s, Bezos as the unfashionable, single-minded geek was largely obsolete. Even the half-reformed nerd from the Fire Phone launch in 2014, who delighted in reciting the technical specifications of the fated smartphone, had bowed from the stage.

Shedding this image as an awkward though self-assured geek, Bezos emerged as a business kingpin who, at first, seemed to have an almost mystical aura of invincibility. Over the summer of 2017, Bezos became the wealthiest person in the world, a mathematical eventuality produced by Amazon's rising stock price and the relatively slower growing fortune of Microsoft cofounder Bill Gates, who was giving his money away in philanthropy, a process Bezos had yet to start in any meaningful way. As Bezos rose to the top of the world's wealthiest chart, a widely circulated photo from the prestigious Allen & Company's conference in Sun Valley showed him wearing a pair of stylish Garrett Leight folding sunglasses and a short-sleeved polo shirt and down vest that exposed enormous biceps. The photo went viral. Jeff Bezos was the action hero of the business world.

At first it was difficult for insiders to discern how much Bezos had truly changed. Colleagues said he remained absorbed in the mechanics of new businesses at Amazon, like Alexa. But other demands required his time, including his fledgling philanthropic efforts, his newly ambitious space company, Blue Origin, and the *Washington Post*, the prestigious newspaper he bought in 2013 that was a frequent target of the impetuous U.S. president, Donald J. Trump.

JPMorgan CEO Jamie Dimon, a longtime friend, said that the "Jeff I know is the same old Jeff." But as Dimon worked with Bezos in forums like the Business Council, a D.C. organization that meets several times a year to discuss policy, and Haven Healthcare, the failed joint initiative between Amazon, JPMorgan, and Berkshire Hathaway to lower employee healthcare costs, he observed his friend's eyes gradually opening. "Jeff was like a kid in a candy store. It was all new to him. He was so focused on Amazon for a long time. Then he gradually became a citizen of the world."

To others, Bezos's metamorphosis indicated the presence of something else: the hubris that comes with unimaginable success. In the fall of 2017, he directed Amazon to stage a contest called HQ2, a bakeoff among cities in North America to land a new Amazon headquarters outside of Seattle. The unprecedented public competition created a seventeen-month frenzy, with 238 regions contorting themselves to attract the tech giant. New York City and Northern Virginia were dubbed the winners, but by then political sentiment had turned sharply against Amazon for (among other things) seeking out rich local tax incentives. Progressive legislators in Queens, like popular congresswoman Alexandria Ocasio-Cortez, and their allies in organized labor were able to make enough noise that Amazon ignominiously rescinded its offer to open the office in Long Island City, New York.

From there things took an even stranger turn. In January 2019,

Bezos tweeted the surprising news of his divorce from MacKenzie, his wife of twenty-five years, stunning even those who believed they knew the couple well. The next day, the *National Enquirer*, the infamous supermarket tabloid, published a eleven-page spread divulging Bezos's extramarital relationship with TV personality Lauren Sanchez that included salacious private text messages between the pair. Bezos ordered an investigation into how the paper obtained his texts and intimate photographs; over the next year, that tawdry drama grew to involve charges of global espionage and hints of a conspiracy that involved Mohammed bin Salman, the crown prince of Saudi Arabia. *How does one of the most disciplined men in the world get himself into a situation like that?* more than one Amazon executive wondered privately at the time.

Amazon's founder was now so many things in the public eye, all at once: an inventor, arguably the most accomplished CEO in the world, a space entrepreneur, a newspaper savior and swashbuckling proponent for a free press—as well as a menacing monopolist, the foe of small business, an exploiter of warehouse workers, and the subject of prurient tabloid fascination. Such a disparate range of responses was also on display in the varied reaction to his February 2021 announcement that he would devote himself more fully to new products and projects at Amazon, as well as to his other interests, by giving the CEO job to longtime deputy Andy Jassy and becoming executive chairman.

Despite his optimism about solutions to global warming at the Climate Pledge press conference, this was clearly *not* the same old Jeff. So I resolved to write this sequel, and to investigate how Amazon had grown to such tremendous size in such a little amount of time. I would once again pose the critical question of whether Amazon and Jeff Bezos were good for business competition, for modern society, and even for our planet.

The task was completed with help from Amazon, the *Washington Post*, and Blue Origin, which facilitated interviews with many senior executives. Amazon did not, in the end, make Bezos himself available, despite repeated requests and personal entreaties. I also interviewed several hundred current and former employees, partners, competitors, and many others caught up in the whirling cyclone of Bezos and his multiple enterprises and personal dramas.

The result is this book. It's the story of a hard-driving CEO who created such a fertile corporate culture that even at massive size it repeatedly shucked its own bureaucracy to invent exhilarating new products. It's also the story of how a leading technology company became so omnipotent over the course of a single decade that many started to worry that it might definitively tilt the proverbial playing field against smaller companies. And it shows how one of the world's most famous businesspeople appeared to lose his way, and then tried to find it again—right in the midst of a terrifying global pandemic that further augmented his power and profit.

It's a tale that describes a period in business history when the old laws no longer seemed to apply to the world's most dominant companies. And it explores what happened when one man and his vast empire were about to become totally unbound.

PART I

INVENTION

Amazon, December 31, 2010

Annual net sales:	$34.20 billion
Full- and part-time employees:	33,700
End-of-year market capitalization:	$80.46 billion

Jeff Bezos end-of-year net worth:	$15.86 billion

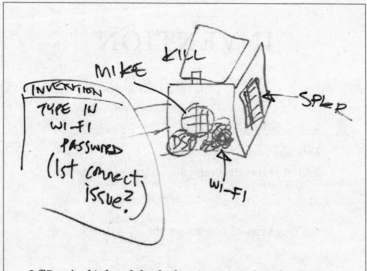

Jeff Bezos's whiteboard sketch of a voice-activated speaker, late 2010

CHAPTER 1

The Über Product Manager

There was nothing particularly distinctive about the dozen or so low-rise buildings in Seattle's burgeoning South Lake Union district that Amazon moved into over the course of 2010. They were architecturally ordinary and, on the insistence of its CEO, bore no obvious signage indicating the presence of an iconic internet company with almost $35 billion in annual sales. Jeff Bezos had instructed colleagues that nothing good could come from that kind of obvious self-aggrandizement, noting that people who had business with the company would already know where it was located.

While the offices clustered around the intersection of Terry Avenue North and Harrison Street were largely anonymous, inside they bore all the distinguishing marks of a unique and idiosyncratic corporate culture. Employees wore color-coded badges around their necks signifying their seniority at the company (blue for those with up to five years of tenure, yellow for up to ten, red for up to fifteen), and the offices and elevators were decorated with posters delineating Bezos's fourteen sacrosanct leadership principles.

Within these walls ranged Bezos himself, forty-six years old at the time, carrying himself in such a way as to always exemplify Amazon's unique operating ideology. The CEO, for example, went to great lengths to illustrate Amazon's principal #10, "frugality": *Accomplish more with less. Constraints breed resourcefulness, self-sufficiency, and invention. There are no extra points for growing headcount, budget size, or fixed expense.* His wife, MacKenzie, drove him to work most days in their Honda minivan, and when he flew with colleagues on his private Dassault Falcon 900EX jet, he often mentioned that he personally, not Amazon, had paid for the flight.

If Bezos took one leadership principle most to heart—which would also come to define the next half decade at Amazon—it was principal #8, "think big": *Thinking small is a self-fulfilling prophecy. Leaders create and communicate a bold direction that inspires results. They think differently and look around corners for ways to serve customers.* In 2010, Amazon was a successful online retailer, a nascent cloud provider, and a pioneer in digital reading. But Bezos envisioned it as much more. His shareholder letter that year was a paean to the esoteric computer science disciplines of artificial intelligence and machine learning that Amazon was just beginning to explore. It opened by citing a list of impossibly obscure terms such as "naïve Bayesian estimators," "gossip protocols," and "data sharding." Bezos wrote: "Invention is in our DNA and technology is the fundamental tool we wield to evolve and improve every aspect of the experience we provide our customers."

Bezos wasn't only imagining these technological possibilities. He was also attempting to position Amazon's next generation of products directly on its farthest frontier. Around this time, he started working intensively with the engineers at Lab126, Amazon's Silicon Valley R&D subsidiary, which had developed the company's first gadget, the Kindle. In a flurry of brainstorming sessions, he initiated several projects to complement the Kindle and the coming Kindle Fire tablets, which were known internally at the time as Project A.

Project B, which became Amazon's ill-fated Fire Phone, would use an assembly of front-facing cameras and infrared lights to conjure a seemingly three-dimensional smartphone display. Project C, or "Shimmer," was a desk lamp–shaped device designed to project hologram-like displays onto a table or ceiling. It proved unfeasibly expensive and was never launched.

Bezos had peculiar ideas about how customers might interact with these devices. The engineers working on the third version of the Kindle discovered this when they tried to kill a microphone that was planned for the device, since no features were slated to actually use it. But the CEO insisted that the microphone remain. "The answer I got is that Jeff thinks in the future we'll talk to our devices," said Sam Bowen, then a Kindle hardware director. "It felt a bit more like *Star Trek* than reality."

Designers convinced Bezos to lose the microphone in subsequent versions of the Kindle, but he clung to his belief in the inevitability of conversational computing and the potential of artificial intelligence to make it practical. It was a trope in all his favorite science fiction, from TV's *Star Trek* ("computer, open a channel") to authors like Arthur C. Clarke, Isaac Asimov, and Robert A. Heinlein whose books lined the library of hundreds of volumes in his lakefront Seattle-area home. While others read these classics and only dreamed of alternate realities, Bezos seemed to consider the books blueprints for an exciting future. It was a practice that would culminate in Amazon's defining product for a new decade: a cylindrical speaker that sparked a wave of imitators, challenged norms around privacy, and changed the way people thought about Amazon—not only as an e-commerce giant, but as an inventive technology company that was pushing the very boundaries of computer science.

The initiative was originally designated inside Lab126 as Project D. It would come to be known as the Amazon Echo, and by the name of its virtual assistant, Alexa.

———

As with several other projects at Amazon, the origins of Project D can be traced back to discussions between Bezos and his "technical advisor" or TA, the promising executive handpicked to shadow the

CEO. Among the TA's duties were to take notes in meetings, write the first draft of the annual shareholder letter, and learn by interacting with the master closely for more than a year. In the role from 2009 to 2011 was Amazon executive Greg Hart, a veteran of the company's earliest retail categories, like books, music, DVDs, and video games. Originally from Seattle, Hart had attended Williams College in Western Massachusetts and, after a stint in the ad world, returned home at the twilight of the city's grunge era, sporting a goatee and a penchant for flannel shirts. By the time he was following Bezos around, the facial hair was gone and Hart was a rising corporate star. "You sort of feel like you're an assistant coach watching John Wooden, you know, perhaps the greatest basketball coach ever," Hart said of his time as the TA.

Hart remembered talking to Bezos about speech recognition one day in late 2010 at Seattle's Blue Moon Burgers. Over lunch, Hart demonstrated his enthusiasm for Google's voice search on his Android phone by saying, "pizza near me," and then showing Bezos the list of links to nearby pizza joints that popped up on-screen. "Jeff was a little skeptical about the use of it on phones, because he thought it might be socially awkward," Hart remembered. But they discussed how the technology was finally getting good at dictation and search.

At the time, Bezos was also excited about Amazon's growing cloud business, asking all of his executives, "What are you doing to help AWS?" Inspired by the conversations with Hart and others about voice computing, he emailed Hart, device vice president Ian Freed, and senior vice president Steve Kessel on January 4, 2011, linking the two topics: "We should build a $20 device with its brains in the cloud that's completely controlled by your voice." It was another idea from the boss who seemed to have a limitless wellspring of them.

Bezos and his employees riffed on the idea over email for a few days, but no further action was taken, and it could have ended there. Then a few weeks later, Hart met with Bezos in a sixth-floor conference room in Amazon's headquarters, Day 1 North, to discuss his career options. His tenure as TA was wrapping up, so they discussed several possible opportunities to lead new initiatives at the company, including positions in Amazon's video streaming and advertising groups. Bezos jotted their ideas down on a whiteboard, adding a few of his own, and then started to apply his usual criteria to assess their merit: If they work, will they grow to become big businesses? If the company didn't pursue them aggressively now, would it miss an opportunity? Eventually Bezos and Hart crossed off all the items on the list except one—pursuing Bezos's idea for a voice-activated cloud computer.

"Jeff, I don't have any experience in hardware, and the largest software team I've led is only about forty people," Hart recalled saying.

"You'll do fine," Bezos replied.

Hart thanked him for the vote of confidence and said, "Okay, well, remember that when we screw up along the way."

Before they parted, Bezos illustrated his idea for the screenless voice computer on the whiteboard. The first-ever depiction of an Alexa device showed the speaker, microphone, and a mute button. And it identified the act of configuring the device to a wireless network, since it wouldn't be able to listen to commands right out of the box, as a challenge requiring further thought. Hart snapped a photo of the drawing with his phone.

Bezos would remain intimately involved in the project, meeting with the team as frequently as every other day, making detailed product decisions, and authorizing the investment of hundreds of millions of dollars in the project before the first Echo was ever released. Using the German superlative, employees referred to him as the *über* product manager.

But it was Greg Hart who ran the team, just across the street from Bezos's office, in Fiona, the Kindle building. Over the next few months, Hart hired a small group from in and outside the company, sending out emails to prospective hires with the subject line "Join my mission" and asking interview questions like "How would you design a Kindle for the blind?" Then, just as obsessed with secrecy as his boss, he declined to specify what product candidates would be working on. One interviewee recalled guessing that it was Amazon's widely rumored smartphone and said that Hart replied, "There's another team building a phone. But this is way more interesting."

One early recruit was Amazon engineer Al Lindsay, who in a previous job had written some of the original code for telco US West's voice-activated directory assistance. Lindsay spent his first three weeks on the project on vacation at his cottage in Canada, writing a six-page narrative that envisioned how outside developers might program their own voice-enabled apps that could run on the device. Another internal recruit, Amazon manager John Thimsen, signed on as director of engineering and coined a formal code name for the initiative, Doppler, after the Project D designation. "At the start, I don't think anybody really expected it to succeed, to be honest with you," Thimsen told me. "But to Greg's credit, halfway through, we were all believers."

The initial Alexa crew worked with a feverish sense of urgency due to their impatient boss. Unrealistically, Bezos wanted to release the device in six to twelve months. He would have a good reason to hurry. On October 4, 2011, just as the Doppler team was coming together, Apple introduced the Siri virtual assistant in the iPhone 4S, the last passion project of cofounder Steve Jobs, who died of cancer the next day. That the resurgent Apple had the same idea of a voice-activated personal assistant was both validating for Hart and his employees and discouraging, since Siri was first to market and with initial mixed reviews. The Amazon team tried to reassure themselves that their product was unique, since it would be independent from smartphones. Perhaps a more significant differentiator though was that Siri unfortunately could no longer have Jobs's active support, while Alexa would have Bezos's sponsorship and almost maniacal attention inside Amazon.

To speed up development and meet Bezos's goals, Hart and his crew started looking for startups to acquire. It was a nontrivial challenge, since Nuance, the Boston-based speech giant whose technology Apple had licensed for Siri, had grown over the years by gobbling up the top American speech companies. Doppler execs tried to learn which of the remaining startups were promising by asking prospective targets to voice-enable the Kindle digital book catalog, then studying their methods and results. The search led to several rapid-fire acquisitions over the next two years, which would end up shaping Alexa's brain and even the timbre of its voice.

The first company Amazon bought, Yap, a twenty-person startup based in Charlotte, North Carolina, automatically translated human speech such as voicemails into text, without relying on a secret workforce of human transcribers in low-wage countries. Though much of Yap's technology would be discarded, its engineers would help develop the technology to convert what customers said to Doppler into a computer-readable format. During the prolonged courtship, Amazon execs tormented Yap execs by refusing to disclose what they'd be working on. Even a week after the deal closed, Al Lindsay was with Yap's engineers at an industry conference in Florence, Italy, where he insisted that they pretend they didn't know him, so that no one could catch on to Amazon's newfound interest in speech technology.

After the purchase was finalized for around $25 million, Amazon dismissed the company's founders but kept its speech science group in Cambridge, Massachusetts, making it the seed of a new R&D office in Kendall Square, near MIT. Yap engineers flew to Seattle, walking into a conference room on the first floor of Fiona with locked doors and closed window blinds. There Greg Hart finally described "this little device, about the size of a Coke can, that would sit on your table and you could ask it natural language questions and it would be a smart assistant," recalled Yap's VP of research, Jeff Adams, a two-decade veteran of the speech industry. "Half of my team were rolling their eyes, saying 'oh my word, what have we gotten ourselves into.'"

After the meeting, Adams delicately told Hart and Lindsay that their goals were unrealistic. Most experts believed that true "far-field speech recognition"—comprehending speech from up to thirty-two feet away, often amid crosstalk and background noise—was beyond the realm of established computer science, since sound bounces off surfaces like walls and ceilings, producing echoes that confuse computers. The Amazon executives responded by channeling Bezos's resolve. "They basically told me, 'We don't care. Hire more people. Take as long as it takes. Solve the problem,'" recalled Adams. "They were unflappable."

———

A few months after the Yap purchase, Greg Hart and his colleagues acquired another piece of the Doppler puzzle. It was the technological antonym of Yap, which converted speech into text. Instead, the Polish startup Ivona generated computer-synthesized speech that resembled a human voice.

Ivona was founded in 2001 by Lukasz Osowski, a computer science student at the Gdańsk University of Technology. Osowski had the notion that so-called "text to speech," or TTS, could read digital texts aloud in a natural voice and help the visually impaired in Poland appreciate the written word. With a younger classmate, Michal Kaszczuk, he took recordings of an actor's voice and selected fragments of words, called diphones, and then blended or "concatenated" them together in different combinations to approximate natural-sounding words and sentences that the actor might never have uttered.

The Ivona founders got an early glimpse of how powerful their technology could be. While students, they paid a popular Polish actor named Jacek Labijak to record hours of speech to create a database of sounds. The result was their first product, Spiker, which quickly became the top-selling computer voice in Poland. Over the next few years, it was used widely in subways, elevators, and for robocall campaigns. Labijak subsequently began to hear himself everywhere and regularly received phone calls in his own voice urging him, for example, to vote for a candidate in an upcoming election. Pranksters manipulated the software to have him say inappropriate things and posted the clips online, where his children discovered them. The Ivona founders then had to renegotiate the actor's contract after he angrily tried to withdraw his voice from the software. (Today "Jacek" remains one of the Polish voices offered by AWS's Amazon Polly computer voice service.)

In 2006, Ivona began to enter and repeatedly win the annual Blizzard Challenge, a competition for the most natural computer voice, organized by Carnegie Mellon University. By 2012, Ivona had expanded into twenty other languages and had over forty voices. After learning of the startup, Greg Hart and Al Lindsay diverted to Gdańsk on their trip through Europe looking for acquisition targets. "From the minute we walked into their offices, we knew it was a culture fit," Lindsay said, pointing to Ivona's progress in a field where researchers often got distracted by high-minded pursuits. "Their scrappiness allowed them to look outside pure academia and not be blinded by science."

The purchase, for around $30 million, was consummated in 2012 but kept secret for a year. The Ivona team and the growing number of speech engineers Amazon would hire for its new Gdańsk R&D center were put in charge of crafting Doppler's voice. The program was micromanaged by Bezos himself and subject to the CEO's usual curiosities and whims.

At first, Bezos said he wanted dozens of distinct voices to emanate from the device, each associated with a different goal or task, such as listening to music or booking a flight. When that proved impractical, the team considered lists of characteristics they wanted in a single personality, such as trustworthiness, empathy, and warmth, and determined those traits were more commonly associated with a female voice.

To develop this voice and ensure it had no trace of a regional accent, the team in Poland worked with an Atlanta area–based voice-over studio, GM Voices, the same outfit that had helped turn recordings from a voice actress named Susan Bennett into Apple's agent, Siri. To create synthetic personalities, GM Voices gave female voice actors hundreds of hours of text to read, from entire books to random articles, a mind-numbing process that could stretch on for months.

Greg Hart and colleagues spent months reviewing the recordings produced by GM Voices and presented the top candidates to Bezos. They ranked the best ones, asked for additional samples, and finally made a choice. Bezos signed off on it.

Characteristically secretive, Amazon has never revealed the name of the voice artist behind Alexa. After canvasing the professional voice-over community, I'm pretty sure I know who she is: Boulder-based singer and voice actress Nina Rolle. Her professional website contained links to old radio ads for products such as Mott's Apple Juice and the Volkswagen Passat—and the warm timbre of Alexa's voice was unmistakable. Rolle said she wasn't allowed to talk to me when I reached her on the phone in February of 2021. And when I asked Amazon to speak with her, they declined.

———

While the Doppler team hired engineers and acquired startups, nearly every other aspect of the product was hotly debated in Amazon's offices in Seattle and in Lab126 in Silicon Valley. In one of the earliest Doppler meetings, Greg Hart identified the ability to play music with a voice command as the device's marquee feature. Bezos "agreed with that framework but he stressed that music may be like 51 percent, but the other 49 percent are going to be really important," Hart said.

Over the ensuing months, that amicable consensus devolved into a long-standing tug-of-war between Hart and his engineers, who saw playing music as a practical and marketable feature, and Bezos, who was thinking more grandly. Bezos started to talk about the "*Star Trek* computer," an artificial intelligence that could handle any question and serve as a personal assistant. The fifty-cent word "plenipotentiary" was used inside the team to describe what he wanted: an assistant invested with full powers to take action on behalf of users, like call for a cab or place a grocery order. With his science fiction obsession, Bezos was forcing his team to think bigger and to push the boundaries of established technology. But Hart, facing pressure to actually ship the product, advocated for a feature set he dubbed "the magical and the mundane" and pushed to highlight basic, reliable features like allowing users to ask for weather reports as well as setting timers and alarms.

The debate manifested itself in endless drafts of the "PR FAQ"—the six-page narrative Amazonians craft in the form of a press release at the start of a new initiative to envision the product's market impact. The paper, a hallowed part of Amazon's rituals around innovation, forces them to begin any conversation about a new product in terms of the benefit it creates for customers. Dozens of versions of the Doppler PR FAQ were written, presented, debated, obsessed over, rewritten, and scrapped. Whenever the press release evolved to highlight playing music, "Jeff would get really mad. He didn't like that at all," recalled an early product manager.

Another early Doppler employee later speculated that Bezos's famous lack of sophisticated musical tastes played a role in his reaction. When Bezos was testing an early Doppler unit, for example, he asked it to play one of his favorite songs: the theme to the classic TV show *Battlestar Galactica*. "Jeff was pushing really hard to make sure this product was more than just music," said Ian Freed, Greg Hart's boss. "He wouldn't let go of it being a more generalized computer."

A related discussion centered around the choice of a so-called "wake" word—the utterance that would rouse Doppler out of passive mode, when it was only listening for its own name, to switch into active listening, where it would send user queries over the internet to Amazon's servers and return with a response. The speech science team wanted the wake word to have a distinct combination of phonemes and be at least three syllables, so the device wouldn't be triggered by normal conversation. It also needed to be distinctive (like "Siri") so that the name could be marketed to the public. Hart and his team presented Bezos with hundreds of flash cards, each with a different name, which he would spread out on conference room tables during the endless deliberations.

Bezos said he wanted the wake word to sound "mellifluous" and opined that his mother's name, Jacklyn, was "too harsh." His own quickly discarded suggestions included "Finch," the title of a fantasy detective novel by Jeff VanderMeer; "Friday," after the personal assistant in the novel *Robinson Crusoe*; and "Samantha," the witch who could twinkle her nose and accomplish any task on the TV show *Bewitched*. For a while, he also believed the wake word should be "Amazon," so that whatever aura of good feeling the device generated would be reflected back onto the company.

Doppler execs argued that people would not want to talk to a corporate entity in their homes, and that spawned another ongoing disagreement. Bezos also suggested "Alexa," an homage to the ancient library of Alexandria, regarded as the capital of knowledge. This was also the name of an unrelated startup Amazon had acquired in the 1990s, which sold web traffic data and continued to operate independently. After endless debates and lab testing, "Alexa" and "Amazon" became the top candidates for the wake word as the device moved into limited trials in the homes of Amazon employees at the start of 2013.

The devices employees received looked very much like the original Echo that would be introduced by Amazon less than two years later. The industrial designers at Lab126 called it the "Pringles can"—a cylinder elongated to create separation between the array of seven omnidirectional microphones at the top and the speakers at the bottom, with some fourteen hundred holes punctured in the metal tubing to push out air and sound. The device had an LED light ring at the top, another Bezos idea, which would light up in the direction of the person speaking, reproducing the social cue of looking at someone when they are talking to you. It was not an elegant-looking device, Bezos having instructed the designers to let function dictate the form.

The experimental Doppler devices in the homes of hundreds of Amazon employees were not smart—they were, by all accounts, slow and dumb. An Amazon manager named Neil Ackerman signed up for the internal beta, bringing one home to his family in early 2013. Both he and his wife had to sign several confidentiality agreements, promising they would turn it off and hide it if guests came over. Every week they had to fill out a spreadsheet, answering questions and listing what they asked it and how it responded. Ackerman's wife called it "the thing."

"We were both pretty skeptical about it," he said. "It would hardly ever give me the right answer and the music coming out of it was inconsistent and certainly not the family favorites." Inexplicably it seemed to best understand their son, who had a speech impediment.

Other early beta testers didn't mince words either. Parag Garg, one of the first engineers to work on the Fire TV, took home a device and said it "didn't work for shit and I didn't miss it when it was gone. I thought, 'Well, this thing is doomed.'" A manager on the Fire Phone recalls liking the look of the hardware, "but I could not foresee what it was going to be used for. I thought it was a stupid product."

Two Doppler engineers recall another harrowing review—from Bezos himself. The CEO was apparently testing a unit in his Seattle home, and in a pique of frustration over its lack of comprehension, he told Alexa to go "shoot yourself in the head." One of the engineers who heard the comment while reviewing interactions with the test device said: "We all thought it might be the end of the project, or at least the end of a few of us at Amazon."

———

Alexa, it was clear, needed a brain transplant. Amazon's ongoing efforts to make its product smarter would create a dogmatic battle inside the Doppler team and lead to its biggest challenge yet.

The first move was to integrate the technology of a third acquisition, a Cambridge, England–based artificial intelligence company called Evi (pronounced *Evee*). The startup was founded in 2005 as a question-and-answer tool called True Knowledge by British entrepreneur William Tunstall-Pedoe. As a university student, Tunstall-Pedoe had created websites like Anagram Genius, which automatically rearranged the letters in words to produce another word or phrase. The site was later used by novelist Dan Brown to create puzzles in *The Da Vinci Code*.

In 2012, inspired by Siri's debut, Tunstall-Pedoe pivoted and introduced the Evi app for the Apple and Android app stores. Users could ask it questions by typing or speaking. Instead of searching the web for an answer like Siri, or returning a set of links, like Google's voice search, Evi evaluated the question and tried to offer an immediate answer. The app was downloaded over 250,000 times in its first week and almost crashed the company's servers. Apple threatened to kick it off the iOS app store for appearing "confusingly similar" to Siri, then relented when fans objected. Thanks to all this attention, Evi had at least two acquisition offers and a prospective investment from venture capitalists when Amazon won out in late 2012 with a rumored $26 million deal.

Evi employed a programming technique called knowledge graphs, or large databases of ontologies, which connect concepts and categories in related domains. If, for example, a user asked Evi, "What is the population of Cleveland?" the software interpreted the question and knew to turn to an accompanying source of demographic data. *Wired* described the technique as a "giant treelike structure" of logical connections to useful facts.

Putting Evi's knowledge base inside Alexa helped with the kind of informal but culturally common chitchat called phatic speech. If a user said to the device, "Alexa, good morning, how are you?" Alexa could make the right connection and respond. Tunstall-Pedoe said he had to fight with colleagues in the U.S. over the unusual idea of having Alexa respond to such social cues, recalling that "People were uncomfortable with the idea of programming a machine to respond to 'hello.'"

Integrating Evi's technology helped Alexa respond to factual queries, such as requests to name the planets in the solar system, and it gave the impression that Alexa was smart. But was it? Proponents of another method of natural language understanding, called deep learning, believed that Evi's knowledge graphs wouldn't give Alexa the kind of authentic intelligence that would satisfy Bezos's dream of a versatile assistant that could talk to users and answer any question.

In the deep learning method, machines were fed large amounts of data about how people converse and what responses proved satisfying, and then were programmed to train themselves to predict the best answers. The chief proponent of this approach was an Indian-born engineer named Rohit Prasad. "He was a critical hire," said engineering director John Thimsen. "Much of the success of the project is due to the team he assembled and the research they did on far-field speech recognition."

Prasad was raised in Ranchi, the capital of the eastern India state of Jharkhand. He grew up in a family of engineers and got hooked on *Star Trek* at a young age. Personal computers weren't common in India at the time, but at an early age he learned to code on a PC at the metallurgical and engineering consulting company where his father worked. Since communication in India was hampered by poor telecommunications infrastructure and high long-distance rates, Prasad decided to study how to compress speech over wireless networks when he moved to the U.S. to attend graduate school.

After graduating in the late 1990s, Prasad passed on the dot-com boom and worked for the Cambridge, Massachusetts–based defense contractor BBN Technologies (later acquired by Raytheon) on some of the first speech recognition and natural language systems. At BBN, he worked on one of the first in-car speech recognition systems and automated directory assistance services for telephone companies. In

2000, he worked on another system that automatically transcribed courtroom proceedings. Accurately recording conversation from multiple microphones placed around a courtroom introduced him to the challenges of far-field speech recognition. At the start of the project, he said that eighty out of every hundred words were incorrect; but within the first year, they cut it down to thirty-three.

Years later, as the Doppler team was trying to improve Alexa's comprehension, Bill Barton, who led Amazon's Boston office, introduced Prasad to Greg Hart. Prasad didn't know much about Amazon and showed up for the interview in Seattle wearing a suit and tie (a minor faux pas) and with no clue about Amazon's fourteen leadership principles (a bigger one). He expressed reservations about joining a large, plodding tech company, but by the time he returned to his hotel room, Hart had emailed him a follow-up note that promised, "We are essentially a startup. Even though we are part of a big company, we don't act like one."

Persuaded, Prasad joined to work on the problems of far-field speech recognition, but he ended up as an advocate for the deep learning model. Evi's knowledge graphs were too regimented to be Alexa's foundational response model; if a user says, "Play music by Sting," such a system may think he is trying to say "bye" to the artist and get confused, Prasad later explained. By using the statistical training methods of deep learning, the system could quickly ascertain that when the sentence is uttered, the intent is almost certainly to blast "Every Breath You Take."

But Evi's Tunstall-Pedoe argued that knowledge graphs were the more practical solution and mistrusted the deep learning approach. He felt it was error-prone and would require an endless diet of training data to properly mold Alexa's learning models. "The thing about machine learning scientists is that they never admit defeat because all of their problems can be solved with more data," he explained. That response might carry a tinge of regret with it, because to the *über* product manager, Bezos himself, there was no question about which way time's arrow was pointed—toward machine learning and deep neural networks. With its vast and sophisticated AWS data centers, Amazon was also in the unique position of being able to harness a large number of high-powered computer processors to train its speech models, exploiting its advantage in the cloud in a way few of its competitors could. Defeated, Tunstall-Pedoe ended up leaving Amazon in 2016.

Even though the deep learning approach won out, Prasad and his allies still had to solve the paradox that confronts all companies developing AI: they don't want to launch a system that is dumb—customers won't use it, and so won't generate enough data to improve the service. But companies need that data to train the system to make it smarter.

Google and Apple solved the paradox in part by licensing technology from Nuance, using its results to train their own speech models and then afterward cutting ties with the company. For years, Google also collected speech data from a toll-free directory assistance line, 800-Goog-411. Amazon had no such services it could mine, and Greg Hart was against licensing outside technology—he thought it would limit the company's flexibility in the long run. But the meager training data from the beta tests with employees amounted to speech from a few hundred white-collar workers, usually uttered from across the room in their noisy homes in the mornings and evenings when they weren't at the office. The data was lousy, and there wasn't enough of it.

Meanwhile Bezos grew impatient. "How will we even know when this product is good?" he kept asking in early 2013. Hart, Prasad, and their team created graphs that projected how Alexa would improve as data collection progressed. The math suggested they would need to roughly double the scale of their data collection efforts to achieve each successive 3 percent increase in Alexa's accuracy.

That spring, only a few weeks after Rohit Prasad had joined the company, they brought a six-page narrative to Bezos that laid out these facts, proposed to double the size of the speech science team and postpone a planned launch from the summer into the fall. Held in Bezos's conference room, the meeting did not go well.

"You are going about this the wrong way," Bezos said after reading about the delay. "First tell me what would be a magical product, then tell me how to get there."

Bezos's technical advisor at the time, Dilip Kumar, then asked if the company had enough data. Prasad, who was calling into the meeting from Cambridge, replied that they would need thousands of more hours of complex, far-field voice commands. According to an executive who was in the room, Bezos apparently factored in the request to increase the number of speech scientists and did the calculation in his head in a few seconds. "Let me get this straight. You are telling me that for your big request to make this product successful, instead of it taking forty years, it will only take us twenty?"

Prasad tried to dance around it. "Jeff, that is not how we think about it."

"Show me where my math is wrong!" Bezos said.

Hart jumped in. "Hang on, Jeff, we hear you, we got it."

Prasad and other Amazon executives would remember that meeting, and the other tough interactions with Bezos during the development of Alexa, differently. But according to the executive who was there, the CEO stood up, said, "You guys aren't serious about making this product," and abruptly ended the meeting.

―――――

In the very same buildings in Seattle and Sunnyvale, California, where the Doppler team was trying to make Alexa smarter, Amazon's campaign to build its own smartphone was careening toward disaster.

A few years before, Apple, Google, and Samsung had staked out large positions in the dawning smartphone market but had left the impression that terrain might remain for innovative newcomers. Typically, Jeff Bezos was not about to cede a critical strategic position in the unfolding digital terrain to other companies, especially when he believed the ground was still fertile for innovative approaches. In one brainstorming session he proposed a robot that could retrieve a carelessly discarded phone and drag it over to a wireless charger. (Some employees thought he was joking, but a patent on the idea was filed.) In another, he proposed a phone with an advanced 3D display, responsive to gestures in the air, instead of only taps on a touchscreen. It would be like nothing else in stores. Bezos clung to that idea, which would become the seed of the Fire Phone project.

The original designers settled on a handset with four infrared cameras, one in each corner of the phone's face, to track the user's gaze and present the illusion of a 3D image, along with a fifth camera on the back (because it could "see" from both sides of its head, the project was code-named Tyto, after a genus of owl). The custom-made Japanese cameras would cost $5 a handset, but Bezos envisioned a premium Amazon smartphone with top-of-the-line components.

Bezos met the Tyto team every few days for three years, at the same time he was meeting the Alexa team as frequently. He was infatuated with new technologies and business lines and loved spitballing ideas and reviewing the team's progress. And while he was inordinately focused on customer feedback in other parts of Amazon's business, Bezos did not believe that listening to them could result in dramatic product inventions, evangelizing instead for creative "wandering," which he believed was the path to dramatic breakthroughs. "The biggest needle movers will be things that customers don't know to ask for," he would write years later in a letter to shareholders. "We must invent on their behalf. We have to tap into our own inner imagination about what's possible."

But many Tyto employees were skeptical of his vision for smartphones. No one was sure the 3D display was anything more than a gimmick and a major drain on the phone's battery. Bezos also had some worrisome blind spots about smartphones. "Does anyone actually use the calendar on their phone?" he asked in one meeting. "We do use the calendar, yes," someone who did not have several personal assistants replied.

As in the Doppler project, the deadlines Bezos gave were unrealistic, and to try to make them, the team hired more engineers. But throwing more engineers at failing technology projects only makes them fail more spectacularly. Kindle was strategically important to Amazon at the time, so instead of poaching employees internally, the Tyto group had to look outside, to hardware engineers at other companies like Motorola, Apple, and Sony. Naturally, they didn't tell anyone what they'd be working on until their first day. "If you had a good reputation in the tech industry, they found you," said a Fire Phone manager.

The launch was perpetually six months away. The project dragged on as they tried to get the 3D display to work. The original top-of-the-line components quickly became outdated, so they decided to reboot the project with an upgraded processor and cameras. It was given a new owl-themed code name, Duke. The group started and then canceled another phone project, a basic low-cost handset to be made by HTC and code-named Otus, which would also use the Amazon flavor of the Android operating system that ran on Amazon's new Fire tablets, which were showing promise as an economical alternative to Apple's iPad.

Employees on the project were disappointed when Otus was scrapped because they quietly believed Amazon's opportunity was not in a fancy 3D display but in disrupting the market with a free or low-priced smartphone. Morale on the team started to sour. One group was so dubious about the entire project that they covertly bought a set of military dogtags that read "disagree and commit," after Amazon leadership principle #13, which says employees who disagree with a decision must put aside their doubts and work to support it.

In his annual letter to shareholders released in April 2014, Bezos wrote, "Inventing is messy, and over time, it's certain that we'll fail at some big bets too." The observation was curiously prophetic. The team was preparing to launch the phone at a big event that summer. Bezos's wife, MacKenzie, showed up for rehearsals to offer support and advice.

On June 18, 2014, Bezos unveiled the Fire Phone at a Seattle event space called Fremont Studios, where he attempted to summon some of the charismatic magic of the late Steve Jobs and waxed enthusiastic about the device's 3D display and gesture tracking. "I actually think he was a believer," said Craig Berman, an Amazon PR vice president at the time. "I really do. If he wasn't, he certainly wasn't going to signal it to the team."

Reviews of the phone were scathing. The smartphone market had shifted and matured during the painful four years that the Fire Phone was in development, and what had started as an attempt at creating a novel product now seemed strangely out of touch with customer expectations. Because it did not run Google's authorized version of Android, it did not have popular apps such as Gmail and YouTube. While it was cheaper than the forthcoming iPhone 6, it was more expensive than the multitude of low-cost, no-frills handsets made by Asian manufacturers, which were heavily subsidized at the time by the wireless carriers in exchange for two-year contracts.

"There was a lot of differentiation, but in the end, customers didn't care about it," said Ian Freed, the vice president in charge of the project. "I made a mistake and Jeff made a mistake. We didn't align the Fire Phone's value proposition with the Amazon brand, which is great value." Freed said that Bezos told him afterward, "You can't, for one minute, feel bad about the Fire Phone. Promise me you won't lose a minute of sleep."

Later that summer, workers in one of Amazon's fulfillment centers in Phoenix noticed thousands of unsold Fire Phones sitting untouched on massive wooden pallets. In October, the company wrote down $170 million in inventory and canceled the project, acknowledging one of its most expensive failures. "It failed for all the reasons we all said it was going to fail—that's the crazy thing about it," said Isaac Noble, one of the early software engineers who had been dubious from the start.

Ironically, the Fire Phone fiasco augured well for Doppler. Without a smartphone market share to protect, Amazon could pioneer the new category of smart speakers with unencumbered ambition. Many of the displaced engineers who weren't immediately snapped up by Google and Apple were given a few weeks to find new jobs at Amazon; some went to Doppler, or to a new hit product, Fire TV. Most importantly, Bezos didn't penalize Ian Freed and other Fire Phone managers, sending a strong message inside Amazon that taking risks was rewarded—especially if the entire debacle was primarily his own fault.

On the other hand, it revealed a worrisome fact about life inside Amazon. Many employees who worked on the Fire Phone had serious doubts about it, but no one, it seemed, had been brave or clever enough to take a stand and win an argument with their obstinate leader.

After Jeff Bezos walked out on them, the Doppler executives working on the Alexa prototype retreated with their wounded pride to a nearby conference room and reconsidered their solution to the data paradox. Their boss was right. Internal testing with Amazon employees was too limited and they would need to massively expand the Alexa beta while somehow still keeping it a secret from the outside world.

The resulting program, conceived by Rohit Prasad and speech scientist Janet Slifka over a few days in the spring of 2013, and quickly approved by Greg Hart, would put the Doppler program on steroids and answer a question that later vexed speech experts—how did Amazon come out of nowhere to leapfrog Google and Apple in the race to build a speech-enabled virtual assistant?

Internally the program was called AMPED. Amazon contracted

with an Australian data collection firm, Appen, and went on the road with Alexa, in disguise. Appen rented homes and apartments, initially in Boston, and then Amazon littered several rooms with all kinds of "decoy" devices: pedestal microphones, Xbox gaming consoles, televisions, and tablets. There were also some twenty Alexa devices planted around the rooms at different heights, each shrouded in an acoustic fabric that hid them from view but allowed sound to pass through. Appen then contracted with a temp agency, and a stream of contract workers filtered through the properties, eight hours a day, six days a week, reading scripts from an iPad with canned lines and open-ended requests like "ask to play your favorite tune" and "ask anything you'd like an assistant to do."

The speakers were turned off, so the Alexas didn't make a peep, but the seven microphones on each device captured everything and streamed the audio to Amazon's servers. Then another army of workers manually reviewed the recordings and annotated the transcripts, classifying queries that might stump a machine, like "turn on *Hunger Games*," as a request to play the Jennifer Lawrence film, so that the next time, Alexa would know.

The Boston test showed promise, so Amazon expanded the program, renting more homes and apartments in Seattle and ten other cities over the next six months to capture the voices and speech patterns of thousands more paid volunteers. It was a mushroom-cloud explosion of data about device placement, acoustic environments, background noise, regional accents, and all the gloriously random ways a human being might phrase a simple request to hear the weather, for example, or play a Justin Timberlake hit.

The daylong flood of random people into homes and apartments repeatedly provoked suspicious neighbors to call the police. In one instance, a resident of a Boston condo complex suspected a drug-dealing or prostitution ring was next door and called the cops, who asked to enter the apartment. The nervous staff gave them an elusive explanation and a tour and afterward hastily shut down the site. Occasionally, temp workers would show up, consider the bizarre script and vagueness of the entire affair, and simply refuse to participate. One Amazon employee who was annotating transcripts later recalled hearing a temp worker interrupt a session and whisper to whoever he suspected was listening: "This is so dumb. The company behind this should be embarrassed!"

But Amazon was anything but embarrassed. By 2014, it had increased its store of speech data by a factor of ten thousand and largely closed the data gap with rivals like Apple and Google. Bezos was giddy. Hart hadn't asked for his approval of the AMPED project, but a few weeks before the program began, he updated Bezos with a six-page document that described it and its multimillion-dollar cost. A huge grin spread over Bezos's face as he read, and all signs of past peevishness were gone. "Now I know you are serious about it! What are we going to do next?"

What came next was Doppler's long-awaited launch. Working eighty to ninety hours a week, employees were missing whole chunks of their family's lives, and Bezos wasn't letting up. He wanted to see everything and made impetuous new demands. On an unusually clear Seattle day, with the setting sun streaming through his conference room window, for example, Bezos noticed that the ring's light was not popping brightly enough, so he ordered a complete redo. Almost alone, he argued for a feature called Voice Cast, which linked an Alexa device to a nearby Fire tablet, so that queries showed up as placards on the tablet's screen. When engineers tried to quietly drop the feature, he noticed and told the team they were not launching without it. (Few customers ended up using it.)

But he was also right about many things. As launch neared, one faction of employees worried that the device wasn't good enough at hearing commands amid loud music or cross talk and lobbied to include a remote control, like the one the company made for the Fire TV. Bezos was opposed to it but agreed to ship remotes with the first batch of speakers to see if customers would use them. (They didn't, and the remote disappeared.)

He also headed off a near disaster when it came to what to actually call the device. For four years there had been no consensus on that topic. The team debated endlessly whether there should be one name or two for the virtual assistant and the hardware. After opting for separate names, they cycled through various options for the speaker and settled on ... the Amazon Flash. The news updates would be called "Flash briefings," and packaging with the Flash brand printed on it was ready to ship.

But then less than a month before the introduction, Bezos said in a meeting, "I think we can do better." Searching for a replacement, they opted to pilfer the name of an Alexa feature, Echo, which allowed a customer to ask Alexa to repeat a word or phrase. (The command was then changed to "Simon says.") There wasn't enough time to print new boxes or user manuals, so the Echo's earliest buyers ended up receiving plain black boxes. Toni Reid, a director Hart hired to launch the product, had to write the user manual without ever actually naming the product. "That's a skill everyone should have," she said.

The introduction of the Amazon Echo on November 6, 2014, was molded by the failure of the Fire Phone only months before it. There was no press conference or visionary speech by Bezos—he was seemingly done forever with his halfhearted impression of the late Steve Jobs, who had unveiled new products with such verve. Instead, Bezos appeared more comfortable with a new, understated approach: the team announced the Echo with a press release and two-minute explanatory video on YouTube that showed a family cheerfully talking to Alexa. Amazon execs did not tout the new device as a fully conversational computer, but carefully highlighted several domains where they were confident it was useful, such as delivering the news and weather, setting timers, creating shopping lists, and playing music.

Then they asked customers to join a waiting list to buy an Echo and reviewed the list carefully, considering factors like whether ap-

plicants were users of Amazon Music and owned a Kindle. Recognizing that it was an untested market, they also ordered an initial batch
of only eighty thousand devices, compared to a preliminary order of
more than three hundred thousand Fire Phones, and distributed them
gradually over the next few months. "The Fire Phone certainly made
folks a little cautious," said Greg Hart. "It led us to revisit everything."

After four years of development, more than one Doppler veteran
suspected that the Amazon Echo might leave another smoking crater
in the consumer technology landscape, right next to the Fire Phone's.
On launch day, they huddled over their laptops in a "war room" from
their new offices in the Prime building, a few minutes' walk from
Fiona, to watch as the waiting list swelled past even their most hyper-
bolic projections.

In the midst of the vigil, someone realized they were letting a significant accomplishment slide by unappreciated. "It was our launch
moment and we weren't ready for it," said Al Lindsay. So, a hundred
or so employees headed to a nearby bar for a long-awaited celebration, and a few of the weary executives and engineers on the project
closed it down that night.

Over the next few weeks, a hundred and nine thousand customers
registered for the waiting list to receive an Echo. Along with some
natural skepticism, positive reviews rolled in, with quotes like "I just
spoke to the future and it listened," and "it's the most innovative device Amazon's made in years." Employees emailed Alexa executives
Toni Reid and Greg Hart, pleading for devices for family members
and friends.

After the Echo shipped, the team could see when the devices were
turned on and that people were actually using them. Bezos's intuition had been right: there was something vaguely magical in sum-
moning a computer in your home without touching the glass of a
smartphone, something valuable in having a responsive speaker that

could play music, respond to practical requests ("how many cups are there in a quart?"), and even banter with playful ones ("Alexa, are you married?").

Many Doppler employees had expected they could now catch their breath and enjoy all their accrued vacation time. But that is not what happened. Instead of stumbling ashore from choppy seas to rest, another giant wave crashed over their heads. Bezos deployed his playbook for experiments that produced promising sparks: he poured gasoline on them. "We had a running success on our hands and that's where my life changed," said Rohit Prasad, who would be promoted to vice president and eventually join the vaunted Amazon leadership committee, the S-team. "I knew the playbook to the launch of Alexa and Echo. The playbook for the next five years, I didn't have."

Over the next few months, Amazon would roll out the Alexa Skills Kit, which allowed other companies to build voice-enabled apps for the Echo, and Alexa Voice Service, which let the makers of products like lightbulbs and alarm clocks integrate Alexa into their own devices. Bezos also told Greg Hart that the team needed to release new features with a weekly cadence, and that since there was no way to signal the updates, Amazon should email customers every week to alert them to the new features their devices offered.

Bezos's wish list became the product plan—he wanted Alexa to be everywhere, doing everything, all at once. Services that had originally been pushed to the wayside in the scramble to launch, like shopping on Alexa, now became urgent priorities. Bezos ordered up a smaller, cheaper version of the Echo, the hockey puck–sized Echo Dot, as well as a portable version with batteries, the Amazon Tap. Commenting on the race to build a virtual assistant and smart speaker, Bezos said, "Amazon's going to be fine if someone comes along and overtakes us," as part of the annual late-summer OP1 series of planning meetings, the year after Alexa's introduction. "But wouldn't it be incredibly annoying if we can't be the leader in creating this?"

Life inside the Prime building, and in the gradually increasing number of offices around South Lake Union inhabited by the Alexa team, became even busier. Many of the new features would be rushed out the door, so that Amazon could start gathering customer feedback. Silicon Valley startups call this style of product development "minimum viable product," or MVP. At Amazon, Jeff Wilke had popularized the idea of calling it "minimum lovable product," or MLP, asking, "What would we be proud to take to the market?" It didn't seem to matter that many Alexa features, such as the voice calling, were initially half-baked and rarely used. Over the course of the 2015 holiday season, Amazon sold a million Echo devices.

Alexa's division-wide motto became "Get Big Fast," the same slogan used in the early years for Amazon. History was repeating itself. An organization of a few hundred employees swelled to a thousand in the first year after the launch, and then, incredibly, to ten thousand over the next five years. Through it all, like a crazed pyromaniac, Bezos kept spraying lighter fluid on the fire, promoting Alexa by paying an estimated $10 million for Amazon's first ever Super Bowl ad in January 2016, starring Alec Baldwin, Missy Elliott, and former Dolphins quarterback Dan Marino.

Despite all this attention, there was a sense inside Amazon that the Alexa organization was not moving fast enough. Greg Hart, who had produced the device out of nothing more than a Bezos email and whiteboard drawing, left the division and moved over to help run Prime Video. "The thing that I got up every day loving doing was the creation of Alexa," he said wistfully years later. But with the Alexa group growing fast, "it was probably a better fit for another leader."

In his place came a longtime Bezos favorite, Mike George, a bald, charismatic, cowboy boot–wearing Amazonian with a penchant for face paint, who liked to walk into meetings with an Amazon Tap under his arm, blasting music.

Mike George had what Bezos called a "fungible" energy. Over the years, Bezos deployed him like a firefighter to douse the flames of chaos and instill order in divisions like human resources, marketplace, payments, and later, Bezos's private philanthropy, Day 1 Academies Fund. Various colleagues endearingly referred to him as a "brute," a "high school jock who never unjocked," and "totally cleaved from Jeff's rib."

Mike George ran Alexa for a year, but the impact is still broadly felt. The Alexa division couldn't recruit fast enough to fulfill its hiring needs, so Amazon instituted a sort of company-wide draft, giving every new hire to other parts of Amazon—like AWS and retail—an alternate job offer to join the Alexa division instead. Unhappy Amazon managers suddenly lost sought-after engineers they thought they had recruited.

George also instituted a dramatic change in the Alexa group's structure. It had been a functional organization, with centralized engineering, product management, and marketing teams. But that wasn't growing smoothly or fast enough for Bezos's liking. George instead reorganized Alexa around the Amazonian ideal of fast-moving "two pizza" teams, each devoted to a specific Alexa domain, like music, weather, lighting, thermostats, video devices, and so on.

Each team was run by a so-called "single-threaded leader" who had ultimate control and absolute accountability over their success or failure. (The phrase comes from computer science terminology; a single-threaded program executes one command at a time.) Alexa, like Amazon itself, became a land of countless CEOs, each operating autonomously. To yoke them all together, George oversaw the creation of a "north star" document, to crystalize the strategy of a global, voice-enabled computing platform.

Meanwhile Bezos approved all these changes and stayed intimately involved, attending product reviews and reading the Friday night compilation of updates from all the various two-pizza teams, and responding with detailed questions or problems that the groups would then have to fix over the weekend. Alexa execs, like leaders elsewhere in Amazon, became frequent recipients of the CEO's escalation emails, in which he forwarded a customer complaint accompanied by a single question mark and then expected a response within twenty-four hours. He was also the chief evangelist for Alexa within the company. "What are you doing for Alexa?" he asked other executives, as he had for AWS years before. Everyone in the company had to include Alexa in the OP1 documents they presented to the S-team, describing their plans for the coming year.

At the end of 2016, after eight million U.S. households had purchased an Echo or Echo Dot, device exec Dave Limp announced internally that Amazon had become the top-selling speaker company in the world. It validated the entire crusade. But of course, Bezos wanted to become the top AI firm in the world, and in that respect, he was about to have significant competition.

That fall, Google introduced the Google Home smart speaker. It looked considerably more stylish, "like something you might plant a succulent in," said *Wired*. It also had a crisper sound and, predictably, searched the web and retrieved answers with aplomb. The Alexa team had "gone into every holiday season just waiting for either Apple or Google to announce something, and when they didn't, we would just high-five each other," said former Alexa exec Charlie Kindel. Even though those companies were allergic to what they considered copycat products, eventually they couldn't resist the fast-growing smart speaker market.

That added to the pressure on the Alexa team to move faster and stay ahead with new features and variations on the hardware. In early 2017, a Swedish customer emailed Bezos to ask why Amazon was waiting to develop language-specific versions of Alexa before introducing the Echo in Europe. Why couldn't they just sell it everywhere in English first? This was actually on the product road map but wasn't a priority. According to one executive, Bezos got that email at 2 a.m. Seattle time, and by the following morning there were a half dozen independent groups working to sell Alexa in eighty new countries.

Later, Alexa execs would say that Bezos's close involvement made their lives more difficult but also produced immeasurable results.

Jeff "gave us the license and permission to do some of the things we needed to do to go faster and to go bigger," Toni Reid said. "You can regulate yourself quite easily or think about what you're going to do with your existing resources.... Sometimes, you don't know what the boundaries are. Jeff just wanted us to be unbounded."

––––––––

But there were drawbacks to the frenetic speed and growth. For years the Alexa smartphone app looked like something a design student had come up with during a late-night bender. Setting up an Echo, or networking Echos throughout the home, was more complicated than it needed to be. It was also difficult and confusing for users to phrase commands in the right way to trigger third-party skills and specialized features.

The decentralized and chaotic approach of countless two-pizza teams run by single-threaded leaders was manifested in aspects of the product that had become overly complex. Basic tasks, like setting up a device and connecting it to smart home appliances, had become "painful, very painful to the customer," agreed Tom Taylor, a sardonic and even-keeled Amazon executive who took over from Mike George as leader of the Alexa unit in 2017. He set out to "find all the places that customers are suffering from our organizational structure."

There was plenty of turmoil that Taylor and his colleagues couldn't quell. In March 2018, a bug caused Alexas around the world to randomly emit crazed, unprompted laughter. A few months later, an Echo inadvertently recorded the private conversation of a couple in Portland, Oregon, and inexplicably sent the recording to one of the husband's employees in Seattle, whose phone number was in his address book. Amazon said the device thought it had heard its wake word and then a series of commands to record and forward the conversation. It was an "extremely rare occurrence," the company said, and that, "as unlikely as this string of events is, we are evaluating options to make this case even less likely." After those incidents, employees had to write a "correction of error" report, which analyzes an incident in detail and tries to get to its underlying root causes by going through a series of iterative questions and answers called "the five whys." The memo went all the way to Bezos, describing what had happened and recommending how the process that created the problem in the first place could be fixed.

Some errors could not be undone, such as Alexa's penchant for assassinating Santa Claus in the minds of younger users. One such incident took place during the Alexa Prize, an Amazon contest among universities to build artificial chatbots that could carry on a sophisticated multipart conversation. When Alexa users said, "Alexa, let's chat," they got to talk to one of the chatbots and rate its performance. During the first competition in 2017, the chatbot from the University of Washington was retrieving some of its answers from Reddit, an online discussion board, and errantly informed a child that Santa was a myth. The parents complained and the chatbot was temporarily pulled from the rotation (but later won the $500,000 grand prize).

The periodic problems with Alexa underscored how far it had come and how far it still had to go. By 2019, Amazon had sold more than 100 million Echo devices. In the span of a decade, a product spawned by Bezos's love of science fiction and infatuation with invention had become a universally recognized product whose miscues and challenges to conventional notions of privacy were widely covered by the media.

Yet Alexa still wasn't conversational, in the way Bezos and Rohit Prasad had originally hoped. And though it had spawned a small cottage industry of startups and other companies pinning their hopes on voice-enabled services and devices, not many people used Alexa's third-party add-ons or "Skills," and developers still weren't seeing much revenue, compared to the way they did on the app stores of Apple and Google.

Bezos fervently believed all that would come in the next few years. Awed employees and Amazon fans who had watched him visualize

Alexa and will it into existence believed the CEO could practically see the future. But in at least one respect, he did not.

In 2016, he was reviewing the Echo Show, the first Alexa device with a video screen. Executives who worked on the project recalled that on several occasions when Bezos demoed the prototype, he spent the first few minutes asking Alexa to play videos that ridiculed a certain GOP presidential candidate.

"Alexa, show me the video, 'Donald Trump says "China,"'" he asked, or "Alexa, play Stephen Colbert's monologue from last night." Then "he would laugh like there's no tomorrow," said a vice president who was in the demos.

Bezos had no idea what was coming.

CHAPTER 2

A Name Too Boring to Notice

I n November 2012, when Donald Trump was still the host of a reality TV show and Alexa prototypes were about to start moving into the homes of employees, Jeff Bezos was asked by the TV interviewer Charlie Rose a question that had become a recurring favorite of journalists: Will Amazon ever buy or open physical stores? "Only if we can have a truly differentiated idea," he replied. "We want to do something that is uniquely Amazon. We haven't found it yet, but if we can find that idea, we would love to."

The answer was only partially true. Because inside Amazon, a small team was already converging on a novel concept for a chain of physical stores, under the direction of Bezos himself. They were getting ready to make what would turn out to be one of the most quixotic and expensive bets in the company's history.

At the time, Bezos was not only observing how advancements in processing power and decreases in computing costs were helping computers understand human speech. He was also tracking the potential for computers with cameras to actually see—to recognize and understand images and video. Earlier that year, he had circulated among Amazon's senior engineers an article in the *New York Times* that described how a Google supercomputer had pored over ten million images and taught itself to recognize cats. "Jeff had faith that this was a really important trend that we should pay attention to," said Joseph Sirosh, chief technology officer of Amazon's retail business at the time. "Just as he got really enthusiastic about computer voice recognition, he was also really excited about computer vision."

The allure of computer vision, along with his interest in pressing Amazon's advantage in the cloud to push the frontiers of artificial intelligence, again sparked the fertile imagination of Amazon's founder. More than 90 percent of retail transactions were conducted in physical stores, according to the U.S. Census Bureau. Perhaps there was a way to tap this vast reservoir of sales with a completely self-service physical store that harnessed emerging technologies like computer vision and robotics.

In 2012, Bezos pitched this broad idea at an off-site meeting to the S-team. Bezos alone handpicked members for the leadership council, and they held such brainstorm sessions every year, usually at some nearby corporate retreat, to spark new ideas and reaffirm the importance of "thinking big." Members were required to write a paper with an inventive idea that might expand Amazon's business.

Judging from the executives he assigned to follow up on his challenge, Bezos considered the opportunity of entering physical retail with a self-service store to be significant. To lead the project, he appointed Steve Kessel, the deputy who had started the Kindle business nearly a decade before. Kessel, a Dartmouth graduate and recreational hockey player who had worked for Amazon since 1999, had the first discussions about the job while he was on sabbatical with his family in the south of France. His new task, in Amazonspeak, was to have a "single-threaded focus" on creating a new line of innovative stores. To manage the project, Kessel in turn lured back Gianna Puerini, a vice president who over the years had run Amazon's home page and recommendations businesses.

Puerini, the wife of S-team member Brian Valentine, was happily retired at the time, restoring and flipping houses in the Seattle area, and had no plans or financial need to return to work. She said she found Kessel's pitch compelling. "When I asked Steve 'Why me?' a key part of his answer was that while we had a lot in common, he thought we would approach problems from different angles and look at things in different ways," Puerini said. "I loved that he acknowledged the diversity of perspective and thought process.... I think I emailed Steve that night and said, 'I'm in!'"

Bezos's technical advisor at the time, Dilip Kumar, the successor to Greg Hart in the coveted aide-de-camp role, would join Kessel and Puerini in early 2013 to run engineering. Because Bezos thought traditional retailers played their appointed roles well, the group had to meet a high bar before they could proceed. "Jeff was very particular that he didn't want to just build any store. He wanted the store to be disruptive—something that no one had attempted before, something that would change the way brick-and-mortar retail had been done for hundreds of years," said Bali Raghavan, who joined as one of the first engineering directors.

The project was to be kept a secret even from other Amazon employees. So the team set up shop above a sporting goods store in a nondescript six-floor building on Westlake Avenue. One of Puerini's first tasks was selecting a code name so boring that no one would pay any attention to them. For the next few years, the team would go by the initials, IHM, short for the nonsensical "Inventory Health Management." Much later, after years of laborious progress toward their ambitious goal, the project would be known by the name of the peculiar store they would create and try to bring to nearly every major city in North America: Amazon Go.

In those early weeks of brainstorming, the IHM crew considered whether they should develop Macy's-style department stores, electronics stores, or Walmart-style supercenters. Bezos had no particular opinion about what they should sell, just that he wanted to disrupt traditional retail. One discarded idea involved two-floor outlets, with mobile robots swarming over an upper level packed with merchandise. Conveyor belts and other robots would then deliver them to customers' waiting vehicles below.

Amazon executives like to say and repeat compulsively that they start with the needs of the customer and "work backwards." Ruminating on the act of shopping in regular stores, Puerini's team made lists of their advantages, such as the instant gratification of walking out with desired items. They also made a list of the drawbacks, chief among them the frustration of waiting in checkout lines. People "are busy. They probably have something they'd rather be doing," Puerini said.

After months of research into customer needs and feasible technology, Amazon's crack team of type A disrupters felt that the waiting problem was one they could solve with technology. The PR FAQs from the time—with Bezos's handwriting scrawled in the margin, according to people who saw drafts—coined a trademark for a system that didn't yet exist: "Just Walk Out technology." Having envisioned the outcome, they would now try to invent a system that would allow shoppers to select items from shelves and get automatically charged without ever queueing up to pay.

An excited Bezos approved the approach in 2013, not knowing that it would take five arduous and expensive years of research to bring it to fruition. "I think in the beginning, even the scientists were a little suspicious whether or not they could actually pull the thing off," said Doug Herrington, the Amazon senior vice president in charge of the North American e-commerce business.

The Amazon Go engineers initially considered using RFID chips in the product packaging to track which items were removed from shelves or asking customers to use their smartphones to scan product barcodes. But Bezos didn't want them to take an easy path; he wanted them to innovate in the field of computer vision, which he saw as important to Amazon's future. So they settled on the idea of cameras in the ceiling and algorithms behind the scenes that would try to spot when customers selected products and charge them for it. Scales hidden inside the shelves would provide another reliable sensor to determine when products were being removed and corroborate who was buying what.

Over the next few years, Dilip Kumar recruited experts from out-side Amazon, such as the University of Southern California's renowned computer vision scientist, Gérard Medioni, as well as engineers from inside who worked on complex technologies like Amazon's pricing al-gorithms. They were entering the hottest crucible at Amazon—a *Jeff project*, one that had the attention of the ever-curious and demand-ing boss. During a normal week, they would put in seventy to eighty hours, pushing against impending deadlines and the boundaries of science. At nights and over the weekends, they answered email, wrote six-page narrative memos, and like their counterparts on the concur-rent Alexa and Fire Phone projects, prepared incessantly for regular reviews with Bezos. "We were all living in a cave," said engineering di-rector Bali Raghavan.

Toward the end of 2013, they decided to focus on groceries. Amer-icans on average shopped for clothes and electronics just a few times a year. They shopped for food an average 1.7 times a week in 2013, according to the Food Marketing Institute, magnifying the inconve-nience of waiting in line. The Go team started to hire executives with grocery experience, who were asked not to change their LinkedIn profiles and were furnished with burner phones and credit cards with no link to Amazon. "In the beginning, it was very 007-like, and it felt cool and important," said Steve Lamontagne, a veteran of the Albert-sons and SuperValu grocery chains. "It's a lonely way to work though, particularly not being able to leverage the contacts you've established over decades."

The Go team presented every few weeks to Jeff Bezos. One notable meeting took place late in the day on June 24, 2014. Team members remember it because Amazon reported weak quarterly earnings that day and its stock sank 10 percent—the biggest drop in a year when Amazon was beset by the failure of the Fire Phone and unusually tepid sales growth. But Bezos was unperturbed. While he could be a remorseless boss capable of terrifying employees when they failed to meet his exacting standards, he seemed to have an unusual wellspring of patience for those at the company who practiced the challenging art of invention. "If there was any time the guy should have been agitated, that was it," said Lamontagne. "Every time I was in a room with him, he never asked us, 'How much is this going to cost me?' or 'Can we make money in X amount of time?' He would look at us and say, 'I know this is really hard and there is a lot of fatigue that comes with inventing something new. You're heading in the right direction.'"

Go execs envisioned large-scale stores of about thirty thousand square feet, roughly the size of a suburban supermarket. After a few months, they decided such a megamarket was overly ambitious and cut the proposed store in half. The midsized grocery store would offer a mix of services, not only rows of shelves with grab-and-go items, but counters with cheesemongers, baristas, and meat butchers. Employees envisioned a warm and welcoming experience and became attached to the idea of selling hot meals and coffee. Puerini's team designed the first concept store in one of their conference rooms, using children's blocks and standard-issue Amazon bookshelves and door desks to conceptualize how customers might behave in such an environment.

As the project neared a hoped-for introduction in mid-2015, Amazon anonymously leased the ground floor of a new luxury apartment building in Seattle's wealthy Capitol Hill neighborhood. Permits filed with the city included plans for a large produce department, dairy coolers, and an on-site kitchen for preparation of fresh foods. The Go team then sought Bezos's sign-off. It would be a typical "Jeff meeting"—the documents endlessly rewritten and polished, the day choreographed to within an inch, and everyone holding their breath and hoping that things didn't go haywire.

To show off the concept, they leased a warehouse in south Seattle, near Starbucks headquarters, and converted part of the ground floor into a fifteen-thousand-square-foot mock supermarket. Plywood faux walls conveyed the perimeter, modular shelves could be moved around, and turnstiles mimicked technology that would scan shoppers' smartphones when they walked in. Bezos and members of the S-team arrived and sat around an imported conference table to peruse the six-page document.

Bezos is usually one of the slowest readers in these sessions; he seems to carefully consider every sentence. But this time, halfway through, he put down the document and said, "You know what, let's go shop," and led the S-team into the dummy store. They pushed grocery carts down the faux aisles with shelves stocked with canned food and plastic fruit and vegetables. Go employees posed as the baristas, butchers, and cheesemongers, taking orders and adding items to their imaginary bills.

It seemed to go well, and afterward Bezos gathered the group in the makeshift conference room. He told them that while they all had done a fine job, the experience was too complicated. Customers would have to wait in line for meat, seafood, and fruit to be weighed and added to their bill, which contrasted with the store's major selling point: the absence of time-wasting queues. He felt the magic was walking out without waiting—the physical equivalent of Amazon's famous one-click ordering—and wanted to focus the effort on that, with a smaller and simpler experience. "It was one of those Amazon things, 'We love it—let's change everything!'" recalled Kristi Coulter, who worked on the project as a brand designer.

Steve Kessel reconvened the Go team in their offices and broke the news: they would be losing the fresh produce, meat, and cheese, and pivoting to a much smaller convenience store format. For the next five years, the storefront on Capitol Hill, where they were going to build the midsized supermarket, would sit abandoned, in the heart of one of Seattle's most well-trafficked neighborhoods, its windows mysteriously covered in brown paper.

By the start of 2016, the Amazon Go project had reached a critical juncture: the path ahead was going to be difficult and expensive.

Kessel called another meeting of Go execs and asked whether they thought they should proceed, move the project into a gestational R&D phase, or cancel it. While a few execs were skeptical, the consensus was to push forward.

Some of the engineers were relieved that they were reducing complexity in the stores by eliminating items with variable weights and prices, like steaks. Others were exhausted from two years of nonstop work and felt captive to an abrasive personality who pushed them relentlessly, generating numerous sprints toward artificial deadlines even as the race started to resemble a grueling marathon. Surprisingly, this time it was not Bezos but the executive who had worked by Bezos's side and exhibited some of the trademark characteristics that executives often need to be successful at Amazon, Bezos's former TA, Dilip Kumar.

Kumar was from Salem, India, the son of a three-star general in the Indian Army. His family moved around when he was a child and spent about "two years everywhere," as he put it. Kumar attended the prestigious Indian Institute of Technology and moved to the U.S. in '94 to get a master's degree in computer science and engineering from Penn State University and an MBA from Wharton. He joined Amazon in 2003, as it was still staggering after the dot-com bust. Over the years, Kumar relieved stress by locking himself in a conference room and teaching himself to juggle and later by performing stand-up comedy at local open-mic nights.

Kumar inhabited a few aspects of the Amazonian leadership template forged by Bezos in his younger, more tempestuous years as CEO: hard-driving, maniacal about the customer, IQ over EQ, raw force of will over innate leadership ability. Colleagues said that Kumar had a remarkable memory and ability to recall even complex technical details. They also say he created an environment in which there were no other options but to succeed. Like every leader at Amazon, he could handily recite the company's fourteen leadership principles—and like his boss, believed that the only way to get to good decisions was to passionately debate hard problems. "If I have to choose between agreement and conflict, I'll take conflict every time," Bezos often said. "It always yields a better result."

But unlike Bezos, Kumar was a skillful wielder of profanity in the workplace, colleagues said. They recall such epic shouting matches between him and Gianna Puerini that once Steve Kessel had to step in. Though instead of breaking up the dispute, Kessel asked them to fight more quietly. "If he was treating you nicely, it meant you were not important," said a senior scientist on the project. Added Bali Raghavan, "He's an intense guy to work for, and it used to drive me nuts. He also brings out the best in people." Of course, the same thing was often said of Bezos as well.

As Go execs decided to move forward, Kumar would need every bit of drive and prickly ingenuity. After the ill-fated demo to Bezos and the S-team, the Go group reduced the project to the size of a 7-Eleven-type convenience store, so that they could focus solely on the capabilities of the technology. Kumar's engineers set up a secret lab on the ground floor of a new Amazon building, called Otter, on the corner of 5th Avenue and Bell Street. Workers could only access it from the inside, swiping their key cards to enter a pair of locked doors. The shelves were packed with fake food fashioned from clay and Styrofoam; shredded green construction paper stood in for lettuce.

Kumar asked Go employees to visit and try to fool the overhead cameras and computer-vision algorithms. They wore heavy coats or walked in on crutches or pushed wheelchairs. One day, everyone was asked to bring in umbrellas to see if they would obscure the view of the cameras; on another, employees all wore Seattle Seahawks jerseys to confuse algorithms that partly distinguished shoppers using the color of their clothing.

The challenge was that while the technology wasn't fooled frequently, it was wrong often enough that it could create vexing problems if Amazon deployed it widely. Changes in lighting conditions and drifting shadows, the depth of a product's placement on shelves, and hands and bodies that concealed customized stickers on products could easily confound the system. Toddlers were a special challenge—small, difficult for computers to distinguish from their parents, and the source of all kinds of anomalous mischief inside stores. Adults might also hoist them on their shoulders, for example, hold them in their arms, or push them in strollers, further confounding the customer identification algorithms, which determined which account would be charged.

While Kumar and his engineers were addressing these challenges, Bezos and Kessel were getting impatient. Despite three years of work, Amazon hadn't opened a single store. So in the peculiar fashion of invention at Amazon, they created separate teams to pursue the singular goal of bringing the company into the vast realm of physical retail. Bezos liked to say Amazon was "stubborn on vision, flexible on details," and here was an illustration: groups working on parallel tracks would essentially compete to fulfill the "Just Walk Out" ideal and solve the problem of the cashierless store.

Kumar's group continued to develop a store with futuristic computer vision technology embedded in the ceilings and shelves. Meanwhile, Kessel asked Jeremy De Bonet, an Amazon technology director based in Boston, to form his own internal startup of engineers and computer vision scientists. They would end up flipping the problem around and integrating computer vision technology and sensors into a shopping cart, instead of blanketing them around the store. In some ways, this was a harder problem. While the Go store could partially deduce the identity of an item based on where in the store it was located, a so-called "smart cart" would have to account for the possibility of a shopper selecting, say, a bag of oranges from the produce aisle but scanning them somewhere else in the store.

This group's efforts would also take years to develop and would culminate in several technologies that were integrated into the Go store, as well as the Amazon Dash Carts equipped with computer vision scanners and touchscreens that would allow customers to check out as they roamed the aisles of a supermarket.

Bezos and Kessel formed a third team to pursue a more modest and immediately obtainable goal: opening bookstores with a more conventional checkout line. Books were the opposite of food—nonperishable, consistently priced, easy to stock—and, of course, the product category Amazon had pioneered online. Customers shopped for books less frequently than food, so waiting to pay was less of a hassle. And books could once again be bait, drawing in shoppers to experience devices like the Fire TV, the latest Kindles, and the new Amazon Echo.

In the fall of 2015, as the company prepared its first Amazon Books outlet in an upscale mall in Seattle, speculation over how it would finally enter physical retail was so feverish that a reporter for the local tech blog *GeekWire* used a pole with a camera attached to it to peek inside. Around the same time, Bezos sneaked in through a back door to see the outlet for the first time and was delighted. He said he felt as if Amazon's business was coming full circle.

The store opened a few weeks later, on November 2, 2015. Employees who worked on the project got to contribute their favorite books to a "staff selections" bookshelf. Bezos himself selected three titles, and in a way, they foreshadowed an unexpected turn of events that lay ahead: *Traps*, a novel by his wife, MacKenzie Bezos; *The 5 Love Languages*, by Gary Chapman, about preserving romantic relationships; and *The Gift of Fear*, by his friend, the famed security consultant Gavin de Becker.

To some longtime Go members, watching Amazon Books open within a few months was disheartening. But by the beginning of 2016, the team was finally preparing for their eventual launch. To decide on a formal name for the store, Puerini's team conducted a series of branding exercises, brainstorming and writing tenets on what the name should communicate to the public. They settled on "Amazon

Go" to convey speed. "Even the word itself is only two characters," she said. "You can literally grab and go."

Inside the Otter lab, fake food was replaced with real items, and Go employees were asked to shop under specific scenarios. For example, Puerini recalled, "You're running to a meeting: buy a salad and a drink for lunch," or "You're in a rush to pick up the kids from day care: grab milk, strawberries, and cereal for tomorrow morning." Continuing to puzzle over the toddler challenge, they asked parents to bring in their kids, who fidgeted, ran around, and grabbed things, further stress-testing the system.

Employees had mixed feelings about their progress. Many loved the convenience, reveling in the ability to run to the Otter lab before an afternoon meeting, grab a sandwich, and return, experiencing the just-walk-out magic they had once hypothesized about in the PR FAQs. But behind the scenes, the technology was not perfect and humans were needed to backstop it. Teams of employees were formed to review footage when the system wasn't certain about a purchase, a so-called "low-confidence event." The creation of these groups, the equivalent of the wizard-behind-the-curtain work being done by contractors that reviewed and improved Alexa's responses, led some employees to question the entire effort. It "was a tricky thing," said designer Kristi Coulter. "If we have an army of people looking at footage, is that scaling properly?"

Humans had another role to play as well: to develop meal-kit recipes and prepare the daily lunch fare, such as lamb sandwiches and caprese salads. To get ready for the opening of an eighteen-hundred-square-foot prototype store on Amazon's Seattle campus in late 2016, the company hired chefs and staff from industrial kitchens and chain restaurants. It then opened both a kitchen inside the prototype store and a commercial-grade cookhouse in south Seattle, to serve as a model for kitchens that the company planned to build around the country as part of a massive rollout of Go stores. Uncharacteristically,

Amazon splurged, buying German commercial ovens that cost tens of thousands of dollars each.

The kitchens brought with them another set of unexpected challenges. When something smelled off in the store's kitchen, Amazon hired a pair of professional smellers to solve the mystery (the culprit: pickled daikon). Because food safety was a top priority, the commercial kitchen was kept bitterly cold, and Amazon initially declined requests from the hourly staff to install mats on the facility's chilly concrete floor, one employee recalled. After a senior manager from headquarters spent a day observing operations at the cookhouse, the company issued the staff hoodies and other cold-weather gear and finally acceded on the mats. The people involved in the food service industry, it turned out, were proving as tricky to manage as Dilip Kumar's algorithms.

The original Amazon Go store opened to all employees in December 2016. The public opening was scheduled for a few weeks later but ended up being delayed a year after an entirely new series of problems surfaced. According to the *Wall Street Journal*, the system tended to freeze when twenty or more shoppers were in the store at the same time, and it lost track of products when shoppers picked them up and set them down on a different shelf. Clerks had to be notified to restock the items in the proper place. The system was also not perfectly accurate, even under the best of circumstances, and Amazon executives could not risk the possibility of it making mistakes, falsely charging shoppers and threatening customer trust.

Shoppers themselves also tended to get confused by the novel format. "We noticed lots of customers hesitating at the exit, asking the entry associate if they really could leave," Puerini said later. "In tests, we put up a big poster that said, 'No, really, you can just walk out!'" A version of the sign is still there in the original store.

When the first Amazon Go store finally opened to the public in January 2018, it was heralded as a peek into the future. ("The whole process was so quick and seamless, I almost forgot the items weren't free," wrote *CNET*.) But with the small size of the store, limited selection of items, and enormous expenses on salaries and operations, the numbers behind the project horrified finance execs. One told me that the original Go store, its adjoining kitchens and data center cost more than $10 million.

"If you were a venture capitalist, this just did not make sense anymore," said another executive privy to the decision-making. But Bezos wanted to forge ahead. "Jeff is master of 'this isn't working today, but could work tomorrow.' If customers like it, he's got the cash flow to fund it," this exec said. In 2017, Amazon spent $22.6 billion on R&D, compared to Alphabet ($16.6 billion), Intel ($13.1 billion), and Microsoft ($12.3 billion). The tax-savvy CEO likely understood that these significant R&D expenses for projects like the Go store and Alexa were not only helping to secure Amazon's future but could generate tax credits or be written off, lowering Amazon's overall tax bill.

Over the next few years, Amazon Go stores opened across Seattle, San Francisco, New York, and Chicago. Amazon closed its kitchens and instead bought food from the same vendors that make the middling salads and sandwiches for Starbucks and 7-Eleven. The pricey German ovens sat unused in the original store and the kitchen staff was dismissed.

Disgruntled, the laid-off staff told tales of declining food quality and of giving away unsold meals to food banks and homeless shelters. "The only thing that's fresh anymore is the vegetables," groused one former employee. "It's heartbreaking to see this project go to hell."

Bezos had envisioned thousands of Amazon Go stores, in urban areas around the country. Seven years into the project there were only twenty-six, hardly producing the financial results he'd had in mind when he conceived the concept. The stores also instigated a political backlash against Amazon for eliminating cashier jobs, the second most popular job in the country according to the U.S. Bureau of Labor Statistics. The stores also threatened to exclude low-income and older shoppers who did not have smartphones loaded with credit cards. Cities such as New York, Philadelphia, and San Francisco passed legislation mandating such stores accept cash.

I spoke to Dilip Kumar in 2019, after he was promoted to run all of physical retail. Kumar alone remained from the original IHM trio—by then, Steve Kessel and Gianna Puerini had both retired. He insisted that it was "still early" for the Go project and noted that "customers love the experience" of walking out without stopping to pay. That, Kumar said, gave the project "a lot of latitude and degrees of freedom to be able to try other kinds of things."

One of those was moving the maturing technology back into mid-sized urban grocery stores. In 2020, right before the onset of the Covid-19 pandemic, Amazon opened its long-dormant site in Seattle's Capitol Hill neighborhood, calling it Amazon Go Grocery. The cheese, meat, and seafood were back, and Kumar hinted that the cashierless system could work even in larger venues. "We've learned a lot," he told the *Wall Street Journal*. "There's no real upper bound. It could be five times as big. It could be ten times as big."

Amazon Go remained a money loser. But Bezos was still looking at it as a bet on computer vision and artificial intelligence, the kind of long-term, high-stakes experiment that was necessary to produce meaningful outcomes for large companies. As he wrote in his 2015 shareholder letter:

> We all know that if you swing for the fences, you're going to strike out a lot, but you're also going to hit some home runs. The difference between baseball and business, however, is that baseball has a truncated outcome distribution. When you swing, no matter how well you connect with the ball, the most runs you can get is four. In business, every once in a while, when you step up to the plate, you can score 1,000 runs. This long-tailed distribution of returns is why it's important to be bold.

Nearly a decade after it was conceived, it was still unclear whether the Go store would produce a 1,000-run windfall for Amazon. But it did lead in interesting new directions. Amazon began licensing the "Just Walk Out" system to several other retailers, such as convenience stores and airport kiosks. Amazon Books spawned a few dozen 4-star stores, where the company used its trove of data about people's buying habits to tailor stores with an eclectic mix of locally popular items. And in 2020, Amazon started opening large Amazon Fresh grocery stores, without Go technology but with the long-gestating Amazon Dash Carts, which allowed shoppers to scan items as they walked the aisles and skip the checkout line.

Another significant outcome was the realization, in early 2016, that Amazon needed to get smarter about physical retail if it ever wanted to seriously compete against giants like Walmart and Kroger in the $700-billion-a-year U.S. grocery industry. Around that time, Steve Kessel joined a cabal of Amazonians that included senior vice president Doug Herrington and members of the Go and M&A teams, to answer a momentous question: whether Amazon should acquire a supermarket chain.

They looked at local grocers, regional chains, and the big national players. Among the calls they placed that year was to the Austin-based Whole Foods Market, the beleaguered organic food chain with cratering same-store sales, a reputation for high prices, and a stock price at a five-year low. But its iconoclastic founder, John Mackey, was confident in his turnaround plan and not ready to sell—yet.

CHAPTER 3

Cowboys and Killers

As Jeff Bezos chased Amazon's next wave of growth by backing ambitious technology projects like the Go store, Alexa, and Fire Phone, he also opened an online store in India, the country of 1.3 billion people whose cosmopolitan cities were rapidly embracing smartphones and broadband internet access. Over the course of several years, Amazon would sink billions of dollars into the country. His bet there was a renewal of Amazon's manifest destiny—to sell not only everything, but everywhere.

Bezos had missed an earlier opportunity to invest in India. In 2004, Amazon opened one of its first overseas software development centers in Bangalore, in a small office above an auto dealership. Employees working on its floundering search engine, A9, and its nascent cloud business, Amazon Web Services, repeatedly pitched plans to start a local online store. But as Amazon recovered from the dot-com bust and concentrated its energies on launching in China, India was practically an afterthought.

As a result, some of Amazon's early employees in India quit to start their own firms. In 2007, two engineers, Sachin Bansal and Binny Bansal—unrelated friends and former classmates at the Indian Institute of Technology (IIT) in New Delhi—left Amazon to start their own company, Flipkart, to try to replicate Bezos's original magic of selling books online. If Amazon wasn't going to serve India's increasingly connected and prosperous upper classes, they would do it themselves.

The Amazon executive who had helped start and run the Banga-lore development center was a Bezos disciple and ardent workaholic named Amit Agarwal, also a graduate of IIT. From 2007 to 2009, Agarwal returned to Seattle to become the technical advisor to Bezos, preceding Greg Hart and Dilip Kumar in the crucial role of shadow-ing the CEO in all of his meetings. At the end of his tenure, he and Bezos had a critical discussion about what the TA would do next. Agarwal asked to join the international division and wrote a business plan to finally introduce Amazon into the country where he grew up.

At the time, Diego Piacentini, Amazon's then senior vice president for its international consumer division, had mixed feelings about ex-panding into India. Though companies like IBM and Microsoft had large and successful operations in India, the country had complex laws in place to protect its vast, decentralized sector of mom-and-pop retail shops. These "foreign direct investment" regulations prohib-ited overseas companies from owning or directly operating a retail business. Piacentini, an Italian who had left Apple to join Amazon in early 2000, also felt that countries with larger gross domestic prod-ucts should take priority. In 2010, he asked Agarwal to help him bring Amazon to *his* native country, Italy. A year later, they opened another foreign-language website, in Spain. Those successful introductions, Agarwal said, gave them confidence about "reigniting global expan-sion."

As Amazon finally prepped for its incursion into India in 2012, the execs carefully considered some of the difficult lessons they were learning in China. Amazon had entered China propitiously in 2004, acquiring the bookselling startup Joyo.com for about $75 million with the belief that the same approach that had worked elsewhere could succeed in the world's most populous country. Amazon planned to patiently invest, winning customers with wide selection, low prices, and reliable customer service.

But after a few years of steady progress, everything seemed to sud-denly go wrong in China. A well-capitalized e-commerce competitor,

Alibaba, opened a popular fixed-price online store for well-known brands, called Tmall, an offshoot of its eBay-like website, Taobao. A few years later, Alibaba expanded a tool called Alipay to let shoppers pay digitally for the products they ordered, while Amazon was still accepting cash from homebound buyers upon delivery. Alibaba and another mounting rival, Jingdong, or JD.com, had cluttered but arresting websites, which catered to the overall design tastes of Chinese internet users. The Amazon.cn website looked like Amazon's other home pages around the world. Amazon's China employees were dependent on technical support and other kinds of help from Seattle, and thus were slow to respond to these and other obvious market signals.

A year prior in 2011, Amazon dusted off another page from its global playbook to introduce a marketplace in China, allowing independent businesses to sell their products on the site. This was a key piece of the heralded flywheel: by adding outside vendors, the company drew in new shoppers and earned money from the fees it charged sellers. The extra revenue was then used to lower prices, which in turn attracted more buyers. But again, Amazon failed to adapt to the idiosyncrasies of the China internet—Chinese sellers were accustomed to paying about 2 to 5 percent of their sales to Alibaba, in addition to ads to make their listings more prominent. Amazon execs were skeptical of the advertising model so instead charged 10 to 15 percent of sales, which seemed unusually high to sellers. As a result, Alibaba raced further ahead.

Then a damaging report on China's state-sponsored television, CCTV, drew attention to counterfeit goods, such as fake brand-name cosmetics, on Amazon's third-party marketplace; any signs of progress in the country quickly evaporated. Amazon.cn executives from that time said that Bezos was totally uninterested in understanding the inner machinations of the Chinese government, cultivating ties with Chinese leaders, or using his budding fame to help Amazon's cause in the country, as Elon Musk would do years later to set up a Tesla Gigafactory in Shanghai.

Without a closer relationship with the Chinese Communist Party, Amazon ended up losing even more ground. In an analysis of the struggling China business they delivered to the S-team in 2014, the international team estimated the company had lost a billion dollars in the decade since the Joyo acquisition. Wary of the gathering red ink, Bezos decided to curtail Amazon's investment in China and set out on a plan to become profitable there instead of accepting the additional losses that would be required to stay competitive in the country.

An Amazon finance exec later described it as the equivalent of "shooting the business in the head." Between 2011 and 2016, Amazon's market share in China fell from 15 percent to less than 1 percent. "There was always the fear that if we invested a lot in China, we'd get screwed anyway and waste a lot of money," Piacentini explained years later. "We were not bold enough to go head-on and compete. We always acted as a timid follower."

On the eve of Amazon's long-awaited incursion into India, Bezos could consider some of those hard-earned lessons: the company hadn't invested or innovated boldly enough in China, didn't cultivate ties with the government, and hadn't set up operations with enough independence from Seattle. With his former shadow Amit Agarwal eager to bring Amazon to his native country, he wouldn't make the same mistakes again.

———

One of Amazon's first moves in India was to try to entice its two famous alumni back. Four years after striking out on their own, Binny Bansal and Sachin Bansal had built Flipkart into a nationally recognized brand that sold not only books but mobile phones, CDs, and DVDs. Amit Agarwal met his former employees at the upscale ITC Maurya hotel in central Delhi to discuss an acquisition. Feeling confident about their progress, the Bansals asked for $1 billion. Agarwal scoffed at the amount, and the talks fell through.

After the Bansals thumbed their noses at Amazon, Agarwal started to build a team to compete against them. He prowled headquarters in South Lake Union, zealously pitching a "once-in-a-lifetime opportunity" to impact Amazon and "change the trajectory" of Indian democracy itself. His target was native Indian Amazonians who understood both the company and the cultural peculiarities and varied languages of the vast Indian market.

By 2012, an Amazon India team of a few dozen engineers occupied an office on the eighth floor of the grandiosely named "World Trade Center," a curved glass high-rise in northern Bangalore. At first, they were uncertain how to proceed. India's foreign direct investment rules seemed to preclude them from opening a standard Amazon web store, where the company bought products from manufacturers at wholesale prices and then sold them to online shoppers.

So in typical Amazon fashion, they tried to get clever, introducing a comparison-shopping website in February 2012 called Junglee. com. By scouring the web and listing all the prices and products for sale on other websites, Amazon could start collecting data and earning referral fees without brokering actual transactions and violating the law. But Flipkart recognized the move as a dangerous giant dipping its toe in their waters and declined to let Junglee trawl its site to gather information. After an initial burst of attention, Junglee failed to get any traction.

By 2013, Agarwal and his team had settled on another approach. They would deviate from the company's playbook and operate Amazon India purely as a third-party marketplace. This would allow outside vendors to sell their wares on the newly christened Amazon.in, with Amazon brokering the transaction and collecting fees but never owning actual inventory. The glaring weakness was that, for the time being, Amazon couldn't set prices or ensure the availability and quality of the most popular products.

After repeated delays, Amazon.in went live on June 5, 2013. A shaky handheld video of the launch posted on YouTube shows a conference room packed mostly with giddy young Indian men. After flipping the switch at 2 a.m., they burst into riotous applause. "Shop with Confidence" the new site blared.

Within a few weeks, Amazon India expanded from media products like books and DVDs to sell smartphones and digital cameras. Beauty products, kitchen gadgets, and Amazon's Kindle Fire tablet soon followed. Agarwal wanted to introduce a new category each week—and, like his boss back in Seattle, he liked to set high expectations. "If there was a week when we didn't launch selection in a category, we used to sit down and say this was a disappointing week," he later recalled.

Although the new Amazon offshoot was eight thousand miles away from home base, Agarwal had managed to import key elements of Amazon's culture. He asked movers to transport the door desk he had built for himself as a new employee in 1999—partly, he says, because he felt bad that his family didn't have enough personal furniture for the shipping company to haul. He introduced Amazon practices like writing six-page narratives and correction of error or "COE" reports, to systematically address problems like delivery delays during the monsoon season. Like Bezos, Agarwal would regularly forward customer emails to his staff with a single question mark—they called them "Amit A. escalations" instead of "Jeff B. escalations"—to highlight problems to be immediately solved, or else.

A few months after launching, in the fall of 2013, Agarwal and his deputies returned to Seattle to present their annual road map to Bezos and the S-team as part of the company's annual OP1 planning process. Their six-page narrative offered a range of conservative to more aggressive investment options for how to expand in India and catch up with six-year-old Flipkart in sales and other critical benchmarks. It also outlined prospects for an experimental advertising campaign, so that the company could test what resonated with Indian consumers.

By then, Amazon's China bet was souring, so Bezos did not want to relinquish his shot at what seemed like the world's next largest prize. In most OP1 sessions, he usually spoke last, not to sway the group with his formidable opinion. But this time, he interjected while Agarwal was still giving his presentation. "You guys are going to fail," he bluntly told the Indian crew. "I don't need computer scientists in India. I need cowboys.

"Don't come to me with a plan that assumes I will only make a certain level of investment," Bezos continued, according to the recollection of two executives who were there. "Tell me how to win. Then tell me how much it costs." Another Indian executive at the meeting, Amit Deshpande, says the message was: "Go big and take risks. Make it happen. We have your backs."

Amit Agarwal, a computer scientist with degrees from IIT and Stanford, was momentarily taken aback. But upon his return to India, he turned that directive into a rallying cry. Bezos's command became such a part of the core mythology of Amazon India that execs would occasionally dress up in cowboy outfits at all-hands meetings. They scotched their meek OP1 marketing plan and became one of the largest advertisers in India, promoting Amazon.in on the front page of newspapers like the *Times of India* and in catchy commercials during Indian Premier League cricket games. One of their new team goals, as Amazon India execs described it, was to grow so fast that it practically forced Bezos to come to India.

The next few months were a blur. Members of the team worked all day, every day, traveling often and taking the first plane in the morning and the last at night. When they weren't flying around the country, they went to China to observe the tactics of Amazon, Alibaba, and JD.com in a similarly competitive environment. "I had a suitcase in my room and a suitcase in the office," says Vinoth Poovalingam, an operations manager who was setting up Amazon warehouses across India. "A couple of folks used to joke, 'Dude, we are working in a labor camp.'"

Amazon had to operate differently in India. Without critical infrastructure like the multilane highways and credit card networks the company enjoyed in the West, execs had to devise distinctive logistics and payment strategies for the country, like hiring bike messengers and accepting cash on delivery. Where the company usually employed a single code base for the retail website across all of its regions, in India Amazon engineers developed new code and a less memory-intensive smartphone app since customers predominantly accessed the site on their phones and via sluggish wireless networks. To move more nimbly, all departments reported into Agarwal, instead of to their peers in Seattle. "At a fundamental level, we questioned everything and asked, 'Is this the right thing for India?'" said an Amazon India executive.

Agarwal, international chief Diego Piacentini, and Peter Krawiec, Amazon's corporate development chief, also found a solution to operating a pure third-party marketplace without being able to have a retail arm that could set prices and ensure the availability of products. In mid-2014, with billionaire Narayana Murthy, cofounder of the Indian outsourcing giant Infosys, Amazon formed a joint venture called Prione Business Services, which Amazon would own 49 percent of. Prione would then run a firm called Cloudtail that would sell popular items like the latest smartphones and consumer electronics. Cloudtail immediately became the largest vendor on Amazon.in, responsible for around 40 percent of sales.

Prione was a transparent hack of India's somewhat murky foreign direct investment regulations. ("Test the Boundaries of what is allowed by law," read an internal Amazon slide from the time, Reuters later reported.) The arrangement allowed Amazon to offer customers exclusives on the hottest new smartphones from companies like Samsung and China's OnePlus. Flipkart, backed by overseas venture capitalists, had paved the way here, setting up its own proxy seller, called "WS Retail," and offering exclusives on phones from Motorola, Xiaomi, and Huawei. The two companies would play this game for years—duking it out with discounts and exclusives, which the vast assortment of mom-and-pop stores around the country couldn't possibly hope to match.

By mid-2014, traffic was exceeding both Amazon's and Flipkart's most optimistic projections. On July 29, a few months after it acquired fashion rival Myntra, Flipkart announced a fresh infusion of $1 billion in venture capital, valuing the company at $7 billion—more than the total of all other Indian internet startups put together. A day later, Amazon, approaching $1 billion in total sales in the country after just a year of operation, put out a rival press release, loudly announcing a $2 billion capital infusion into Amazon India. The e-commerce opportunity in India was a lucrative echo of the previous battle in China—and this time, Bezos was determined not to lose.

That September, he fulfilled his promise to Agarwal, visiting India to use his budding business fame to advance Amazon's cause. Flipkart greeted his arrival with an advertising campaign of billboards outside the Bangalore airport and around Amazon's offices, promoting a new Flipkart-minted online holiday, Big Billion Day, to mark the upcoming Diwali festival.

Bezos planned his public appearance himself, hoping to make a big enough statement that even Flipkart's investors might hear it. He wanted to present an oversized $2 billion check to Agarwal while riding an elephant—a symbol in India that represents wisdom and strength. But all the elephants were occupied in a religious festival at the time, and after stubbornly pressing his colleagues to find one, he agreed to perform the publicity stunt instead atop a Tata flatbed truck festooned with ceremonial decorations. Sporting a formal cream-colored *bandhgala* suit and maroon *dupatta* scarf, Bezos presented the mock check as Agarwal played along.

The local press devoured the pageantry and the crosstown rivalry between Amazon and Flipkart. Bezos tried to play it down, even as he worked to defeat Flipkart in battle. "My own view is that most companies spend too much time thinking about the competition," he told the Indian publication *Business Today*. "What they should be doing is thinking about their customers."

Meanwhile, responding to Big Billion Day, Bezos conceived of a competing day of deals celebrating the successful orbit of Mars by an India-launched space probe, which dovetailed with his own passion for space. Amazon initiated a fresh marketing blitz to advertise the promotion, and traffic poured into both Amazon.in and Flipkart.

During a quieter moment of his trip, Bezos talked to his local executives at a nearby hotel. He reiterated that he wanted them to think like cowboys, with India as the Wild West frontier of e-commerce. "There are two ways of building a business. Many times, you aim, aim, aim, and then shoot," he said, according to three executives who were there. "Or, you shoot, shoot, shoot, and then aim a little bit. That is what you want to do here. Don't spend a lot of time on analysis and precision. Keep trying stuff."

Bezos, Piacentini, and Agarwal also had lunch with their new corporate partner, Narayana Murthy, the sixty-eight-year-old Infosys cofounder. He regaled them with stories of backpacking through Europe as a broke college graduate, and about Infosys University, the company's massive internal training program to furnish recent college graduates with practical technical skills. Bezos listened intently; Piacentini recalled that Bezos and the elder Murthy had "an immediate chemistry."

From there, Bezos and Agarwal flew to Delhi to meet with the true figure who controlled Amazon's prospects in India: Prime Minister Narendra Modi. In interviews before the meeting, Bezos touted India's entrepreneurial spirit, dangled the possibility of placing AWS data centers in the country, and said of the newly elected leader, "I am completely at his disposal; he has a fantastic international reputation."

But Modi said little publicly in return. Local merchants, a key part of his governing coalition, were eyeing Amazon suspiciously. If Modi ever needed to shore up their support by tightening the rules around foreign investment, he could blow up the economics of Amazon's most promising overseas venture in an instant.

———

Back in Seattle, Amazon's progress in India was emboldening. Bezos and the S-team figured that if e-commerce could take off in India, there must be untapped opportunity in other developing countries. Their next priority for international expansion, in 2014, came via the French-Canadian Amazon executive Alexandre Gagnon. Having served as the technical advisor to S-team member Diego Piacentini and helped with the launches in Italy and Spain, Gagnon had also been in charge of bringing Amazon north into Canada. He realized that one of their primary advantages in that move had been the proximity of U.S. warehouses, which helped to fulfill some items that were not popular enough to be stored in Canada's local FCs. A single, networked continental supply chain could also work in Mexico, which had the fifteenth largest GDP in the world at the time. The episode that unfolded over the next year would include one of the more curious experiments in Amazon's international expansion as well as one of the most notorious characters in its history.

At the time, Walmart was the largest physical retailer in Mexico and had the largest e-commerce presence. The Argentine startup MercadoLibre also operated there, but the country represented less than 7 percent of its total sales in Latin America. E-commerce was constrained in Mexico by the same factors that had stifled it in India: low internet usage, balky wireless networks, and low credit card penetration. But Amazon now had experience solving these problems.

Gagnon brought his plan for Mexico to the S-team in March 2014. His six-page proposal drew parallels with India. It also pointed out that many wealthy Mexicans were already buying from the U.S. website, paying extra to ship products across the border. One of Gagnon's colleagues later said they were nervous going into the meeting, after hearing that Bezos was in a particularly foul mood that day. But the session, scheduled for ninety minutes, lasted only forty-five—always a good sign. "His reaction was generally that we were not early but not too late either," Gagnon said. "He felt that we had a good plan and that we should launch as soon as we could."

Mexico received only a fraction of the multibillion-dollar investment that flowed into India. And while Bezos would make most of the important decisions about investment levels in India himself—a sign of the importance he placed on the country—Gagnon reported to Jeff Wilke, the head of the global consumer business, who was in charge of "anything that touches the I-5," the interstate that threads down the western coast of the U.S.

One of the first orders of business in Mexico was finding a local CEO who could manage the rollout and be the face of Amazon in the country. After a months-long search, Amazon's lead recruiter, Susan Harker, reached out to Walmart de México e-commerce executive Juan Carlos Garcia, who was ready for a change after an infamous bribery scandal in the country had forced several of his colleagues to resign and eroded company morale. Garcia had previously founded and sold several e-commerce startups.

Garcia visited Amazon headquarters that October and spent two days in back-to-back interviews. He was asked to write a six-page document explaining "the most innovative thing I've ever done" and "the most customer obsessed thing I had ever done in my career." At the end of the grueling session, he was ushered into a surprise final meeting that wasn't on his schedule: with Bezos himself. Bezos likes to say that he gets "all weak-kneed around entrepreneurs," and the ten-minute talk stretched into an hour. Bezos revealed what no one had yet explicitly stated to Garcia—that Amazon was launching a business in Mexico.

Garcia got the job and took over the small Amazon Mexico team, which moved into an office at a Regus coworking space in the affluent Polanco neighborhood of Mexico City. And they started planning. Garcia's initial six-page proposal for the project—dubbed Project Diego, after Mexican painter Diego Rivera—was rejected by Bezos for being too conservative. Garcia had modeled the approach after the methodical rollouts in Italy and Spain, where the company introduced a few product categories to start, then later added others along with a third-party marketplace. But Bezos, capitalizing on what he had learned in China and India, wanted to quickly catch up with Walmart and MercadoLibre. Garcia rewrote the plan and "threw everything in."

The following March, as Amazon Mexico approached its launch date, Garcia was skiing on Whistler Mountain north of Vancouver when he was summoned to Seattle for an emergency meeting. Jeff Wilke was tired of paying Google $3–4 billion a year for search ads to promote product listings at the top of its monolithic search engine. At the time, Google was also expanding the Google Express shopping service to more cities and investing in a number of e-commerce start-ups to challenge Amazon around the world. Wilke wanted to know if it was possible to launch Amazon in a foreign country without using search advertising at all—as a test, to see if Amazon could wean itself from its dangerous dependency on an avowed rival. Wilke suggested using Mexico as the guinea pig.

Garcia joined the meeting and pored over the document outlining the plan. He recalled Bezos walking in after an hour and asking anyone who was against it to raise their hand. Garcia later told me he was the only one who did. Google was the dominant search engine in Mexico, with some 24 million unique visitors a month. According to the analysis in the document, which I later obtained, Amazon estimated it would forgo 20 percent of its overall potential traffic to Amazon Mexico by spurning paid Google search. The document also estimated that cutting off Google ads would reduce the overall percentage of visitors who clicked on regular free search links from 14 to 11 percent.

To recover that lost traffic, the paper concluded, they'd have to dangle discounts, offer free shipping, and wage a brand advertising campaign to get customers to begin their shopping searches on Amazon instead of Google. Later, Jeff Wilke explained his support for such a move by saying, "We have a reliance to varying degrees on Google in all of our established countries. I always want to ask the question, 'Is the advertising that we do worth it?'"

In the meeting, Bezos was circumspect, Garcia recalled. He seemed to side with Garcia against the plan. But then Wilke convinced him that it was a "two-way door"—Bezos's phrase for a decision that can always be reversed later, as opposed to "one-way doors," in which the choice is permanent. He agreed to try it out. Garcia had to "disagree and commit," Amazon's lingo for committing to a course of action you oppose.

Amazon.com.mx went live on June 30, 2015, becoming the company's first comprehensive online store in Latin America. The site was entirely in Spanish, promising "*millones de productos en nuestra tienda en línea.*" The Amazon Mexico team flew to Seattle for the launch, since the Wi-Fi in their local Regus office was spotty. They held a small party that night in a lounge on the ground floor of Day 1 North, where Wilke introduced Garcia to international chief Diego Piacentini, who told him, "Enjoy your five minutes of fame." A few weeks later, the Amazon Mexico execs held a flashier affair at the St. Regis Hotel in Mexico City, where Garcia hired a popular Mexican party band, Moderatto, to play.

For the next few quarters, Amazon avoided buying Google ads in Mexico and tried to compensate with billboards, radio, and TV ads, and shipping discounts. As Garcia had feared, it hobbled the site. The offline ads were more expensive and less effective. Google brought in $70 billion in annual advertising revenues because search ads *worked* and were a relatively inexpensive way for websites to attract visitors. "I wanted to see if we could get traction in a country launch without using Google," Wilke later said, "and it turned out, the answer was no.... We weren't reaching enough customers."

Garcia and his colleagues then ended the experiment, employing the internal system Amazon uses to manage its massive Google ad-buying campaigns, called Hydra (for the multiheaded sea organism, but also, Amazon employees snickered, for the terrorist organization in Marvel comics). A year later, in 2016, Amazon Mexico's P&L statement recovered and started to show promise.

Nevertheless, in Seattle, Garcia's reputation was declining. Some executives complained that he "didn't get Amazon culture," and according to several accounts, he did not get along with Jeff Wilke or his direct manager, Alexandre Gagnon. While several Amazon Mexico employees remembered Juan Carlos Garcia as an approachable leader who often stayed at work late at night and represented the company well in the press, one colleague recalled a moment when Garcia revealed an alarming temper, leading up to Black Friday in 2015. He was arguing about matching a smaller website's heavily discounted price on a sixty-inch television with a category manager, who insisted that the rival's price must be a mistake and that Amazon would lose too much money if it matched it. As the debate grew tense, Garcia banged his hand on the table and said, "I am CEO! Do it!" Amazon matched the price, quickly sold thousands of TVs, and indeed lost a lot of money.

In late 2016, Garcia later recalled, tensions with his Seattle bosses reached a boiling point when an Amazon board member ordered a shipment of shoes from his vacation home in Punta Mita and only some of them arrived. The problem was relayed to Jeff Wilke, to see if it might indicate a larger issue. Wilke forwarded it to Garcia and then asked him about it in a meeting. The resulting discussion grew heated, and Garcia later said he felt disrespected. He was fired from the company shortly after, in February 2017.

Garcia reached out to me in September 2019 to relay his Amazon story over a long conversation in a café and a walk around downtown San Francisco. He said that he had looked into the board member's shoe purchase and concluded that he had mistakenly ordered from the U.S. website, not the Mexican one. He said that before he was fired, he pointed that out to Wilke, who never responded.

Alexandre Gagnon spent more time in Mexico after Garcia left, and eventually handed over the role to one of his U.S. deputies. Under their management, with full access to Google ads, Amazon Mexico thrived. By the end of that year, it was a leading player in the country's $7.1 billion e-commerce market—slightly ahead of MercadoLibre and Walmart.

But there's a startling postscript to this story. After our talk, Garcia and I agreed to keep in touch. Despite sending a few follow-up emails, I didn't hear from him for several weeks. Then, in November 2019, a news report caught my eye: ex–Amazon Mexico CEO Juan Carlos Garcia was wanted for questioning in the murder of his wife, Abril Pérez Sagaón.

The horrifying tale started the previous January, eight months before I met with Garcia. After a fight, he had allegedly beaten his wife with a baseball bat and slashed her face with a knife. Their fifteen-year-old son witnessed the incident and their teenage daughter documented her mother's injuries in grisly photographs. Pérez recovered and obtained a restraining order against Garcia, who was sentenced to pretrial detention for the next ten months. News reports differ on when he was actually held, but somehow he was allowed to travel to San Francisco. I was clueless about the earlier incident, which hadn't made the news.

Then a few weeks later, on November 25, 2019, Pérez flew to Mexico City for a custody evaluation for their three children. On the trip to the airport afterward, she was sitting in the passenger seat of an automobile driven by her lawyer, with two of the children in the back seat, when an assassin on a motorcycle drove alongside the car and shot her twice through the window. She died that night.

The killing sparked a furor in Mexico and abroad. "Ex–Amazon Mexico CEO on the Run in the U.S. After Wife's Mysterious Murder" one newspaper headline blared. Protests erupted around the country, with activists accusing the government of failing to protect women in abusive relationships or to take seriously the crime of *femicide*. In a terrible irony, an Amazon Mexico employee told me the company had to temporarily suspend its Google ad buying program, so that

Amazon ads didn't inappropriately pop up when users searched for updates on the crime.

In March 2020, two men were arrested and charged with the murder. But police and even his children were convinced that Juan Carlos Garcia had hired the assassins, and he remained the primary suspect. According to Mexican police, he entered the U.S. on foot near Tijuana days after the killing and, as of this writing, hasn't been seen since.

———

Back in India in 2015, Amazon and Flipkart swung at each other like heavyweight prizefighters. They jockeyed for exclusive deals with smartphone makers, offered steep discounts during their holiday bonanzas, and built warehouses around the country at a dizzying pace. Amazon's catchy TV ads ("*Aur Dikhao*," or "Show Me More," what Indian customers tell salespeople at small shops) littered the airwaves. To help teach small Indian vendors how to buy and sell online, Amazon procured a fleet of three-wheeled wagons, dubbed Chai Carts, which rolled into India's colorful local markets offering free tea, water, and lemon juice. Employees introduced sellers to tools like email and apps and showed them how to register on Amazon.in and upload their inventory.

That fall, Agarwal and his execs returned to Seattle for the annual OP1 planning sessions. Two years prior, they had been asked to revise their conservative projections, and by now, Agarwal had internalized Bezos's directive to put aside caution and pesky concepts like operating profit. The plan for the next year showed dramatic levels of investment, sales growth, and red ink. Still buzzing from the entrepreneurial energy he had witnessed in India, Bezos was inspired. "The future is going to be the U.S., China, and India," he declared, according to a colleague who reports hearing him say it multiple times. "For Amazon to be a truly world-class global company, we have to be relevant in two out of the three markets." At the end of the discussion, Agarwal and the India execs received a standing ovation from the S-team, an unusual commendation in a usually solemn and intimidating environment.

On the ground in India, little applause existed, just intricate problems to solve. Agarwal realized early on he couldn't depend solely on logistics partners like the India Post, the federal mail carrier. So Amazon, like Flipkart, created its own network of couriers in vans, motorcycles, bikes, and even boats to reach the remotest parts of the country. To get Indians more comfortable with the idea of digital payments, it introduced the option to deposit the change from a cash transaction as credit in their Amazon accounts.

All these moves showed promise. By the summer of 2016, Amazon was preparing to introduce its Prime two-day shipping guarantee in the country. And in a momentous turn of market leadership, it was set to surpass Flipkart in sales. Galvanized, Bezos again met with Prime Minister Modi that June at the U.S.-India Business Council in Washington, D.C., and announced that Amazon would plug another $3 billion into Amazon India. Modi, on a goodwill tour to cultivate foreign investors, seemed more receptive to Bezos's entreaties this time. He posed for photos with business leaders, and called India "much more than a market" and a "reliable partner" that would continue to make it easier to conduct business in the country.

As Amazon doubled down on its progress, its rival began to look shaky. Flipkart's CEO, thirty-three-year-old Sachin Bansal, was grappling with the same problem of Google's web dominance that had led Amazon to suspend search advertising in Mexico. Studying Google's ad fees and India's relatively low level of PC ownership, Bansal declaimed that Flipkart and the fashion site it had acquired, Myntra, would concentrate their energies and investments on their smartphone apps and scrap their desktop and mobile websites altogether. He then fired most of his management team, which had strenuously objected to the move.

The strategy backfired. Customers were alienated by the inconvenience of having to download apps; meanwhile, Amazon took out full-page newspaper ads with a letter from Jeff Bezos, thanking Indians for making Amazon.in the most visited e-commerce site in the country. Flipkart sales slowed and the company laid off workers. Nevertheless, private investors were still besotted; the following year, Flipkart raised an additional $1.4 billion from a consortium that included the Chinese tech giant Tencent, eBay, and Microsoft. But it had to accept a reduced valuation of $11.6 billion from its previous round. "If someone gave us a model of how to fuck it up, we followed it," said a Flipkart board member. Soon after, Sachin Bansal was replaced as CEO by his cofounder, Binny Bansal, though he remained executive chairman, a largely ceremonial role at Flipkart.

The company's stumble was one factor in a complex strategic landscape that Jeff Bezos was surveying by 2017. Investors had bid Flipkart's valuation into the stratosphere, but both Amazon.in and Flipkart were losing well over a billion dollars a year. The retail giant Walmart, under CEO Doug McMillon, was looking afresh at global e-commerce and trying to stem Amazon's advance around the world; it had previously explored the prospect of investing in Flipkart.

Meanwhile, as Modi prepared to run for a second term, he was making it more, not less, difficult to conduct business in India, despite his previous promises. His ruling Bharatiya Janata Party proposed a new set of rules that would prevent a single seller on a foreign-owned online marketplace like Amazon.in from brokering more than 25 percent of the site's total sales. This was a dart aimed directly at Amazon and Flipkart's arm's-length subsidiaries, Cloudtail and WS Retail—and a way for Modi to placate his powerful base of small retailers, which were increasingly unsettled by the e-commerce frenzy.

Amid that piquant set of facts, Sachin Bansal met Jeff Bezos at The Weekend, an elite conference in Aspen, Colorado, organized by Ari Emanuel, CEO of the entertainment and media agency Endeavor, and Google chairman Eric Schmidt. He pitched an acquisition that would end the capital-intensive conflict between the two companies but keep both websites independent. Amazon.in would broker everyday items like groceries and books, while Flipkart would sell higher-value products, giving it additional leverage to reach better deals with vendors like smartphone makers. After being sidelined following the disastrous attempt to go mobile only, Bansal could use this as his route back into Flipkart's leadership.

Bezos, as always "weak-kneed" around a brash young entrepreneur, was intrigued by the proposal. He asked M&A chief Peter Krawiec to start negotiations.

Krawiec started off with a lowball offer, backed up by numbers that showed Amazon India had grown larger than Flipkart. Flipkart disagreed with that market analysis. Both sides, which professed publicly not to care about the competition, adamantly insisted that they were winning. Since they couldn't even agree on a common set of facts, negotiations proceeded slowly over the next few months.

In October, some of Walmart's management team heard about the talks from Goldman Sachs bankers. Intoxicated with India's potential and with fear of losing out to Amazon in a critical growth market, they jumped back into the fray. That month Flipkart executives made a pilgrimage to Walmart headquarters in Bentonville, Arkansas. Amazon then heard about those talks and got more serious as well.

Flipkart's investors and board members split into camps favoring three different strategies: sell to Amazon, sell to Walmart, or stay independent. Sachin Bansal backed a deal with Amazon since it might allow him to resume running the company.

But most Flipkart investors were skeptical that India's antitrust authorities would sanction a merger with Amazon, which would consolidate around 80 percent of the e-commerce market. Bezos seemed to have faith in his budding relationship with Narendra Modi and expressed confidence that he could get the deal done. He pursued the acquisition earnestly, according to several colleagues—even over any concerns from Amit Agarwal, who would have the frightening responsibility of integrating two disparate brands and money-losing supply chains.

In March 2018, Bezos hosted Sachin Bansal and Flipkart CEO Kalyan Krishnamurthy in the boathouse behind his home on Lake Washington. A few weeks later, he spoke over the phone with two of Flipkart's most influential backers, Tiger Global partner Lee Fixel and SoftBank chairman Masayoshi Son, aka "Masa," who particularly favored a deal with Amazon over Walmart and seemed determined to enlist Bezos as a long-term ally.

The sticking point in the Amazon-Flipkart talks was a breakup fee. Flipkart's investors feared the uncertainty of the regulatory review process and knew of Amazon's infamous reputation for engaging in discussions only to not follow through, or to try to raise the price for a more determined rival. So Flipkart demanded a $4 billion breakup free, with the cash paid up front, so that if the merger review took eighteen months and resulted in rejection, Amazon wouldn't benefit from having impeded a competitor. Amazon balked at that arrangement, which would amount to funding its rival. Though Masa clung to hope until the end, the Flipkart board turned down the Amazon deal.

Meanwhile, Walmart had played its hand well. CEO Doug McMillon, Walmart International CEO Judith McKenna, and board member Greg Penner built a rapport with the Flipkart executive team, never forced exclusivity provisions into the talks (which would have required Masa to relinquish his dreams of a bromance with Bezos), and dangled the prospect of allowing Flipkart to continue to operate independently.

After a process that stretched on for six months and had assaulted the calendars of everyone involved with never-ending conference calls, the fractious Flipkart board finally agreed to sell a stake to Walmart. At first the deal talks had called for the retailer to only take a minority position, but by then most of Flipkart's weary investors wanted to sell their shares and cash out. Even at this late moment, drama dogged Flipkart; Sachin Bansal almost scuttled the deal by insisting Walmart guarantee him future control in the management of the company. Exasperated, the Flipkart board finally insisted that he leave the company for good.

In May 2018, the companies announced that Walmart would pay $16 billion for a 77 percent stake in Flipkart. Walmart CEO Doug McMillon visited India after the deal was announced and told Flipkart employees, "It is our intention to just empower you and let you run. Speed matters. Decisiveness matters."

Despite the stormy previous months, Sachin and Binny Bansal were now billionaires and widely lauded as two of the most successful entrepreneurs in Indian history. But who can say what assails the judgment of exorbitantly wealthy and famous men as they enter middle age? Binny Bansal was promptly ousted from his role as chief executive of the Flipkart Group in late 2018 after Walmart investigated an allegation that he had conducted a consensual extramarital relationship with a former employee and tried to cover it up. And in 2020, ugly divorce proceedings between Sachin Bansal and his wife spilled into public view.

Inside Amazon India, which had lost out on the hard-fought deal, executives were consumed with more pedestrian affairs. While they had a formidable new rival in India, they were confident that Walmart would find the road ahead as difficult to navigate as a rutted Indian highway. "If there was one thing we all knew, it was that Walmart had no idea what they were buying," said a longtime Amazon India executive. "It really requires seven or eight years of living out here and working in an environment like this before you truly understand how complicated this mess is."

———

At noon on a Saturday in the fall of 2018, SP Road, Bangalore's wholesale electronics market, felt desolate. In the tiny, mostly empty stores that lined the street, shop attendants arranged and rearranged their goods. As sales of smartphones and computers skyrocketed on Amazon and Flipkart, they were cratering here.

Caught in the downdraft was Jagdish Raj Purohit, the owner of a store that billed itself as Sunrise Telecom. In a shoebox of a space, Purohit was seated behind the cash register at the entrance. Along one side were hundreds of cases for every conceivable smartphone model. On the other was a combination of low-end and mid-price phones, as well as a Vivo V11, an upscale model from China that sold for 26,000 rupees.

Purohit didn't expect to sell many phones. "All mobile sales have gone online," he groused, when asked the customary Hindi question "*Dhanda kaisa hai?*" ("How's business?"). "Flipkart and Amazon are always advertising discounts on such phones, so who will come here?" He was trying to make up the shortfall by selling accessories.

At Raj Shree Computech down the street, Mahendra Kumar and his two brothers had been selling computers and accessories for a dozen years. For the last few, business had been "*thoda thanda*"—a bit cold. It wasn't a great mystery why. "Whoever comes here quotes laptop prices from Flipkart and Amazon straightaway, even before we say anything," said Kumar. Or "they'll come here and try many headphones for sound and then walk out saying they'll be back later. We know they aren't coming back." Like his fellow shop owner down the street, Kumar was reluctant to become a seller on Amazon or Flipkart because margins were slim and returns created headaches.

India's competition regulations had been created to prevent this sort of bloodletting. Amazon and Walmart were trading blows, expanding into the delivery of apparel and fresh food and groceries, and each losing more than a billion U.S. dollars a year. It seemed like the noose of global capitalism was being fitted over the necks of millions of Indian small businesses.

After Modi won reelection in 2019 amid the country's most serious economic slowdown in years, the pendulum swung dramatically against the overseas retail giants. As Modi's government had threatened, it tightened foreign investment laws. Amazon and Flipkart had to sell their ownership stakes in their affiliated subsidiaries and were barred from entering into exclusive arrangement with manufacturers or offering steep discounts.

Small retailers and their trade organizations weren't the only ones trying to enlist the state to protect them from the U.S. giants. India's wealthiest person, Mukesh Ambani, was also lobbying the government to strengthen foreign investment rules for his own interest. In 2019, his company, Reliance Industries, which owned India's largest chain of grocery stores, also entered the e-commerce fray. Its site, JioMart, would not be subject to the same restrictions as Amazon and Flipkart. Ambani, a political ally of Modi, tapped into growing strains of Hindu nationalism and called on his fellow citizens to "collectively launch a new movement against data colonization."

In response to the new hurdles, Bezos diversified his investments in India and expanded his ambitions, investing in a digital payments service, promoting the Kindle and Alexa, and adding a catalog of Bollywood films and various Indian-language TV shows to its local Prime Video service. Amit Agarwal would not concede that Amazon's India adventures were veering off course. "Jeff would say, 'it's still day one,' and I think it's not even minute one of day one in India from where we are," he told me.

By many measures, Amazon had made remarkable progress in India. Customers in not just cosmopolitan cities but around the country were buying online, paying digitally instead of with cash, and leaning into the technological future that Jeff Bezos had envisioned for them. Small businesses were learning how to sell online and finding buyers well outside the outdoor markets whose essential character hadn't changed in a century. But Amazon would remain grossly unprofitable in India for the foreseeable future, and its intense competition with Flipkart had created a disorienting set of social and economic discontinuities that helped to summon the dogs of nationalism and divisive populism. The entire saga was a preview of the political headaches that were waiting for Bezos back home.

CHAPTER 4

A Year for Eating Crow

I n October 2014, a few weeks after Jeff Bezos returned from his first trip to India, former Microsoft CEO Steve Ballmer appeared on the talk show *Charlie Rose* and threw serious shade at his company's crosstown rival. "I don't know what to say about Amazon. I like Amazon. Nice company. [But] they make no money, Charlie! In my world, you're not a real business until you make some money."

Amazon's performance at the time seemed to merit Ballmer's assessment. The company had lost $241 million that year, and over the holiday season it logged its slowest growth in sales since the disastrous days of the dot-com bust. By December 31, 2014, after declining 20 percent over the previous twelve months, Amazon's market capitalization sat at a meager $143 billion.

Which is why 2015 was such a critical year for the company and its CEO: it marked the true beginning of Amazon's climb toward the lofty altitudes beyond a trillion dollars in market capitalization.

Ballmer and other Amazon skeptics, like the hedge fund investor David Einhorn, who added Amazon to his "bubble basket of stocks" that fall, were looking at Amazon's reported losses and significant investments in new initiatives. They were also underestimating the true performance of its older business units, which the company shrouded in secrecy. Amazon *was* profitable, particularly mature retail categories like books and electronics in the U.S. and UK. But rather than accumulating record amounts of cash and reporting it on its income statement, as companies like Microsoft and Apple were doing at the time, Bezos invested Amazon's winnings like a crazed gambler at the craps table in Las Vegas.

Years ago, he had learned that there were no annuities in retail. Customers were fickle and could change their loyalties at the moment they were presented with a better offer elsewhere. Amazon could only stay ahead of rivals if it kept inventing new technologies and improving levels of service. As we have seen, Bezos avidly pursued that goal by plunging billions into projects like Alexa, the Fire Phone, and the Go store, as well as future dominance in India and Mexico and other secret initiatives never known to the public.

None of those bets had yet borne fruit. But in 2015, an earlier wager finally started to pay off. In its April earnings report, Amazon revealed for the first time the financial health of its ten-year-old cloud business, Amazon Web Services, and shocked Wall Street with its underlying sales growth and profitability. Then in June, Amazon copied a competitor in China and introduced the first Prime Day, capitalizing on a decade of growth from its two-day shipping program. Both Wall Street and the media began to show a newfound interest in Amazon, and shortly after the twentieth anniversary of its launch, the company came under a new kind of scrutiny commensurate with its growing size. That August, an explosive newspaper article in the *New York Times* turned Amazon's combative corporate culture into the subject of national attention.

Over the course of that eventful year, 2015, Amazon stock more than doubled. Because he owned about 18 percent of the company, Bezos was vaulted into the ranks of the top five wealthiest people in the world, according to *Bloomberg*'s Billionaire's Index. It turned out that Steve Ballmer's broadside against Amazon was a perfect contrarian indicator; it would mark almost precisely the start of one of the most dramatic increases in corporate value and personal wealth in the entire history of capitalism.

———

Of course, Ballmer had little grasp of how Amazon's eventual engine of profitability, Amazon Web Services, was performing—and that was how Jeff Bezos wanted it. Over its first decade, AWS's revenues and profits were a closely guarded secret. The division generated $4.6 billion in sales in 2014 and was growing at a 50 percent annual clip. But Amazon disguised those numbers, along with nascent advertising revenues, in a sundry "other" category on its income statement, so that potential competitors like Microsoft and Google would not recognize how attractive a business cloud computing actually was. Observers and analysts could only guess at the financial dimensions of a unique enterprise computing business, anomalously tucked inside an online retailer.

In the years after the introduction of its first products in 2006, AWS was used mostly by startups and university labs that needed extra processing power and signed up with a credit card to run their software over the internet on Amazon's servers. When engineers inside corporations and governments wanted to run their computing experiments via AWS, they often quietly routed around their organizations' stringent procurement processes. Like many other technology revolutions, cloud computing was first the provenance of geeks, and then spread outward.

The first companies to embrace AWS became its beta testers and evangelists. Silicon Valley startups like Uber, Airbnb, Dropbox, and the photo-sharing site SmugMug ran their operations on AWS and could quickly order up more servers as their businesses grew at unprecedented rates. It was one of the greatest enablers of the post-recession technology boom—arguably more important than even the iPhone, though outsiders understood very little about it. NASA's Jet Propulsion Lab in Pasadena, California, signed up in 2009 and used AWS to store and stream images from the Curiosity Rover on the surface of Mars. "I still have the presentation I gave to colleagues," said Tom Soderstrom, JPL's chief technology officer. "They thought I was talking about earth science, literal clouds."

Even some of AWS's earliest executives had little sense for cloud computing's enormous potential. "This business could be really big someday, maybe even $1 billion in revenue," product manager Matt Garman once told an incredulous fellow Amazon newbie, Matt Peterson, his former business school classmate, over lunch in 2006. "Are you kidding, there is no way this will be a billion dollars. Do you know how big that would be?" Peterson responded. Garman is now an AWS vice president and member of the S-team; Peterson is an Amazon corporate development director; and AWS generated $45.4 billion in sales in 2020.

Amazon's original cloud products were conceived by Jeff Bezos in concert with other technical leaders between the years 2004 and 2006. The Simple Storage Service, or S3, and the Elastic Compute Cloud, or EC2, provided most of the functionality of a back-office computer room—but one that could be accessed remotely, and existed inside the massive, air-conditioned data centers that Amazon would construct elsewhere in the country. These would be the dial tones of the twenty-first-century internet explosion. In 2007, Amazon also introduced a primitive database called SimpleDB, to allow customers to store and retrieve organized or "structured" sets of their data.

Entering the business of databases, a seemingly boring bit of commerce that is actually a thriving and competitive $46-billion-a-year industry, would be one of AWS's most important pathways to success. Amazon itself used Oracle's relational database to manage Amazon.com, and the company's ever-growing traffic strained the software and periodically threatened the stability of the site, frustrating Bezos. Across its fulfillment centers and in its online store, Bezos always wanted to minimize Amazon's dependencies on other companies, because their own primitive database capabilities weren't up to the task. When SimpleDB also proved to be too clunky and complex to use, AWS engineers started working on a more fast and flexible version, called DynamoDB, to handle the massive volumes of traffic that were endemic to the internet.

SimpleDB was also used avidly by another early AWS customer to store the titles and thumbnail images of its entertainment catalog: Netflix. Reed Hastings's DVD-by-mail startup wanted to move other parts of its technology operation to the cloud as it transformed itself into a streaming company. To accommodate that, Amazon would need to build the cloud versions of relational databases and a tool called a data warehouse. In 2010, Andy Jassy, the head of the AWS unit, and a vice president named Raju Gulabani started working on the project and then updated the S-team on their progress.

In the meeting, according to a participant, Gulabani projected it would take a decade for Amazon to succeed in relational databases. "I will bet you it will take more than ten years to get this done," Bezos said, causing momentary consternation among the assembled AWS crew. "So, you better get started now." Understanding that robust databases would be one of the biggest opportunities in cloud computing, Bezos significantly increased Jassy's budget request.

Gulabani poached another Indian-born executive, Anurag Gupta, from Oracle, and they opened an office in Silicon Valley. Over the next few years, Gupta assembled a team that would build several AWS databases around free and increasingly popular open-source software tools like MySQL and Postgres. In 2012, AWS introduced Redshift, a so-called data warehouse that allowed companies to analyze the data they stored in the cloud; in 2015, it rolled out Aurora, a relational database. These were typically Amazonian names: geeky, obscure, and endlessly debated inside AWS, since according to an early AWS exec, Bezos had once mused, "You know, the name is about 3 percent of what matters. But sometimes, 3 percent is the difference between winning and losing."

The name "Redshift" was suggested by Charlie Bell, a former engineer for Boeing on NASA's space shuttle and the senior vice president in charge of AWS's operations; it's the term for the change astronomers see in light, the fastest thing in existence, that's emitted from a celestial object like a star as it moves away from the observer. Nonetheless, Larry Ellison, then the CEO of Oracle—whose logo happens to be red—saw it as corporate trash talk and began to see red himself. That "never even occurred to us," Jassy said. "When we were told later that Oracle believed that, we thought it was kind of funny." A bitter rivalry between Oracle and Amazon, already simmering with Amazon's entry into databases, intensified.

AWS's portfolio of cloud-based databases, on top of the classics like S3 and EC2, drew companies big and small toward cloud computing and further into Amazon's embrace. Once they moved their data onto Amazon's servers, companies had little reason to endure the inconvenience of transferring it back out. They were also more likely to be attracted to the other profitable applications that AWS introduced. Over the next few years AWS sales and operating margins started to shoot upward. "Of all the services we added, it was the database portfolio that broadened AWS's appeal," said Taimur Rashid, a former AWS manager.

Nearly as remarkable as AWS's evolution into a profitable business over the first half of the 2010s was its emergence as its own distinctive organization, an ablation calved from the glacier of Amazon itself. In 2011 the division broke off from the company's main campus in South Lake Union and moved a half mile away to 1918 Eighth Avenue, a five-hundred-foot-tall glass skyscraper that Amazon dubbed Blackfoot. Ever the Bezos disciple, Jassy hung on the walls not the admiring articles but the critical ones, including a 2006 *Businessweek* story whose sub-headline read: "Amazon's CEO wants to run your business with the technology behind his Web site. But Wall Street wants him to mind the store."

AWS's culture was a microcosm of Amazon's: tough, unrelenting, and focused on meeting impossibly high standards. Jassy and his fellow managers asked searing questions of their underlings and hammered anyone without suitable answers or who didn't embrace accountability for a problem within their purview. Daily operations were driven by data-filled six-page narratives and the obsessive contemplation of the needs of customers. When employees returned strong results, attention always turned to the ways in which they could have done better. One former executive described the mentality this way: "We were really good at going up to the gold medal podium and complaining that our medals weren't shiny enough."

Engineers were given pagers and were assigned to on-call rotations, when they were expected to be available at all hours to address system outages. If a serious technical problem erupted while the pagers were muted during meetings at AWS, Amazon's pager program would automatically circumvent "silent mode" and the meeting would erupt in a rolling orchestra of electronic pings.

In many respects, Jassy's business philosophies were a distillation of Bezos's. A few years after he joined Amazon from Harvard Business School in 1997, Jassy had narrowly avoided getting fired in an early purge of Amazon's marketing department. Bezos saved him, dubbing him as "one of our most high potential people," according to former S-team member Diego Piacentini. For eighteen months, he was Bezos's first full-time shadow, or technical advisor. This brand-new role entailed the almost slavish following of the CEO, and colleagues gently teased Jassy for it.

Jassy totally embodied Amazon values like frugality and humility. He usually wore inexpensive sport coats and loudly trumpeted his enthusiasms for diversions like New York sports teams, buffalo wings, and the Dave Matthews Band. Even as his net worth skyrocketed along with AWS's value—he received a $35 million stock grant in 2016 alone—he shunned the ostentatious trappings of success, like traveling via private aircraft. He held an annual Super Bowl party in the replica sports bar that he'd fashioned inside the basement of his own Seattle home. Bezos attended every year until 2019, when in another glimpse of dramatic changes ahead, he showed up *at* the actual game, sitting in the commissioner's box.

Bezos liked to say that "good intentions don't work, but mechanisms do." Inside AWS, Jassy applied that adage ferociously. The

rhythms of a week at AWS revolved around several formal "mechanisms" or well-honed processes or rituals. Ideas for new services,
their names, pricing changes, and marketing plans were meticulously written as six-page documents and presented to Jassy in his
twentieth-floor meeting room, dubbed "the Chop" (the name Jassy
and his roommate had given their Harvard dorm room, from a novel
they were assigned in European literature, Stendhal's *The Charter-
house of Parma*). Executives asked hard technical questions and Jassy
usually spoke last. Colleagues said he exhibited almost inhuman levels of discipline, sitting in meetings for ten hours a day and digesting
dense and complex documents without flagging.

The highlights of the AWS week were two Wednesday morning
meetings. Jassy ran the ninety-minute midday business review, where
the top two hundred managers discussed the minute details of customers, competitive developments, and the financial health of each
product unit. But the real centerpiece of the week was the forum that
preceded that meeting: the two-hour operations review to assess the
technical performance of each web service. Held in the large conference room on the third floor, it was run by the intimidating and direct
Charlie Bell, the former space shuttle engineer.

AWS execs and engineers typically describe this remarkable session with a combination of awe and post-traumatic stress disorder.
Around the big table at the center sat more than forty vice presidents
and directors, while hundreds of others (almost all of whom are men)
stood in the wings or listened over the phone from around the world.
On one side of the room was a multicolored roulette wheel, with different web services, like EC2, Redshift, and Aurora, listed around
the perimeter. Each week the wheel was spun (until 2014 when there
were too many services and software mimicked the function of the
wheel), with the goal being, Jassy said, to make sure managers were
"on top of the key metrics of their service all week long, because they
know there's a chance they may have to speak to it in detail."

Getting selected could be a career-defining moment at AWS.

Managers could boost their prospects with a comprehensive and confident presentation. But if they employed ambiguous language, erred with their data, or conveyed even the whiff of bullshit, then Charlie Bell swooped in, sometimes with awesomely patronizing flair. For managers, a failure to deeply understand and communicate the operational posture of their service could amount to career death.

Nevertheless, as AWS approached its ten-year birthday, and as its revenues increased and profits mounted, it became the most desirable division for Amazon's tech elite, a kind of Ivy League among all of its business units. Staying and thriving amid the geniuses and their diabolical rituals amounted to earning the medal of honor.

———

In the early years, Bezos waded into the details of AWS himself, editing web pages for the first products and reviewing revenue reports from EC2 and occasionally replying with smiley faces. Over time, as he fixated on newer things, like Alexa and the Amazon Go stores, he allowed Jassy to run AWS autonomously. He receded from regular view, save for reviewing significant investment decisions and overseeing the annual OP1 and OP2 sessions, where he usually pressed for ways to connect AWS with other parts of Amazon's business. "Jeff was very involved almost as an investor in AWS," said Joe DePalo, a former AWS exec. "He would ask questions and poke and review. But day to day, Andy operated it independently."

Bezos also served as a kind of strategic guru for Jassy and his leadership team. As Google and Microsoft awoke to the potential of cloud computing and began investing heavily in their competing initiatives, he urged Jassy to think about ways to protect Amazon's advantages. "You've built this lovely castle, and now all the barbarians are going to come riding on horses to attack the castle," Bezos said, according to a former AWS exec who reports hearing the comment. "You need a moat; what is the moat around the castle?" (Amazon denied that Bezos said this.)

In January 2015, one of Jassy's answers was Amazon's $400 million acquisition of an Israel-based chipmaker, Annapurna Labs, to build low-cost, high-performance microprocessors for Amazon servers, and seek a cost advantage in Amazon's data centers that competitors couldn't match.

Bezos had one other impact at AWS: both he and Jassy lobbied to conceal the division's financial details from public view, even amid the widespread skepticism that throttled the company and its stock price in 2014. But in 2015, Amazon's finance department argued that the division's revenue was approaching 10 percent of Amazon's overall sales and would eventually trigger reporting requirements under federal law. "I was not excited about breaking our financials out because they contained useful competitive information," Jassy admitted.

Nevertheless, that January, Amazon signaled that it would report AWS's financial results in its quarterly report for the first time, and investors girded in anticipation. Many analysts predicted that AWS would be revealed as just another Amazon "science project"—a lousy, low-margin business that was sapping energy from the company's more advanced efforts in retail.

In reality, the opposite was true. That year, AWS had a 70 percent growth rate and 19.2 percent operating margin, compared to the North American retail group's 25 percent growth rate and 2.2 percent operating margin. AWS was gushing cash, even as it rapidly consumed most of it to build even more computing capacity and keep up with the fast-growing internet companies like Snapchat that were piling onto its servers.

This reporting was a huge surprise for the analysts and investors who monitored and scrutinized Amazon, and likely even a bigger one for Microsoft, Google, and the rest of the enterprise computing world. Analyst Ben Thompson facetiously called that April 2015 earnings report "one of the technology industry's biggest and most important

IPOs." After the reveal, Amazon's valuation jumped almost 15 percent in a day, crossing the $200 billion mark for the first time and laying to rest the myth of Amazon as a perpetually money-losing machine.

———

A few months before that earnings report, the S-team had been analyzing their deteriorating competitive position in China and the success of Alibaba's annual holiday shopping extravaganza, Singles Day. For the last five years, Jack Ma's e-commerce juggernaut had turned the date of 11/11 into a hybrid of Black Friday and Valentine's Day, offering a frenzy of deals which in 2014 generated more than $9 billion sales and a dependable tsunami of free press.

In his presentation on China, international boss Diego Piacentini proposed that Amazon might fashion its own such shopping holiday. Jeff Bezos thought it was a good idea, but at the time he was consumed with linking everything to Amazon's seductive Prime service. He suggested that the company roll out the holiday globally and use it to try to add new members to Prime.

The assignment was passed to Greg Greeley, a vice president in charge of Prime, who in turn handed it to one of his deputies, longtime Amazon executive Chris Rupp. Rupp knew that Amazon customers were accustomed to spending freely on Black Friday and Cyber Monday and that another Christmas shopping event would simply shift their discretionary spending by a few weeks. She also knew that Amazon was not particularly adept at tapping the summer shopping season known as "back to school," a period marked by such retail rituals as Nordstrom's Anniversary Sale.

Rupp's subsequent proposal to hold the event midsummer sparked contentious debate inside Amazon. She argued that customers had money to spend over the summer, while Amazon could exploit the excess warehouse space built for the peak season. Amazon's supply chain executives, who spent their comparatively tranquil summers preparing for the holidays, had little interest in handling a midyear surge. "I got every kind of pushback on that, but I had darn good reasons for doing it," Rupp said.

Greeley and Rupp presented the paper to the S-team in January 2015 and got a sign-off from Bezos. "Don't make this convoluted. Prime Day needs to mean one thing, and we have to do it really well," he told them. In the appendix, he highlighted a section that targeted ten thousand deals for Prime Day, a larger selection than Black Friday. To accomplish that, they would have to persuade Amazon's merchandising teams to coalesce behind the goal and harangue their vendors to supply the discounts.

In early March, the event was assigned to a member of Rupp's team, a thirty-year-old product manager named Meghan Wulff. Wulff would be Prime Day's "single-threaded leader," with her sole focus on the event (as well as trying to blot out the characteristically Amazonian paranoia that, at any moment, she might screw things up and get fired). Because it was a global event and meant to be chock-full of surprises, Wulff and a colleague code-named it "Project Piñata," requiring an awkward keyboard maneuver every time she wrote the name in a document or email. "I will never put an *enye* in a project name ever again," Wulff joked.

Wulff now had to mint an entirely new shopping holiday on an impossible deadline. Amazon wanted to hold it on July 15, to mark the twentieth anniversary of the first sale on Amazon.com. In May, she embarked on a whirlwind trip, traveling to Tokyo, London, Paris, and Munich, to try to yoke together a confederation of Amazon's merchandisers, marketers, and supply chain executives to get behind an initiative that almost everyone was dubious about. Prime Day did not exist yet, so there was little reason for Amazon's retail and advertising teams to drop everything and convince suppliers to support it. "I felt like I was running a Ponzi scheme," Wulff said. Only the imprimatur of Bezos motivated other Amazon execs to abandon their apathy and fall into line.

As the date approached, Wulff and Rupp started to realize there might be more riding on Prime Day than they'd suspected. Bezos wanted to wade into the details and review the promotional materials. *Good Morning America* was interested in previewing the event. "At first we thought, 'this is fantastic,'" Rupp said, "and then 'uh-oh, wait a minute, this might be bigger than we thought.'"

Amazon in 2015 had moved into the zeitgeist in a way that perhaps even its own executives hadn't yet recognized. The event kicked off in Japan, where the local website promptly crashed due to overwhelming interest, then cascaded into Europe, and finally into the U.S., where social media reaction was swift—and brutally negative. Armchair shoppers ignored Amazon's proposed hashtag, #HappyPrimeDay and took to Twitter to criticize the company for sold-out items, discounts on trivial products like dishwashing detergent, and an abundance of underwhelming deals. "I keep going back to the Amazon #PrimeDay sale like a girlfriend who is convinced it's going to get better," said one typical Twitter post. "The best deal I've seen so far is 15% off a box of pop tarts," read another.

Rupp and Wulff and their team had turned a Seattle conference room in Amazon's Arizona building into their designated war room. They spent two days and nights monitoring the traffic and promoting whatever deals they could. Wulff recalled going home to sleep for a few hours and then returning. In the middle of the chaos, Jeff Wilke stopped by and gave a pep talk. The event was ultimately the biggest shopping day in Amazon's history, but considering her struggles to bring Amazon's merchandisers on board that first year, Wulff was not surprised by the negative reaction on social media.

Behind the scenes, "Jeff lost his mind" over the negative online reaction, said Craig Berman, a senior PR vice president, who was at his son's swim meet in Oregon when all hell broke loose. "He was screaming at me and my team that we needed to be clear that these aren't shitty deals. He was being maniacal, saying, 'Get this fixed! You've got to show this is a success!'"

Berman and a PR colleague, Julie Law, started poring through the sales numbers and releasing as much data as they could find on what products were being discounted and how quickly they were selling out. It didn't satisfy the social media mob, but press accounts of the first Prime Day were more balanced. "To Jeff's credit," Berman said, "you only get one chance to make a first impression. He was personally vested."

A few days later, the Prime Day team gathered in their office kitchen in the Arizona building to acknowledge the end of their exhausting journey and took turns whacking a real piñata. But there was little time for celebration. Rupp and Wulff were asked to write a six-page narrative summarizing the day's mixed results: 34.4 million items purchased, including twenty-four thousand Instant Pot 7-in-1 Programmable Pressure Cookers, and 1.2 million new Prime accounts started worldwide, according to an internal document. It also highlighted that a "subset of our members and the press were quite vocal, particularly in the U.S., claiming the deals were random, the experience was clunky, and that the event was a disappointment."

Years later, Wulff reflected on that wistfully and considered it an illustration of the Amazon leadership principle that stipulates leaders must be "vocally self-critical." "That's when I learned a lesson that regardless of whether you just delivered the biggest revenue day in Amazon's history, your first sentence is, 'We fucked up.'"

———

After the Prime Day review, Chris Rupp was exhausted. She took time off for an overdue sabbatical and while on leave, she accepted an offer to join Microsoft's Xbox unit. Of that first Prime Day, she said, "It was hard, hard, hard."

In the wake of her globe-trotting stint as a single-threaded leader, Meghan Wulff was just as tired. "I was totally depleted, emotionally and physically, and took a few weeks off to recover and reflect," she said. As Greg Greeley and the Prime team got to work on next year's event, Wulff declined to lead it again and sought another job inside the company. Over the next few years, she would take a variety of roles at Amazon, including serving as technical advisor for the new senior vice president of human resources, Beth Galetti.

In 2019, Wulff took a sabbatical from the company and went to visit family in North Carolina. She had grown up with four older brothers, in a family with financial hardships. In an unguarded moment, she used some of that Amazon-style critical feedback on her adored mother, who responded quietly, "Please stop using the leadership principles in our relationship."

As if a heavy fog had suddenly lifted, Wulff started to think about her time at Amazon in a new light. She was grateful for the experience but conflicted about it. She loved the "beautiful collaboration machine," how she had learned about operational discipline and made lasting friendships. At the same time, she also felt like she had "given more than I got back" and didn't like who she was becoming as a leader or a person.

Wulff started to ask herself: Was the overall impact of Amazon's customer obsession on local businesses, the climate, and warehouse workers worth it? Why weren't there more women and underrepresented minorities on the S-team? Why was the work environment so punishing, and why was she perpetuating it? As an Amazonian, she had to earn the trust of her colleagues and superiors every day she had worked at Amazon. Had Jeff Bezos, she wondered, earned her trust?

Now Wulff joined the ranks of a crowded club: she was a disillusioned former Amazon employee. "At some point along the way it moved from an admirable mission to an uncomfortable awareness that, for me, Jeff Bezos too often didn't make admirable choices," she said. "He continues to amass an obscene amount of money and do very little with it for the good of society."

She even questioned the annual spree of discounts that she had helped create. When an article in *Fast Company* suggested that Prime Day cynically manipulated shoppers into buying things they didn't need, it resonated with her. "It was a shopping holiday," Wulff said flatly. "We were convincing people to buy Instapots and join a loyalty program geared at having them spend more at Amazon."

Wulff left the company in 2019 and joined the Seattle online real estate company Zillow. She canceled her Prime membership shortly after, recycled her Amazon Echos, and closed her Amazon account permanently.

———

Only a week after the first Prime Day, Amazon announced its second consecutive gangbuster earnings report on July 23, 2015, recording another profit and capitalizing on its AWS-fueled momentum. The stock surged 18 percent overnight and yielded a momentous realignment of the business universe. For the first time, Amazon's market capitalization surpassed Walmart's; it was now the most valuable retailer on the planet. To celebrate both the official twentieth anniversary of the company's first sale, but also undoubtedly their new success, employees flooded into Seattle's CenturyLink Field the day after earnings to enjoy a private concert by the local hip-hop duo Macklemore and Ryan Lewis.

But the revelry would be fleeting. If the emergence of AWS and the rapid execution of Prime Day were testaments to Amazon's fleet-footed and inventive culture, negative effects were on display as well—namely, the relentless pace and self-criticism that unmoored many employees and contributed to the company's robust turnover rate. That August, those discontents burst into the open when the *New York Times* published a 5,800-word gut punch of an article, titled "Inside Amazon: Wrestling Big Ideas in a Bruising Workplace."

The reporters, Jodi Kantor and David Streitfeld, described an environment of combative meetings, unreasonably high standards, eighty-hour workweeks, and employees who regularly wept at their desks. They reported that some workers who suffered from critical illnesses, miscarriages, or other personal crises were penalized professionally. And they described the practice of "stack ranking," or regularly dismissing the least-productive workers, amounting to "purposeful Darwinism" that created an environment of fear.

In response to the piece, Amazon's combative new senior vice president of policy and communications, Jay Carney, broke with the company's aversion to battling publicly with critics and penned a *Medium* post charging that the story "*misrepresented Amazon.*" A high-profile hire earlier that year, Carney was the former White House press secretary to President Barack Obama and director of communications for then Vice President Joe Biden. He claimed the reporters violated journalistic standards and attacked a primary source with private details of his Amazon employment record, alleging he was fired for impropriety and had an axe to grind with the company. From that point forward, Amazon would become far more outspoken and confrontational when it came to defending itself in the press. Executives were no longer comfortable simply telling themselves that they were "misunderstood."

Carney's post had followed an internal email that Jeff Bezos sent to all of its 220,000 or so full-time employees, encouraging them to read the article but asserting that it "doesn't describe the Amazon I know or the caring Amazonians I work with every day." Bezos asked employees to send any similar stories of callous management behavior to the human resources department or directly to him at his well-known email address, jeff@amazon.com. A few hundred of them would, and those responses would get directed to one of Amazon's longest serving human resources executives, David Niekerk.

A West Point graduate and U.S. army veteran with combat stories that he was not at liberty to discuss, Niekerk was in Brazil when the *Times* article hit, preparing for Amazon's launch in the country. He had the same protective reaction as many other Amazon employees: the article, he felt, was sensationalized and used negative anecdotes to reach unfair conclusions. "Working at Amazon is like being in an Olympic training camp," Niekerk told me a few years later. "There are very high standards and a push to get everything done, all the time." At the same time, he had seen plenty of examples of bad management and could admit that there was something familiar in the *Times* account.

Bezos himself was the architect of Amazon's culture and skeptical of the unoriginal way that human resources was run at many companies. Other Silicon Valley CEOs had varying levels of disinterest in getting involved in the muck of HR and culture building. Steve Jobs, for example, upon returning full-time to Apple in 1997, had addressed an audience of the company's human resources employees in Cupertino and bluntly told them, "It seems to me you are all just a bunch of barnacles."

Bezos, on the other hand, dove into the tedious details of HR and tried to formulate mechanisms that would substitute for good intentions. He was a student of organizations, culture, and innovation. Early on, he always wanted to hire the smartest people over the best leaders and told HR execs like Niekerk that it was their responsibility to train them to be good managers.

Bezos also advocated for the practice of stack ranking, where employees were rated by their managers on the basis of job performance, with the lowest performers pushed out the door. Niekerk recalled that Bezos had absorbed that practice from *Topgrading*, by Bradford Smart, who had helped legendary CEO Jack Welch set up a hiring system at General Electric that classified job candidates as A Players, B Players, and C Players. Bezos wanted to apply those principles, not just in recruiting, but inside the company as well.

"The greatest pain any leader will feel are the open jobs in their organization," he once told Niekerk. "That means leaders will be very hesitant to let anyone go." Bezos suspected that managers couldn't be counted on to voluntarily embrace the hassle of additional hiring and feared that a tolerance for mediocre performers would spread through the company and erode the "Day 1 mentality." Stack ranking would force managers to upgrade the talent on their teams. "People thought it was a mean-spirited process and to a certain extent it was," Niekerk said. "But in the big picture, it kept Amazon fresh and innovative."

But as Amazon expanded, booting the poor performers wasn't enough. Bezos appeared to believe that an overly comfortable or exceedingly wealthy workforce might also doom Amazon. Did employees still have passion for their jobs? Or were they hanging on for ever-larger compensation rewards, draining the company of energy while awaiting riches and retirement? Bezos eschewed any financial hooks, like steadily increasing stock grants, that might keep people at the company even if they were no longer engaged in their work.

The typical compensation package at Amazon reflected these priorities. It featured a standard base salary of around $150,000, a signing bonus, and a grant of stock that vested in 5, 15 and 40 percent portions over each of four years; the combination of salary and stock vesting then comprised an employee's total compensation target.

If employees couldn't cut it at Amazon and lost their jobs in the first few years, they didn't get their entire stock grant and wouldn't receive the remaining portion of their prorated signing bonus. And if Amazon's share price increased more than 15 percent in a year, the employee's total annual compensation then exceeded their target, and their annual performance stock grants would reflect that and be correspondingly lower, vest farther out into the future, or could even disappear altogether.

That meant that after years of Amazon's stock price increasing well beyond 15 percent, many employees encountered what they called a total compensation "cliff." They were making well in excess of their target and saw their stock grants drop precipitously. This was another reason why valued, experienced Amazon executives like Chris Rupp left the company for opportunities elsewhere. (Bezos himself made just under $82,000 a year and received no additional stock-based compensation beyond his large initial ownership stake;

his wealth was generated purely by Amazon's steadily increasing stock price.)

Bezos understood that in some quarters, all this might make Amazon an unpopular place to work. But he also felt that the perks factored into those high-profile media surveys of workplace desirability—like lavish compensation, unlimited vacation time, and free meals and massages—had little to do with the passion and purpose employees brought to their jobs. "He once told me, 'If we ever appear in the "100 best places to work in America,"' you've screwed this place up,'" Niekerk said. (Alas, Amazon would soon become a mainstay of those lists.)

Despite the fact that Niekerk was preparing to retire in 2015, Amazon had one more mission for the old soldier. When some 250 Amazon employees sent their horror stories directly to the CEO and to HR after the *Times* article and Bezos's email to the company, they were then all forwarded to Niekerk. Over the following four months, he consolidated and reviewed the stories and pulled together a paper, offering ten courses of action the company might take to address the issues that had emerged. For example, he suggested that every leader should be required to take a course called "As Life Happens," to learn how to sensitively manage an employee whose personal life might be interfering with their work obligations.

Niekerk recalled that colleagues who read his paper said that it was among the best analyses they had seen of the cultural challenges that were so obviously plaguing the company at its twentieth anniversary.

But before the paper got any further, Amazon's lawyers killed it. The stories that employees had volunteered and submitted at Bezos's urging, they asserted, were one-sided and unverified. The recommendations, the lawyers said, were thus "fruit from a poisoned tree." Niekerk retired from Amazon soon after and his report never made it to the S-team.

Nevertheless, after the *Times* story, Amazon made several changes to its culture that it said (somewhat dubiously) were already underway before the article was published. Even as Bezos was publicly defensive, he seemed to acknowledge privately there were valuable aspects to the critique and that a culture forged to support the maniacal pace of a startup needed to evolve alongside a maturing company with 230,000 employees.

For example, the practice of stack ranking, or setting attrition targets for each team, was largely discarded; managers were no longer forced into contentious sessions over whom to fire. Employees were offered the chance to change jobs anytime they wanted, even if they had recently joined the company, so that they could always escape a bad manager. This forced managers to be extra solicitous to their employees. Amazon also instituted an internal appeal process to adjudicate cases when employees were put on performance improvement plans or faced termination. The company added a unique parental leave program that allowed employees to divide their time off into different intervals within a twelve-month period, or to share it with a spouse whose job didn't offer such a benefit. It also instituted smaller changes, such as allowing new mothers to expense Milk Stork, a service that let them send refrigerated breast milk home when they were traveling for business. After the *Times* article, one female executive said, "We got a lot more latitude to make human decisions."

The biggest change may have been to Amazon's decade-old performance review system. The former system had required all of a worker's peers to write lengthy appraisals and send them to the worker's direct manager, who then wrapped them all into a single evaluation for a one-on-one conversation with the employee, which tended to culminate in a contentious tangle over the worker's shortcomings. "We found that when we surveyed Amazonians, 90 percent were more demotivated after their review than before, even if they were the best employees," said HR chief Beth Galetti, who was asked to "radically simplify" the review process after she took over as head of HR a few months after the *Times* article was published.

In this revamped performance review system, peers and managers were asked to write sixty words describing an employee's "superpower," and another sixty to describe a "growth idea" for the year ahead. "It was all about looking forward and being motivational," Galetti said.

Bezos also conceded that the old process had grown too negative, explaining his sudden appreciation for its flaws to a group of large Amazon investors at a private meeting: "Imagine if you sit down with your wife once a year. You tell her all these great things that you love about her, but then at the end you say, 'Also, you're just a little bit fat.' That's the only thing that's going to stick with her from that entire conversation!"

As Bezos delivered the punch line, he burst into laughter, according to an investor who was at the meeting: "We want to have a performance review system that doesn't tell our employees that they're fat."

———

By the end of 2015, there was little doubt left about Amazon's ascendance. The company posted its third consecutive quarterly profit, along with 69 percent growth in sales at Andy Jassy's booming AWS division. Amazon's market capitalization had doubled in the span of a year and stood at $315 billion. For Steve Ballmer and the other skeptics, it was a year for eating crow. At the same time, Amazon became the fastest company in history to surpass $100 billion in annual sales, meeting a long-standing goal of Bezos and the S-team.

In his annual letter to investors the following April, Bezos trumpeted that benchmark and tried to get in the final word in the debate over Amazon's culture. "You can write down your corporate culture, but when you do so, you're discovering it, uncovering it—not creating it," he wrote. "It is created slowly over time by the people and by events—by the stories of past success and failure that become a deep part of the company lore."

The events of 2015 would be added to that already rich history. Over the course of a critical twelve months, the dramatic transformation of Amazon in the eyes of the world was matched in scope only by the makeover in the image of the founder himself. He was now known as a corporate taskmaster who had architected a culture of unquestionable efficiency; the genius inventor behind the Kindle and Alexa, but also a versatile CEO who had authored an enterprise computing platform capable of generating lucrative profits. He continued to be dubious of most media coverage of Amazon; yet at the same time, through a set of unlikely circumstances, Jeff Bezos was about to become known as the voluble defender of a free press.

CHAPTER 5

"Democracy Dies in Darkness"

Who can say what set Donald J. Trump on a tirade against the *Washington Post*? It could have been the months of critical coverage of his presidential campaign from the nation's third largest newspaper. Or perhaps it was the edition of the column "Fact Checker," published by Glenn Kessler on December 7, 2015. That morning, the reporter scrutinized the Republican's absurd claim that he had foreseen the threat posed by Osama bin Laden before September 11. "I predicted Osama bin Laden," Trump had declared on the campaign trail in Knoxville, Tennessee. "I predicted terrorism. I can feel it, like I can feel a good location in real estate." For this assertion, Kessler assigned Trump the highest grade on his scale of mendacity: "four Pinocchios."

A little after 7 a.m. EST that morning, Trump responded with a fusillade of tweets aimed at Amazon.com, the *Post*, and the man who owned it: Jeff Bezos.

Donald J. Trump
@realDonaldTrump

The @washingtonpost, which loses a fortune, is owned by @JeffBezos for purposes of keeping taxes down at his no profit company, @amazon.

 7:08 AM

Donald J. Trump
@realDonaldTrump

The @washingtonpost loses money (a deduction) and gives
owner @JeffBezos power to screw public on low taxation of @
Amazon! Big tax shelter

 7:18 AM

Donald J. Trump
@realDonaldTrump

If @amazon ever had to pay fair taxes, its stock would crash
and it would crumble like a paper bag. The @washingtonpost
scam is saving it!

 7:22 AM

Trump's claims were as tenuous as his boasts about bin Laden;
the *Post*'s financial results had no impact whatsoever on Amazon's
corporate taxes. Bezos had personally acquired the ailing newspaper in August 2013 for $250 million in cash and tried to keep his two
high-profile concerns separate. Now the opportunistic GOP candidate
was trampling over Bezos's careful attempts at compartmentalization.

Later that morning, across the country in Seattle, Bezos emailed
Jay Carney, his senior vice president for global corporate affairs. The
response not only exhibited Bezos's surprising fondness for emoti-
cons but kicked off a revealing exchange that was forwarded to me a
few years later.

> From: Jeff Bezos
> To: Jay Carney
> Subject: Trump trash talk
>
> Trump just trash talked Amazon/me/WaPo. Feel like I should
> have a witty retort. Don't want to let it go past. Useful opportunity

(patriotic duty) to do my part to deflate this guy who would be a scary prez. I'm an inexperienced trash talker but I'm willing to learn. :) Ideas?

Also tactically I'm about to be interviewed by some German pubs set up a long time ago and they might ask about it.

Carney's style with the media on articles about Amazon that the company didn't like (e.g., most of them) was nakedly pugilistic. He had helped to persuade Bezos, who felt that responding to media critics only gave their attacks more oxygen, to allow him to challenge coverage like the *New York Times* exposé of Amazon's corporate culture. But when it came to Donald Trump, the politically savvy Carney recognized a cynical game and advised Bezos to stay out of it:

> From: Jay Carney
> To: Jeff Bezos
> re: Subject: Trump trash talk

We've been discussing and decided to make sure reporters know WaPo and Amazon are not connected. He's playing to his base of disaffected voters by bashing the press and big business in one tweet. For him politically, it doesn't matter that he's got his facts all wrong. Much as I'd love to have you slap him down, I personally think you'd be helping him by trash talking him back. Every fight he gets into gives his campaign more energy.

If you get asked about [it] with the Germans, I recommend you say, 'you know Amazon and the Washington Post are two entirely separate companies. I'm not sure what he's talking about.'

For years, Bezos would have readily agreed with Carney's advice and stayed quiet, but now their positions were reversed. Trump's targets at that point had included his rivals in the GOP primary, high-profile journalists, and major business figures like Barry Diller.

Bezos was seemingly eager to join that distinguished club and had a desire to engage Trump, counter his inaccuracies, and defend the newspaper.

> From: Jeff Bezos
> To: Jay Carney
> re: Subject: Trump trash talk
> This seems like one of those times when I might disregard really good advice! :) Can you guys come up with some good options just so we can look at the specifics.

Over the next few hours, Carney brainstormed over email and on the phone with Amazon PR deputies Drew Herdener, Craig Berman, and Ty Rogers. They considered and discarded the idea of proclaiming that Amazon and the *Post* "are as separate as the two sides of Trump's hair." Berman suggested reserving a seat for Trump on a Blue Origin spacecraft, a clever bit of misdirection that drew in a third Bezos company. Carney liked that idea and suggested it to Bezos, who asked that they include his feeling of being "left out" until now of Trump's unmoored denunciations.

Finally, after an afternoon of wrangling over the precise wording and the decision to include a link to a Blue Origin launch video, Ty Rogers responded from Bezos's Twitter account:

Jeff Bezos
@JeffBezos

Finally trashed by @realDonaldTrump. Will still reserve him a seat on the Blue Origin rocket. #sendDonaldtospace http://bit
.ly/1OpyW5N

 3:30 PM

Inexorably drawn to chaos and conflict, Trump eagerly responded, charging in a television interview that Bezos had acquired the *Post* for political influence and promising that Amazon was "going to have such problems" if he got elected. He later honed his attempt to delegitimize the newspaper by branding it the *#AmazonWashingtonPost*.

Jeff Bezos had officially entered the political fray.

———

"Why would I even be a candidate to buy the Post*? I don't know anything about the newspaper industry."*

With such indifference, expressed to investment bankers representing the *Washington Post*, Jeff Bezos kicked off one of the more illustrious chapters of his career. The *Post* would expand and fortify Bezos's reputation as one of the most successful businesspeople of his generation, an organizational theorist whose management practices could be applied not just inside fast-growing tech companies but outside them as well.

The *Post* was owned by the venerable Graham family and run by Donald Graham, the son of legendary owner Katharine Graham, and for years it had been on shaky financial footing. It remained a local paper serving the D.C. region, with a specialization in national politics, at a time when local advertising was moving to the web and the classified ad business was being vaporized by websites like Craigslist. The financial crisis of 2008 only compounded that decay. Seven straight years of revenue declines tended to "focus the mind," as Don Graham liked to say.

Graham was beloved in the *Post* newsroom for his first-name familiarity with staff and his zeal for the journalistic mission. But under his cautious eye, the *Post* had reached an impasse. Graham had reached an agreement in 2005 with Facebook founder Mark Zuckerberg to invest in the budding social network, but then he allowed Zuckerberg to withdraw from the deal and take money at a higher valuation from the Silicon Valley venture capital firm Accel instead. Having forfeited a historic company-enriching windfall, Graham joined Facebook's board of directors, where for the next few years he listened to Zuckerberg preach that content on the web should be free. When major media organizations like the rival *New York Times* started adding paywalls in 2011, the *Post* was late to the trend; its paywall was porous and easily circumvented by readers.

By 2013, an atmosphere of melancholic decline had gripped the boxy, mid-century concrete headquarters of the Washington Post Co. at 1150 15th Street NW in downtown Washington. Its once profitable Kaplan educational division had been decimated by a regulatory overhaul of the often scammy for-profit education industry. The newsroom, once more than a thousand journalists strong, had been reduced by waves of layoffs to around six hundred. Morale was low, with deep distrust between the business and editorial divisions. The company didn't have the resources to invest in national and international news and distribution, or to free itself from the straitjacket of regional news and its deteriorating economics. So Graham agreed to sell the paper.

Post executives sought a wealthy, technologically sophisticated individual who cared about the paper's journalistic mission. Jeff Bezos was at the top of the list, alongside other internet billionaires like eBay founder Pierre Omidyar. Bezos's initial response to the *Post*'s investment bankers, and sporadic conversations with Graham, a longtime friend, was cool. Only that July 2013, when Bezos asked Graham to meet privately at the annual Allen & Company conference in Sun Valley, did Graham realize that Bezos had researched the opportunity and was more interested than he had previously let on. In the brief talks that followed, Bezos accepted Graham's initial $250 million asking price and paid cash. Amazon's founder acquired the newspaper—not via Amazon but personally.

Bezos was the platonic ideal of a *Post* owner—a leader with boundless resources, a widely known reputation as a digital innovator, and a corona of credibility that seemed to extend to whatever he touched. He expressed a staunch commitment to the paper's editorial independence and seemed to have little interest in using it to serve any political agenda. When Fred Hiatt, editor of the opinion page, offered to resign that fall, explaining that "it's entirely legitimate for an owner to have an editorial page that reflects his world view," Bezos declined the offer.

Bezos had a traditionalist's view of the media business. In his first address to *Post* employees at the 15th Street building in September, he declared his faith in "the bundle," the collection of news, culture, and entertainment coverage that makes up a newspaper. He also lamented the rise of so-called aggregators, which summarized other organizations' work, like the *Huffington Post*. But he had no compunctions about casting aside the paper's local ambitions and deprioritizing its print edition in favor of a more ambitious future online. "You have to acknowledge that the physical print business is in structural decline," he told his new employees. "You have to accept it and move forward. The death knell for any enterprise is to glorify the past, no matter how good it was—especially for an institution like *The Washington Post*."

Their new owner was ready to break from the disciplines of that past. And when Bezos invited the *Post*'s management team to spend a weekend with him in Seattle that fall, he wanted its cerebral executive editor, Marty Baron—the former *Boston Globe* chief who would later be depicted in the movie *Spotlight*—to be included. "If you are going to change the restaurant, the chef has got to be on board," he reasoned.

Baron joined publisher and CEO Katharine Weymouth, president Steve Hills, and chief information officer Shailesh Prakash on the cross-country trip. On the first night, they had dinner with Bezos at Canlis, an upscale restaurant with majestic views over Lake Union; during the meal, they saw a perfect double rainbow over the lake (the future name of the paper's magazine-like national edition for tablets: the Rainbow app). The next morning, the group met MacKenzie and the four Bezos children at their twenty-nine-thousand-square-foot home on the shores of Lake Washington. Bezos made everyone pancakes for breakfast (afterward the *Post*'s leadership team called themselves "the Pancake Group"). During the daylong review of the *Post*'s editorial and business strategies, Bezos never once looked at his cell phone. If he had other things on his mind, he kept them completely compartmentalized.

For the next few years, friends occasionally teased him about the purchase of the *Washington Post*. "The joke was 'Jeff, when MacKenzie asked you to pick up a newspaper, she meant just one copy,'" said his high school pal, Joshua Weinstein. But interviewers and colleagues always asked the question: Why had he bought, of all things, that anachronistic digital relic, a *newspaper*?

It may have been that with his own fortunes soaring along with Amazon's, Bezos understood that he could use his resources for things he valued, such as ensuring a strong and independent press. Saving the *Post* would not only help his friend Don Graham; it would be a significant boon to the American media establishment, as well as a symbolic contribution to the country, and democracy. But his public answer to that question was always much simpler and more earnest: "It's the most important newspaper in the most important capital city in the Western world. I'd be crazy not to save [it]," Bezos said a few years later in an onstage conversation with Axel Springer CEO Mathias Döpfner. "I'm going to be very happy when I'm eighty that I made that decision."

A year after the purchase, Fred Ryan, a cofounder of the politics news site *Politico*, asked Bezos the same question while they were having breakfast in the Amazon building Day 1 North. The conversation would lead to Bezos hiring Ryan to replace Weymouth as the company's chief executive and publisher. Ryan, a former aide to Ronald Reagan, had been invited to Seattle after sending Bezos an unsolicited email expressing admiration for the paper. He later recalled thinking at the time that "sometimes wealthy people have passions and toys or might want to own a publication so they can influence things."

Bezos surprised him with his response. "I remember his answer because he has lived it to this day," Ryan said. "He said he feels that it is essential to have a strong and independent press for the health of our society and democracy."

———

If members of the Pancake Group had fanciful notions that Bezos was going to rescue the *Post* by spending uncontrollably, he quickly dispelled them. In early 2015, they trekked back to Seattle and presented him with a multiyear operating plan that called for the paper to lose more than $100 million over the next four years. Bezos shot it down immediately. "Yeah, I'm not interested in that" is how one participant recalled his understated reaction. After the meeting, Bezos and Fred Ryan sat down and hashed out a plan to run the paper as a disciplined, stand-alone business, not as the hobby of someone with limitless resources. Over the next few years, there would be a quiet, targeted series of layoffs in the company's print advertising division, which were partially offset by a smaller but louder number of hires of digital media specialists.

In addition to wanting the *Post* to operate within its means, Bezos applied elements of his well-tuned business philosophy to the paper. He preached the wholesale embrace of technology, rapid experimentation, and optimism about the opportunities of the internet instead of despair. "You've suffered all the pain of the internet but haven't yet fully enjoyed its gifts," Bezos told his new employees. "Distribution is free, and you have a massive audience."

One of his first ideas was to give subscribers of other newspapers free online access to the *Post*. Some 250 papers, like the *Toledo Blade* and the *Dallas Morning News*, signed up for the new *Post* partnership program. While it didn't result in a surge of new subscribers, the program, plus Bezos's patina of digital coolness, generated a fresh wave of buzzy news stories about the *Post*.

Another Bezos principle resulted in a more tangible outcome. The Amazon founder always looked for ways to "weave a rope" of connections between his different business units. Careful not to overtly push, he introduced *Post* execs to their Amazon counterparts and suggested it would be a good idea for them to talk. In the fall of 2014, Amazon's Fire tablet owners got a free six-month digital subscription to the *Post*'s national edition on an app that was preinstalled on the device. A year later, tens of millions of Prime members got the same deal.

Between 2014 and 2015, unique visitors to the *Post*'s websites and apps grew by 56 percent. In October 2015, the *Post* briefly surpassed the *New York Times* in unique monthly visitors. Taking an opportunity to strafe a competitor and rally the troops, Bezos declared on *CBS This Morning* that the *Post* was "working on becoming the new paper of record." The paper then took out ads that declared, "Thank you for making *The Washington Post* America's New Publication of Record."

Though the advertising staff was being pared back, Bezos did agree to methodical increases in hiring in the newsroom and the technology department. In the two years after the acquisition, Marty Baron added 140 full-time journalists, boosting his staff to around 700—compared to some 1,300 reporters and editors at the *Times*. The additions came mainly on the national, political, and investigations desks, as well as in business and technology coverage. Resources devoted to regional news, the unprofitable mainstay of the *Post*'s previous leadership, remained largely flat.

Bezos also had a few strange notions about how the journalism process might be streamlined. He wondered aloud whether the paper would need so many editors if it simply hired great writers. Baron responded that if anything, the paper probably needed more editors. Bezos repeated that refrain so often that a few editors took to sending him the raw copy of high-profile journalists. Amazon said Bezos never received or read any such emails, but he eventually came to agree with Baron.

Marty Baron recalled Bezos defying his expectations at every turn. For example, he assumed that Bezos would want to personalize the *Post*'s home page for every reader. But Bezos observed that readers came to the paper in part because they trusted the staff's editorial judgment. Baron said that Bezos "didn't try to reinvent the paper; he tried to capture what made it special."

But Bezos did try to reinvent the systems behind the paper, with a flood of Amazon-style rituals. The Pancake Group, which occasionally expanded to include finance and audience development execs, spoke to Bezos every other week on Wednesdays at 1 p.m. EST for an hour. Bezos asked *Post* managers to "bring me new things"; he wanted to see everything, including changes in pricing and how to expand the paper's audience and revenue, in the form of six-page Amazon-style narratives, subject to Bezos's careful reading and detailed questions.

It was a Bezos-style repeatable process, or forcing function, designed to push his team to think creatively and innovate. *Post* execs said that Bezos read every memo beforehand save for once, when he apologized for not getting to it and took the time to read it quietly at the start of the meeting. He also exposed them to a steady stream of *Jeffisms*: about one-way and two-way doors; how double the experimentation equals twice the innovation; how "data overrules hierarchy" and there are "multiple paths to yes"—an Amazonian notion that an employee with a new idea who gets a negative reaction from one manager should be free to shop it to another, lest a promising concept get smothered in infancy.

Bezos had only one conspicuous misstep, at least in the eyes of many current and former *Post* employees. In late 2014, acting on concerns that he had expressed during his due diligence before the acquisition, he froze the *Post*'s pension plans, cutting retirement benefits for longtime employees and converting newer employees' plans to 401(k) retirement accounts with a relatively miserly matching grant from the company.

The pension had been on perfectly stable footing, thanks in part to the fund's stake in Warren Buffett's Berkshire Hathaway. The changes nevertheless reduced the *Post*'s obligations toward its longest-serving employees and gave current employees less financial incentive to stay at the paper for their entire careers. Bezos's scuttling of the pension fund, and a twin hostility to the Washington Post Guild, was in line with how he operated Amazon, as well as his long-standing aversion to unions and to lavishing employees with ostentatious perks. "The only explanation anyone ever got was that he doesn't believe that a company has any obligation to its workers once they walk out the door," said one *Post* writer. (Amazon said this does not accurately represent Bezos's views.)

The move initiated a frosty relationship between Bezos and the guild. During the difficult negotiations every few years, a smattering of employees would protest the changes to their contracts in picket lines outside the *Post*'s offices. But they remained a vocal minority. Many *Post* employees were grateful for the paper's revival and remained card-carrying members of the Church of Bezos. Only Donald Trump, lobbing Twitter grenades from afar, noticed the discord and tried to stir the pot:

Donald J. Trump
@realDonaldTrump

Washington Post employees want to go on strike because Bezos isn't paying them enough. I think a really long strike would be a great idea. Employees would get more money and we would get rid of Fake News for an extended period of time! Is @WaPo a registered lobbyist?

Predictably, Bezos took the most interest in the *Post*'s products and technology. He forged a partnership with CIO Shailesh Prakash, a graduate of the Indian Institute of Technology in Bombay, and boasted that the newspaper had better engineers than many Silicon Valley startups. He obsessed over shaving milliseconds from the time it took web pages and complex graphics to load. He also asked for customized metrics that could measure the reader's true interest in stories, and whether an article was truly "riveting."

When Bezos acquired the paper, Prakash had been developing a content system for the *Post*, called Arc Publishing, to manage functions like online publishing, blogging, podcasting, and advertising. Naturally, Bezos loved the idea of supplying that technology to other papers and encouraged Prakash to license it to broadcasters and any company that needed publishing software. By 2021, Arc powered fourteen hundred websites and was on a path to generating $100 million in annual revenue.

Bezos and Prakash's team also spent eight months developing the magazine-like Rainbow app for tablets. This digital edition of the paper, updated twice daily, had no home page. It presented articles in a magazine-like layout and allowed users to scroll through a series of pages containing two articles each and then zoom into any story that interested them. Prakash described Bezos as "chief product officer" on the app; he recalled that the owner articulated an overarching goal of solving the problem of "cognitive news overload" by allowing readers to hover high above the day's events, like a glider soaring through the sky. The *Post* released the app in July 2015 and made it standard on Amazon's Fire tablet.

In Prakash, Bezos had found a kindred spirit. They agreed on everything—almost. When Apple (an Amazon rival) solicited the *Post* to join a bundle of publications in a new service called Apple News+, Prakash and other Pancake Group members saw the gaudy potential of 1.5 billion iPhones and iPads and wrote a six-page memo outlining the pros and cons of joining. But Bezos reasoned that it would undermine the *Post*'s identically priced subscription offering and argued against it passionately. *The Post* passed on the opportunity.

When the *Wall Street Journal* tried to poach Prakash to be their CTO in early 2017, Bezos persuaded him to stay—in part by endowing him with a separate role on the advisory board of his private space company, Blue Origin. On the occasional Saturday, Prakash would fly across the country to Kent, Washington, to help the company with its supply chain systems. "The most important thing Jeff has brought is a culture of experimentation," Prakash said. "None of us feel that if we spend money and screw up some big project that we're going to have to face an auditing committee. We are not afraid to fail."

Bezos's imprimatur did more than just allow the *Post* to take bigger risks. On the advertising side, the mere proximity of the world's most famous businessperson seemed to cast an effervescent glow. A sales deck developed by the ad team screamed "the Bezos Effect" on its second page, next to a smiling headshot of the bald tech impresario. *Post* ad executives said that sponsors were drawn to the paper because of Bezos's involvement, even if the execs did find themselves constantly explaining that no, Amazon did not own the paper. "The story is what helped us more than anything else," said one business-side executive. "That is part of the magic of Jeff Bezos—that he is Jeff Bezos."

The *Post* was now a private company, so it no longer released financial information. But between the years 2015 and 2018, according to an executive privy to the numbers, ad revenues jumped from $40 million to $140 million and digital subscribers rose by more than 300 percent, exceeding 1.5 million for the first time. (That number would reach 3 million by the time of Marty Baron's retirement in January 2021.) While the paper had lost around $10 million in 2015, it made more than $100 million in the three years after that—a remarkable turnaround from the projected losses Bezos had rejected. "I can't believe how fast this is happening," he said to the Pancake Group after witnessing the extent of the turnaround.

Luck certainly played a role: the chaotic presidency of Donald Trump generated record levels of interest in political news. But Bezos, his management methods, and his deference to the realities of a changing news business had also delivered a blast of strategic clarity to a 140-year-old institution.

———

A year after Bezos acquired the *Post*, its reporter in Tehran, Jason Rezaian, was imprisoned by the Iranian government and charged with espionage. Rezaian would spend the next eighteen months in jail, held often in solitary confinement in "the city I called home," according to his 2019 memoir, *Prisoner*. Initially after his arrest, *Post* execs thought the detention would amount only to short-term harassment. As weeks stretched to months, they realized the situation was more dangerous and that Rezaian might be tried and executed by the country's hard-line religious clerics.

In the U.S., Rezaian's family, along with Marty Baron, Fred Ryan, and many other representatives of the *Post*, reached out to officials at every level of the U.S. government. When foreign leaders visited the capital, Ryan requested private meetings and asked them to exert their influence with the Iranian government on Rezaian's behalf. From Seattle, Bezos asked for frequent updates and at one point briefly considered running a "Free Jason" advertisement in the 2015 Super Bowl. Later that year, when it appeared that the U.S. government had reached a complex and later controversial financial deal with the Iranian government that included freeing Rezaian and three other prisoners, Bezos wanted to fly over personally and bring him home.

So on January 21, 2016, Bezos flew his new $65 million Gulfstream G650ER private jet and met the recovering Rezaian and his family at the U.S. Army's Landstuhl Medical Center in Germany. He had stocked the plane with streamers, #FreeJason signs, and burritos and beer, since prior to his captivity, Rezaian had told TV host Anthony Bourdain that it was the food he missed the most. They flew to

Bangor, Maine, an accessible entry point with little air traffic, where despite Rezaian and his wife having parted with their passports and other identification during the ordeal, an ICE official ushered them in, saying that the Iranians needed to know "you screw with one of us, you screw with all of us." Bezos then personally shuttled Rezaian and his wife to Florida for a brief respite in Key West.

A few days later, they were all back in D.C. having dinner with *Post* execs, and on January 28, they attended the ceremonial opening of the *Post*'s gleaming new headquarters on K Street, overlooking historic Franklin Square. The offices were state-of-the-art, with new workstations, and spots for developers and designers, who would now sit alongside journalists, as well as video studios so reporters could easily appear on cable TV. Rezaian spoke emotionally at the opening, and then Bezos, wearing a #FreeJason lapel pin, addressed employees. "Important institutions like the *Post* have an essence, they have a heart, they have a core—what Marty called a soul," he said. "And if you wanted that to change, you'd be crazy. That's part of what this place is. It's part of what makes it so special."

Bezos had saved the *Post*. But he was also, in a way, benefiting from the refracted glow of its noble journalistic mission. In 2016, *Fortune* magazine placed Bezos in the top spot on its list of the world's 50 Greatest Leaders—above Angela Merkel, Pope Francis, and Tim Cook. The accompanying article spent as much space on the turnaround at the paper as it did on the momentum at Amazon. "We used to joke that Jeff changed retail completely, built a 10,000-year clock, and sent rockets into space. But he wasn't called the greatest leader in the world until he helped a newspaper company," a former *Post* executive told me.

Washington, D.C., seemed to appreciate Bezos, and he returned the sentiment. That fall, he paid $23 million for the largest home in the city, the former Textile Museum and an adjoining mansion in the fashionable Kalorama neighborhood; his new neighbors were Barack and Michelle Obama, along with Ivanka Trump, the daughter of his adversary, and her husband, Jared Kushner. Bezos would spend the next three years and $12 million renovating the 27,000-square-foot structure, with its eleven bedrooms and twenty-five bathrooms. He planned to spend more time in the city and use the residence to hold the kind of exalted dinner parties for the rich, powerful, and interesting that were once the hallmark of a previous owner, Katharine Graham.

"Now I get it," Bezos had told Sally Quinn, widow to the *Post's* celebrated former editor, Ben Bradlee, at Bradlee's funeral. The *Post* wasn't just a business to be reinvented with Amazonian principles and integrated into its ecosystem of Kindle devices and Prime membership. It was also a mission to be protected and a community where he was welcomed and even revered. And if an enemy of the institution attacked it—like, say, a candidate for the presidency of the U.S.—Bezos was going to throw caution to the wind and respond.

During the presidential campaign, Bezos asked the Pancake Group to come up with a unique national branding statement, something that would neatly encapsulate that mission. "If this was a club, would you want to join that club?" Fred Ryan recalled Bezos saying as he described what he wanted in the slogan. "If this was on a T-shirt, would you want to wear it?" Bezos offered a single suggestion—something he had heard in speeches by Watergate reporter Bob Woodward, who had read a version of the phrase long ago in an appellate court decision: "Democracy dies in darkness."

Post execs spent a year trying and failing to come up with something better. They hired outside branding agencies and then fired them in frustration. Finally, they gathered around a table and spent hours brainstorming. They wanted something optimistic and hopeful, but out of hundreds of ideas like "Freedom moves in light," none were quite as poetic or resonant, particularly after Donald Trump's shocking victory. So they ended up going with Bezos's original suggestion, which they later put on a T-shirt and mailed to him.

Over the next few years, irritated by the *Post's* penetrating coverage of his tumultuous administration, Trump would grow even more vindictive on Twitter toward Bezos and the paper. He threatened Amazon with onerous new regulations and attacked its relationship with the U.S. Postal Service. The paper's reporting on human rights violations would also antagonize authoritarian governments in other countries around the world, from Russia to the Kingdom of Saudi Arabia. In response, they would try to take out their ire on Amazon and its high-profile CEO. Bezos's easy compartmentalization of all the swirling concerns from multiple entities in his growing business empire was swiftly proving untenable.

Bezos and his unique management practices and optimism about technology had been undeniably good for the newspaper. But in the end, owning the *Washington Post* would exact more of a toll on Amazon—and on Bezos himself—than he ever could have imagined.

CHAPTER 6

Bombing Hollywood

A s reporters and editors at the *Washington Post* grappled with the surprising victory of Donald Trump in late 2016, publicists for Amazon's television and film division were immersed in a much different challenge: how to conduct a buzz-generating campaign for its Oscar-worthy movie, *Manchester by the Sea*. The publicists were brainstorming when one had the idea of asking the boss himself whether he would consider hosting a party for the film in Los Angeles. They emailed him and later recalled getting an unusually speedy reply: "Yes! Let's do it at my house."

On Saturday evening, December 3, a cool, cloudless night, celebrities descended on Bezos's twelve-thousand-square-foot Spanish-style estate in Beverly Hills, which he had purchased nine years earlier for $24 million. An extravagant tentlike structure was erected in the backyard, on a decoratively tiled outdoor patio near the swimming pool. One of the film's producers, Matt Damon, and its star Casey Affleck held court, while actors, directors, and agents lined up at the well-stocked open bar.

Here was a substantial slice of Hollywood's A-list, invited either because they worked with Amazon's production arm, Amazon Studios, or were members of the Academy of Motion Picture Arts and Sciences: Michelle Williams (also in the film), Gael García Bernal, Joseph Gordon-Levitt, Andy Garcia, and Megan Mullally; the directors Joel Coen and Kenneth Lonergan (who directed and wrote

Manchester); Hollywood legends Faye Dunaway, Diane Keaton, John Lithgow, and Ben Kingsley; the musicians T Bone Burnett and Beck; Maria Shriver and her daughters; and many more.

In the middle of it all was Bezos, wearing a plain charcoal-gray suit with an open-collared white shirt—still, back then, the cautious choice of a reforming technology geek. MacKenzie did not attend. "Jeff is the opposite of me," she had told *Vogue* magazine in a rare interview. "He likes to meet people. He's a very social guy."

Indeed, Bezos was laughing and enjoying himself. The room was full of stars radiating high-powered wattage, but as the host and CEO of the company that had hired the event photographers, attention gravitated toward him. Among the many pictures snapped that evening, one would later be closely scrutinized and reprinted. Bezos was standing with Patrick Whitesell, the powerful executive chairman of entertainment and media agency Endeavor, and his wife, former television news anchor Lauren Sanchez, who stood comfortably between them.

Bezos's minders tried to make sure he spoke to as many guests as possible. At one point, they had to interrupt his conversation with actress Kate Beckinsale and her plus-one, the skier Lindsey Vonn, who wore a striking cream-colored jumpsuit. Intermittently towering over him was his longtime deputy Jeff Blackburn, a six-foot-four-inch former college football player who oversaw Amazon's streaming video business, Prime Video. Also by Bezos's side but leaving early was Roy Price, head of Amazon Studios, who sported jeans and a black motorcycle jacket over a white V-neck T-shirt.

As an event designed to generate buzz and to amplify Amazon's presence in Hollywood, the party worked magnificently. Trade publications carried multiple photographs and covered it like a high-society ball of yore. Bezos's "intent this weekend was clear," wrote the entertainment columnist Peter Bart in *Deadline*. "He wants a bigger presence in town for both himself and his company."

Over the next few weeks, Bezos would be ubiquitous in Hollywood. He was the target of a joke in Jimmy Fallon's opening monologue at the Golden Globes ("He actually arrived yesterday, but there was no one around to sign for him"). That night, he hosted one of the buzziest after-parties of the evening in the Stardust Ballroom of the Beverly Hills Hilton. Casey Affleck collected the Golden Globe for best actor in a dramatic film; the following month, he won the equivalent award at the Oscars, despite a gathering storm of controversy involving past allegations of sexual harassment levied against him by former colleagues.

Amazon was now mentioned in the same breath as Netflix, another Hollywood upstart composing a radical future for the entertainment business. But inside Amazon Studios, far away from the glamour, tensions were rising. Independent movies like *Manchester by the Sea* and niche TV hits like *Transparent*, about a Jewish family in L.A. navigating issues of gender identity, garnered acclaim and accolades. But they were not the kind of mainstream entertainment that could attract large audiences around the world and nurture other parts of Bezos's e-commerce empire.

So Bezos issued an edict to Roy Price and the already embattled executives at Amazon Studios. It would hover above them like the sword of Damocles and contribute to an unlikely chain of events that would remove the luster from Amazon's Hollywood effort and temporarily embroil it in controversy: "*I want my* Game of Thrones."

It had all started, as these things usually do at Amazon, with a counterintuitive decision by Bezos that confounded his colleagues and looked smart only with the passage of time. In late 2010, Amazon was one of several companies selling online access to an identical catalog of movies and TV shows. Customers could spend a few dollars to stream a title once over the internet or they could pay more to "own" it and access it repeatedly.

Meanwhile, Netflix had introduced an $8-a-month service totally

independent from its original DVD-by-mail program; it allowed subscribers to stream the older TV shows and films in the company's digital catalog at any time. Even though Netflix's library generally did
not include new releases and the company was not yet producing its
own content, its customers, as well as investors, were responding favorably to its push for a less restrictive and more customer-friendly
future for home entertainment.

Amazon executives had periodically considered acquiring Netflix over the years but always considered the price too high and so
never seriously pursued it. Now it seemed like they had missed their
chance—the Los Gatos, California, company was evolving into a serious competitor. Characteristically, Bezos was unwilling to cede a significant opportunity to a rival. He asked Bill Carr, the vice president
in charge of digital music and video, to come up with a way to compete in the emerging business of subscription video on demand, or
SVOD. They met frequently over the course of the next few months,
and then one day Bezos presented the answer himself: they would
offer a subscription video service for free—to members of Amazon
Prime.

To Carr and other execs, the idea was perplexing. Prime, originally $79 a year, guaranteed Amazon customers that their purchases
would show up in two days without an extra shipping charge. Bezos
now wanted to define Prime as something different and less transactional: an all-access entry pass to a library of digital content. "I didn't
get it at first," Bill Carr said. "But what I had learned at that point of
my career is that when Jeff comes up with a novel idea, you listen
carefully, ask a lot of questions to get clarification of how to think
about it, and then come back to him later with details."

In retrospect, the solution was ingenious. Amazon customers
would have balked at paying extra for a service that was inferior to
Netflix's more established offering. Introducing streaming as a "free"
benefit—people do tend to gravitate toward free things—could tip
some Prime members into rationalizing their annual membership

fee, even if they only ordered from the site a few times a year. (Amazon would then raise the price of Prime twice: to $99 in 2014 and $119 in 2018.)

These were still lean times for Amazon, so Carr was given what he felt was a considerable budget, of around $30 million, to launch the service, called Prime Video. He had no idea that four years later, Amazon executives would be gathering to consider paying $240 million to license a library of programming from 20th Century Fox, including hit shows like *24*. During the meeting, they debated whether Amazon had ever spent that much on *anything* in its twenty-year history, including the new headquarters they were building a few blocks away from South Lake Union in Seattle's Denny Triangle neighborhood.

They did the deal and didn't stop there. Amazon licensed the hour-long drama *Justified* from Sony Pictures, *Downton Abbey* from PBS, *Orphan Black* from BBC America, and countless other popular shows. Netflix struck a wide-ranging deal with Disney for its Marvel and Pixar films and animated classics, as well as with ABC for shows like *Scandal* and The CW for *Gossip Girl*. In 2014, Amazon had forty thousand titles in its video catalog; Netflix had sixty thousand. Reed Hastings and Netflix stayed ahead of Amazon at every turn. "Netflix drove our strategy a lot," Carr said. "I'm not ashamed to say we learned from them."

By then, Jeff Wilke had handed over the supervision of digital video to his more artistically inclined peer on the S-team, Jeff Blackburn, the former jock who was now the company's cerebral and soft-spoken M&A and business development chief. In addition to overseeing the content licensing spree, Blackburn supervised the effort to get the Amazon Prime Video app onto as many set-top boxes, video game consoles, and smart TVs as possible. In late 2015, his team started negotiating with cable giant Comcast to preinstall the service on the new Xfinity X1 cable box, which would end up in tens of millions of U.S. households. But according to several executives who worked on that long-gestating deal, one of Blackburn's underlings, a temperamental manager named Jim Freeman, became uncomfortable with the look of Prime Video on the Comcast home screen and declared, "Netflix would never do this deal!"

The talks died. A few weeks later, Comcast did the deal with Netflix instead, even though Reed Hastings hadn't made many friends there by calling its proposed 2014 merger with Time Warner Cable anticompetitive. Comcast would end up promoting Netflix in all of its marketing. Amazon had to tuck its tail between its legs, and a few years later reached its own agreement with the cable company.

Such duels with Netflix to acquire premium programming and distribution were expensive, exhausting, and in the end, did little to change the competitive balance of power. Both companies had learned a valuable lesson, gleaned a generation ago by premium TV channels like HBO and Showtime: by competing to pay top dollar to license various films and shows, they had enriched the Hollywood studios and other entertainment industry incumbents but ended up with cash-draining services that were difficult to distinguish from each other.

If they wanted to attract viewers with truly unique video offerings, it made much more sense to try to create hit TV shows and films themselves.

———

The companies reached this conclusion early in their race to develop streaming video services. At Amazon, Bill Carr dispatched one of his deputies, Roy Price, to set up an outpost in Los Angeles and explore the idea of original programming.

Having grown up in Beverly Hills, Price was literally descended from Hollywood royalty. His maternal grandfather, Roy Huggins, was a well-known film and TV writer who in the 1950s was branded a Communist, blacklisted, and forced to testify in front of the House Un-American Activities Committee. He later created hit shows such as *The Fugitive* and *The Rockford Files*. Price's father, Frank Price, was a Tinseltown giant: he ran Columbia Pictures in the late seventies and early eighties and released classics like *Gandhi* and *Ghostbusters* in addition to Universal Pictures and overseeing *The Breakfast Club*, *Back to the Future*, and the infamous *Howard the Duck*. The younger Price grew up among celebrities—vacationing in the Bahamas with Sidney Poitier and learning to swim from Lee Majors, star of *The Six Million Dollar Man*.

Price had worked at Disney and McKinsey & Company before joining Amazon in 2004 to create the company's digital video strategy. For years he advocated for creating shows and films to distinguish Amazon's video offering. He was, in company parlance, strong on the "think big" leadership principle, capable of elucidating his ideas persuasively in six-page documents. Bezos was also attracted to the idea, but typically, he wanted to rethink the entire Hollywood development process. He looked askew at the "gatekeepers" who used their subjective judgments to decide what people could read or watch—with only a marginal success rate, as evidenced by the many shows with weak concepts that flopped.

Bezos proposed an entirely new approach, which he dubbed "the scientific studio." Anyone would be able to send in a script, not just the L.A. and New York elite; customers and independent judges could evaluate them and their accompanying storyboard illustrations. Their feedback would then produce objective data that Amazon could use to decide what it should actually make. "It was very much a Jeff idea," Price later said of the original thesis for Amazon Studios. "Instead of a 10 percent hit rate, we would have enough data where we could move it up to 40 percent."

Starting in 2010, Amazon invited anyone to submit screenplays and offered hundreds of thousands in cash prizes for the best scripts. It didn't work, of course. Accomplished writers stayed away and overall the submissions weren't very good. It took eight years for Amazon to retire the system (which produced one program for kids: *Gortimer Gibbons Life on Normal Street* and another pilot, *Those Who Can't*,

which was made into a series by the WarnerMedia network truTV).
But Bezos quietly acknowledged that he would need professionals
after all to identify and cultivate promising concepts.

In 2012, Price started traveling regularly from Seattle to L.A. and
hiring content development executives to oversee development and
strategy for comedy and kids' programs. Back then, Amazon was
still avoiding sales tax in California, so the group was set up as an
independent subsidiary called the People's Production Company and
forced to carry special business cards and use non-Amazon email addresses. They shared an office with IMDb, the Amazon subsidiary
that maintains a popular database of films and TV shows, in Sher-
man Oaks, above a Fuddruckers restaurant, before later moving to a
slightly more upscale but bland office complex in Santa Monica called
the Water Garden.

That year, Price and Bezos tweaked their original premise. Amazon Studios executives would meet with agents and writers, review
scripts, and identify pilot opportunities. But then they would let viewers vote and help influence their decisions on which shows should
be extended into full series. In April 2013, two months after Netflix
scored an immediate hit by debuting its first show, from the production company Media Rights Capital—the political drama *House of
Cards*—Amazon unveiled its first so-called "pilot season."

Customers could sample fourteen pilots. The political comedy
Alpha House (operating in the same vein as HBO's subsequent, fun-
nier *Veep*) and a dot-com sendup called *Betas* (ditto for HBO's *Silicon
Valley*) were among those that made the cut. But when the seasons
premiered later that year, they garnered media attention but gained
little traction with viewers. Writers on those shows received positive
feedback from Amazon, but later expressed disappointment about
the absence of Nielsen ratings for online shows, or any significant
promotional support.

With deputies overseeing drama, comedy, and kids' programming, Price honed a unique sensibility for Amazon Studios: it would

produce high-quality episodic shows that were more akin to serial-ized films than stand-alone installments. Taking high-quality indie films as their inspiration, and sensitive to the fact that customers already had lots of TV options, they set out to create TV that was distinctive and sophisticated, and that added to people's entertain-ment selection. The programs would offer windows into unfamiliar lifestyles and worlds. They would pursue the kind of programs that the major networks, obsessed with pumping out different versions of mainstream fare like *NCIS*, would never touch. Amazon "had the brand of a retailer," Price said. "We had to surprise people and focus on quality."

The approach paid off quickly. Among the pilots that Prime mem-bers could sample in early 2014 were *Mozart in the Jungle*, about hijinks in the fictional New York Symphony; *Bosch*, about a hard-scrabble LAPD detective; and *Transparent*, featuring a transgender matriarch named Maura Pfefferman. Bezos brought the Amazon Stu-dios team to Seattle that March to discuss which pilots to pick up. The *Transparent* pilot had garnered a litany of gushing reviews praising it for its daring subject matter and open-ended final scene, but it wasn't the most watched of the new shows. Bezos nevertheless started the meeting by walking into the conference room and declaring, "Well, I guess we're going to pick up *Transparent*."

They did, and the show furnished Amazon Studios with a repu-tation as a backer of visionary creators and historically overlooked material. In January 2015, *Transparent* became the first streaming series to win a Golden Globe—both for best musical or comedy TV se-ries, and best actor for Jeffrey Tambor.

If Price had entertained the fanciful notion that he would be the public face of this success, it was quickly dashed. Bezos wanted to at-tend the awards ceremony too. He brought MacKenzie and sat at a table during the Golden Globes with Price; his head of comedy, Joe Lewis; show creator Joey Soloway; and the principal cast.

Later, they attended after-parties hosted by HBO and Netflix.

With his wife by his side, Bezos basked in the glow of Hollywood adulation. "She always seemed like she was having a good time," one Amazon Studios exec recalled of the couple at Hollywood events, "while he seemed like he was having a great time."

A few weeks later, Bezos appeared on *CBS This Morning* with Tambor and Soloway to accept more kudos for *Transparent*'s win. He said that Amazon had backed the show because it was a remarkable piece of storytelling. "Every time we do something, we don't want to do me-too," he said. "We'd like to do some wrinkle on it, some improvement, something that customers have a chance of responding to. *Transparent* is a perfect example."

———

Bezos, a film lover, was now excited by the idea of creating original content. It was evolving into another significant long-term bet, alongside Alexa, the Amazon Go stores, the expansions in India and Mexico, and Amazon Web Services. To the surprise of Amazon Studios execs, who often wondered whether the chief of a $100-billion-dollar company didn't have better things to do, he regularly asked them to come to Seattle to discuss which shows to green-light. "The best part of this pilot is that it's only a half an hour," he complained in an early 2015 debate over whether to pick up *The New Yorker Presents*, a docuseries by the iconic Condé Nast magazine.

Bezos asked trenchant questions but deferred to Price's judgment even when he disagreed with it. "You can do what you want, but I'd sleep on it if I were you," he said of the news magazine show. The following week, Price and his head of drama, Morgan Wandell, picked up the dystopian drama *The Man in the High Castle*, based on the novel by Philip K. Dick, a few other series, as well as the relatively inexpensive *The New Yorker Presents*. One Amazon Studios executive who was at the meeting said she wondered to herself at the time whether Price was defying a direct order.

By then Price was working full-time in L.A. and ingratiating himself in a new Hollywood lifestyle. He had separated from his wife and moved to an apartment downtown. Amazon Studios employees couldn't help but notice his transformation. Back in Seattle, he had favored sport coats, khakis, and the occasional bow tie. Now in Los Angeles, he slimmed down, started wearing Valentino shoes and a leather jacket, got the logo of the seminal L.A. punk band Black Flag tattooed on his right shoulder, and bought a Dodge Challenger muscle car. "He presented as someone who was going through a midlife crisis," one employee said.

But Amazon was on a roll. *Mozart in the Jungle* was well reviewed and would make Amazon Studios the first network to win consecutive Golden Globes for Best Comedy in years. Bezos and Price's strategy was validated—and so Price was empowered to take bigger bets and to move faster. He had hired a friend, Conrad Riggs, a former partner of *Survivor* producer Mark Burnett, to develop reality TV shows for Amazon. On a trip to London in June 2015, Riggs went to a Who concert with Jeremy Clarkson, the former host of BBC's reality TV show about cars, *Top Gear,* who had been ousted from the program for verbally and physically attacking a BBC producer. Riggs observed that Clarkson was a bigger star than even the members of the classic rock band. Amazon then outbid Apple and Netflix to sign him and his cohosts to a three-year, $250 million deal to make a similar show, *The Grand Tour.* It was one of the largest deals in unscripted television history. Riggs recalled that Bezos approved the expenditure via email in "about 15 seconds."

Roy Price could seemingly do no wrong. The next month, he attended Comic-Con in San Diego, where Amazon was screening the first two episodes of *The Man in the High Castle* to the annual gathering of sci-fi and fantasy aficionados. For Amazon Studios, the show represented the possibility of tapping the growing audience for big-budget genre fare, and at its first showing at Comic-Con, it got an exuberant reception by fans. Studios executives were exhilarated.

That night, Price enjoyed a celebratory dinner with colleagues and the show's creators, which included numerous champagne toasts. Afterward, Price shared an Uber to an after-party with Amazon colleague Michael Paull and someone he was meeting for the first time: Isa Hackett, the show's executive producer and the daughter of legendary science fiction author Philip K. Dick.

There are several versions of what happened in that car and at the party after, which differ on some of the substantive facts. Everyone agrees, though, that Price, who relished casual and occasionally boundary-pushing banter, had had a few drinks and made several off-color jokes and sexual comments to Hackett, whom he knew was gay and married. Hackett found the remarks to be inexplicably vulgar and inappropriate.

Outside the Uber, Price insisted that Hackett take a selfie with him, explaining that if people believed they were dating, it would help promote the show. Hackett was dismayed. Inside the party, she encountered Price again, and he allegedly continued to blurt out graphic sexual remarks.

Clueless, Price didn't realize he had offended Hackett and the next day tried to add her as a friend on Facebook. But she was infuriated. She reported the incident to an executive at Amazon Studios, who referred the matter to Amazon's legal department. Amazon then contracted with an L.A. firm specializing in workplace misconduct to get to the bottom of the incident. One of its senior investigators started to interview Amazon's Hollywood employees about their boss. They also talked to Hackett, who told them that she hoped the deplorable incident was a catalyst for significant changes at the studio.

The overall picture that emerged was unflattering. Several of Price's female employees in particular were disapproving, saying he had a pattern of making inappropriate jokes in the workplace. They described some of his off-putting habits—for example, squatting in meetings with his feet tucked underneath him, as well as closing his eyes and rocking back and forth. They also criticized him as a poor manager who delegated most of his responsibilities and seemed to prefer going to meals with celebrities and chronicling them for his Instagram feed.

Amazon had an opportunity to quietly remove Price from his position of leadership and avoid a future calamity. But it did not. He had helped conceive and build the studio, which was showing signs of promise. Bezos's weak-kneed fondness for builders appeared to be shared by others at Amazon, including Jeff Blackburn. Price was also remorseful and wanted to apologize to Hackett, though Amazon's lawyers asked that he have no further contact with her. They told him to stop drinking at company parties and to get additional training on workplace conduct and how to be a better manager. The company later said in a statement that it "acted appropriately in responding to the incident, including by hiring an outside investigator."

When a female Amazon Studios employee asked a friend in the legal department what had become of the investigation, and why it hadn't resulted in any obvious disciplinary action, he told her that the company had concluded of the allegations: "That's not the Roy we know."

———

Roy Price had kept his job but now faced a more ominous threat: Jeff Bezos was fully attuned to the opportunities and challenges of building a successful film and TV business. And when Amazon's CEO paid close attention, he generally wanted everything to be bigger, bolder, and more ambitious. The company spent an estimated $3.2 billion on Prime Video in 2016 and nearly $4.5 billion in 2017. Even its usually agreeable board of directors was apprehensive over the growing expenditure and asked pointed questions about it. "Jeff was ahead of us in thinking about the relationship between content and Prime" is how former board member and venture capitalist Bing Gordon put it.

Bezos contended that the media business enhanced the appeal and "stickiness" of Amazon Prime, which in turn motivated people to spend more on Amazon. "When we win a Golden Globe, it helps us sell more shoes," he said on stage at a technology conference in 2016.

At least some of his Hollywood employees were dubious of that characterization. They did not consider themselves to be shoe salespeople, although everyone appreciated having the backing of a profitable e-commerce company subsidizing their creative risks. They tracked each show and analyzed how many people watched and then converted from free Prime trial periods or extended their current membership. But there was little evidence of a connection between viewing and purchasing behavior—especially one that justified the enormous outlay on video. Any correlation was also obfuscated by the fact that Prime was growing rapidly on its own.

The truth was this: Bezos *wanted* Amazon to make TV shows and films. He could see that the decades-old way that TV shows and movies were produced and distributed was changing and sought a principal role for Amazon in that future. As in the early days of Alexa, the Go store, and Amazon India, the economic justification might be flimsy today, but opportunities for making money would always present themselves tomorrow.

At the time, the company was preparing to introduce Prime Video in 242 countries and to charge for it separately; the project, code-named Magellan, would be Amazon's introduction to many parts of the world where it didn't yet operate an online retail business. Video was the introductory product for new markets, as books had once been. But the third season of *Transparent*, which revolved around the main character's exploration of gender confirmation surgery, wasn't the greeting that Bezos had in mind for countries like Kuwait, Nepal, and Belarus.

Thus the stage was set for a series of tense meetings between Bezos and the Amazon Studios team during the latter half of 2016 and throughout 2017. It was now utterly pressing that they find a big show akin to HBO's blockbuster *Game of Thrones*. But Price was still putting out middling fare like *One Mississippi*, *Good Girls Revolt*, and *Mad Dogs*. He had overseen the acquisition of *Manchester by the Sea*, which led to awards and the memorable party at Bezos's L.A.

house, but that had also associated Amazon with the accusations of sexual harassment against star Casey Affleck. Price also laid out an astonishing $80 million for Woody Allen's first TV series, the poorly received *Crisis in Six Scenes*. (Price was a big Allen fan and had a long-standing relationship with Allen's longtime agent, John Burnham; colleagues said the series was Price's "dream project.") Not only was Price doing business with a filmmaker whose work would later be enveloped in controversy, he was still making prestige American content for awards consideration at precisely the time that Bezos wanted to abruptly change direction and turn Prime Video into a broadly appealing global business.

Price understood Bezos's directive but argued that those kinds of shows took years to develop. In January 2017, he hired an Israel-born TV exec, Sharon Tal Yguado, who had helped distribute the popular zombie series *The Walking Dead* around the world. The hire, which Price didn't properly alert colleagues about before it was publicly announced, created another set of internal frictions inside Amazon Studios. Nevertheless, Tal Yguado bonded with Bezos over their love for literary sci-fi sagas like *The Culture* and *Ringworld*. Later that year, Tal Yguado would help Amazon secure a reported $250 million deal to acquire the global rights to undeveloped material in J. R. R. Tolkien's *Lord of the Rings* books.

For Bezos though, the changes were not happening fast enough. In combative meetings, he impatiently demanded his *Game of Thrones*. Price tried to reason with him. There was not going to be another breakout hit like it—the next one would be something that felt as fresh and daring as HBO's fantasy blockbuster had. He asked for more time and argued there were promising candidates on the way, like a series based on Tom Clancy's character Jack Ryan.

Bezos also quizzed Price on whether he was sufficiently testing titles and concepts with an online focus group of early viewers that Amazon had built, called the preview tool. Among other things, the tool had helped steer a Billy Bob Thornton show, originally called *Trial of the Century*, to a winning new title, *Goliath*. But Price reported that the tool was unreliable—you can't use the same crowd-sourcing principles to gauge the virtues of story ideas as you can to appraise the value of kitchen appliances on the aisles of an endless virtual store. The development executives often had to move fast to close competitive deals with in-demand TV producers and filmmakers; sometimes they had to bypass the data and just go with their instincts. Price also felt that crowd-sourcing creative concepts was suspect: shows like *Seinfeld* and *Breaking Bad* were unpopular at first, after all. Do you trust storytellers, or do you trust data; the ingenuity of artists or the wisdom of the crowd?

Bezos had encountered the same questions at the *Washington Post*, where he had pressed for more ways to measure article popularity but ultimately deferred to the judgment of his newsroom experts. At Amazon, which was his own personal canvas for ruthlessly remaking industries with computer science, experimentation, and copious amounts of data, he was more impatient. He wanted a scientific approach to creative decision-making and to see results quickly. And on that point, Bezos and Roy Price were increasingly not aligned.

———

By early 2017, Amazon had moved into its new thirty-seven-floor tinted-glass office tower, dubbed Day 1, like its previous headquarters a half mile away. Bezos's old ideas about corporate anonymity were now impractical for a company of Amazon's prominence. The building was flanked by the first Amazon Go store and bore a giant yellow light sign with the computer science phrase "Hello World" on it, looking out over the park on its eastern side.

Bezos's new office and spread of conference rooms were on the sixth floor—the same as the old building—so he could take the stairs and get in extra exercise. That March, Amazon Studios executives traveled to Seattle to meet him there, amid the busy, clanging construction of another skyscraper across the street and the three interconnected Amazon Spheres—company meeting places that, when finished, would double as nature conservatories.

In one of the conference rooms, the frustrated CEO laid into the tepid storytelling of *The Man in the High Castle*. "The execution is terrible," he complained. "Why didn't you guys stop it? Why didn't you reshoot it?"

Bezos continued to reproach Price. "You and I are not aligned," he said. "There must be a way to test these concepts. You are telling me that we are making $100 million decisions and we don't have time to evaluate whether they are good decisions? There must be a way for us to see what will work and what won't, so we don't have to make all these decisions in a vacuum."

After more debate, Bezos boiled it down: "Look, I know what it takes to make a great show. This should not be that hard. All of these iconic shows have basic things in common." And off the top of his head, displaying his characteristic ability to shift disciplines multiple times a day, then reduce complex issues down to their most essential essence, he started to reel off the ingredients of epic storytelling:

- A heroic protagonist who experiences growth and change
- A compelling antagonist
- Wish fulfillment (e.g., the protagonist has hidden abilities, such as superpowers or magic)
- Moral choices
- Diverse worldbuilding (different geographic landscapes)
- Urgency to watch next episode (cliffhangers)
- Civilizational high stakes (a global threat to humanity like an alien invasion—or a devastating pandemic)
- Humor
- Betrayal
- Positive emotions (love, joy, hope)
- Negative emotions (loss, sorrow)
- Violence

Price helped riff on the list and wrote it all down dutifully. Afterward, Amazon Studios executives had to send Bezos regular updates on the projects in development that included spreadsheets describing how each show had each storytelling element; and if one element was missing, they had to explain why. But Price also told colleagues to keep the checklist from the outside world. Amazon shouldn't dictate to accomplished auteurs the ingredients of a good story. Good shows should break such rules, not conform to them.

Price's risky decisions seemed to be compounding. He authorized a docuseries on Novak Djokovic, the premier men's tennis player in the world, which shot hundreds of hours of footage before the Serbian star got injured and withdrew from the project. He also struck a deal with Danish director Nicolas Winding Refn for a violent and plodding crime series, *Too Old to Die Young*; Matthew Weiner's meandering show *The Romanoffs*; and a never-titled work by director David O. Russell that was supposed to star Robert De Niro and Julianne Moore, about a family that ran a winery in upstate New York. The first two shows were canceled after their initial seasons; the last, produced by the Weinstein Company, blew up before production started, amid the explosive revelations of producer Harvey Weinstein's history of grotesque sexual misconduct.

According to several former employees, Weinstein had an amicable relationship with Bezos, Jeff Blackburn, and Roy Price, and traveled frequently to Seattle to help steer Amazon through its early challenges in Hollywood. It was a relationship that later no one was particularly eager to discuss. But Prime Video employees said that at one point, the notorious producer worked with Amazon to develop a service called Prime Movies, which would have given Prime members a certain number of free tickets to see some films in cinemas. The program, which presaged the doomed startup MoviePass, never got off the ground.

Price's deals with Woody Allen and Harvey Weinstein would later reflect poorly on his judgment. He displayed other questionable conduct as well. In 2017, Price got engaged to actress and writer Lila Feinberg and tried to persuade his employees to acquire her idea for a TV series, called *12 Parties*. Colleagues pointed out that this was a conflict of interest; so instead it was optioned by the Weinstein Company. They also complained that Price was developing his own script, called *Shanghai Snow*, featuring stereotypical ethnic characterizations and gratuitous sex and violence, that was received poorly by anyone who read it.

Many female employees at Amazon Studios in 2017 continued to be unhappy with their boss or their work environment. One described a conference room at the Amazon Studios office with walls that were covered in portraits of Jeffrey Tambor, Woody Allen, and Kevin Spacey (star of an Amazon film, *Elvis & Nixon*). All three would fall in the gathering backlash against sexual misconduct, known as #MeToo. The movement was also about to ensnare Roy Price and entangle Amazon in a scandal that its executives thought they had put behind them.

That October 2017, a few hundred or so tastemakers, thought leaders, authors, musicians, actors, producers, and their families were whisked by a fleet of private jets from the Van Nuys Airport in L.A. to Santa Barbara. From there, they were taken by another convoy of black sedans to the nearby Four Seasons Resort. The five-star hotel was closed to the public that weekend, as was the Coral Casino Beach & Cabana Club across the street. Counselors greeted each family, with one for every child. Waiting for the guests in their hotel rooms were thousands of dollars of free swag, including premium luggage to transport it all back home.

This was Campfire, Amazon's private retreat for the literati and glitterati. The company started the annual event in 2010 in Santa Fe, New Mexico, as a weekend salon for storytellers and their families. In 2016, when the event grew too big for its original venue, Amazon moved it to Santa Barbara. Bezos liked to call it "the highlight of my year" and seemed to love it when others did the same. The shift to Southern California happened to coincide with the evolution of Amazon's ambitions from the book business to the broader entertainment world.

The weekend, entirely paid for by Amazon, consisted of talks, lavish meals, intimate conversations, and hikes. Bezos was bringing together some of the world's most interesting people and relished being in their company. He usually sat in the front row of every talk and was the center of much of the attention, with his arms draped over the shoulders of his wife and four kids, laughing louder than anyone. Guests were asked to sign confidentiality agreements and never to mention or discuss Campfire with the press.

The guest list that year included Oprah Winfrey, Shonda Rhimes, Bette Midler, Brian Grazer, and Julianne Moore, as well as indie actress and musician Carrie Brownstein, the novelist Michael Cunningham, *Post* executive editor Marty Baron, and musician Jeff Tweedy. Benjamin Berell Ferencz, the last surviving prosecutor from the Nuremberg trials, gave a talk. Also invited to the festivities were several Amazon Studios executives, including Price, who brought his fiancée, Lila Feinberg.

As Campfire was set to begin, Price stood on perilous ground in the company. The previous month, Hulu and HBO had collected a host of Primetime Emmys while Amazon was shut out. The *Wall Street Journal* acknowledged this shortfall in a critical story that reported that Amazon Studios had passed on hits like *The Handmaid's Tale* and *Big Little Lies*. The article quoted David E. Kelley, the creator of *Lies* as well as *Goliath*, calling the entire operation "a bit of a gong show," and saying of Amazon, "they are in way over their heads."

But that was the least of Price's problems. For the past few months, enterprising L.A. journalist Kim Masters had been pursuing the story of Price's inappropriate comments to Isa Hackett after the 2015 Comic-Con and Amazon's subsequent internal investigation. Numerous outlets, including the *New York Times*, *BuzzFeed*, and the

Hollywood Reporter, which hadn't shied away from other #MeToo reporting, passed on the story. Price had personally hired some of the same attorneys who had represented Harvey Weinstein. But in August, the technology online news site *The Information* printed a short version of Masters's piece. Hackett declined to comment, other than calling her encounter with Price a "troubling incident."

By the start of Campfire weekend, #MeToo momentum was building. Ronan Farrow had just published his damning investigation into Harvey Weinstein's behavior in the *New Yorker*. (Weinstein had attended and spoke at previous Campfires but was now persona non grata.) On the afternoon before the first day, actress Rose McGowan, a Weinstein victim, started tweeting at @JeffBezos that she had told Roy Price of Weinstein's crimes and urged Amazon Studios to "stop funding rapists, alleged pedos and sexual harassers." Price had told her to report the crime to the police. Still, Amazon *had* done plenty of business with the Weinstein Company and with many other Hollywood figures accused of sexual harassment and other illicit behavior. That was an impeachable fact in a fraught social climate—and a particularly embarrassing one at the start of Amazon's big weekend.

Then the *Hollywood Reporter*, where Masters was an editor at large, reversed its stance and published her full story. This time, Isa Hackett had gone on the record and confirmed the "shocking and surreal" experience and inappropriate things Price had said to her in the Uber after Comic-Con more than two years before. Amazon Studios executives were required to be at Campfire a day before the event officially started, so Price was in his hotel suite when the story hit; Feinberg, his fiancée, was downstairs with other Amazon Studios execs and started to cry when she read it on her phone.

It was a seminally awkward moment. Price and Feinberg were immediately asked to return to L.A. "It was totally upsetting and humiliating. How could it not be?" Price said later. Other Amazon Studios execs jumped on an emergency conference call with Jeff Blackburn, who told them to stay for the conference.

Behind the scenes, Amazon struggled again with what to do. Blackburn placed Price on a temporary leave of absence while revisiting his loyalty to the person who had initiated Amazon's foray into original content, hiring and managing a team that had won a haul of prestigious awards. Roy Price had carved a path for Jeff Bezos in Hollywood. Leaders *are right, a lot,* according to the hallowed leadership principles.

That had been enough for Bezos—until suddenly it wasn't. There was still no *Game of Thrones*. Price had also lost the confidence of much of his team; and his social awkwardness and occasional impropriety was off-putting and, in the situation with Hackett, disturbing. Amazon execs had known about that behavior but believed it had been addressed. Could they really support a beleaguered executive in the midst of a widespread cultural reckoning? By Tuesday, Price had agreed to resign.

In the middle of all this, Blackburn called Isa Hackett to try to make amends. It was now excruciatingly clear that Amazon management, with its predominantly male S-team, had failed to take her charges seriously enough. With the accumulated exhaustion of trying to privately relay a traumatic experience to Amazon's investigators and, when that failed, having to go on the record in the media, Hackett was overcome with emotion. She started to cry over the phone: "I tried to tell you. And for so many months you had the opportunity to do something about it! You put me in this position, and it caused a lot of pain for my family and me." Blackburn listened and agreed to her entreaty that he try to use Amazon's plentiful resources to address pervasive sexism in Hollywood and corporate America.

A few days later, Blackburn was in Santa Monica talking to groups of Amazon Studios employees. Some demanded to know why Price hadn't been fired in 2015; others wondered if Amazon was firing Price to distract from its affiliations with other #MeToo characters, like Harvey Weinstein. Price's few defenders believed he had been scapegoated and noted that under his leadership, Amazon had backed more female creators than any other studio. Blackburn, according to several people who were in the meetings, acknowledged that the situation should have been dealt with sooner but said that new information had come to light. The explanation rang hollow to at least some employees. By the end of that week, Blackburn was trying to bring closure to the entire unseemly episode. "Amazon Studios has been in the news recently for the wrong reasons," he wrote in an internal email to Studios employees. "We should be generating buzz about the terrific programming we are creating for customers and the new shows we are planning for next year."

Price would later seek to apologize publicly and clear his name from Hollywood censure, with little success. "I sincerely apologize for any discomfort caused by my comedy faux pas with Isa Dick Hackett in 2015," he wrote to me in an email. "I wish Amazon had allowed me to apologize to her then, as I desperately wanted but was not permitted to do.... In any case I truly aspired to nothing but to keep us amused as we all Ubered a few blocks from one party to another."

Price's fiancée quickly left him after the scandal, a few weeks before their planned wedding, and although he was never convicted like Weinstein, he was expelled from the entertainment industry, his name relegated to the same broad category as others like Les Moonves and Matt Lauer, accused of sexual impropriety. Considering what his grandfather had been through a generation before during the infamous witch hunt for Communist sympathizers, Price saw bitter historical parallels.

He didn't expect to hear from Bezos and never did. After all, this was Amazon, where employees were there to produce results, not create personal bonds. After Price was ousted, Amazon installed his deputy, Amazon Studios COO Albert Cheng, in the role on an interim basis, and he started to sweep out many of the original executives, including Joe Lewis, who had helped develop such groundbreaking shows as *Transparent* and *The Marvelous Mrs. Maisel*. (Lewis was given a two-year production deal and would produce *Fleabag*, adding to Amazon's growing awards tally.) Soon after, Amazon hired NBC executive Jennifer Salke to take over the role permanently and announced plans to finally leave the bland office park in Santa Monica and move into a historic film complex in Culver City—the mansion used in *Gone with the Wind*.

A new regime was taking over Amazon Studios. Ironically, many of the shows that the scandal-plagued old guard put into production, like *The Boys* and *Jack Ryan*, would turn out to be global hits. Bezos continued to spend heavily on video. Prime Video consumed $5 billion in 2018 and $7 billion in 2019. There was continued debate over the actual return on this investment, though the objections from Amazon's board and investors were not quite as loud. As rivals like Walmart and Target caught up to Amazon in their ability to guarantee two-day shipping, free media became a more important part of Prime's bundle of perks. Amazon's original shows and films also helped to solidify its position just behind Netflix, and alongside Disney, Apple, Paramount, HBO, and other companies in the race to define the future for home entertainment.

Prime Video was yet another of Jeff Bezos's big bets over a fruitful decade. By pointing the way for his employees over and over, closely monitoring their efforts, and using his own budding fame to magnify their visibility, Bezos had blazed a path into promising new technologies and industries. Alexa, Amazon Go, Amazon India, Prime Video, and the rest could still prove disappointments relative to their massive investments—or they could set up Amazon to reap new potential windfalls.

But as a result of Bezos's immersion in the invention process, he managed other parts of Amazon much less closely—like the buying, selling, stocking, and distribution of products. This was Amazon's original and largest business, of course. And as the public profile of the company and its impresario continued to rise, the gears of that unrelenting machinery were starting to turn ever faster.

PART II

LEVERAGE

Amazon: December 31, 2016

Annual net sales: $135,987 billion

Full- and part-time employees: 341,400

End-of-year market capitalization: $355.44 billion

Jeff Bezos end-of-year net worth: $65.4 billion

CHAPTER 7

The Selection Machine

On a rainy Sunday morning in October 2016, a Miami criminal defense attorney named Victor Vedmed was tinkering in his garage when there was an unexpected knock on the front door. Vedmed's wife and two children were in the living room in their pajamas watching television, so he wiped his hands clean, walked through the house, and answered it. Standing in the humid drizzle were two middle-aged men and a teenage boy. No car was parked out front. One of the men introduced himself as Joshua Weinstein, a former resident of the neighborhood, and was about to introduce his companion when Vedmed had a flash of recognition and blurted out: "I know you!"

Jeff Bezos greeted Vedmed and conceded that yes, people often recognized him. He explained that he had spent his high school years in Vedmed's Palmetto Bay house over thirty-five years ago. He and his second oldest son, George, were in town for the day to visit the family of Weinstein, Bezos's childhood friend whose father had just passed away, and they had walked over in the rain. He asked if they could come inside and take a look around.

Vedmed was thunderstruck. He had never known that his modest three-thousand-square-foot bungalow was the former home of one of the world's richest people. "There is a good luck feeling about this house" was the only thing the previous owner had told him when he purchased it in 2009. But his wife, Erica, still sitting on the couch in the living room, didn't recognize their guest at all. Bezos was familiar to avid followers of business and media news, but perhaps not yet to the general public. She assumed her husband had let in a candidate for local public office and glared at them. Vedmed, flustered by the unexpected situation, failed to introduce their guests or even explain what was going on to his wife and kids.

Now they were all standing in the foyer. To the right was the kitchen and the high-ceilinged two-car garage, where Bezos and his friends had once built a science club float for their homecoming parade. To the left, down a hallway, were the four bedrooms where Bezos had grown up with his parents and two younger siblings, Mark and Christina. On the far side of the hall was a bathroom with a door that opened to the backyard, which a teenage Bezos had sneaked out of late one night after a verbal altercation with his father, Mike, worrying his mother, Jackie. One of the bedrooms facing the front of the house had been Bezos's, where he had written his high school valedictorian speech, outlining an audacious vision of orbiting space stations that could take polluting factories off the Earth and turn the planet into a nature preserve.

Bezos kept looking around, marveling at the changes and what had remained the same. Peering through the sliding glass doors that opened to the backyard, he noticed that the screen enclosure for the pool, common in many South Florida homes to keep out insects, was gone. Vedmed told him it hadn't been there when they moved in.

After a few more minutes, the visitors prepared to leave. Erica finally stood up and, still confused, asked George whether he attended Miami Palmetto Senior High School, Bezos's alma mater. George politely informed her that no, they lived in Seattle and he attended school there.

The group took a photograph together, memorializing the encounter, and said their goodbyes. Afterward, Vedmed recalled that Bezos was down to earth and sociable. But he would replay those unlikely fifteen minutes in his mind and wish that he had handled the visit more gracefully.

"I'll tell you, it's hard to communicate when you are at such different levels," Vedmed said a few years later. "It would have been better if I didn't know who he was." He was describing the intimidating bubble that surrounds many famous people, distorting the behavior of those around them. With Jeff Bezos getting richer by the day, it was only going to get worse.

———

To fully appreciate the rise of Bezos's trillion-dollar empire and the accompanying growth in his personal fortune, we need to rewind the clock to understand the acceleration of Amazon's e-commerce business and some of the unintended consequences resulting from it. In 2015, Amazon's domestic retail sales were growing at a respectable 25 percent clip; by 2017, they were increasing at an even faster rate of 33 percent. Amazon was generating more sales, and was more profitable, than it ever had been in its history. Even with more than $100 billion in annual North American retail revenues alone, the hormones of a much younger company seemed to course through its corporate veins.

Amazon executives explained this as a triumph of their flywheel, the virtuous cycle that guided their business. Once again, it worked like this: Amazon's low prices and the loyalty of its Prime members led to more customer visits, which in turn motivated more third-party sellers to list their wares on its marketplace. More products attracted more customers. And the commissions that marketplace sellers paid to Amazon allowed the company to further lower prices and invest in speedier delivery for a greater percentage of items, making Prime even more attractive. Thus the fabled flywheel fed on itself and spun ever faster.

Another way to understand Amazon's fervid growth as a large company was by its successful pursuit of operating leverage, or growing revenues at a faster rate than expenses. Operating leverage is a little like trimming the sails of a sailboat as it picks up speed. Bezos and his lieutenants on the S-team asked the same questions of the executives in their older, more mature business units: How could they reduce costs in their operations while maintaining sales growth? How could they maximize the productivity of every hour they were getting from their employees? Where could automation and algorithms stem the growth in headcount or replace employees altogether?

Each year the company would try to get more efficient and improve leverage by even the smallest margin. The resulting changes could make employees' jobs more difficult. One such project gathered momentum in the summer of 2013, after the release of the animated movie *Despicable Me 2*. An employee in Amazon's toys group was apparently enthusiastic about the film and initiated a significant purchase of its licensed merchandise, since in-stock managers in the retail division were manually placing orders for products at the time. This employee's order included stuffed animals based on the Minions, the film's Twinkie-shaped henchmen.

The movie performed reasonably well at the box office, but unfortunately for Amazon, the toys didn't sell for whatever reason, and ended up sitting on the shelves of Amazon's FCs, gathering dust. "It was just a thud of a license," recalls Jason Wilkie, a former in-stock manager in the toys group. "You couldn't even discount it. Nobody wanted it." Analyzing the mistake, Amazon's retail execs concluded that capricious human emotion had interfered with the cool-headed evaluation of the available data, which might have led to a more conservative purchase order.

The project that emerged was called "Hands Off the Wheel." Over the next few years, in-stock managers across the retail group were moved to different jobs or booted from the company and replaced by automated systems. Software, not people, would crunch the numbers and place purchase orders. Algorithms might not be able to perfectly gauge demand for cinematic toy licenses, but they could predict the surge of interest in, for example, canine anxiety jackets to soothe dogs before the July 4th fireworks display, or snow shovels before a predicted winter storm in the Midwest, and so on.

Bezos and his deputies believed that algorithms could do the job better and faster than people. They could even determine where to place the merchandise in Amazon's fulfillment network to meet the anticipated demand. Amazon also developed systems to automatically negotiate terms with vendors and to allow brands to initiate their own promotions, without any help from Amazon employees.

Building such systems required a significant up-front investment and added to Amazon's fixed costs. But over the ensuing years, those expenses paid off as they replaced what would have been even larger, variable costs. It was the ultimate in leverage: turning Amazon's retail business into a largely self-service technology platform that could generate cash with minimum human intervention.

The quest for leverage gained momentum in Amazon's marketplace for third-party sellers and an accompanying service, Fulfillment by Amazon, or FBA. The counterintuitive idea behind FBA was to allow sellers to send their merchandise to Amazon's warehouses, and to let Amazon store and ship it to customers. These companies still owned their inventory and set their own prices, but their products qualified for two-day shipping to Prime members. Bringing independent merchants onto the site and into Amazon's fulfillment centers allowed the company to increase the volume of products it pushed through its warehouses and to increase its revenues compared to its fixed costs.

When Amazon first introduced the service back in 2002, under the name "Self-Service Order Fulfillment," sellers were wary at the potential loss of control. But eventually many recognized that storing and shipping products to people's homes was not their strength, while using FBA guaranteed a good customer experience and made their products more visible on the Amazon website. After a few years, products of every size, including hard-to-store items like bowling balls and whiteboards, began to stream into Amazon's warehouses. "For me, it was a nightmare," recalled Marc Onetto, a former GE executive and Amazon's senior vice president of worldwide operations between 2006 and 2013. "These guys were emptying their attics on me. But of course, I realized, we had to make it work."

Bezos managed FBA closely during the late 2000s, reviewing minutiae like the rate card for sellers and declaring that Amazon should keep it simple until the service grew to a certain scale, even if it meant losing money. "I'm not sure it's time yet," he said every time FBA execs tried to raise Amazon's rates for certain kinds of inventory in order to inch toward profitability.

"What's this?" he demanded of an FBA executive in a memorable October 2008 review, pointing to a statistic in an Excel appendix of a six-page narrative outlining FBA's overseas economics. This was back in the formative years of Bezos's maturation as a CEO, before he managed to occasionally suppress his temperamental management style and bad habit of punishing underlings with scathingly direct feedback. Cynthia Williams, the finance director who'd prepared the document, had suspected something was wrong with her analysis but hadn't been able to identify the problem beforehand. "I looked down and sure enough, it was blatantly obvious," she said years later. "I am telling you, my heart sank all the way to my toes."

Bezos then said: "If this number is wrong, I don't know how I can trust any of these numbers. You've wasted an hour of my time." He tore the paper in half, threw it down the table at Williams, and walked out the door, leaving the room in stunned silence.

"Well, that didn't go as planned, did it?" cracked Tom Taylor, the executive who ran FBA over its first ten years, as he chased Bezos out of the room.

That afternoon, Williams emailed Bezos with an apology and the amended data, then went home and opened a bottle of wine. Bezos responded at 8 p.m. that night. He didn't address his outburst but thanked her for the update and wrote that he didn't know anyone who hadn't made that type of error despite the same diligence. Williams, who stayed at Amazon for another decade and was eventually promoted to vice president before defecting to Microsoft, said she felt good about the email and presented the revised proposal to Bezos again a few weeks later.

The story was discussed and celebrated inside Amazon for years—not as an example of volatile leadership, but as an illustration of the high standards of company leaders, and the grit and resilience of employees, which were needed to execute complex services like FBA.

Bezos believed that FBA had a chance both to succeed and to have an outsized impact on the company. "I need you to deliver so that we can fund the portfolio of other businesses" that also have enormous potential, he said, according to Tom Taylor, instructing the FBA team that they should be moving three times faster than normal Amazon teams.

Other "Jeffisms," recorded by the FBA team in their annual OP1 planning session with Bezos, further shaped their perspective. Among his greatest hits, recorded in a memo that was later passed to me:

"Focus on lowering cost structure. It is better to have low costs and then charge to maximize your value versus charging to cover costs."

"Having a stupid rate card equals stupid things happen. Rate cards must be equal to the value."

"We do not charge more because we can't figure out how to make it cost less. We invent to make it cost less."

"We should be able to fulfill 100% of the 3P business. I do not know what the debate is, yes, we must fulfill low priced selection, it is crucial."

"Averages are bad measures. I want to see actuals, highs, lows and why—not an average. An average is just lazy."

By 2014, after more than a decade of such blunt guidance, the service became profitable for the first time and the number of sellers using FBA was growing briskly. "Don't pretend that anyone else on the project was some kind of genius, because that is just not true," said Neil Ackerman, a former FBA executive. "Jeff was the one who challenged everyone to lower fees and not focus on income, but instead to put our attention to adding sellers and growing selection. He knew that was how we could get the business to scale and become profitable. Jeff always said that when you focus on the business inputs, then the outputs such as revenue and income will take care of themselves."

At the same time Bezos was shaping FBA, he was nurturing its conjoined twin, the Amazon Marketplace, which allowed third-party sellers to register on Amazon's website and display their new or used products. In 2007, the marketplace was already a few years old but was basically just a dusty repository for used books, accounting for a meager 13 percent of all units sold on the site. Bezos was frustrated by its lack of progress and tore up the team's documents in OP1 meetings and demanded more ambitious rewrites. "How would you get a million sellers into this marketplace?" he asked the stream of executives whom he interviewed to take over the group.

Eventually, he found the right person. In early 2009, Peter Faricy, the head of Amazon's thriving music and movies business in the years before Prime Video, invited the actor Tom Cruise to speak at an all-hands meeting at Benaroya Hall in downtown Seattle. Backstage, Bezos and Cruise fell so deep into conversation about airplanes and space travel that Faricy couldn't get the CEO out on stage on time for his Q&A with employees. Afterward, in appreciation for his department's success, Bezos invited Faricy to lunch with the S-team. A month later, he asked him to run what he described as one of the most underachieving teams at the company.

Faricy understood that there was only one answer to Bezos's interview question—you couldn't possibly reach out to sellers and recruit a million of them one by one. You would have to build a machine that would have to be self-service, and sellers would have to come to Amazon instead of the other way around.

Over the next few years, Faricy and his team rebuilt Seller Central, the website for third-party merchants, giving merchants the ability to easily list their products on Amazon.com, set prices, and run promotions—all with a minimum of oversight by Amazon employees. As he had with FBA, Bezos supervised the project closely at first. "I think in my first two weeks, I got seven question mark emails from Jeff," Faricy recalled. "Right out of the gate, it was like throwing me into the fire and a once-in-a-lifetime learning experience."

What helped Amazon to recruit third-party merchants was its rival eBay, which was alienating its unruly seller community by raising fees and giving favorable deals to large retailers. At the inaugural Amazon sellers conference in 2010 in the Marriott hotel near the Seattle-Tacoma International Airport, Faricy addressed "all of you in the audience who mostly sell on eBay." He said that Amazon was committed to a fair marketplace and level playing field for all sellers and invited them to double down on their business with the company. They gave him a standing ovation. But that reservoir of goodwill wouldn't last for long.

Like other Amazon execs, Faricy appeared to adopt a few of the severe management tactics Bezos had popularized in the company. Originally from Detroit, he had spent time at McKinsey & Company and the Borders book chain before Amazon, but he quickly acclimated to his new workplace. If deputies were late to deliver their weekly metrics reports, for example, Faricy would casually suggest they might be getting paid too much or weren't right for the job. He also battled with his counterparts on the retail team, whose priority was a premium selection of merchandise to guarantee a good customer experience, versus the anything-goes anarchy that accompanied the seller platform, where anyone could sign up and start selling cheap, low-quality products.

The perennial debate inside Amazon was pitting the *quality* of products versus the *quantity*. The fights often had to be arbitrated by Faricy's boss, senior vice president Sebastian Gunningham, or by

Bezos himself. Both leaned heavily toward expanding the breadth of selection as fast as possible. "Jeff and Sebastian's view was that all selection is good selection," said Adrian Agostini, a longtime marketplace executive. "They wanted rules in place: don't offend, don't kill, don't poison. Other than that, you take what you get and let customers decide."

In the first few years of the 2010s, attentive entrepreneurs in Amazon's primary markets in the U.S. and Europe recognized a lucrative new opportunity. They could develop a unique product, find a manufacturer, often in China, and sell it to millions of online shoppers. Faricy and his team considered sellers to be their customers and cultivated them with programs like Amazon Exclusives, to highlight unique products, and Amazon Lending, to help finance sellers' growth, using the inventory they stored with FBA as collateral. They regularly convened focus groups, asking sellers to identify issues that needed to be fixed and new tools that should be built.

"Amazon at the time actually cared about helping brands thrive," said Stephan Aarstol, whose firm sold a popular line of stand-up paddleboards on Amazon and was featured on an episode of *Shark Tank*. By 2015, Aarstol employed ten people in San Diego and was bringing in more than $4 million a year—one of countless entrepreneurs who minted small fortunes on Amazon's flourishing platform. But his opinion about the marketplace would gradually evolve.

Bezos was delighted by the progress. That year, for the first time, the value of goods sold through marketplace surpassed sales from Amazon's retail side. Best of all, since the business was largely self-service, revenues were growing much faster than headcount. "Finally, a business that is able to get some leverage after it becomes successful," Bezos crowed at the team's OP1 meeting that year, holding the six-page narrative to his chest. "I'm going to take this document home and sleep with it."

Bezos then told Faricy that he no longer needed to individually review the marketplace during the annual OP1 session and only wanted to spend time on new initiatives like Amazon Lending. The CEO was devoting more of his attention to new products at the company while the details of Faricy's business were getting so complex that he felt like he could provide only limited guidance anyway.

He told the FBA team the same thing. He would still continue to audit the businesses, adjudicating disputes and sending question mark emails when he learned of problems. But he no longer needed to be so intimately involved in the planning stages.

Which would put Bezos at some distance from the coming chaos.

As the Amazon Marketplace and Fulfillment by Amazon grew, the executives in charge were eyeing a potentially disruptive competitor. In 2010, Peter Szulczewski, a Polish-Canadian former Google employee, cofounded an online advertising startup called ContextLogic. When it didn't gain traction, he pivoted the company toward e-commerce with an ingenious twist—a kind of geographic arbitrage. Most internet sellers sourced their products from manufacturers in China, shipped them in bulk to the West, and marked them up for rapid delivery to relatively affluent online urban shoppers. Why not instead allow merchants in China to sell inexpensive, unbranded goods directly to customers in the West who might not care if it takes several weeks for products to get to their doorstep?

Szulczewski renamed his company Wish.com and in late 2012 started hiring Chinese staff to recruit sellers and handle customer service. His timing was perfect. Alibaba had helped to spawn a vibrant community of resourceful Chinese internet merchants who were looking for new customers outside their home country. In fact, Alibaba had the same idea and was developing a cross-border commerce site called AliExpress, which was enjoying early traction in Mexico and Europe.

The Wish.com and AliExpress websites were crowded with prod-

ucts and difficult for novice online shoppers to navigate. But customers seemed to relish the treasure hunt–like pursuit of disposable
fashion, such as $12 faux leather sneakers. In 2014, Wish raised $69
million from venture capitalists and was featured in the *Wall Street
Journal.* After one conversation about the startup, Bezos looked at
Sebastian Gunningham and said, "You're on this, right?" Gunningham later noted that "Wish inspired us. They hit a nerve."

Amazon's strategy toward such disruptive startups is usually to
develop a relationship with them and learn what it can—often by
dangling the possibility of an acquisition. That year, Szulczewski and
his cofounder Danny Zhang were invited to Seattle, where they spent
the day talking to a dozen marketplace executives. They came away
with the impression that the Amazon execs were skeptical of their
business model.

But over the next two years, Wish continued to raise capital and
grow. In 2016, Amazon reached out again, inviting Szulczewski to
meet with Bezos. By then the Wish CEO was dubious of Amazon's intentions and said he would only meet with Bezos one-on-one. When
he later noticed other Amazon executives on the calendar invite, he
said he canceled and never went.

By now Amazon was hurriedly adapting to a changing e-commerce
landscape. The flood of Chinese sellers onto the internet represented
a potential Cambrian explosion of new, low-priced selections. Such
generically branded goods might not appeal to everyone, but they
could draw younger or lower-income buyers to online shopping, and
they later might graduate to more expensive products and even sign
up for Amazon Prime.

Amazon had conspicuously failed to develop an online marketplace for Chinese sellers *within* China. This represented another opportunity to do business in the world's most populous country. As part
of a new initiative dubbed Marco Polo, after the thirteenth-century
Italian explorer, Amazon hired teams in Beijing to sign up local sellers, translate Seller Central into Mandarin, and provide live customer

support for merchants. To lower freight costs and streamline the process of shipping overseas, the company also developed an initiative called Dragon Boat. The service consolidated merchandise in coastal hubs like Shanghai and Shenzhen, moved them in bulk through customs, and then shipped them in containers that Amazon reserved at wholesale rates from shipping companies like Maersk.

New employees who joined the new global selling teams were pushed to move quickly—to *get big fast*. Internal documents, shared with me by a former employee, describe the team's goals from that time, such as quickly growing headcount in China to recruit local sellers and teach them how to use FBA. Though AliExpress hadn't gained much traction in the U.S., execs noted that Alibaba's fees were lower than Amazon's and worried that its hypercompetitive CEO, Jack Ma, might suspend the fees altogether to secure a foothold in Western countries. "Are we doing enough to capture the China-based seller opportunity?" asked one Amazon document. "Should we reduce the friction in our China-based seller onboarding by relaxing our listing standards to accelerate selection growth?"

While it's not clear whether Amazon actually relaxed those standards, what's evident is that they weren't very high to begin with. Throughout 2015 and 2016, thousands of Chinese sellers registered on Amazon's marketplace *each day*. "The numbers were astronomical. No one had seen volume like that," said Sebastian Gunningham. Predictably, quality varied dramatically. "People would see a bestselling coat in the U.S. and literally it would appear on the site from a Chinese seller within hours," Gunningham said. "Then a customer would pay for that coat and they'd leave a review about the sleeves falling off in the first minute."

Gunningham, a member of the S-team, was in charge of global selling as well as FBA and the marketplace. He'd grown up on a ranch in Argentina, earned a mathematical sciences degree at Stanford University, and worked with Larry Ellison at Oracle and Steve Jobs at Apple before scoring a kind of high-tech hat trick by joining Jeff Bezos at Amazon. Colleagues said he was creative and empathetic—and a *big thinker*, in Amazon's lexicon.

Gunningham quickly recognized that the flood of Chinese merchandise would stir controversy among sellers in the West who would not be able to match the low prices. One solution, at first, was to publicly and somewhat disingenuously downplay the shift. "The risky downside to this is that U.S.- and EU-based sellers do not find this avalanche of China-based sellers very amusing," he wrote to fellow S-team members, in an email that was later submitted as testimony and made public in congressional antitrust hearings. "I have coached the team to be aggressive marketing in China to sell globally, but [to] take a low-key approach in the import countries."

The low-cost merchandise was also divisive inside Amazon, so Gunningham devised symbolic ways of illustrating both the benefits and the challenges. One day, he started wearing a gaudy 80-cent stainless steel necklace with a dangling owl pendant. Amazon was selling tens of thousands of them per month, with Chinese sellers recouping a tiny profit margin on shipping charges. His point was that Amazon should not dismiss such low-priced items. "Everybody thought that lots of trash was coming onto the site, but trash is in the eye of the beholder," Gunningham said. "Lots of it was very fashionable to many."

Gunningham also bought dozens of black cocktail dresses of various sizes and styles on the marketplace and displayed them on a rack in his conference room. Amazon was selling thousands of such garments, no-name brands of variable quality made in China. Some were long, some short; some cost a few hundred dollars and others were as cheap as $20; some seemed durable, while the zippers on others seemed to spontaneously self-destruct on the first use. Colleagues recall that the rack of dresses sat there for months. His point was that his team needed to do a better job of distinguishing the various dresses from one another, giving customers the ability to evaluate them individually, so that the well-proven reviews system could penalize the low-quality sellers. The dresses "illustrated the broad set of dilemmas that mostly stemmed from the stuff coming out of China," he observed.

Despite these demonstrations, the influx of Chinese products onto the marketplace remained contentious within Amazon and between the company and its partners. It was an accelerant, sprayed onto the already combustible frictions between sellers in the U.S. and China, and between Amazon's first-party (or 1P) retail division and its third-party (or 3P) marketplace group. Quality was once again being pitted against quantity. Did Amazon want a calm, orderly store with only well-known and trustworthy brands? Or did it favor a more chaotic marketplace with a more extensive variety of products and prices?

Execs didn't have to guess which customers preferred: their choice was clear in numerous trials and experiments. Amazon's German website, for example, allowed third-party merchants to list and sell a wide variety of branded and generic shoes, while Amazon's UK site featured a curated shoe store with only more expensive, brand-name footwear. The German site performed markedly better, because of the greater selection and cheaper options.

This finding was significant, because Amazon's corporate compass only pointed one way: toward what customers wanted. And it turned out that plenty of people will buy dirt cheap sneakers on the internet, even if they suspect the shoes are not destined to last that long.

Nevertheless, Amazon's retail execs continued to object to the inundation of low-quality Chinese merchandise, and the debate regularly made its way to the S-team. In one meeting, Jeff Bezos was asked to resolve a version of it: What should Amazon's broader strategy be in apparel? Should the company prioritize the sale of high-end clothing, usually from premium Western brands, on carefully curated, dedicated websites? Or should it favor low-end generic apparel and private-label products across Amazon.com and via the Amazon Marketplace?

The room went silent while everyone waited for Bezos's decisive answer.

"I think we should target everybody who wears clothes; I haven't seen that many people naked over the last few days," he finally said, laughing uproariously. "I believe people are going to be wearing clothes for a long time."

———

It was one of those questions that Bezos believed should not be answered. He wanted Amazon to do it all. But by not answering, he was also casting a vote for uninhibited, low-priced selection on the marketplace—one that would have enormous ramifications.

Chinese startups, some quite formidable, arose almost out of thin air to sell on Amazon.com. In 2011, a software engineer named Steven Yang had quit his plum Silicon Valley job at Google and moved to Shenzhen to start an electronics company called Anker to sell accessories like replacement laptop batteries. Over the next few years, his product line expanded to include just about every kind of cable, charger, and battery imaginable, many of which soared to the coveted top spot of Amazon's bestseller lists.

Yang developed close relationships with local factories, so Anker could quickly change and improve its products based on market trends and customer feedback. It paid its employees a fraction of the wages Western sellers paid theirs, and because it was based in China, the company didn't have to collect the same income and VAT taxes as its U.S. and European counterparts. It also enjoyed heavily subsidized shipping rates to the West, thanks to an arrangement between the China Post and the U.S. Postal Service, making it cheaper to ship from China to the U.S. than within the U.S. itself.

In other words, Anker and Chinese sellers like it had significant advantages that in a highly competitive marketplace like Amazon's would make a material difference. Yang was friendly with Bernie Thompson, founder of the Seattle area–based Plugable Technologies, which sold similar computer accessories. Both recognized that Chinese brands selling to a global audience were going to radically tilt the e-commerce playing field. "Bernie, I'm sorry, but I'm going to run you over," Yang once told Thompson at an industry conference, Thompson recalled (though Yang does not remember saying this).

Many Chinese sellers like Anker sold high-quality products at attractive prices. But there were also plenty of bad actors on China's unruly capitalist frontier. To safeguard their sites and increase the cost of committing fraud, local e-commerce players like Alibaba and JD.com required safety deposits from new merchants and sometimes waited months after product sales to remit payments to sellers. They also regularly purged their sites of the worst actors. Amazon had ported over its U.S. marketplace system to China with few of those protections in place at first and had little ability to discriminate good sellers from bad. As a result, it became an appealing target for fraud, counterfeit, and sellers with shoddy merchandise.

Bezos never wanted to compromise on quality—there were no trade-offs allowed at Amazon, after all. He wanted quality *and* quantity, and he expected that Amazon's engineers would create new tools to block dangerous products and counterfeits. But the wheels of change turned faster than Amazon could create systems to police its own site.

Bogus vitamins, dangerous Christmas tree lights, and other unsafe products, as well as books replete with typos, all made their way onto the shelves of the everything store. So-called hoverboards were the hot ticket during the 2015 holiday season; several Chinese models had an unfortunate penchant for bursting into flames and burning down homes. Amazon pulled the hoverboards from the site on December 12 that year and emailed buyers referencing "news reports of safety issues" and offering refunds. A *Wall Street Journal* investigation later concluded that faulty lithium-ion batteries in the hoverboards led to fifty-seven fires and caused $2.3 million in property damage; about half were purchased on Amazon, more than any other retailer, generating a bevy of lawsuits against the company.

Over the ensuing months, defective batteries in cell phones, laptops, and vape pens bought on Amazon also led to injuries, more lawsuits, and more news coverage. Bezos was apoplectic about the problems and the bad publicity, colleagues said, even though he had helped to create the situation with his relentless pursuit of expanding product selection and obtaining leverage. "Jeff's tone was 'how can you guys not have foreseen this?'" said Adrian Agostini, the market-place VP. "There were tough lessons learned." In response, Amazon execs rushed to expand the trust and safety team, which developed tools to scan the site and identify fraud and policy violations. But the program was ineffective at first, since abusers were often booted from the site only after their abuse was detected and had impacted customers.

Western sellers were afraid of crossing the line and getting into trouble with Amazon. But in China, they didn't know where the line was and often didn't care. Scrappy Chinese sellers adopted deceit-ful tactics, like paying for reviews on the Amazon website, which at the time—before Amazon embraced advertising within search results—was the only way to boost their products to the top of the page. If they got caught and their accounts were shut down, they sim-ply opened new ones.

Amazon execs saw what was happening but struggled to tame the chaos; the marketplace team considered sellers their customers, after all, who were innocent until proven guilty. "We were all very ide-alistic," said a former Beijing-based Amazon executive. "I feel like I should have moved much faster and more aggressively. I bought into a narrative that all sellers were good."

In 2016, Faricy and his deputies traveled to China to try to better understand the complicated seller dynamic. They traveled to Hong Kong and Shanghai, then split up into groups focusing on electronics and apparel. The former went to Shenzhen, the latter to Guangzhou, Zengcheng, and Beijing, among other cities. Then they all met back in Shanghai to compare notes.

The executives on the trip were amazed by what they saw. The group on the fashion leg visited an apparel factory that was making $9 sport coats for the retailer Abercrombie & Fitch, which then sold them at retail for $500. The same factory was also selling the coats with a different button pattern directly online for $90—and still making a fat profit. They also visited a factory that made women's tops for the retail chain Zara. As the Amazon execs looked down from a balcony onto the factory floor, one asked their host about a group of workers separate from the rest, making similar clothing as the others. They sold on Alibaba, the host said, under the factory's own private label.

Execs on the electronics leg of the trip saw similar things. Factories across China were going straight to shoppers online, bypassing traditional stores, and providing great value for consumers. In other words, massive disruption was coming to retail, despite the problems of fraud, counterfeits, and low-quality items. "It was unbelievable what we saw," Faricy said. "We realized that people charging ten to fifty times what products actually cost to make, based on a brand name, wasn't going to last and consumers would be the winners."

———

On the last day of May 2016, a hundred or so apparel sellers gathered in Seattle for Amazon's first Fashion Seller Conference. Held in the company's brand-new meeting center on 7th Avenue, a block from the new Day 1 tower, the summit consisted of a day and a half of speeches, seminars, and meetings. Sebastian Gunningham kicked off the festivities with a fireside chat.

Gunningham had predicted that the "avalanche" of Chinese sellers would alienate U.S.-based merchants. Now he reaped that expected harvest. During his Q&A session, the sellers stood up, one after another, took the microphone, and leveled a blistering set of questions and accusations at him: *How did Amazon expect them to compete with Chinese sellers? They didn't play by the rules! Why was Amazon not protecting authorized rights-holders and resellers and booting infringers? Why did the search results always favor their competition?*

Several attendees recalled that one woman commandeered the microphone for fifteen minutes. She described herself as a T-shirt seller from the Midwest and said that every time she had a successful design, a Chinese seller quickly copied it, undercut her on price, and pilfered her sales. She asked how many of her fellow merchants were having such problems; a collective murmur intimated at an angry consensus.

Gunningham stood patiently onstage, addressing the complaints, and pledging to fix what he could. But the inexorable forces of cross-border trade and globalization were part of the problem, and he couldn't alter those. "It was extremely tense," said Brad Howard, CEO of the online retailer Trend Nation, who was in the room. "It was a revolt in their building, on their dime, as they were asking us to send questions their way." Amazon execs and attendees of the fashion conference still talked about the near mutiny years later.

Many apparel brands echoed the frustration of the merchants. In July 2016, the sandal maker Birkenstock loudly pulled its merchandise from Amazon and banned all of its authorized third-party resellers from selling its products on the site. Companies like Nike and Ikea would follow suit, provoking speculation that Amazon's inability to stop counterfeits was damaging its relationship with brands.

Inside Amazon, the employees in charge of the retail fashion business, where Amazon bought merchandise at wholesale from established brands, were now in a difficult situation, caught between angry vendors and the unbridled growth of the marketplace. With fanfare back in 2009, Jeff Wilke had hired Cathy Beaudoin, a senior executive from The Gap, and tasked her with bringing high-end fashion to a site that was barely even considered a destination for buying clothes. Beaudoin had opened a forty-thousand-square-foot factory in Williamsburg, Brooklyn, where photographers and models churned out high-quality imagery for the site. She also enlisted Jeff and MacKenzie Bezos to attend the Met Gala in 2012, their first highly publicized encounter with the celebrity elite. At the ball, they hobnobbed with celebrities, sitting at a table with Mick Jagger and Scarlett Johansson.

Now the unruly marketplace was undoing all that meticulous relationship building. Generic handbags, jeans, and evening gowns that all looked uncomfortably similar to established makes and styles led to an endless series of tense conversations. In meetings, Beaudoin railed against the poor customer experience of the marketplace, colleagues recalled; she believed that the third-party merchandise cheapened the site and alienated Amazon's partners. She left the company in 2017, just as Amazon became one of the leading apparel retailers in the U.S. on the back of its extensive, low-priced selection.

Despite its success, Amazon still had a significant problem. Counterfeits, unsafe and expired items, and shoddy products threatened to tarnish its reputation and destroy the trust it had cultivated with its customers. In 2017, Amazon introduced an initiative called Brand Registry, which allowed brands to claim their logos and designs, and to report potential violations to Amazon. Amazon executives insisted the project was already underway before the seller mutiny at the fashion conference. But in the months after the revolt, they hired a senior manager for the effort, grew its team of employees to review complaints, and spared little expense in improving its fraud detection tools. Over the next few years, three hundred and fifty thousand brands would sign up.

That was only a start. Brand Registry would lead to an entirely new set of complaints about the length of time it took Amazon to address claims, and it still didn't solve the problem of abusive Chinese sellers who, once their accounts were closed, simply signed up for new ones. "Brand Registry improved things, but it was a pretty low bar," said Larry Pluimer, a former Amazon executive who started a digital retail consultancy to help brands navigate these problems.

By that point, the marketplace division was losing its influence on the S-team. Sebastian Gunningham, who had reported directly to Bezos for years, was moved underneath Jeff Wilke, a former peer, after

Wilke and Andy Jassy were promoted to CEOs of the retail and AWS divisions in a 2016 company-wide reorganization. In 2018, Gunningham left Amazon and, ruining his streak of working for visionary tech leaders, headed to the ill-fated office-sharing startup WeWork.

With the champion of third-party sellers gone, along with Gunningham's direct access to Bezos and Wilke, Peter Faricy and his team were moved under Doug Herrington and the retail group—their intellectual foils in the perennial debate between the first- and third-party businesses, and between quality and quantity. Bezos had incubated the two divisions separately for more than a decade; now he was merging them, with retail asserting itself over the marketplace.

That fall, Faricy also left Amazon, along with many of Gunningham's longtime deputies. They described an environment that was no longer as much fun; too much time was spent on taming the marketplace rather than growing it, and on giving depositions for the legal cases that were one legacy of the service's unrestrained expansion. The team was also subject to an unrelenting barrage of escalation emails from Bezos, highlighting the marketplace's problems and demanding immediate answers. "I think I received a question mark from Jeff on a weekly basis," said Ella Irwin, general manager of a team that worked on seller abuse.

Amazon executives were now in an awkward position. They wanted to boast about the achievements of the marketplace and the way in which Amazon supported hundreds of thousands of independent entrepreneurs. In his shareholder letter published in April 2019, Jeff Bezos wrote that independent merchants were now responsible for 58 percent of all units sold on the site. "Third-party sellers are kicking our first-party butt," he wrote.

But executives also had to frequently defend the marketplace. "The facts are that the vast majority of the merchandise is great, but there's a small fraction of sellers who are gaming the system or committing fraud in some way," Jeff Wilke told me. "Our job remains to protect customers and root out the fraud as fast and as completely as we can. Look, our reputation is built on customer trust, and it's something we have to earn every day because it's so easy to lose it."

In 2019, Amazon spent $500 million on fraud prevention; it said it stopped bad actors from opening 2.5 million accounts. It also introduced a new anti-counterfeit tool, called Project Zero, that allowed approved brands to zap suspected infringers automatically, without going through an approval process. And it started testing a system aimed at verifying sellers one by one, via video-calls. Amazon, it seemed, was quietly retreating from the idea of a completely frictionless and self-service selling platform.

What execs still didn't like to admit, particularly at a politically sensitive time in bilateral trade relations, was that 49 percent of the top ten thousand largest sellers on Amazon were based in China, according to Marketplace Pulse, a research firm that monitors the site. In April 2020, the Office of the U.S. Trade Representative listed Amazon sites in five countries as "notorious markets" with dangerous levels of counterfeit and pirated products. Amazon called the report a "purely political act" and part of a vendetta by the administration of Donald Trump.

Despite all these tribulations, the selection machine had met Jeff Bezos's lofty goals and positioned Amazon at the forefront of a rapidly globalizing retail landscape. The higher-margin proceeds from the third-party marketplace, which were at least double the profits from Amazon's own retail efforts, would go on to nourish other parts of his business empire, such as Prime Video and the construction of new fulfillment centers, just as Bezos had always hoped.

They would also help to fund Amazon's unprofitable, multiyear effort to finally crack the $700-billion-a-year domestic market for groceries. There was, it turned out, a whole lot you could do with leverage—even when the journey to obtain it was difficult and the costs to society were unexpectedly high.

CHAPTER 8

Amazon's Future is CRaP

John Mackey was in trouble. By the spring of 2017, same-store sales in his 460 Whole Foods supermarkets had steadily declined for two years while the company's stock price had plummeted by half since 2013. Things were going poorly for the entrepreneur who was perhaps most responsible for popularizing the manifest notion that humans should be more mindful about what they eat.

I had met the iconoclastic Mackey a few years before, when he took me on a tour of the eighty-thousand-square-foot flagship store that adjoined Whole Foods Market headquarters in Austin, Texas. Even back then the founder and CEO, a vegan with habitually tousled hair, seemed frustrated with how things were going—particularly when I referred to the chain's disparaging moniker, "Whole Paycheck." Journalists "always want to take pictures of our $400-dollar bottles of wine, not the $2.99 wine," he said, walking through the market with a slight limp, the result of osteoarthritis after years of jogging and basketball. "We are meeting all these price points, but the story they want to tell is about the expensive things. That's become our narrative—that Whole Foods is broken."

Over four decades, Mackey had charted a path between the natural food purists (who couldn't abide selling alcohol or white sugar) and the supermarket industry's pragmatists (who wouldn't know an organic carrot if they bit into one). He had occasionally violated the bounds of CEO decorum—for example, by adopting an alias on internet bulletin boards and posting hundreds of messages over the years attacking rivals and critics. But he always stuck to his principles: Whole Foods would never sell Diet Coke, Oreos, Cool Ranch Doritos, or other popular but unhealthy fare. Along the way, he built a company worth $21 billion at its peak that promoted the once-fringe notion of selling healthy food to the masses.

But Wall Street can be an unforgiving place for stagnating public companies that are "grounded in an ethical system based on value creation for all stakeholders"—as Mackey's 2013 book, *Conscious Capitalism*, put it. One problem was that Whole Foods was no longer unique: Walmart, Costco, and Kroger were expanding the number of aisles devoted to organic and natural products. Another was that the company had grown over the years by acquiring regional chains, which led to an unwieldy patchwork of back-end technology systems. Without a frequent shopper program, which Mackey refused to implement, it knew next to nothing about even its most loyal customers. A decentralized operating structure limited the company's dexterity at precisely the time when it needed to evolve quickly to meet changing tastes, as well as to introduce home delivery and new digital payment methods.

In an unusual arrangement, Mackey was running the company at the time with a co-CEO, Walter Robb, who managed day-to-day operations. They recognized the looming challenges, and hired teams of data scientists in Austin and contracted with the San Francisco–based grocery delivery startup Instacart. But things were progressing slowly—and then they ran out of time.

In 2016, the New York investment firm Neuberger Berman started sending letters to Whole Foods leadership and to other shareholders, complaining about complacent management, the unconventional CEO structure, and highlighting deficiencies like the absence of a rewards program. Their letter-writing campaign didn't get much traction until that November, when Mackey responded to the pressure by taking over as sole chief executive—exactly the opposite of what the firm wanted.

The move piqued the interest of hedge fund Jana Partners, a so-called "activist investor," whose managing partner, Barry Rosenstein, believed Whole Foods was "lost and broken." Jana bought stock in distressed companies, agitated for change, and usually minted money when it forced a firm to slash costs or found an acquirer to pay a premium for it.

Quietly amassing Whole Foods stock that winter, Jana revealed itself as the company's second largest shareholder in April 2017. It demanded changes on the management team and board of directors; Rosenstein later said the firm was prepared to take over the company and "fix it ourselves." But Whole Foods executives worried that Jana's plan was to merge the organic grocer with another food giant it had a stake in: Albertsons Companies, an amalgamation of traditional supermarket chains like Safeway and Vons. In that scenario, the conglomerate would take Whole Foods' esteemed brand name and relatively unlevered balance sheet; it would also likely ship out the intractable John Mackey and ship in Coke, Doritos, and other crowd-pleasing fare.

Dismayed, Mackey and his executive team scrambled a defense. They recruited five new independent directors to replace longtime board members who had an average tenure of more than fifteen years. They also sought a white knight, contacting private equity firms as well as billionaire Warren Buffett, according to a former board member. But since earnings were flat and the grocer wasn't generating enough cash to borrow money, the math on a leveraged buyout didn't work.

One option remained, which almost everyone at Whole Foods Market considered fanciful. Over the years, they had engaged in several fruitless conversations with Amazon. John Mackey was an admirer though, and the year before had vividly dreamed his grocery chain had been acquired by the e-commerce giant. ("That's crazy," his wife, Deborah, had told him.) When *Bloomberg News* reported that Amazon executives had recently discussed acquiring Whole Foods, Mackey asked one of his advisors to place a phone call and try one last time to save the company.

———

Jeff Bezos placed prospective business opportunities into one of two buckets. There were land rushes, when the moment was ripe, rivals were circling, and Amazon had to move quickly or else it would lose out. Then there was everything else, when the company could bide its time and patiently experiment.

Amazon's attempts at a third-party marketplace and with the Kindle and Alexa were land rushes. Bezos pushed his employees to move with urgency and they had the battle scars to prove it. But for years he took a more passive approach to home delivery of food—that is, until he saw formidable competition emerge and abruptly changed his mind. The resulting shift in strategy would have significant consequences for the massive grocery market and the way customers, competitors, and regulators viewed the e-commerce juggernaut forever after.

The Amazon executive who brooded over the grocery business the longest and who agitated for a more aggressive approach was Doug Herrington, the senior vice president of Amazon's consumables unit. Herrington often wore plaid shirts and a Patagonia vest in the office and talked in such a low voice during meetings that employees often had to lean forward to hear him. Earlier in his career, he had worked at the first-generation grocery delivery flameout Webvan, which raised close to a billion dollars in private and public financing during the dot-com boom and then went out of business in 2001.

Internet historians would view Webvan as the ultimate symbol of Silicon Valley's arrogant rush to create a future that people didn't want. According to Herrington, a Princeton University and Harvard Business School alumnus who ran product development and marketing at Webvan, the real story was more complex. CEO Louis Borders—cofounder of the eponymous book chain—and his team erred by building a network of warehouses that were so costly to operate that the company lost money on every order. Before they could rectify that mistake or even open for business in many cities where they had set up operations, Wall Street stopped funding unprofitable startups during the early 2000s recession. The company's sales and customer base were growing, but it couldn't withdraw from its financial commitments fast enough and declared bankruptcy. "I walked away saying, 'theoretically this model can work,'" Herrington said. "We made the wrong choices, we did some inefficient things, but customers loved it."

After joining Amazon in 2005 to run consumables—goods that are used up relatively quickly, like laundry detergent and food—Herrington assembled a team of employees to meet at night on an ambitious project, which would be outside the bounds of their daily responsibilities. The mission was to develop a plan for Amazon to launch a national grocery service. He wanted to solve the problem of home food delivery and finally vanquish the acrid taste of the Webvan bankruptcy. A year or so after, in late 2006, back when Amazon was in the old Pacific Medical Center, Jeff Bezos reviewed their plan, which called for a $60 million up-front investment, and rejected it. "The feedback was 'love the vision, hate the numbers,'" Herrington recalled. Instead, he got $7 million to open a limited service beta test in Seattle. Then-CFO Tom Szkutak asked him to try not to let it distract the rest of the company.

Amazon Fresh launched in August 2007. In Bellevue, east of Seattle, Herrington's team leased an old Safeway distribution center, which was sitting fallow amid the collapse of the local real estate market and was "horror movie scary," according to Ian Clarkson, Fresh's first general manager. Everything about the new service had to be different than other parts of Amazon: rooms in the warehouse had old walk-in refrigerators, while the website displayed multiple products on each page instead of just one and gave customers the option of choosing a specific window of time in the day for delivery. Bezos frequently reviewed Fresh's progress and at one point, scrutinizing the ballooning delivery costs, suggested Amazon offer predawn drop-offs. Like garbage collection trucks, they could take advantage of the dearth of traffic in the early morning.

Seattle customers appreciated waking up to groceries on their doorstep. But Fresh's other challenges were more formidable. Unlike other Amazon services, which instantly had national or even global reach, Fresh's potential was bounded by the zip codes where its fleet of drivers could make deliveries. The Fresh team also had to solve a nest of thorny problems, like what to do with expired food, how to manage the complex banana ripening process, and how to respond when customers complained they had found something unseemly in their dinner. Still, over the course of six years, they made slow but steady progress that crept toward profitability.

During that time, Herrington regularly pitched plans to the S-team to replicate Fresh in other cities. But Amazon was smaller back then, and the land-rush opportunities, such as the doomed expansion in China and the Fire Phone, took precedence. Consumer adoption of home grocery delivery, Bezos believed, was going to be a more gradual process. Forced to stay local, Herrington was frustrated by the perpetual delay.

Then in April 2012, Bezos convened the S-team at Willows Lodge in Woodinville, Washington, about a half hour northeast of Seattle, for their annual off-site retreat. Each executive was asked to bring a one- to two-page memo that contemplated a significant new opportunity for Amazon. Herrington had joined the vaunted leadership council a year before, and his blunt memo would resonate inside the S-team for years. Even its title was provocative: "Amazon's Future is CRaP."

In company parlance, CRaP stood for "can't realize a profit" and had several meanings. CRaP included items like stepladders and whiteboards, which couldn't be put in boxes or efficiently shipped to customers. But in his memo, Herrington was talking largely about the inexpensive, bulky items stocked by supermarkets, such as bottled water, Diet Coke, or even a bag of apples. In the wake of the Webvan fiasco, most online retailers at the time considered these types of products to be economic quicksand. To the extent it sold them at all, Amazon had developed an "add-on" program to minimize their harmful financial impact. Customers could only include CRaP in their orders when they were making a broader assortment of purchases, such as books or electronics at the same time.

Herrington's memo pointed out that Walmart, Carrefour, Tesco, Metro AG, and Kroger were the world's five largest retailers at the time. "All of them anchor their customer relationship in groceries," he wrote. If Amazon's retail business was going to grow to $400 billion in gross merchandise sales, it needed to transform a model based on infrequent shopping for relatively high-priced goods to more regular shopping for low-priced essentials. In other words, if the company was going to join the ranks of the biggest retailers, the S-team had to figure out a way to profitably sell supermarket items. If they didn't, Amazon was going to be vulnerable to rivals who already enjoyed the shopping frequency and cost advantages of the grocery model.

He concluded the memo by subtly needling his colleagues, including Bezos, who considered himself implacably bold. "We should be less timid in investing in this future," Herrington wrote. "We have the capacity to put a much more significant bet on the table, if we have the will."

Bezos typically responded well to this type of critical introspection, especially when it was coupled with a proposal for aggressive expansion. Such thinking reflected his own mindset. After the S-team sat in silence for several hours reading one another's papers, the CEO picked up Herrington's and said, "This one really made me think." A few months later, Herrington got a green light for a limited expansion of Fresh into Los Angeles and San Francisco.

He had won the battle. The problem was that he hadn't yet figured out how to wage the war. The introduction of Amazon's grocery service into California in June 2013 was initially greeted with fanfare by the press. But it didn't quite work, at least not at the scale that Herrington had hoped. To defray shipping costs, Amazon charged customers a hefty $299 annual Fresh subscription fee. To fashion a new supply chain for perishable groceries, it created chilled rooms inside existing Amazon fulfillment centers an hour or so to the east of each city, in San Bernardino and Tracy, California. Then Amazon routed trailer trucks twice a day into staging areas in each region, where orders were moved to bright green Fresh vans for the last-mile delivery to customers' homes.

Logistics employees who worked on the California service said this hub-and-spoke model ended up being inefficient and unreliable; one said that Amazon was "basically stapling a $10 or $20 bill to every order." The Fresh team also tracked a metric called "perfect deliveries"—when an order was promptly delivered and included every item. They found they were hitting that target less than 70 percent of the time.

Grocery industry veterans belittled the effort from afar. "Amazon Fresh is their Waterloo," John Mackey told me during our chat in 2014. "What's the one thing people want? Convenience. You can't do that with distribution centers and trucks."

Aside from its quiet introduction into parts of Brooklyn a year later, the expansion of Fresh into new markets slowed down considerably after the California expansion. Success in delivering online groceries relied on getting the logistics exactly right and amassing enough demand to make it profitable to send drivers into residential neighborhoods. Amazon had set up warehouses too far from customers, made it too expensive for them to sign up, and saddled them with bulky tote bags and sacks of dry ice after each delivery. Bezos had finally agreed with Doug Herrington that Amazon needed to reinvent its retail business, but they were going to have to find a different way to do it.

———

Then, as so often happened in Amazon's history, the arrival of competitors onto a shifting landscape injected some resolve into the calculations of Bezos and the S-team. The race for online ordering and rapid delivery of groceries was about to turn into the one thing that reliably captured their attention and investment dollars: a land rush.

Two rivals introduced same-day delivery services, using similar business models. The San Francisco startup Instacart was founded by Apoorva Mehta, a former Level 5 senior engineer in Amazon's logistics division (in other words, a relatively low-level worker on a hierarchy that stretched from Level 1 warehouse recruits to Bezos at Level 12).

Instacart raised millions from venture capital firms including Sequoia, the original backer of Webvan, and struck partnerships with grocery chains like Whole Foods Market, Costco, and Safeway. It then contracted with smartphone-toting pickers to select orders off the shelves of retail stores and with drivers to transport them in their own cars to customers' homes. There was no inventory risk or costly employment contracts, since the workers were all independent contractors. With few of the fixed costs that sank Webvan, the startup had tremendous leverage.

After Instacart burst onto the scene in 2012 and started furiously expanding into new cities, Amazon's M&A team tried to reach out to learn more about the company. Wise to Amazon's methods, Apoorva Mehta didn't return the call.

The second challenger seemed even more dangerous at the time. Amazon's archrival, Google, introduced a service called Google Shopping Express—later Google Express—offering customers unlimited same-day delivery from retailers like Costco, Target, and Smart & Final for a $95-a-year annual subscription. In 2014, the service expanded to Chicago, Boston, Washington, D.C., and soon after would land in Bezos's backyard in Seattle. In case there was any confusion about the search giant's intentions, Google chairman Eric Schmidt cleared it up at a speech that fall in Berlin. "Many people think our main competition is Bing or Yahoo," he said. "Really, our biggest search competitor is Amazon. People don't think of Amazon as search, but if you are looking for something to buy, you are more often than not looking for it on Amazon."

Amazon execs and employees expressed varying opinions about which rival posed a bigger threat. Jeff Wilke acknowledged that Google Express, which offered a broad assortment of merchandise from both regular stores and supermarkets, was "demonstrating that customers preferred a faster delivery option." But both were dangerous. In the past, Amazon simply acquired competitors like Zappos and Quidsi (owner of Diapers.com) that offered superior selection and delivery speed in a focused product category. With Instacart and Google, it faced a pair of challengers that couldn't be bought and weren't going anywhere.

With Bezos spending his time on newer initiatives like Alexa, he was leaving the daily maneuverings in Amazon's consumer business to his retail chief. That September, in the midst of the Google Express expansion, Wilke was conducting a quarterly business review with the Amazon Prime team and asked his top lieutenants to propose a response to the threat. His deputies pitched expanding the selection of items that were available to Prime members for same-day delivery at an extra charge. Wilke didn't think that would be enough to match the new offerings, rejected the idea, and, as he put it later, "blew up the meeting."

Wilke announced that he wanted to attack this problem from a totally different angle. They were going to form an independent team to build a service that was separate from the Amazon website and singularly devoted to ultra-fast delivery. The goal, he declared, was to launch it within a hundred days. Dave Clark, Amazon's head of operations, would oversee the effort in conjunction with Herrington.

Sitting next to Wilke in the meeting and taking notes was his technical advisor, a ten-year Amazon veteran named Stephenie Landry.
While she was dutifully typing, a chat window popped up on her
screen, from Clark, who was sitting across the room. Did she want to
spearhead the new project? In fact, she did.

Landry was a fast-rising star who exhibited some of the management qualities—detail-oriented, dogged determination, a merciless
driver of underlings—of the Bezosian leadership template. She was
originally from New York City and had attended Wellesley College,
where she majored in women's studies. After graduation, she received
a grant from the school to spend a year building, of all things, wooden
boats. After that, she joined a struggling internet company during the
dot-com bust, earned an MBA from the University of Michigan, and
then joined Amazon in 2003 in operations, working on how to trans-
form its warehouses to accommodate products other than books,
DVDs, and small consumer electronics. In her first employee badge
photo, she sported a quasi Mohawk.

Landry joined the original Fresh team in Seattle and then managed another of Herrington's beleaguered efforts to crack the CRaP
problem, Prime Pantry. That service, which was perpetually unprofitable, allowed customers to load up heavy boxes of household staples
like cereals, pasta, and bottled water at steep discounts.

In her new job, Landry's first task was writing the PR FAQ, the
preliminary press release that conjured the kind of service that Wilke
wanted. The paper and its subsequent revisions described a smartphone app-based service that Landry first dubbed Amazon Magic,
and then Amazon ASAP. She proposed forming three separate teams,
each with a magic-themed name, which would all take different approaches toward the same goal of ultra-fast delivery.

One group would develop a retail service, code-named Houdini,
which would store and sell a limited selection of the most popular
products on Amazon from strategically located urban warehouses.

That would allow Amazon to deliver frequently purchased items to customers within a few hours.

Another group would take a third-party marketplace approach, dubbed Copperfield. That team would seek to form partnerships with retail and grocery stores and list the products they had on their shelves on a new Amazon smartphone app, just like Google Express and Instacart.

Finally, a third group was formed to pursue an idea called Presto. It called for assembling an even smaller selection of top-selling products and driving them around in a truck or van to deliver items in less than ten minutes to surrounding neighborhoods. This approach proved complex and risked overlapping with the others, causing confusion, so it was quickly shelved.

Bezos approved these plans but wasn't as immersed in their development as he was in new technology projects, like Alexa. He reviewed the weekly updates that Landry emailed the S-team and occasionally responded with questions. He did make one significant contribution though: in a November 2014 meeting, he scrapped the Amazon ASAP name and rechristened the service Prime Now, to tie it more closely to Amazon's expanding subscription club. Landry and her team had to scramble to change their branding at the last minute.

By then, they were all working eighteen-hour days and seven-day weeks, sprinting to meet their one-hundred-day goal. In Seattle, engineers pumped out the new Prime Now app and a corresponding smartphone tool, dubbed Rabbit, to guide drivers through the delivery routes. The company planned to introduce the business with full-time drivers and then transition to the kind of freelance contractor model popularized by Uber and Instacart.

In midtown Manhattan, where Amazon decided to introduce the Houdini portion of Prime Now, employees set about stocking popular merchandise like Beats headphones, coffee grinders, toilet paper, and bottles of seltzer water in a fifty-thousand-square-foot warehouse inside an office tower across the street from the Empire State Building. For the first few weeks of December, they scattered around Midtown, placing test orders in the initial service area. Landry, who practically moved to an Airbnb in Brooklyn with her partner and their two-year-old son, ordered a pair of Havaiana flip-flops while she was getting a pedicure; they arrived before it was done.

After abandoning a marketing plan to promote the launch by wrapping the entire Empire State Building in gift paper, Amazon introduced Prime Now on December 18, 2014. Due to some last-minute delays, Landry and her team missed their deadline by eleven days—a trivial number that qualified them for gentle ribbing, instead of a more serious rebuke. Wilke was satisfied. The service offered free two-hour delivery for Prime members in select areas of Manhattan and delivery within an hour for an extra $7.99, then gradually expanded outward from there. After the launch, Bezos was photographed holding a brown paper Prime Now bag outside his Central Park West apartment, next to a seemingly oblivious delivery person.

But Houdini was the relatively easy part. Copperfield, the initiative to sell affiliated grocery store products online for the stores, was arguably the more important initiative; people didn't mind waiting a few days for Beats headphones or a pair of slippers, but they usually wanted their groceries right away. Seeking a partnership, Prime Now executives and their counterparts in Amazon's business development group visited the headquarters of Kroger in Cincinnati, Safeway in Pleasanton, California, and Gelson's Markets in Los Angeles. The grocers were all afraid of Amazon, indifferent to Prime Now, and concerned about Amazon Fresh, even though it only operated in a few cities.

Bezos was particularly enthusiastic about signing up another chain: Trader Joe's. Colleagues said he was infatuated with the store and its wide variety of distinctive, high-quality private-label products. Amazon's country manager in Germany, Ralf Kleber, was dispatched to the western city of Essen to meet with the chain's owners, the reclusive Albrecht family of the European supermarket conglomerate

Aldi Nord. He reported back that it was a short meeting and that the Albrechts did not want to work with Amazon.

Finally, Copperfield execs flew to Austin, where they pitched Prime Now to Whole Foods Market. John Mackey did not attend the meeting, but his deputies delivered a swift rejection. Whole Foods already had an exclusive partnership with Instacart. Plus, they asked to know more about Amazon Fresh and said they were not happy to hear about Fresh delivery trucks being parked in a Whole Foods parking lot; they viewed it as a cheap promotional stunt. Amazon execs left without a deal; they never seemed to understand why so many companies viewed Amazon as a pernicious threat, even as it scrambled the economics of every industry it entered. But the meeting was not entirely futile. In preparation for it, Amazon's business development staff reviewed Whole Foods' portfolio of real estate and observed that it neatly aligned with the geographic distribution of Prime members.

Copperfield was supposed to launch in New York City in March 2015 to complement Houdini. But the absence of large partners and the added complexity of picking items from store shelves delayed the rollout by several months. It finally went live with only a smattering of local stores and a single national brand: Sprouts Farmers Market, a Whole Foods competitor. Nevertheless, Prime Now spread throughout New York City and expanded to cities including London, Los Angeles, San Francisco, Atlanta, Dallas, and Miami.

Prime Now employees later admitted that they had rushed the service. It initially lacked some crucial features, like the ability for customers to return products. When customers had problems, Amazon simply refunded their money with no questions asked and ate the charge. The cost of rapid delivery was also significant, as was leasing and operating warehouses in metro areas with high real estate costs. As a result, Prime Now would be a significant money loser for years.

But the program closed Amazon's open flank and addressed the competitive threat posed by Instacart and Google Express. The entire Prime Now effort was heralded inside Amazon as a success under challenging conditions, and Stephenie Landry was asked to address the company at the biannual all-hands meeting at Seattle's KeyArena. The failed discussions with hostile retailers had also been a revelation. With limited opportunities for partnerships, Amazon itself would have to push much deeper into the supply chain of everyday household products and groceries if it was ever going to be successful in a brutally competitive business.

———

In the midst of Prime Now's blitz into new cities, Doug Herrington pitched another phase of his ongoing grocery campaign to Jeff Bezos. In the fall of 2015, employees on the project listened in via phones from their offices three blocks away in the Roxanne building while Herrington and his deputies met Bezos in his Day 1 North conference room. They were there to discuss Bloom Street, a heavily focus-grouped house brand they planned to affix to a wide range of grocery and home-care staples like coffee, snacks, wine, and razors. The goal was to create the equivalent of Costco's sweeping Kirkland Signature brand, which at the time was responsible for a staggering $30 billion in annual sales.

As with many such Bezos reviews at Amazon, Herrington's team had prepared for this moment for months. They conceived of the products, found factories to make them, negotiated prices, and designed labels. Herrington even brought the inaugural product, Bloom Street coffee, for Bezos to sample. According to two employees who attended the meeting, Bezos tasted it privately, then walked into the conference room and announced that he liked it quite a bit. Then he said that he didn't like the brand concept at all.

Amazon later said in a statement, "Jeff simply thought we didn't think we hit the mark with Bloom Street, and thought we could find something more interesting and creative." But several employees who worked on the project heard a more nuanced explanation. Bloom Street was explicitly tied to the company, with the Amazon Smile logo and other corporate trademarks on the product packaging. These employees were told that Bezos didn't want to risk Amazon's name and reputation on a single, relatively uncreative brand for food products. He asked for a total redo, and for the team to test various house brands with and without Amazon in the name. Since this would be a highly visible area of innovation, he now wanted to closely review the team's subsequent work. "Jeff just slammed on the brakes," recalled JT Meng, an employee on the project.

The meeting delayed the introduction of private-label products by Amazon's consumables group by six months. But they had good reason to keep pushing: in-store brands made up around 20 percent of all retail in the U.S. and above 40 percent in European countries like the UK, Germany, Spain, and Switzerland. By working directly with manufacturers, retailers lowered prices, increased their profit margins, and cultivated loyalty among shoppers with exclusive products. "We were kind of late to the game," Herrington said. "The vendors that I talked to were always asking me, 'When are you guys going to do this? Practically everyone else has.'"

Amazon already had private-label goods, mostly in its hardline and softline divisions. Its track record was mixed so far. There had been a few notable successes—like batteries, HDMI cables, and other electronics accessories that Amazon sold under the umbrella of Amazon Basics—but there had been some debacles as well. Amazon's Pinzon bed sheets were once recalled because the company missed a labeling requirement, according to an employee who worked on the brand. One of its outdoor furniture lines was discontinued after quality problems; many pieces were returned and had to be thrown out. Most famously, Amazon introduced diapers and baby wipes with fanfare in December 2014, under the mantle of Amazon Elements. The diapers were promptly buried in an avalanche of one-star reviews by parents complaining about poor fit and leaks. Amazon ignominiously withdrew the diapers from the market a few weeks later, and some employees felt that the public relations disaster contributed to Bezos's reticence to the idea of a single, high-profile consumables brand.

After the Bloom Street meeting with Bezos, Herrington and his team retooled their private-label strategy, creating several brands, including a few that weren't obviously linked to Amazon. With an assortment of slightly bizarre names, they started to appear on the website over the summer of 2016. There was Happy Belly coffee, snack items, and spices; Presto! household cleaning products; and Mama Bear provisions for new parents, including a relaunched diaper, manufactured this time by consumer goods giant Kimberly-Clark.

Wickedly Prime, a gourmet label that Bezos developed with Herrington and one of his deputies, Sunny Jain, debuted in late 2016 with eclectic snacks like coconut toffee roasted cashews, plantain chips, and fiery mango trail mix. A few months later, Amazon Elements was relaunched and preserved the brand's novel approach to ingredient transparency. The packaging of vitamins, supplements, and protein powder displayed an "authenticity code" that users could scan with a smartphone app to call up information about the product's ingredients and where it was made. Few customers took advantage of it.

Nevertheless, Bezos and other Amazon executives wanted the whole effort to move even faster. They set "S-team goals" such as requiring the team to grow product selection by a certain amount. Around five hundred such goals were established inside Amazon and approved by the leadership committee at the end of every calendar year, establishing the most important metrics for each business unit at the company. Teams that owned those goals were required to supply frequent updates on their progress and explanations if they fell behind schedule. It was a crucial way that the S-team managed a sprawling amalgamation of loosely affiliated business units.

With aggressive new benchmarks, the private-label team was now in the hot seat. They were being asked to fill gaps in Amazon's catalog with a steady stream of new products while keeping the quality level high and doing nothing to damage the company's reputation. Employees from that time describe a high-pressure environment, with various brand teams pitted against one another and everyone held accountable for their individual P&L statement. Meanwhile, Bezos was reviewing everything up to the artwork for new products and issuing a constant edict to *go faster*.

Numerous private-label employees later admitted to taking a shortcut out of this predicament: they exploited Amazon's massive treasure trove of data. Years later, this fact would become a significant focus of attention for regulators in the U.S. and Europe. They would demand to know: Did the company take advantage of the unique tools and proprietary information at its disposal as a retailer to give its house brands an unfair advantage? Did Amazon, in effect, *cheat* in its effort to compete directly with its own vendors and sellers?

One of Amazon's databases, Heartbeat, had all customer reviews across the website; accessing it allowed employees to look for revealing patterns that might indicate how they could improve well-established products. For example, customer reviews in the all-important category of dog poop bags indicated regular confusion about which end of the bag opened. So the Amazon Basics version included a blue arrow and the words "open this end." Another valuable tool was Amazon's Vine program, in which influential product reviewers received free samples in return for their written appraisals—and were thus more likely to produce more exuberant critiques.

Speaking on the condition of anonymity, several private-label managers admitted to exploiting a resource that was even more precious than product reviews—prominence in Amazon's search results. When they introduced a new brand, like Mama Bear diapers, a practice called "search seeding" allowed the brand managers to pin the initial relevancy score for the new product to the score of an established product, such as Pampers, at least for the first few days. The Amazon product would then appear at the top of search results, rather than starting on the unseen last page with other new brands.

When I asked Doug Herrington whether Amazon changed search results for its private-label products, he flatly denied the practice occurred. "We don't manipulate search results at all," he said. He added that Amazon brands were sometimes given prominent advertising slots in search results when they were a "great deal for the customer," and if customers didn't respond, the Amazon products quickly vanished. He also compared Amazon's tactics to those of competing physical retailers, who put generic products like painkillers right next to Tylenol and Advil, taking up limited shelf space. Amazon, on the other hand, had "infinite aisles," Herrington said, and customers could make selections from an extensive variety.

But Amazon's brand managers said these practices did occur, and that the impacts were substantial. JT Meng, the former private-label employee, recalled having to back off search seeding for Amazon Essential baby wipes because unit sales were exceeding 20 percent of the category's overall volume, which risked damaging the company's relationships with Procter & Gamble and Kimberly-Clark. An Amazon economist who worked with the private-label team added, "Brand managers were given really big goals and were like bulldogs. They would do anything they possibly could to get their stuff out there. That is just the Amazon way."

Amazon's critics and some of its sellers accused the company of exploiting another significant advantage. By looking at the sales data in the company's third-party marketplace, Amazon's private-label managers could rapidly identify new consumer trends and determine what products were selling well and should be copied. Amazon executives claimed they had safeguards in place to prevent this kind of data snooping from happening. "We don't use data about an individual seller to decide what items to produce for a private label," Jeff Wilke told me. The company also asserted this in congressional testimony in 2019: "We don't use individual seller data directly to compete," Amazon lawyer Nate Sutton testified.

But three managers from the push into private brands said this was simply not the case.

One who worked on a new lifestyle brand called Solimo said she originally assumed third-party data was off limits when she joined the company in 2016. A year into her job, her boss showed her how to access the sales data and told her to ask Amazon's data analysts if she needed help. The employee, who asked that her name not be used, subsequently examined third-party sales to determine the fastest-selling vitamin supplements, how many units were sold, and the average selling price and profitability of each.

To prove it, she shared a spreadsheet of probiotics sold by third-party sellers that she had kept from her time at Amazon. It showed individual marketplace sellers and their products, including the trailing twelve months of sales and average prices for each. "We would look at what our competitors were doing and sometimes copy it exactly, or just semi-customize it and throw a label on it," she said. "All along I was told there was a firewall, and then I learned it was a sort of a 'wink wink.'"

An article in the *Wall Street Journal* in 2020 reported similar accusations from former private-label employees, who dubbed the practice "going over the fence." The story recounted the ordeal of a four-person Brooklyn merchant, Fortem, which sold a foldable trunk organizer. Amazon spotted its success and prepared a competing product under the Amazon Basics banner. "We strictly prohibit our employees from using nonpublic, seller-specific data to determine which private label products to launch," Amazon told the *Journal*. The revelations added fuel to antitrust investigations in the U.S. and Europe.

The question, ultimately for regulators, was whether all this gave Amazon unfair advantages. Back in 2017, when Doug Herrington's private-label expansion was in full swing, the data and internal tools almost certainly helped amplify the team's efforts and meet their ambitious S-team goals. But much of the data they gleaned was also easily available to competitors, either by scraping the Amazon website or via research companies that collect data on consumer trends, like Nielsen. At least in consumables, many of the private-label products from that time—from Happy Belly peanut granola bars to Wickedly Prime roasted almonds—didn't appear to hurt rival brands, at least any more than the similar efforts of other large retailers. In a statement, Amazon added that "All retailers have information about brands and products that are popular in their stores, or that customers frequently ask about, and use that information to decide which private label products to offer."

The new products also did little to accelerate the popularity and profitability of Amazon's dueling home grocery initiatives, Prime Now and Amazon Fresh. The house brands had little of the appeal and salutary financial impact of the private labels at major grocery chains—like Whole Foods Market. Its 365 Everyday Value brand, attached to everything from milk to meat to maple syrup, conveyed a sense of being economical and wholesome while accounting for a significant percent of the chain's sales. Amazon, which remained largely the land of engineers, MBAs, and a CEO who considered himself a swashbuckling inventor, still didn't know how to harness that kind of magic.

———

But Bezos intended to keep trying. He had two additional ideas for how to forge a connection with grocery shoppers and solve the quandary of CRaP. They remain among the strangest projects in Amazon's history and provide an additional glimpse into its odd corporate rituals.

The first, which Bezos proposed in a free-flowing brainstorm session in 2014, started as a notion he called "the steak truck." Imagined as "an ice cream truck for adults," the original suggestion was to stock a van or truck with steaks, drive into neighborhoods with lights flashing and horn blaring, and sell them to residents, as Doug Herrington remembered it. It would be convenient and a great deal for customers, since the meat was being sold in bulk. Eventually, the company might even predict demand and eliminate the inefficiencies and wasted food of supermarkets.

The idea was perhaps just kooky enough that an executive was assigned to write a PR FAQ, the Amazon memo that kicks off the development of a new project by imagining its press release. The document gave the idea an official name: Treasure Truck. Bubble machines and digital displays would convey a carnival-like atmosphere while the truck sent out text alerts to the smartphones of nearby customers, announcing the item on sale that day.

Herrington assembled a two-pizza team to develop the project over the fall of 2014, alongside Prime Now and the private-label push. Though the idea itself was whimsical, the technical problems behind it were challenging, such as how the truck would announce its presence only to customers in the vicinity and keep meat and seafood properly chilled.

By the spring of 2015, the team had applied for two patents, but the project still hadn't launched. Employees started working long days and nights. They designed and purchased a prototype truck from a custom-vehicle maker in Chicago; it looked like a giant cardboard box that unfurled like a Transformer robot to reveal giant screens, blinking lights, and a spinning wheel bedecked with plastic salmon. Employees who worked on the project said the prototype cost about a quarter of a million dollars. They hid it in a South Lake Union parking garage and prepared to introduce the service that June with something far less perishable than steaks: a $99 deal for stand-up paddleboards.

Then the night before, after the press had been alerted to the unveiling, internal testing revealed a software bug that might erroneously inform customers who purchased the product that it was sold out. The launch was delayed, and beleaguered project members had to come in on a Saturday to analyze the issue. Amazon also sent in the "principal engineers": an elite squad of about a dozen technical wizards at the company who parachute into troubled projects to diagnose problems.

The principal engineers interrogated Treasure Truck employees for two weeks and authored the "correction of error" or COE report, the top-secret document prepared inside Amazon when something goes awry. In the middle of this painful self-examination, disaster struck again: a junior employee accidentally triggered the release of text messages to all the customers who had signed up for Treasure

Truck, incorrectly announcing the imminent sale, and the $99 paddleboards. The Seattle tech blog *GeekWire*, which had vigorously covered the entire saga, declared that the project was "quickly reaching the status of the most-bungled product launch in Amazon history."

Seven months later, with the old project managers swept out and new ones installed, the Treasure Truck finally started rolling over the hills of Seattle, hawking GoPro cameras at a 64 percent discount. Over the next few months, the truck would sell Shigoku oysters, wild king salmon, Thanksgiving turkeys, new models of the Amazon Echo, and *Harry Potter and the Cursed Child*. The team commissioned new trucks, not as garish or pricey as the original, and expanded to twenty-five major U.S. cities.

But the service was never as ubiquitous or as endearing as Jeff Bezos and Doug Herrington had hoped. Internet critics were baffled by the project and sneered at some of the more inexplicable deals ("bidet sprayers for $19.99, 33% off!"). One empty Treasure Truck burst into flames in a West Philadelphia parking lot at 1:30 a.m. Bezos briefly touted the initiative in his 2017 shareholder letter, but an executive on the finance team told me that it never performed particularly well or was close to profitable. If Amazon wanted to arouse excitement and loyalty for its fledgling grocery services, it needed something else entirely—like a unique product that customers were passionate about.

Well, Bezos had an idea for that as well and it was just as bizarre. In August 2015, the *Washington Post* published an unappetizing article about how a single hamburger might contain the meat of up to a hundred cows. Sourcing a burger from just a single cow could theoretically produce a superior-tasting patty but that "would be hard and expensive," a meat distributor told the paper.

That caught Bezos's attention. He seemed to have increasingly adventurous tastes, later sampling an iguana, for example, at a meeting of New York City's Explorers Club. In another brainstorming meeting with Herrington, he suggested they find a ranch to produce a "single cow burger" and make it a unique item that customers could only buy from

Amazon. "I really think you should try this," Bezos told Herrington, who recalled thinking at first it was a joke. "How hard can it be?"

The project was assigned to a new culinary innovations team inside Amazon Fresh and immediately established as an S-team goal—a high-priority benchmark monitored closely by Bezos and the leadership council. A product manager named Megan Rosseter was then charged with finding a way to actually produce it. The meat vendors she initially contacted told her that such a thing was totally impractical and would in fact be disruptive to their operations. "I felt like I was always getting crazy daunting goals that seemed almost impossible," she said.

Somehow, Rosseter and her colleagues found a ranch in San Diego County, near the Mexican border, that could produce the burger. They worked with the ranch that spring, devising ways to freeze the meat for transport and designing packaging that wouldn't leak when it was defrosted. In June 2016, Amazon splashed Single Cow Burger promotions on the Fresh website and smartphone app, advertising half-pound Wagyu beef burgers with 80 percent lean meat and 20 percent fat. The company also prepped Alexa with an answer should anyone ever ask it for a definition: "Single cow burger: a beef burger made with meat from just a single cow."

The initial feedback from customers was promising. "These burgers are HUGE, JUICY and DELICIOUS!!!" wrote a reviewer on the Amazon website. But a few months later, Bezos sent an email to Fresh executives. He felt that the packaging was too difficult to open and complained that the burger was so fatty that dripping fat had caused his grill to flame up.

Rosseter believed that premium Wagyu beef should be cooked in a cast iron skillet and not on a grill. But she was not about to give unsolicited cooking advice to her CEO. She was also astonished that Bezos seemed to care so much. "It was definitely one of those 'I can't believe this is actually happening moments' in my life," she said.

So Rosseter went back to her supplier, who subcontracted the work to another ranch in Georgia that could produce Heritage Aberdeen Angus beef burgers with 91 percent lean meat and only 9 percent fat. After repeated trips to taste-test variations, Rosseter had a second single cow burger, with easy-to-peel packaging, ready to go by January 2017. The Fresh team sent a sample to Bezos's office, and word came back a few days later that he was satisfied.

The project once again represented a different style of innovation within Amazon. Employees didn't "work backwards" from their idealized customers, who had never asked for such a creation. They worked backwards from Bezos's intuition and were catering to his sometimes eclectic tastes (literally). Bezos was right a lot, particularly when it came to cutting-edge technology. But in the end, the single cow burger and other culinary innovations introduced within Amazon Fresh generated little buzz or increased business.

Rosseter stuck it out for a few months but felt her efforts were not being recognized. She called the work environment "stressful and unhappy." So she prepared to leave Amazon Fresh, right as a bomb was dropped on top of it.

———

On April 21, 2017, Matt Yale, the head of regulatory affairs at Tusk Ventures, one of the firms advising Whole Foods amid the assault from activist investors, called Jay Carney, an acquaintance from the Obama administration. Would Amazon be interested in meeting with the organic grocer to discuss a strategic transaction? Carney referred the contact to Bezos and Jeff Wilke, who passed it along to Peter Krawiec, Amazon's vice president of worldwide corporate development. On April 27, the two companies started negotiating under the veil of a strict nondisclosure agreement.

Amazon did not appear to equivocate much when deciding to respond favorably to the outreach. The company had expanded: Prime Now was in thirty-three U.S. cities and a handful overseas; Amazon Fresh in fourteen metro regions, as well as London and Germany.

But they remained unprofitable and were achieving neither leverage nor scale. Prices were high and product selection was unremarkable. While the private-label efforts inside Amazon's electronics and fashion divisions had taken off, thanks in part to the unique and controversial search and data tools employees used, the strangely named brands from the consumables group had not. Few customers were clamoring for Wickedly Prime fiery mango trail mix. Treasure Trucks and single cow burgers weren't making much of an impact either.

Another rising competitor to worry about had also emerged, in addition to Instacart and Google Express. In 2016, Walmart acquired the e-commerce startup Jet.com for $3.3 billion. Its founder Marc Lore was now running Walmart's domestic e-commerce efforts and still held a grudge over the way Amazon had outmaneuvered and acquired his previous company, Quidsi, which operated the website Diapers.com. He was smartly focusing on the online grocery opportunity, using the retail giant's forty-five-hundred-plus U.S. stores as delivery hubs and pickup points and making real headway where Amazon had not.

So on Sunday, April 30, 2017, John Mackey and three deputies flew from Austin to Seattle to meet Bezos, Krawiec, Steve Kessel, and Doug Herrington in the boathouse of Bezos's home on Lake Washington. Mackey recounted the long, proud history of Whole Foods Market, noting that the grocer had almost single-handedly popularized the consumption of kale. But now there were rapacious activist investors at his door. "I love this company. I want to stay independent, but it doesn't look like that's going to happen," Mackey said, according to Doug Herrington's recollection. "If I have to be acquired, there's one company that I have respect and admiration for, and that is Amazon."

Mackey would later describe the conversation "like falling in love. . . . We were finishing each other's sentences before the first meeting was over." Bezos, of course, had a fondness for entrepreneurs. He and Mackey were a lot alike in some ways: detail-oriented, stubborn about their visions, and pugnacious in response to public criticism. But Mackey didn't have the same mastery of technology or talent for constant reinvention as Bezos. Whole Foods stores hadn't changed much in decades, and as a result, his brand of corporate consistency and idealism was endangered.

Throughout May, as it continued to indulge proposals from Albertsons, Whole Foods negotiated in secret with Amazon, responding to a constant stream of requests for more information. On May 23, Amazon offered to buy the company for $41 dollars a share, nearly a 27 percent premium over its share price. Amazon added that it wouldn't negotiate further and threatened to withdraw the offer if it leaked. Whole Foods responded by asking for $45; Amazon upped the amount, barely, to $42 per share, and said that was its final offer.

The companies announced the $13.7 billion deal on June 16, 2017, shocking the world. The most famous e-commerce company was buying one of the most iconic grocery chains. Jeff Wilke flew to Austin that morning, where he joined Whole Foods' executives at an all-hands meeting in the company auditorium. Mackey triumphantly announced that he would remain as CEO under the marriage with Amazon—"until death do us part." He also mocked Wilke mercilessly for appearing to refer to quinoa as a vegetable.

In a remarkable sign of Wall Street's confidence in Bezos's every move, the deal sent shares of Amazon skyrocketing that day and added $15.6 billion to its market cap, pushing it past $475 billion. (It also temporarily sent the stocks of rival grocers spiraling downward and was a boon for Instacart, which was quickly the beneficiary of their panicked scramble to move online and counter the Amazon threat.) Charles Kantor, managing director of Neuberger Berman, who had arguably started the entire chain of events with his letter-writing campaign, told Reuters that because of the stock appreciation, "there's the argument that Amazon acquired Whole Foods for free."

But there would be a price to pay, although it remained largely invisible to outsiders. Amazon now had to reconcile a decade of overlapping grocery initiatives and combine them with 465 physical stores and their accompanying supply chain and antiquated technology systems. When the next discussion between Bezos and Wilke turned to which executive should take charge of the herculean effort and oversee Mackey and his team, they gave it to Steve Kessel, who ran Amazon Go and the bookstores, and had the smallest organization.

The Federal Trade Commission approved the merger in August, judging that the companies were not significant rivals and that the acquisition did not substantially lessen competition. Afterward, Kessel implemented some quick changes. Discounts for Prime members, Amazon Lockers, and Kindle and Alexa devices all arrived at Whole Foods stores. On Amazon's website and smartphone apps, the struggling private brands were quickly complemented by Whole Foods' much larger selection of 365 Everyday Value products. The grocery chain also got credit for lowering its prices—John Mackey's perpetual bugaboo—for perhaps the first time ever. And Amazon introduced uniform standards and stricter financial terms to Whole Foods suppliers.

One thing Amazon didn't do was turn over the Whole Foods management team. The activist investors had darkly joked about how many days it would take Bezos to fire John Mackey. But Bezos often allowed acquired companies and their eccentric CEOs to operate autonomously, as he had years before with the late Tony Hsieh and Zappos. He preferred to learn from their experience and harvest the data and business lessons that emerged.

Now Bezos had to find alignment among Amazon's divergent approaches in the trickiest product category it had ever encountered. So he also gave Steve Kessel authority over Prime Now and Amazon Fresh. Over the next few years, Kessel would combine the two services into a curious hybrid: the website, smartphone app, and brand name of Amazon Fresh largely supplanted Prime Now (though the Prime Now app was preserved for its fans). The new Fresh experience was then overlaid on Prime Now's supply chain of centrally located urban warehouses and flexible fleet of contract drivers. And the products in Whole Foods stores and warehouses were added to the selection—which had been Amazon's goal years before, with the Copperfield effort, proving once again that acquisitions, rather than partnerships, were the more viable path for a company of Amazon's size and forbidding reputation. Kessel also unified the disparate, often warring grocery teams behind a single manager—Stephenie Landry, who had successfully rolled out Prime Now.

Back in 2012, Doug Herrington had predicted that Amazon's future was in the low-price and barely profitable items that people bought every day. "We can't reach our $400 billion aspirations with today's business model, and there's good reason to fear we won't make the necessary transformation," he had warned solemnly in his memo. But it turned out the fear was unfounded; five years later, Amazon sold an enormous assortment of CRaP. That left the truly hard work: storing it and getting it to customers' doorsteps, via one of the largest armies of low-wage workers and drivers that the world has ever seen.

CHAPTER 9

The Last Mile

To understand how Amazon came to operate one of the largest and most sophisticated logistics and transportation networks anywhere, we must again go back, even further this time, to the company's life-or-death struggle during the dot-com boom and bust. When a bespectacled twenty-six-year-old former middle-school band teacher named Dave Clark joined Amazon in 1999, the company operated only seven warehouses in the U.S. and three in Europe, which were barely able to handle the frenetic holiday sales peak. By the time he took over as head of global operations in 2012, Amazon ran around forty fulfillment centers in the U.S. and another two dozen overseas. But the massive buildings were mostly located in remote areas, a strategy to minimize Amazon's labor expenses and tax burden, not to best serve customers. They also relied on lower-wage employees walking an average of twelve miles a day to find and pick the right items from shelves.

By August 2017, after it had agreed to collect sales taxes in most U.S. states and completed its acquisition of Whole Foods Market, Amazon's supply chain looked dramatically different. It was comprised of around 140 FCs in the U.S. and another few dozen abroad, many of them in urban areas and crowded with squat orange robots zooming to and from employees, carrying yellow stacks of shelves crammed with merchandise. Amazon also had hundreds of new smaller buildings: sortation centers that organized packages by zip codes, Prime

Now centers for groceries, delivery stations where contract drivers picked up packages for transport to customers' homes, and airport hubs for a new fleet of gleaming white cargo jets with "Prime Air" written in blue font on the side.

Along with the booming growth in the number of its facilities, Amazon's treatment of its warehouse workers had also become the subject of increasing scrutiny. Media accounts portrayed Amazon as a callous employer that prioritized profit over safety and evaded responsibility for the injuries and even deaths caused by its delivery operations. Clark, by then one of the few executives on the S-team who bantered with Amazon's critics and challenged criticisms online, responded aggressively to every charge, proclaiming that safety was Amazon's top priority. "Senator, you have been misinformed," Clark tweeted at Connecticut senator Richard Blumenthal in September 2019, after he accused the company of taking a "heartless" and "morally bankrupt" approach toward public safety.

Dave Clark grew up in the small town of Dalton, Georgia, the self-proclaimed "carpet capital of the world" for its high concentration of rug factories. His father was a tinkerer and itinerant entrepreneur, according to Clark, who worked on radio technology and built nine-hole golf courses as well as several houses and often conscripted his only child to dig the footings for the foundation walls. When he was nine years old, his parents piled carpet into a fifty-three-foot moving truck and moved to a suburb of Jacksonville, Florida, to open a rug store.

Clark's mother fought a losing battle with cancer when he was in high school, and to "get out of their hair a little bit," he got a job as a bag boy at a Publix supermarket, and later at the defunct chain Service Merchandise—good training for when Clark took oversight of another physical retailer, Whole Foods Market. He paid his way through Auburn University as the equipment manager for the music department, and after graduating with a degree in music education, he directed the beginner's marching band at his former junior high school for a year. "Teaching 250 seventh graders who have never played an instrument before prepares you for a lot of challenges in life," he later told me.

While Clark attended business school at the University of Tennessee in Knoxville, he met Jimmy Wright, a charismatic former Walmart executive whom Jeff Bezos employed briefly in the late 1990s to try to build a new class of Amazon distribution centers. At Wright's prompting, Clark and several classmates went to Seattle to interview, even though others at the company back then considered Amazon a haven for engineers, not MBAs. "We know why you're here," a recruiter told Clark as he waited in the lobby. "We don't like it, so don't expect to have a great day."

Clark nevertheless got an entry-level analyst job in the operations division after graduation. One of his first tasks was studying compensation rates for hourly employees; then he was sent to Tokyo, to help set up Amazon's first warehouse there. He had to get his very first passport for the trip. After that, Clark was deployed to a fulfillment center in Campbellsville, Kentucky, which would have an even bigger impact on him. The web of relationships he formed there would end up shaping both his personal life and the future of Amazon's operations.

The facility's general manager was Arthur Valdez, whose mother had traveled to the U.S. from Cuba in the same mass migration, Operation Pedro Pan, as Bezos's father, Mike Bezos. Growing up in Colorado Springs, he had been steeped in the world of logistics; both of his parents drove for UPS and the family ran a pharmaceutical delivery business on the side.

But none of that prepared Valdez for the deluge of orders and insanity that inundated Amazon's warehouses every holiday season. Valdez recalled having so much trouble even paying the temp agencies that were supplying Amazon with seasonal labor that Bezos had to wire money into his personal account so he could write them checks. Whenever the FC was late to ship orders, he had to email

Bezos and Wilke, explaining what happened and how he would fix it. At one point, Valdez was so inundated that his message to Seattle contained a single world of capitulation in the subject line: "uncle."

In response, Wilke sent reinforcements. Dave Clark oversaw the flow of packages out of the Campbellsville FC. To manage the inbound flow from suppliers, Wilke also transferred Mike Roth, a German logistics executive from Amazon's subsidiary in Leipzig. Both reported to Valdez.

Together, the trio navigated daunting challenges. In 2000, Amazon bolstered its fragile balance sheet by agreeing to handle online sales for the retail chain Toys "R" Us, with all merchandise sent to Campbellsville. The following year, it struck the same arrangement with Target. The excess inventory overwhelmed the 770,000-square-foot building. To keep up, Valdez, Clark, and Roth leased some six hundred tractor trailers, stocked them with overflow, and parked them around the tiny town (population: nine thousand). "It was pure survival," Valdez said.

In 2002, a snowstorm hit the Midwest during the crucial days before Christmas. Amazon had contracted with a line-haul trucking company to transport orders from the FC to the UPS hub in Louisville, ninety miles away. With the storm moving in, the anxious driver departed early, leaving scores of boxes behind. Amazon workers loaded the remaining boxes into a rented Ryder van; Clark drove, navigating the icy roads, while Valdez sat in the passenger's seat. Along the way, they stopped at a Burger King drive-thru.

In Louisville, they encountered a closed gate at the UPS facility. The building was run by the International Brotherhood of Teamsters, and only union members were permitted to unload packages. Amazon was anti-union, maintaining that they interceded between the company and its workers and made it more difficult to serve the hallowed customer. Valdez, whose only goal was to off-load those packages in time for Christmas delivery, got the facility manager on the phone and convinced him to let them in.

But the manager warned the Amazon execs they better move quickly. Clark backed the Ryder van into the loading dock, and nonunion UPS managers off-loaded the boxes while the Teamsters sprinted over, incensed. They jumped onto the van, pounding on the windows and hood, yelling at Clark and Valdez to leave. Clark would later recount that story to employees; it was an example of Amazon's "customer obsession," he said, but it also happened to convey one of the reasons for Amazon's deep antipathy to organized labor: union workers often seemed reflexively opposed to the many improvised adjustments that were necessary for Amazon to fulfill its promises to customers.

Overall, the Campbellsville FC experience was a formative one for Valdez, Clark, and Roth. They spent considerable time with Bezos and Wilke, who visited each fall as part of their old whistle-stop tour of all Amazon's warehouses. They introduced Bezos to cigars and bourbon on one visit. Clark also met his future wife, Leigh Anne, in town; she was the daughter of the family that owned the restaurant at the local golf club.

After their stint in Campbellsville, Valdez, Clark, and Roth each circulated through a series of increasingly prominent positions at Amazon. Their development into senior leaders was the story of Amazon operations itself—a human one, full of ingenious solutions to hard problems, as well as petty grudges and deeply held orthodoxies that would have consequences for the company and society. At its heart was a friendship that would last for fifteen years. When Clark and Leigh Anne got married at the Fairmont Olympic Hotel in downtown Seattle in May 2008, Mike Roth was an usher, and Arthur Valdez was his best man.

After their tour of duty in Campbellsville, Roth transferred to the UK to address problems with the fulfillment network there, while Valdez moved to Dallas to oversee the network of non-sortable FCs, which stored and shipped big and bulky items like furniture and flat-screen TVs. With a hearty endorsement from Valdez, Dave Clark was promoted to general manager of a fulfillment center in New Castle, Delaware, about forty-five minutes south of Philadelphia.

Colleagues said that Clark had raw management skills and a temper that flared when employees didn't carefully follow his instructions. He earned a nickname, "the Sniper," for his proclivity to lurk quietly on the sidelines and identify and fire slacking underlings. He could also be cavalier toward his employees. At all-hands meetings, he would invariably brush aside questions by answering, "I'll get back to you on that," but rarely would. Finally, at one meeting, fed-up workers packed the first few rows wearing T-shirts that read, "I'll get back to you on that." Clark later insisted that he appreciated the feedback and even kept one of the shirts.

Still, results from the Delaware FC were good, and Clark was impressing the only person who mattered at the time: operations chief Jeff Wilke. "He proved to me that with authentic leadership, he could get a large group of people, including a very tenured and opinionated workforce, to follow him," Wilke said.

Clark's purview over Amazon's East Coast operations gradually expanded over the next few years, until he was promoted to Seattle in 2008 to take a job as director of a program called ACES or the Amazon Customer Excellence System. It required him to advocate for the principles of Lean manufacturing, a methodology popularized by Toyota in its factories that called for minimizing waste, maximizing productivity, and empowering employees. The role gave him a front-row seat to a philosophical debate that would end up shaping life inside Amazon's rapidly growing fulfillment network.

Clark's new boss and the primary evangelist for the Lean method was Marc Onetto, a boisterous French executive from General Electric who took over for Jeff Wilke as head of operations when Bezos promoted Wilke to run all of domestic retail. Onetto was a Lean fanatic. He introduced roles like the "water spider," a helper in the fulfillment centers who brought workers anything they needed, like extra packing tape; and he pushed the concept of "poka-yoke," or designs that prevent human errors, such as a cafeteria trash can whose opening is too small for a meal tray to be carelessly discarded.

One of Onetto's goals was to promote empathy and teamwork in Amazon's operations, which Seattle managers worried had grown heartless and punitive. At the time, the company was measuring worker productivity in every way possible and aggressively "stack ranking," or firing the lowest performing percentile of workers every year. Toyota's Lean method, on the other hand, modeled a lifetime of work for the same company. But Jeff Bezos vehemently disagreed with that approach, and his and Onetto's marked differences in philosophy and style led to a series of significant clashes.

In 2009, Onetto's human resources deputy, David Niekerk, wrote a paper titled "Respect for People," and presented it at an S-team meeting. The paper drew from Toyota's proven Lean ideology and argued for "treating people fairly," building "mutual trust between managers and associates," and empowering leaders to inspire employees rather than act as disciplinarians.

Bezos hated it. He not only railed against it in the meeting but called Niekerk the following morning to continue the browbeating. Amazon should never imply that it didn't have respect for people embedded in the very fabric of how it operated, he said. Bezos also solemnly declared that one of the biggest threats to the company was a disgruntled and entrenched hourly workforce—like the unionized workers that impaired U.S. automakers with strikes and onerous contract negotiations. (Amazon later denied that Bezos said this.) He encouraged Niekerk and Onetto to focus on ensuring that FC workers who weren't advancing within Amazon stayed for a maximum of three years.

Amazon then made several changes in its warehouses to ward off this danger. Where previously workers had been eligible for small raises in their hourly wage every six months for five years, now raises were cut off after three years, unless an employee was promoted or the compensation plan for their entire facility was adjusted upward. Amazon also instituted a program called Pay to Quit, inspired by a similar one at Zappos, which it had recently acquired, that offered several thousand dollars to workers who were no longer engaged in their jobs and wanted to leave the company.

Bezos expressed this stern paternalism in other ways as well. When Onetto and Niekerk proposed a broad employee education program that would furnish FC workers with up to $5,500 per year in tuition assistance toward a four-year college degree, Bezos replied, "I don't understand why you are so determined to set up our employees for failure." He then explained that for a vast majority of Americans, a standard college degree with majors in subjects like art and literature won't lead directly to better opportunities with higher pay outside the warehouses. The resulting program, Career Choice, offered on-site classes and tuition reimbursement tied specifically to in-demand professions like IT, healthcare, and transportation.

After these battles, Marc Onetto's tenure at Amazon grew increasingly turbulent. In S-team gatherings, he liked to talk about his time at GE working for famed CEO Jack Welch. But the leadership meetings were supposed to be all about checking your past experiences and ego at the door. Eventually, Onetto's standing with Bezos became so poor that his teams would ask him to remain silent or not even attend when they were presenting.

Among the final straws for Onetto was a September 2011 story in the *Morning Call* newspaper in Allentown, Pennsylvania. The paper reported that the company's warehouse in the Lehigh Valley had gotten so swelteringly hot that summer that workers were passing out and being transported to nearby hospitals by ambulances that Amazon had waiting outside. An ER doctor even called federal regulators to report an unsafe work environment.

It was a disaster that should have been avoided. Before the incident, Onetto had presented a white paper to the S-team that included a few paragraphs proposing to install rooftop air-conditioning units in Amazon's facilities. But according to Niekerk, Bezos bluntly dismissed the request, citing the cost. After the *Morning Call* article drew widespread condemnation, Bezos approved the $52 million expense, establishing a pattern of making changes only after he read criticism in the media. But he also criticized Onetto for not anticipating the crisis.

Fuming, Onetto prepared to remind Bezos of his original proposal. Colleagues begged him to let it go, but he couldn't. As they anticipated, the meeting did not go well. Bezos said that as a matter of fact, he did remember the paper and that it was so poorly written and ambiguous that no one had understood what course of action Onetto was recommending. As other S-team members cringed, Bezos declared that the entire incident was evidence of what happens when Amazon puts people in top jobs who can't articulate their ideas clearly and support them with data.

Years later, Onetto, unfailingly polite, was generous in his recollections of the tensions with Bezos and expressed pride in his time at Amazon. "When you run operations, there are always tough moments because you are a cost center and you are always the one who screwed up," said Onetto, who announced his intention to retire in 2012. "There were instances where I would pitch something to Bezos and let's say in a nice way that he was not happy. But I don't want to be critical. Many times, he was right."

By that point, Dave Clark had been promoted to vice president overseeing all the North American fulfillment centers and was about to make a bet that would position him as Onetto's successor while inexorably altering the nature of work inside Amazon warehouses.

Bezos didn't want another empathetic business philosopher to replace Onetto as the head of Amazon's operations; he sought an uncompromising operator who could gain operating leverage by slowing down the growth of costs in the FCs relative to Amazon's skyrocketing sales. Fulfillment expenses had jumped by 58 percent in 2011 and 40 percent in 2012. Amazon hired fifty thousand temporary workers in its domestic FCs over the 2012 holidays alone; those numbers would keep going up and up and up to meet anticipated increases in sales. The new operations leader would have to take a hard-nosed run at the entire supply chain and figure out how to use technology to get more efficient.

Clark was a leading contender for the job. A major part of his candidacy was his bid to acquire the North Reading, Massachusetts–based robotics startup, Kiva Systems, which made the Roomba-like mobile robots. Instead of pickers walking a dozen miles a day to select items from shelves spread out over giant warehouses, Kiva robots maneuvered portable containers of merchandise around the building, an orchestral symphony conducted by the invisible hand of software.

The idea behind Kiva was born from the same disaster that had inspired Doug Herrington to propose Amazon Fresh. After Webvan went bankrupt, one of its executives, Mick Mountz, realized that e-commerce companies were essentially paying people to spend two-thirds of their time walking. He conceived of a robotics system that would instead transport shelves of merchandise to workers, increasing their productivity and eliminating potential bottlenecks in warehouse aisles. A few years later, his startup, Disrobot Systems, changed its name to Kiva, a Hopi word relating to ant colonies.

Over the next few years, Mountz and his colleagues developed prototypes, raised venture capital, and sold their robots to companies like Staples, Dell, and Walgreens. They pitched Amazon unsuccessfully a few times and even conducted a pilot for Herrington and Amazon Fresh. Amazon then acquired two of Kiva's customers, Zappos and Quidsi in 2009 and 2010 respectively, but afterward mothballed their robots. Mountz believed Amazon was trying to incite skepticism about the startup in the tech industry. Then Amazon made a low-ball offer to buy Kiva over the spring of 2011. Mountz rejected the proposal.

At the same time, Amazon began quietly evaluating other robotics companies and asking them to build a mobile warehouse robot. The effort failed though, and Amazon increased its offer for Kiva. An investment banker who represented Kiva said that the subsequent talks "were the most painful negotiations I've ever been through," with Amazon characteristically arguing every point. After the $775 million deal closed in early 2012, Kiva execs visited Seattle and saw one of Amazon's unsuccessful robot prototypes parked in a conference room.

The deal to acquire Kiva Systems was Dave Clark's baby—he implicitly understood its potential to remake the FCs and turn Amazon's surging variable labor costs into a more predictable fixed investment in robotics and software. In a meeting to discuss the acquisition, according to a *Bloomberg* profile of Clark years later, he pushed an imaginary pile of chips on the conference room table and said, "I only know one way to play poker—that's all-in."

Before the deal with Amazon closed, Mountz was adamant about continuing to grow Kiva's business of selling robots to other retailers. Clark said he was fine with that. "I don't care if you sell to Walmart. com if you want to, they can fund our growth," he told Mountz. Mountz relayed those reassurances to Kiva's customers, but he didn't get Clark's promise in writing. Two years after the acquisition, Clark and Wilke decided the tactical advantage conferred by the robots was too valuable and, one by one, turned off the supply of Kiva robots to other companies.

Mountz was disappointed. "I was burning relationships I had built in the industry for years," he said. "I was pretty sour on the whole experience." He tried to appeal directly to Bezos but didn't get anywhere.

Instead Bezos, Mountz recalled, was mostly fixated on the potential of robotic arms in the FCs. As a way to indulge the CEO's interest and stimulate research in the field, his Kiva cofounder, Peter Wurman, proposed a competition among universities called the Amazon Picking Challenge to try to find a robot that could do a better job than humans lifting items off a shelf. The contest, with a meager top prize of $20,000, lasted three years and probably attracted more media hand-wringing about the potential of robots to steal human jobs than actual advancements in robotics.

Over the next few years, Amazon methodically redesigned the Kiva robots and moved Kiva's software to AWS. Then it introduced the machines into its newer FCs, with profound results. As Clark had hoped, they magnified worker productivity and decreased the rate of growth of Amazon's seasonal labor needs relative to its sales. They also allowed Amazon to build denser fulfillment centers, with the shelf-toting robots swarming over the ground floor as well as a series of reinforced mezzanines. In a 2014 TV interview, Clark estimated that Amazon was able to get 50 percent more products per square foot into new fulfillment centers than the previous generation.

The robots also transformed labor that was physically exhausting, characterized by endless walking, into work that was instead mentally straining, with employees standing in place and monotonously repeating the same movements over and over. (A 2020 report in the Center for Investigative Reporting's *Reveal* magazine cited an OSHA letter to Amazon that said the robots exposed employees to "ergonomic risk factors" including stress from repeated movements and standing for up to ten hours a day.) Just as the tyrannical invisible force of software guided the robot swarms, it also monitored worker performance, flagging any quantifiable decrease in productivity and subjecting employees to performance improvement plans and possible termination.

The acquisition of Kiva established Clark's credentials as the kind of transcending leader Bezos sought to run operations. He took over the role from Marc Onetto in 2012 and was promoted to senior vice president the following year. Clark now had a spot on the S-team, and his old Campbellsville buddies, Mike Roth and Arthur Valdez, were back by his side in Seattle as deputies—ready to help him implement Jeff Bezos's most audacious vision yet.

———

Like many of the managers at Amazon who so snugly fit the Bezosian leadership template, Clark's intellect trumped his emotional intelligence. He liked to talk about his family and Auburn football and could speak with eloquence and even a sense of romanticism about Amazon's mission of serving customers. But dozens of operations employees also described their boss as a truculent personality who hardly acknowledged others in the halls and was reluctant to meet with anyone below the rank of vice president as his organization grew.

On one of his first conference calls with his direct reports after taking the top operations job from Onetto, Clark stunned his subordinates by casually recalling his old nickname from the East Coast FCs—the Sniper. Many later recalled with trepidation his notorious sayings, such as "There's no room for art degrees here" (even though he himself was a music education major). At one memorable meeting to review a team's proposal to put RFID chips into Amazon pallets and packages, to better track them through the FCs, Clark walked in, apparently unimpressed with the plan, and said: "Tell me why I shouldn't just fire all of you right now."

But all of that was handily overshadowed by Clark's strengths—a sharp, analytical mind and masterful ability to dive into the most intricate level of detail to identify problems and negative trends. He possessed a crucial skill at Amazon that was about to prove exceedingly useful: he could take Bezos's ambitious visions, convert them into something approximating reality, and then grow them into systems that didn't blow apart at Amazon's tremendous size.

Over Christmas 2013, UPS, Amazon's primary shipping partner, was overwhelmed by the volume of last-minute orders amid a confluence of bad weather and the sharp increase in the popularity of online shopping. UPS's 5.2-million-square-foot Worldport center in Louisville, one of the largest package handling facilities in the world, choked on the onslaught and failed to deliver an estimated hundreds of thousands of Amazon packages in time for the holiday. Clark was furious, colleagues recalled, castigating UPS execs over the phone and browbeating them into helping Amazon compensate disappointed customers with $20 gift cards and refunds on shipping charges.

But the "Christmas fiasco," as Amazon operations employees dubbed it, was not entirely the shipping company's fault and may have been inevitable. It is worth slowing down for a moment to examine why. Amazon's famed flywheel was beginning to spin faster at the time, with the ranks of Prime members growing by millions every holiday season and merchandise streaming into its FCs from third-party sellers.

Amazon ran its fulfillment centers seven days a week, to keep up with customers ordering from its website around the clock. But UPS and FedEx, a less significant Amazon shipping partner, didn't operate on Sundays or on national holidays. The difference didn't matter for most of the year, but after the extended Thanksgiving holiday—which included the Black Friday shopping extravaganza—the delivery companies' networks became woefully backlogged.

Amazon harangued UPS and FedEx to deliver over the weekend and to build more capacity to keep up with Amazon's surging growth. But they were wary; Amazon alone could stretch the shipping companies' employees to the breaking point and devour all of their shipping capacity, leaving no room for other customers. Amazon also negotiated ferociously every few years to procure ever-steeper discounts. For the shipping companies, the online retailer generated increasing revenues while eroding the fat, double-digit profit margins that kept their investors happy and stock prices buoyant.

UPS and FedEx tried to mitigate Amazon's corrosive effects by levying surcharges and capping its use of their air freight networks over the holidays. Amazon executives didn't appreciate that. Four

employees from that time told me they heard Clark and other senior Amazon executives gripe about FedEx and say that its founder,
Fred Smith, "surrounds himself with sycophants and has completely
off-the-charts arrogance." The obvious irony, even to Clark's employees, was that this could describe Amazon's senior leaders too.

All of these tensions culminated after UPS failed so prominently
over the 2013 holiday season. Amazon executives had had enough.
If they couldn't reliably count on the shipping companies to support
their growth, the company would have to build an in-house logistics
network—controlling merchandise from the warehouses of its suppliers to its fulfillment centers, and all the way to customers' doorsteps.

The day after the 2013 holiday meltdown, Clark called Michael
Indresano, a former FedEx executive who had joined Amazon as a
transportation director, and asked how many "sortation centers" they
could build before the next holiday peak. These were the facilities
that consolidated packages by zip code and injected them into the
U.S. Postal Service for last-mile delivery to people's homes.

Indresano estimated that he could open sixteen by the end of
2014. "Build 'em all!" Clark replied. Inside Amazon, the rapid creation of sort centers in cities like Atlanta, Miami, and Nashville was
dubbed "the Sweet 16."

During this buildout, Amazon packages also began showing up
to customers' homes on Sundays. Bezos, said an ops executive, was
frustrated with UPS and FedEx's refusal to deliver over the weekends.
Clark and his colleagues had found an ingenious solution: a deal with
the USPS to deliver on the proverbial day of rest. The arrangement
quickly reinforced the post office as Amazon's top carrier by volume
and allowed Amazon to achieve a total lower cost per delivery than it
could achieve by using UPS and FedEx.

Amazon's sort centers, combined with Sunday delivery, changed
the experience of being a Prime member. Customers no longer had
to abandon their online shopping cart on a Friday afternoon and visit
the mall for instant gratification. Proud of the achievement, Bezos

brought Amazon's board of directors to San Bernardino, California, to tour one of the new facilities.

But the sort centers and Sunday delivery were only the first step toward the goal of an in-house logistics network. Amazon was never entirely comfortable relying on the USPS, just as it was distrustful of UPS and FedEx. The post office was subject to unpredictable political forces and the lingering public perception that it provided a less reliable service. So Clark and his colleagues began pitching their most ambitious move yet: a so-called "last mile" network to customers' homes. If it couldn't count on the giant package carriers to keep up with its growth, it would simply oversee the delivery of orders itself.

A primary concern, said executives who were in those meetings, was not whether Amazon could effectively build such a complex network. Rather, it revolved around whether getting into the transportation business would increase Amazon's exposure to unions. Delivery stations would have to be placed in the urban areas where most of Amazon's customers lived—places like New York City and New Jersey that were the locus of the organized labor movement.

Clark and his colleagues assuaged themselves by considering the nonunion workforces of FedEx Ground, DHL, and pretty much every other ground delivery firm that competed with UPS and its unionized delivery workforce. Amazon would use the exact same model in creating Amazon Logistics, its new transportation division. It wouldn't directly hire anyone but instead create relationships with independent delivery companies—DSPs (delivery service partners)—that employed nonunion drivers. That would allow it to pay lower labor rates than UPS and to avoid the prospective nightmare of drivers bargaining collectively for higher wages, which could destroy the already fragile economics of home delivery.

Such arm's-length deals with drivers would indemnify Amazon from all of the unseemly and inevitable corollaries of the transportation business—such as botched deliveries, driver misbehavior, or worse, car accidents and deaths. Economists called this kind of arrangement, where companies outsourced specialized forms of work to subcontractors, "the fissured workplace," and blamed it for eroding labor standards and fomenting a legalized form of wage discrimination that exacerbated inequality. This was a decades-long trend propagated not just by transportation providers like FedEx and Uber but by hotels, cable providers, and other tech companies like Apple. Amazon's size, of course, spread it that much further, and policymakers, whose job it was to protect workers, were caught flat-footed.

As Amazon gradually spread its arms around home delivery, Clark and his colleagues moved to take over another important stage of the supply chain. Until that point, the company had relied on big freight transporters to move merchandise from suppliers to Amazon's FCs and between the FCs and sortation centers. In December 2015, as Amazon was building new sort centers and Amazon Logistics slowly opened in new cities, Amazon announced that it had purchased thousands of truck trailers with the Amazon Prime logo on their sides, a program called Mosaic that was executed in part by Mike Roth. Once again, Amazon employees wouldn't do the actual driving—the company would rely on a mosaic of line-haul service providers to attach their truck tractors to the Prime-emblazoned semitrailers.

Colleagues viewed the older Roth as a masterful strategist, saying that he was playing the game Go, while everyone else was playing checkers or chess. They also saw him as an empathetic leader who was more inclined to check in on an employee's well-being after a bad meeting or to discuss their long-range career plans. "Mike covered up a lot of Dave's sins," said a longtime Logistics executive. "He was the people person, the guy behind the scenes who put his arm around you and fluffed you up after Dave tore you apart."

But there were limits to his compassion. When a Mosaic driver apparently showed up intoxicated to a supplier's facility, the resulting email of complaint went right to Bezos's public email address.

Bezos forwarded it to an Amazon executive—who asked not to be named—going beyond the customary question mark by adding three ominous letters: "WTF."

The executive showed it to Mike Roth, who said in his inimitable German accent, "Oooh, you got one! Oh, that's from Jeff. It says 'WTF'! Oh, that's Jeff, that's very Jeff. Good luck with that."

Roth's old Campbellsville boss, Arthur Valdez, was having a rougher time. Valdez had moved back to the U.S. from the UK to take over the new Amazon Logistics division. In 2013, he recruited a talented logistics executive from FedEx in Europe named Beth Galetti to help him build a delivery capability akin to FedEx Ground. But when Clark interviewed her, he decided that she would make a perfect replacement for David Niekerk, the team's retiring human resources director.

Even though Clark's instincts were right and Galetti would later join the S-team as the head of all HR at Amazon, Valdez was annoyed and felt his independence was being usurped. He and Clark lived a mile from each other in Seattle's eastern suburbs and their families remained close. But after that episode, their relationship began to fray.

Under Valdez's stewardship, Amazon Logistics had gotten off to a rocky start. As anticipated, the company was building an entirely new type of smaller facility in urban areas, called a delivery station, to organize packages and hand them off to the delivery service providers. But the system was disorganized and prohibitively expensive at first, while the drivers were proving unreliable and were periodically caught engaging in a variety of uncouth acts, such as fighting with customers or flinging packages onto front porches from afar. Employees received so many question marks from Bezos about these reported incidents that they nearly lost track of them.

Bezos also couldn't understand why the original metrics for last-mile delivery were so poor. Paperboys and pizza delivery drivers, he remarked, visited homes for $5 a trip! Some of the early per-package transportation costs for Amazon Fresh were many times that amount. "I'm okay with you making sophisticated mistakes, but this is just us being stupid," Bezos said in one review of Amazon Logistics, according to an operations exec.

Fairly or not, Valdez caught the blame for the transportation network's embarrassing start. In early 2015, Clark reassigned him to work on Amazon's operations in emerging markets like Brazil and Mexico, reporting to Mike Roth. It was essentially a demotion and a major comedown for an executive who had been both Clark and Roth's manager in Campbellsville and whose career at Amazon was now clearly off track.

A year later, John Mulligan, Target's chief operating officer, approached Valdez about taking over as executive vice president of the retailer's supply chain. Valdez initially replied that he planned to be "an Amazonian until the day I die," but then started to consider the offer in the context of his recent setbacks, and accepted the job.

Target planned to announce the hire on the last day of February, to coincide with a speech that CEO Brian Cornell was delivering at an industry conference. Valdez couldn't bear to face Roth with the news, so he called Clark and asked if they could meet privately in his office. But Clark was taking the day off to attend a school event for one of his children. Valdez had to tell him over the phone that he was leaving. Clark responded genially at first. "Where are you going?" he asked.

Valdez informed him it was Target—and Clark erupted. Here was one of the more naked hypocrisies at Amazon, which aggressively poached employees from competitors but considered it an act of absolute treachery when an executive left for a rival. "He told me that if I made that decision, Amazon was coming after me," Valdez recalled painfully years later. Clark then hung up the phone.

A few minutes later, Beth Galetti called Valdez to tell him that he would have a big problem if he left to work for Target. "Beth, my role is to manage the replenishment of eighteen hundred stores and a very small e-commerce business," Valdez pleaded. Galetti said that Amazon didn't see it that way. Valdez then texted Jeff Wilke, saying that he would "cherish the opportunity to speak" but never got a reply.

Amazon sued Arthur Valdez in King County Superior Court, a week before he was due to start at Target, for violating his noncompete agreement and sharing proprietary information with a competitor. The lawsuit asked a judge to exclude Valdez from working for Target for eighteen months. It was eventually settled privately, as many such Amazon lawsuits are, after Target agreed to trivial adjustments in Valdez's contract.

But the damage to a fifteen-year personal friendship was done. After their contentious phone call, Dave Clark never talked to the best man at his wedding again.

———

Clark had proven himself a true Amazonian, putting loyalty to the company above personal friendship while pursuing Bezos's vision of an independent supply chain. But to really accomplish that mandate, he had to do more than put cars and truck trailers on the road; he also had to get planes in the air.

UPS Next Day Air and FedEx Express were key links in the Amazon fulfillment network, whisking less frequently purchased items to Prime customers across the country when they weren't stocked in nearby fulfillment centers and available for ground delivery. But as the shippers started to view the online retailer warily, Amazon was discovering that it could no longer count on them.

This was manifestly demonstrated at the end of 2014, a year after the Worldport fiasco, when UPS again was rationing access to its network and restricted Amazon cargo on flights into—of all places—Seattle. The company's last deal-of-the-day of the season, free next-day delivery of Kindles, wouldn't be available to Seattle residents. Since that was evidently an intolerable outcome, Clark called Logistics VP Mike Indresano and asked if he could get an airplane.

"What do you mean, an airplane? Are we talking about a plane ticket and an overhead compartment, or an actual plane?" Indresano asked.

"Just get an airplane," Clark replied.

Indresano asked Mike Roth whether Clark was serious, then enlisted a member of his sortation center team, Scott Ruffin. Ruffin called an old friend who operated an air charter service and rented two Boeing 727s. Amazon had the planes filled with the stranded orders and merchandise from its fulfillment centers in Southern and Northern California and flown to Sea-Tac Airport. As a joke, Indresano bought a Santa hat that was stored in the Ontario, California, FC and had it gift wrapped and delivered to Clark's home with a holiday greeting.

That was the unofficial birth of the service that would come to be known first as Prime Air, then Amazon Prime Air, and finally, Amazon Air. The confusion was born from Bezos using the former name in his infamous *60 Minutes* interview in 2013 to announce that the company was working on aerial drones to ferry individual packages to people's backyards. Several operations executives told me they were embarrassed by that stunt (which seven years later, had progressed no further than private tests). They used an old internal Microsoft term to describe it: "cookie licking," or the act of claiming to do something before you actually do it, in order to capture notoriety and prevent others from following.

Unlike the drone program, the effort to lease planes delivered immediate results. After the first two charters in 2014, Ruffin was put in charge of developing the business case for creating an air cargo network. He recruited a half-dozen colleagues and holed up in a windowless conference room in the Ruby-Dawson buildings in South Lake Union, where they met regularly with Clark.

In the resulting white paper, they argued that owning air capacity would allow Amazon to shorten its delivery times and pay only the true cost of transporting cargo in the air rather than the public rates charged by UPS and FedEx Express. Bezos was dubious about buying planes outright and wondered what Amazon would do differently from other logistics companies if it operated a freight airline. Executives were also undoubtedly aware that operating an airline would come with plenty of actual baggage: it could expose the company to a potentially belligerent pilots' union, a surfeit of regulations, and an oversight authority, the FAA, that had a dim view of Silicon Valley–style corner-cutting and innovation.

The solution they came up with, which Clark successfully proposed to the S-team, allowed Amazon to avoid those drawbacks. Like Amazon's parallel initiatives on the ground, the plan called for controlling air freight while not necessarily owning it or exposing the company to the dangerous messiness of the aviation industry. The details provide a fascinating window into the self-amplifying advantages of Amazon's size and power.

Over the spring of 2016, Amazon announced it was leasing forty Boeing 767 freighters from a pair of airlines: ATSG, based in Wilmington, Ohio, and Atlas Air, based in Westchester County, New York. The airlines would continue to maintain and operate the aircraft, but the planes would be rebranded with the Prime Air logo and requisitioned into Amazon's service for a period of five to ten years.

As part of those deals, Amazon purchased warrants to buy 19.9 percent of ATSG stock at $9.73 a share and 20 percent of Atlas's parent company at $37.50 a share. Amazon knew that investors in those companies would be excited by the partnership with the e-commerce giant and want to participate in the upside.

Sure enough, after each company announced the news, their stock prices soared—49 percent and 14 percent respectively over the month after each deal was announced. "Fantastic job—that is how it's done!" Bezos crowed, replying to an update that Clark emailed the S-team. By the second anniversary of the deals, based on the numbers in each airline's 8K public filings, Amazon had simultaneously achieved its goal of securing exclusive access to air routes and earned nearly half a billion dollars on its investments.

The planes, emblazoned with Prime Air on their sides and the Amazon smile logo on their tails, made their debut at a Seattle air show over the summer of 2016. The press was enthralled by the implications; could Amazon disrupt FedEx, UPS, and the USPS and their hold over the domestic e-commerce delivery business? On an earnings call with investors, FedEx CEO Fred Smith called such talk "fantastical," specifying that he chose the word carefully.

Publicly, Clark answered questions about the initiative by saying that FedEx and UPS were "great partners" and that Prime Air was supplemental. But Clark's antagonism toward Fred Smith, borne from the tension in the companies' relationship, wasn't very well concealed. "Ho!Ho!Ho! Have a Fantastical Holiday everyone!!!" Clark tweeted later, along with a photo of a Prime Air model airplane in front of a Christmas tree.

Amazon added ten more aircraft to its fleet in 2018, twenty more in 2019, twelve in 2020, and another eleven as of January 2021. The Prime Air fleet allowed Amazon to exploit its increasing sales volume and pack the planes full of bulky yet lightweight items that would be more expensive to ship via traditional carriers. It also allowed Amazon to cater to its peculiar around-the-clock cycle—routing the aircraft from sort centers at 2 a.m. on a Sunday, for example. UPS and FedEx Express, which served thousands of other companies, couldn't offer that kind of flexibility to a single customer.

Now that he had airplanes, Clark also needed something else: air hubs, to load and unload cargo before and after flights. In January 2017, Amazon announced it would build a Prime Air hub at the Cincinnati/Northern Kentucky International Airport, the location of DHL's international hub, which Amazon would pay to use while its new facility was being constructed. The $1.49 billion deal was negotiated by Holly Sullivan, Amazon's director of economic development, who extracted $40 million in tax incentives from local and state governments.

But if Clark thought he would get another commendation from Bezos, he was wrong. Amazon's new air hub was going to create around two thousand new jobs. In contrast, electric automobile maker Tesla—run by Elon Musk, Bezos's chief rival in the private space industry as well as for public adulation—had secured $1.3 billion in tax breaks a few years before for a battery plant in Nevada, dubbed the Gigafactory. Tesla was projecting it would create 6,500 jobs. It had earned about thirteen times more in tax incentives, per job, than Amazon.

Bezos, of course, had spotted the difference. Three employees independently recalled his response to the news of the Kentucky deal and considered it a fateful harbinger of the belabored public process, nearly two years later, that would go by the infamous name HQ2. Bezos's email went something like this: "Why does Elon Musk have this superpower of getting big government incentives and we don't?"

In the midst of the Amazon Logistics buildout, the prospect of Bezos agitating for additional government succor was ironic. Amazon had already displaced significant costs onto the public. It didn't provide healthcare coverage for its drivers, maintain the congested roads to and from its FCs and sort centers, or sustain the temporary employees who got jobs in its FCs over the holidays and then were unemployed and collected public benefits for the rest of the year. In building out a transportation network with considerable speed, Amazon had avoided many of the risks that often accompanied the unsexy business of moving items from one place to another.

But those challenges hadn't disappeared. And in the press and court of public opinion, at least, Amazon wasn't going to be able to dissociate itself from them altogether.

On December 22, 2016, an eighty-four-year-old Chicago grandmother named Telesfora Escamilla was struck and killed by a white Nissan NV1500 cargo van emblazoned with the Amazon logo on its rear door. It was operated by a company called Inpax Shipping Solutions, one of the independent delivery firms that existed almost solely to deliver packages for Amazon.

Inpax had a shady record, according to subsequent media accounts. The Department of Labor later found the firm had underpaid dozens of employees and violated labor laws by failing to pay overtime. Its driver, twenty-nine-year-old Valdimar Gray, was fired from a previous job at another Amazon delivery company for what was later characterized in legal filings as a "preventable hit and run." He did not possess a commercial driver's license but nevertheless got a job with Inpax and worked there for two months before the tragic incident.

Gray was charged with reckless homicide—and acquitted. A Chicago judge agreed with the defense that it was an accident. But a civil lawsuit brought by the Escamilla family against Amazon and Inpax alleged that Amazon had contributed to her death by putting excessive pressure on drivers to make deliveries on time. A week before, Amazon had emailed Inpax and other DSPs in the area about "some struggles the last few days with route coverage and route performance" and proclaimed: "Our #1 priority is getting every package to the customer on time." Amazon and Inpax quietly settled the suit in March 2020 and agreed to pay the Escamilla family $14 million.

There were similar tragedies, many exposed by investigative reports in *ProPublica* and *BuzzFeed News* over the course of 2019. The publications revealed that drivers delivering Amazon packages had been involved in more than sixty serious crashes, including at least thirteen that resulted in fatalities. In 2018, a sixty-one-year-old legal secretary named Stacey Hayes Curry was killed in her office parking lot by a driver delivering Amazon packages for a firm called Letter Ride. The driver told police he never saw Curry and thought he'd hit a speed bump. Her son later wrote (but never sent) a letter to Jeff Bezos, saying, "I think this attitude of reckless speed stems from the top and trickles down," according to *ProPublica*.

Amazon executives told me that safety was their top priority and that the company met or exceeded all public safety laws. In an interview, Jeff Wilke said that Amazon's transportation partners had collectively driven 700 million miles in 2019—and asserted that Amazon had a better safety record than the national benchmark. This claim was impossible to check without specific data about Amazon's accident rate, which the company declined to provide. "I have not seen a deterioration in the safety culture; in fact, I've seen just the opposite," Wilke said. "I just don't think it's true that we had to sacrifice safety in order to build this capability."

Many former operations employees agreed that Amazon did not deliberately dilute its safety standards, noting that delivering packages is an inherently dangerous business for all companies. But they added that the act of contracting with delivery service providers, instead of acquiring them or simply hiring drivers directly, limited Amazon's ability to control what was happening on the road.

In its FCs around the world, Amazon was accustomed to wielding almost tyrannical authority and could deploy that power to prevent accidents. Workers began each day with lectures on safety and stretching exercises, for example; drivers, however, received no such support from Amazon, lest they be reclassified as its employees. "You had this weird dichotomy," said Will Gordon, a senior manager on Amazon's operations team for three years. "Safety meant different things when you were talking about FCs, versus the contractors who made last-mile deliveries."

Unable to impose the same culture of safety and efficiency on its delivery partners, Amazon used technology to try to guide them. The company distributed an app to drivers, internally called Rabbit, that scanned packages, displayed addresses, and algorithmically generated the fastest routes for delivering packages.

Rabbit was originally developed for a separate, Uber-like delivery service called Amazon Flex, which allowed individual drivers to sign up online and pick up and deliver Amazon packages for an advertised $18 to $25 an hour. Drivers could set their own schedules but had to supply their own vehicles, fuel, insurance, and smartphones. Flex was meant to deliver Prime Now orders (thus the Rabbit name, which was part of Stephenie Landry's taxonomy of magical brands).

But it quickly became the de facto tool for all drivers delivering packages for Amazon.

Former employees who worked on the app said the development of Rabbit was haphazard and rushed. At first it was missing features that might remind drivers to take breaks or that would choose routes in such a way as to minimize the statistically dangerous act of making a left turn—a key safety feature long known to UPS and FedEx. "Like a lot of things at Amazon, it was ready, fire, aim," said Trip O'Dell, the former head of the design team that worked on Rabbit. "They just rapidly expanded it and assumed they would fix it later."

O'Dell said that he and members of his team worried that the app was distracting drivers on dangerous city streets and complained to their superiors. They pointed out that the presentation of information on the app was dense and difficult to read in sunlight, and that constant notifications for new workloads vied for drivers' attention when their eyes should have been planted on the road ahead.

Issues with the app cascaded, O'Dell said. Routing was poor, and drivers found it difficult to progress from one delivery to another. Fraud was prevalent, with drivers finding loopholes to get paid for work they didn't do. One problem was that dueling two-pizza teams in Seattle and Austin worked concurrently on versions of Rabbit for iOS and Android, magnifying the confusion among delivery firms. "All of the things were wrong with it all at once," O'Dell said. "It was not a good app."

But employees said that Clark was more concerned with resolving the tricky economics of Amazon Logistics, like maximizing the shipments per truck and getting the pay for drivers just right. He made decisions based on cold, hard data, while employees' initial concerns about safety were based on anecdotal evidence. The Rabbit team occasionally observed drivers and watched them skip meals, rush through stop signs, and tape their phones to their pant legs so they could easily glance down at the screens, all to meet the challenging delivery deadlines.

Without quantifiable evidence of a widespread safety problem though, Clark and other execs largely dismissed the complaints. "I don't think safety was the number one problem or priority," said Will Gordon, the senior manager. "It was productivity and cost-effectiveness."

After the damning articles in *ProPublica* and *BuzzFeed*, Amazon cut ties with several delivery firms, including Inpax and other companies linked to accidents. A spokeswoman said that Amazon had "a responsibility... to ensure these partners meet our high standards for things like safety and working conditions." Implicit in the statement—as close as Amazon ever got to a mea culpa—was that some of the partners it had previously chosen to work with did not meet those safety standards.

There would be no comparable admission about Amazon Air, despite similar circumstances. On February 23, 2019, an Atlas Air cargo flight ferrying Amazon and USPS packages from Miami crashed into a muddy marsh while approaching George Bush Intercontinental Airport in Houston, killing two pilots and one passenger. Atlas had grown quickly over the past three years, in large part because of its deal with Amazon. It employed around 1,185 pilots at the start of the relationship and 1,890 by the time of the accident less than three years later—a 59 percent jump, according to the airline's public filings.

In the weeks leading up to the crash, the news website *Business Insider* talked to thirteen pilots who worked for Amazon's airlines; all thirteen said their pay and benefits were below industry standards, and twelve said the pilots there were less experienced overall than their counterparts elsewhere. One of the pilots alleged that Atlas Air overworked its pilots and that the situation was "a ticking time bomb."

———

By the fall of 2017, Amazon Logistics was delivering about 20 percent of its own packages, a larger share than FedEx, and was on the verge of permanently surpassing UPS, according to the research firm

Rakuten Intelligence. After years of effort, it had spurred the creation of hundreds of new small delivery companies and generated a fair amount of chaos and negative headlines. It was also just starting to meet some of the lofty goals executives had set for it.

But Amazon still needed more drivers, particularly during the busy holiday peak. Clark then made two additional moves to attract more delivery firms. In June 2018, he introduced a new program for delivery service providers with fewer than forty vans, offering discounts on Amazon-branded vehicles, uniforms, fuel, and insurance—while still requiring them to operate independently and provide healthcare and pay overtime. The addition of multiple, smaller firms in each city would guarantee Amazon had plenty of partners to work with and ensure that it had yet another kind of leverage: the ability to dictate terms and cut ties with any disruptive or poorly performing companies without compromising the level of service for customers.

A few months later, Clark then authorized the purchase of twenty thousand dark blue Sprinter vans from Mercedes-Benz and leased them at discounted rates, along with blue-and-black Amazon uniforms and caps, to the new delivery firms.

The gambit worked, helping over a thousand new delivery businesses get off the ground. And in early 2019, Amazon eclipsed both UPS and the U.S. Postal Service to become its own largest carrier in the U.S. It was a momentous achievement, even if there had been significant costs along the way.

Clark's decade-long retrofit of Amazon's fulfillment centers and its last-mile delivery network had inexorably changed Amazon's retail business. It allowed the company to place its merchandise closer to dense population areas and to lower its transportation costs, since Amazon no longer had to pay the inflated retail rates of the big carriers. It also aligned Amazon's delivery expenses with its growth; the more customers signed up for Amazon Prime and Amazon's grocery delivery services, Prime Now and Amazon Fresh, the more efficient and cost-effective it became to send drivers into those neighborhoods.

The last-mile network also protected Amazon from the exigencies of UPS and FedEx, and the political winds that battered the USPS. When Donald Trump accused Amazon of ripping off the U.S. Postal Service and threatened to raise rates, the company disagreed, but the result of the dispute hardly mattered. Amazon now had the leverage to shift that volume to its own network and to another shipping partner, UPS.

The carrier had recognized that Amazon had changed the dynamics of the industry. In 2019, UPS announced that it would finally deliver on Sundays, bowing to customer expectations and the pressure that Amazon's around-the-clock cycle was exerting on its e-commerce rivals. As the post office had years before, UPS had to renegotiate its contract with the Teamsters to allow it to create a new category of drivers who would work weekend shifts at a reduced pay scale.

FedEx, relegated to a low single-digit percentage of Amazon's network, also started working Sundays, but opted to stop delivering for Amazon altogether. The cold war between Dave Clark and Fred Smith continued, unabated and entertaining. FedEx loudly announced the end to its air and ground contracts with Amazon and said it was devoting itself to other customers, including Walmart and Target. Smith doubled down on his view that Amazon was not a disruptive threat to FedEx, again calling the prospect "fantastical" in the *Wall Street Journal*. Clark temporarily banned third-party merchants from using FedEx Ground. In his Seattle office, he had a set of golf balls printed with the word "fantastical."

Meanwhile, Amazon Logistics was providing that most coveted of Amazonian objectives: leverage, which Bezos promptly turned into a customer benefit and a competitive moat. In April 2019, Amazon announced it would shift Prime from two-day to one-day shipping. It was a large but manageable expense, mainly because Clark had already laid the groundwork in the FCs and transportation network. Later that year, Amazon was also able to retire the $15 monthly subscription fee for grocery delivery, adding free Amazon Fresh and

Whole Foods delivery to the perks of Prime membership. This would prove propitious a year later, when the Covid-19 pandemic turned millions of desperate home-bound shoppers on to online grocery delivery.

Clark had fulfilled Bezos's vision of a liberated supply chain and established himself as the highest embodiment of an Amazon leader: a big thinker, who placed methodical, long-term bets that would be unpalatable to the impatient executives at more short term–oriented companies—and almost certainly to more cautious and socially conscious business leaders. "I'm a simplifier," Clark said, when I asked about the set of skills that had enabled him to progress from the Campbellsville FC, all the way to the upper echelons of the S-team. "I can take complicated stuff and figure out how to boil it down into what you need to do to actually make it big."

Along the way, the former middle-school band teacher had busted through obstacles of every kind, fractured a major friendship, squeezed additional productivity out of Amazon's low-wage workers, and levered the significant costs onto society at large. And Amazon's reputation was only slightly grazed in the process.

In other words, Dave Clark had proven himself to be nearly every bit as creative and ruthless as Jeff Bezos himself.

CHAPTER 10

The Gold Mine in the Backyard

Many longtime Amazon employees had a sneaking, unspoken fear in the run-up to the pivotal OP1 planning meetings in the fall of 2017: that their esteemed leader was backing away from the company. Bezos remained deeply involved with new initiatives, where he believed his ideas and support could make a difference, such as Alexa, Amazon Studios, and the Amazon Go stores. But he was coming into the office less often and had largely ceded control of the company's increasingly complex main businesses—retail and AWS—to the co-CEOs who reported to him, Jeff Wilke and Andy Jassy.

Plus, Bezos was spending more time with the *Washington Post* and at his private space company, Blue Origin. A noticeable development in Bezos's life was the fact he was also contending with the impact of his steadily increasing fame and wealth. That May, he was trailed by paparazzi while vacationing in Italy with his wife, MacKenzie, and his parents, siblings Mark and Christina, and their spouses. On June 15, pressured by the media to begin giving away his fortune, he bought himself time to craft a philanthropic strategy by tweeting "a request for ideas" to address pressing societal problems. In July, he was photographed at the annual Allen & Company conference in Sun Valley, Idaho, his biceps bulging from a black polo shirt and down vest, an image that spawned countless internet memes as well as the redolent phrase "swole Bezos." He had come a long way from that *Time* "Person of the Year" cover with the Styrofoam peanuts.

Amazon's founder had plenty of reasons to relax, get in shape, and step back from daily operations at the company he founded. Its stock price had tripled over the past two years, boosting its market capitalization to a little over $500 billion that summer. The Amazon flywheel was spinning briskly, and as a result, Bezos was the second wealthiest person in the world, with a fortune of $89 billion.

Bezos also had a growing staff of assistants, PR professionals, and security consultants managing his daily schedule and public image. They applied the same precision to his daily movements as they might for a state leader—and made certain his speeches and social media posts were always harmlessly anodyne. That October, he introduced a new Amazon wind farm in Texas by smashing a bottle of champagne atop a windmill and tweeting the aerial video. The next month, he was interviewed at an event called Summit LA by the gentlest of interlocutors: his younger brother, Mark, an investor and Blue Origin advisor who once gave a TED talk about being a volunteer firefighter. They chatted about craft cocktails, space exploration, their grandparents, and how Jeff and MacKenzie left New York City and drove across the country to start Amazon in Seattle.

While they would never publicly admit it, Amazon's senior leaders were happy to operate with more independence, and with fewer of the founder's impossibly probing questions and demanding ambitions. Meetings with Bezos could still go sideways, resetting projects and depleting employee morale. Even the most inconsequential of utterances from the sagacious chief executive could instigate a flurry of wheel-spinning and white paper–writing inside the company. Many executives were relieved to be meeting with Bezos less often and wondered openly if his interest in Amazon was waning. Perhaps they could finally take a breath.

Then Amazon entered the annual end-of-summer planning cycle

known as OP1, and the tantalizing possibility of an overbearing CEO in retreat all but vanished—at least for the time being.

The first and most ominous sign emerged in the annual review of the North American consumer retail unit. The meeting took place on the sixth floor of the Day 1 tower, around a large square of adjoining tables in a giant conference room with views to the west. Bezos sat at the center of one table, with his chief financial officer, Brian Olsavsky, to his left, and his technical advisor at the time, Jeffrey Helbling, to his right.

Doug Herrington sat across the room, facing Bezos. Herrington's longtime finance chief, Dave Stephenson, sat to his left, almost like a consigliere in the *Godfather* films. Jeff Wilke and S-team members and executives from retail, marketplace, and other departments ringed the tables and sat along the walls; others listened in on Chime, the company's erratic teleconferencing app. The meeting started in the customary fashion, in total silence, with everyone reading the retail group's OP1 report, full of charts detailing its past financial performance and the operating plan for the years ahead.

Executives later wondered whether Bezos planned the ambush beforehand or reacted when reading the document. What they noticed in the moment, while Bezos turned the pages, was that his brow furrowed, his eyes narrowed, and his head cocked ever so imperceptibly before he asked: "I wonder what unit profitability was in 2017 without advertising?"

Banner ads had long decorated the Amazon home page. More recently, sponsored listings, paid for by vendors like Procter & Gamble and smaller Amazon sellers in the third-party marketplace, populated the top of its search pages, intermingled with the unpaid results generated by Amazon's search engine. Analysts estimated that such ad sales generated $2.8 billion in 2017 and were growing at a 61 percent annual clip. But retail executives considered ads to be a key part of their unit's performance—not a separate element to be plucked out of their profit-and-loss statement.

"Hang on, Jeff, let me get that," said Stephenson, the retail group's finance chief. There was no easy way to calculate it. Sitting behind a stack of binders, the seventeen-year Amazon veteran did the math on his smartphone calculator while the rest of the room sat in stressful silence.

After five minutes or so, Stephenson produced a result. The room exhaled in relief. But Bezos was still regarding Herrington and Stephenson icily across the table. "What was it for 2016?" he asked.

Stephenson returned to his binders for another five minutes of oxygen-deprived tension. Stephenson produced another number, and then Bezos asked for 2014. "You can't underestimate how intimidating that room is, especially when Jeff's brain is going and onto something," said an executive who was in the room. "It's an unnerving environment. I was very impressed with how calm Dave was." Without advertising, the financial picture of Amazon's domestic retail business suddenly looked far less rosy. Its underlying economic health had actually been deteriorating.

Bezos had tugged on a string, and the entire quilt started to unravel. Now he kept pulling. In the multi-hour discussion that followed, he argued that the growth of advertising was concealing stagnation in online retail. Bezos was constitutionally tolerant of losing money over the first decade of a promising new business; but retail was well past that point. He wanted to go as far back as possible to find when this troubling trend had started. Then he insisted that Wilke and his team throw out months of careful planning that had gone into their OP1 document and present a revised version to him. He insisted that they radically scale back their hiring plans and other investments and commit to returning to the underlying profitability they had achieved years before—without the safety blanket of advertising.

For executives on the consumer retail team, this was a stunning development—a "root canal," in the sardonic parlance of the finance team's grizzled veterans. Bezos had personally insisted on matching the low prices of rivals and getting into unprofitable categories of merchandise. Increasing perks and service levels for customers was expensive, but they could always rely on more profitable parts of the company to subsidize those investments. So execs on the finance team had never even contemplated devising their internal systems in such a way as to exclude the revenue from ads.

For more than two decades, Bezos had emphasized the tactical advantages of low margins and low prices, in order to win points of market share as if they were continents on a Risk board. But now his thinking had shifted; he was frustrated that retail wasn't more profitable and that two of his most trusted deputies, Jeff Wilke and Doug Herrington, weren't getting more leverage out of their operation. The numbers suggested executives might be backsliding in their mandate to relentlessly improve operating performance, and that Amazon was inheriting some of the attributes of what Bezos ominously called "Day 2" companies. "Day two is stasis, followed by irrelevance, followed by excruciating, painful decline, followed by death," he had said earlier that year on stage at an all-hands meeting. "And that is why it is always Day one."

S-team members appeared to cast blame on Stephenson, who would leave the company a year later to become the CFO of Airbnb. "The tone of it was 'how did you miss it?'" said another executive privy to the discussions. "But we had been missing it together for this whole time."

The retail OP1 set the tone for other contentious meetings that month. Bezos issued a similar mandate to Russ Grandinetti, senior vice president of the international consumer group, whose division's finances looked even bleaker without advertising. Bezos wanted to see better unit results in countries that Amazon had been active in for longer, like the UK, and to take a hard look at investments that were unlikely to ever grow large. He fixated on the money-losing marketplace in China, where the company had competed unsuccessfully for more than a decade against Alibaba and JD.com. After that session, he also asked Grandinetti's team for a series of follow-up meetings.

In another OP1 meeting that combined the reviews of legal, HR, and global corporate affairs, Bezos ran through headcount requests line by line and demanded justifications for them. He skeptically questioned anything that resembled gratuitous expansion. At one point, he grumbled about a planned staff increase for members of the consumer retail public relations team and stunned some employees by wondering why Amazon needed to do any PR at all for its original business of selling books—since its dominance in the category was already secure.

Only AWS avoided the same withering scrutiny. Sessions with Andy Jassy to review AWS's 40 percent growth rate and 30 percent operating margins were typically feel-good festivals. Bezos nevertheless prodded Jassy and his longtime CFO, Sean Boyle, about whether their financial projections were truly automated, in the way the retail team's were, or whether inefficient human sentiment was guiding them.

The message from OP1 that fall, and from a subsequent CEO directive later that year that would scramble Amazon's organizational charts, was clear: even as he became wealthier and more famous, Amazon remained Jeff Bezos's company. And he had bigger plans for a decade-old advertising initiative than simply covering up the sins of his other business units.

———

In perhaps an indication of Bezos's initial trepidation about advertising, he had kicked off the effort in the mid-2000s by thinking not about the type of ads the company could accept but the kinds that it shouldn't. S-team members remember Bezos handing out a list of products that he felt should never be promoted on the site, such as guns, alcohol, online dating sites, dietary supplements, and financial services that pushed people into high-interest loans. The S-team spent hours debating the list and the relative merits of getting into the advertising business.

Despite these reservations, Bezos was a proponent of bringing ads onto Amazon and using them to support low prices. He talked about two hypothetical e-commerce websites: one with ads that subsidized low prices and another that was ad-free but had higher prices. Customers, he said, would always flock to the website with better deals. "We are stupid if we don't do it" was his usual conclusion, according to several S-team members.

Amazon could have established itself quickly as an online advertising juggernaut. While Google knew what people searched for and Facebook knew what they liked, Amazon had one of the most substantive data points of all: what they actually bought. Yet it was only after online ads fueled the historic rises of Yahoo, Google, and Facebook that Amazon entered the advertising business in a meaningful way—and even then, it was with an abundance of caution and a number of false starts.

In the late 2000s, Amazon began hiring employees in the advertising capital of the world, New York City. To avoid Amazon having to collect sales tax in the state, they initially worked for a subsidiary called Adzinia and were furnished with accompanying business cards and email addresses. Their first major office was located on Sixth Avenue, with a view of the famous "Love" sculpture on the sidewalk of 55th Street.

But Amazon never quite fit into the clubby confines of New York City advertising. Though the age of *Mad Men* had long passed, the industry still revolved around personal relationships and expensed lunches. Ad execs were accustomed to taking their clients to premier sporting events and traveling to glamorous industry conferences, like the annual Cannes Lions festival on the French Riviera.

Amazon, frugal to the bone, refused to do any of that. Even employees taking international flights were relegated to coach class unless they personally secured an upgrade. "You would get flagged if you paid over a certain amount for a plane ticket," said Andrew James, an account executive for five years. "Google and Facebook were lavishing customers with big parties. It put us at a disadvantage."

Amazon moved hesitantly to grow its New York–based ad sales team. It didn't throw people at problems, it threw brainpower, went the common internal refrain. In one OP1 review, Jeff Wilke flipped to the appendix of the ad team's document and skeptically regarded their hiring plans. "How many new sales people are we going to have carrying account executives' luggage next year?" he cracked.

Amazon rejected other industry norms as well. The CEOs and chief marketing officers of firms like Procter & Gamble wanted to meet their C-Suite counterparts at the companies where they spent their ad dollars. At Facebook, big advertisers could expect to sit-down with COO Sheryl Sandberg, for example. But aside from a breakfast one year with advertisers and ad agencies, Bezos declined to play that game; and Wilke and Jeff Blackburn, the S-team member who managed the advertising group for years, were also reluctant (though Wilke did once greet the CMO of Burberry wearing his blue Burberry blazer).

In 2013, a senior marketing executive from Unilever, one of the largest package goods companies in the world, showed up in Seattle with a contingent of colleagues to discuss the expanding relationship between the companies. Bezos and Wilke declined to take the meeting. "They were disappointed," said Shiven Ramji, an Amazon ad executive at the time. "They had all these people and PowerPoints and photos. We had a one-pager printed telling them all the glorious things we could do."

Though he wasn't meeting with advertisers, Bezos nevertheless made his presence felt. In the early years of the ad effort, he wanted to review each large campaign, particularly when they ran on the Kindle Fire tablets that debuted in 2011 and featured full-screen color ads. Jeff Blackburn and Paul Kotas, the engineer who managed the technology side of the advertising business at the time, also personally reviewed ad campaigns. Their exacting standards and peculiar aesthetic requirements drove Amazon's ad execs and their clients crazy. But Blackburn and Kotas had good reason: they didn't want Amazon to do anything to harm customer trust or interfere with online purchases, at the time the true revenue engine of the company. Often, their reactions consisted simply of a single word: no.

No, advertisers couldn't make vague claims in their ads. They couldn't use exclamation points; that would be shouting at the customer. Their colors couldn't garishly stand out because it might distract shoppers. They couldn't use images that showed excessive skin. And on and on.

Advertisers accustomed to getting rich sets of demographic data about customers from Silicon Valley firms were also rebuffed. No, advertisers couldn't access Amazon data about its customers' age, ethnicity, and shopping habits. No, Amazon wouldn't allow companies like Adobe and Acxiom to put their third-party software tags onto ads and track their performance, a common practice elsewhere on the web. Advertisers would have to settle for getting reports about their ads' effectiveness directly from Amazon.

Inside the advertising group, a few of these battles became notorious. Over one holiday, Paul Kotas vetoed the particular hue of blue in ads by the Ford Motor Company, because the display campaign felt "Sunday circular." Amazon also told the wireless carrier T-Mobile that its trademarked magenta-pink logo was too bright and distracting. And it informed Sony Pictures that a banner for the James Bond film *Skyfall* violated the policy on showing weapons. The studio "was like, 'screw you!'" an Amazon ad executive recalls. "Who is James Bond in silhouette without a gun? Literally, he's just a random dude."

Amazon compromised in many of these disputes—and ultimately allowed 007 to hold his iconic weapon, reasoning that it wasn't pointed at anyone in particular. But advertisers came to view the company as arrogant and remote. "We would be met with warm handshakes to start the relationship, and by the end they were tired of us," said Steve Susi, an Amazon creative director for five years.

The stubbornness spoke to Amazon's ambivalence about display advertising and a religious refusal to violate the trust of customers in any way—a philosophical departure from the approach of its Silicon Valley peers, such as Facebook. For Bezos, during the first part of Amazon's journey into advertising, the sanctity of the customer experience took absolute precedence over any business relationship or incremental boost to the balance sheet.

There was also internal suspicion toward any ads that directed a clicking customer off the Amazon website and away from making a purchase. For years, the ad team offered a service called Product Ads that allowed other retailers, such as Nordstrom and Macy's, to promote their wares on Amazon's website. The goal, to allow customers to see more selection and competitive prices, was misunderstood and unpopular inside the company. "The retail team spent all their time trying to drive traffic to Amazon and we were driving traffic off Amazon," said Colleen Aubrey, Amazon's vice president of performance advertising. "I remember having regular meetings with retail leaders where they were like, 'What are you guys doing?' We would have to talk it through."

By 2014, Amazon was close to retiring Product Ads, with the overall enthusiasm for advertising inside the company waning. The financial results were good but not great. Restrictive guidelines and inaccessible senior executives were alienating advertisers. The division was constantly fighting for resources, and its execs were putting in sixty-hour weeks but felt unappreciated and under attack. "We were bad for a long time and people held us accountable for that," said one advertising executive.

———

In a shake-up that summer, Paul Kotas was promoted to senior vice president and placed in charge of the entire advertising group. Lisa Utzschneider, Amazon's longtime global VP of ad sales, who had previously reported directly to S-team member Jeff Blackburn, quit in frustration six months later to work for Yahoo. Amazon's nascent advertising effort was in tatters.

Kotas had joined Amazon in 1999 from D. E. Shaw, the Wall

Street quantitative hedge fund where Bezos had conceived the original idea for an online bookseller. He liked to tell employees the story of how Bezos had actually recruited him to join Amazon in 1997. His bags were packed for Seattle when he decided to stay at the hedge fund at the last minute. The change of heart ended up costing Kotas millions.

Other than a fondness for punk and new wave music, Kotas was, like many of his colleagues, obsessed about metrics, like the length of time it took for ads to load, and fanatical about the leadership principles, such as frugality. "Tell me more about this dinner on your expense account" was a familiar refrain to his direct reports. When ad execs gathered in "war rooms" at the start of the peak season to monitor the performance of the holiday ad campaigns, Kotas could be relentless: "If any of you are thinking about going to grandma's house and turning off your phone and not being available, think again!" an ad exec recalls him saying one year.

Kotas took over as sole manager of the beleaguered advertising group just as the possible answer to its perennial problems began to reveal itself. At the time, Amazon's marketplace business was clicking into high gear. Third-party sellers—including the flood of merchants coming online from China—were eager to boost the visibility of their products on the increasingly crowded pages of search results. The solution was obvious: charge them for it, just as Google taxed web publishers to promote their websites in its search engine.

Amazon's Google-style-search ad auction was called "sponsored products." It allowed a third-party seller of bedsheets, for example, to place a bid to feature its linens whenever customers entered terms like "bedding" into Amazon's search engine. At first the ads showed up at the bottom of the first page of search results; if a user clicked on a sponsored listing, they were transported to the product page and Amazon collected a fee.

As Amazon expanded sponsored products into more product categories and the ads migrated to the right-hand side of the page alongside search results, the advertising team had trouble developing the necessary technology fast enough. It had to build a search auction system to take bids from advertisers and a tool to track the effectiveness of the ads and report the results back to them. Amazon's first search advertisers recalled that early versions of these services were flimsy. "The reports you would get back about the success or failure of the campaigns we ran were very, very poor," said Jeremy Liebowitz, the former global e-commerce vice president of Newell Brands, maker of Sharpie markers and Elmer's glue. "It was almost impossible to tell if something actually worked."

Amazon also needed to make the right semantic connections between ads and specific search terms. Google had two decades of experience in the complex field of search relevance, whereas Amazon was a relative novice. Every time Bezos or Wilke saw a misplaced ad, they fired off an email to Kotas, who in turn forwarded it to his engineers in frustration. One ad technology engineer recalled a memorable ruckus when a sponsored listing for a sex toy popped up in the results for children's toys.

Search ads were controversial inside Amazon and even in the ad group itself. Amazon ad sales execs in New York, L.A., and London, whose mission was to sell conventional banner ads, were given aggressive sales goals every year. Now their clients were being distracted by a whole new way to spend their ad budgets with Amazon. Engineers working in Amazon's Silicon Valley–based search division, A9, loathed the new search ads; their job was to elevate objectively useful products in search results, not the listings of sellers who had paid the most money for an ad.

Yet sponsored ads clearly worked. Customers clicked on them, often failing to distinguish between sponsored placements and objective search results. While they grumbled about the expenditure, sellers and brands were already accustomed to search advertising on Google and seized on it as a way to stand out on Amazon. By 2016, the S-team was confronting the ads' increased popularity and debating a key question: Should it allow search ads to appear on the top half of the search page—mixed with organic search results?

The debate over so-called "above the fold" placement was fierce and played out over countless meetings, pitting the sanctity of the customer experience against a promising new revenue stream. Ad execs argued that sellers and vendors would benefit from having their products appear at the top of search results. Retail executives worried customers might be led astray by ads for low-quality products, have a bad experience, and decrease their overall spending on the site.

In one debate, Doug Herrington, chief of the domestic retail division, used the parable of the scorpion and the frog to frame the issue. In the story, the scorpion asks the frog if it can climb onto its back for passage across a river, then can't help but sting the frog along the way, dooming both. His counterparts in advertising were the scorpion—they weren't evil, per se, but it was simply in their nature to pervert the more egalitarian playing field of the authentic search results.

Eventually Bezos had to settle the argument. His predictable answer was to methodically test sponsored ads at the top of search results, first in a small percentage of search queries. The engineers who administered the tests never thought their instrumentation or data was very reliable, but the results were fairly consistent. When sponsored ads were prominently displayed, there was a small, statistically detectable short-term decline in the number of customers who ended up making a purchase. The longer-term effects were unknown. The scorpion wasn't killing the frog, but lightly nicking it—and it wasn't clear yet whether the bite was poisonous.

While there would almost certainly be collateral damage—fewer customers finding what they wanted—sponsored products also made money. A lot of it. And in that respect, Bezos's decision whether to expand ads to the top of all search queries also consisted of a single word: Yes. Amazon should continue to expand the percentage of search results that included sponsored listings. Yes, it should increase the number of sponsored listings on each page of search results, even if that meant a small corresponding drop-off in customer clicks.

Back in the days of display advertising, Bezos had resisted compromising on the customer experience. But now, while he cautioned against alienating customers by serving too many ads, he opted to vigorously move forward, saying that any deleterious long-term consequences would have to be implausibly large to outweigh the potential windfall and the investment opportunities that could result from it.

Search ads had all of the business characteristics that Bezos loved. Customers weren't transported off Amazon when they clicked but sent to individual product pages, where they made purchases and fed the flywheel. Few expense account–wielding mad men were needed to administer it; the system was largely self-service. And once the technology was in place, search ads would produce tremendous leverage—and a huge windfall that Bezos could use to finance new inventions.

"Moving ads to the top of search pages was the game changer," said an Amazon computer scientist who worked on the ad business. "Sponsored products would be nothing close to what it is today if that decision wasn't made, and Jeff was the one who signed off on it."

———

Once Bezos showed a willingness to convert the relative meritocracy of search results into a domain that prioritized Amazon's commercial interests, the possibilities were endless. For example, Bezos had received an email from a customer in Florida a few years before, who described visiting Amazon.com to buy a selfie stick. There were hundreds of choices and the customer had no idea which one to buy; then he went to a local store and got advice from a salesperson. Why couldn't Amazon, the customer wrote, offer such a recommendation?

The S-team was already deliberating that question when Bezos forwarded the email, which kicked around in the retail organization and ultimately landed with a team working on voice shopping for Alexa. Their product was called Amazon's Choice. It weighed variables such as customer reviews, prices, and shipping speed to bestow a recommendation on certain products in an otherwise crowded category when users asked Alexa to order it.

Voice shopping grew rapidly on Alexa, and the Amazon's Choice badge started appearing prominently in search results in 2016 alongside sponsored products. Its meaning was ambiguous—the company did little to explain what the endorsement actually meant, but it seemed to fill the role of an informed salesperson at least somewhat. Customers nevertheless flocked to products that were assigned the badge and, by one independent account, lifted sales by a factor of three. Not surprisingly, when merchants weren't trying to fool the system and earn the badge by generating positive reviews, they were desperate to know how they could pay for it. Amazon execs replied that it wasn't for sale. "We said it's fairly simple," said Assaf Ronen, a voice shopping vice president. "Take your best products, make them cheap, and make customers happy."

But Amazon's Choice served the company's interests in another way. The groups working on private-label products, such as Amazon-Basics batteries, clamored for the badge when they saw it assigned to rival brands like Duracell. That sparked another round of tense internal debate, pitting private-label teams against A9 search engineers and even Paul Kotas and the ad team, who argued that giving house labels prominence in search results would undermine the company's advertisers and corrupt the impact of the badge. Nevertheless, the badge gravitated toward many of Amazon's private-label products, giving them another advantage over competitors in search results. A *Wall Street Journal* story in 2019 about Amazon's Choice found that 540 AmazonBasics items were awarded the badge, more than any other brand.

Naturally, aggrieved vendors complained when they saw the Choice badge assigned to Amazon's house brands. Though Amazon's

After Jeff Bezos quit his high-paying job on Wall Street, he launched his seemingly modest business, an online bookstore, in July 1995. The company's first warehouse was in its office basement. *Jim Lott/Seattle Times*

(*Below*) Thirty-five-year-old Jeff Bezos and wife MacKenzie at home in Seattle in 1999. Amazon's market cap hit $25 billion that fall, and he was named *Time*'s "Person of the Year," right before the internet economy crashed and Amazon barely survived the fallout. *David Burnett/Contact Press Images*

As a child, Bezos's parents sent him every summer to the Cotulla, Texas, ranch of his retired grandfather, where he learned the value of self-reliance and developed a love for science fiction and space. He revisited the family ranch in 1999. *David Burnett/ Contact Press Images*

Jeff Bezos wanted Amazon to create a totally unique smartphone. The Fire phone, which he conceived in 2010 and closely managed, could present the illusion of a 3D image on its screen. But Amazon's engineers were skeptical of its appeal, and the phone bombed after its introduction in June 2014. *David Ryder/Getty Images*

When Amazon India executives presented a conservative growth plan, Bezos told them, "I don't need computer scientists in India. I need cowboys." He rewarded their resulting ambition with a visit in September 2014, unveiling an oversize $2 billion investment check atop a decorated flatbed truck. *Manjunath Kiran/AFP/Getty Images*

(*Left*) Bezos wanted legendary executive editor Marty Baron involved in his strategy meetings with *Washington Post* executives. "If you are going to change the restaurant, the chef has got to be on board," he said. They spoke onstage in May 2016. (*Right*) Jason Rezaian, the *Washington Post*'s Tehran bureau chief, was unjustly convicted of espionage and imprisoned in Iran for eighteen months. Upon his release in January 2016, Bezos took his personal jet to Frankfurt to return the journalist and his family back to the United States. *Alex Wong/Getty Images*

Bezos's fascination with Hollywood and *Star Trek* converged with his cameo in the 2016 film *Star Trek Beyond*. He attended the premiere with then-wife MacKenzie and their four kids. *Todd Williamson/Getty Images*

Roy Price, the first head of Amazon Studios, greenlit critical hits like *Transparent*, helping launch Amazon—and Bezos—in Hollywood. He was a mainstay at Amazon parties, including at this one after the Emmys in September 2016. Price resigned the following year after allegations of inappropriate behavior. *Charley Gallay/Getty Images for Amazon Studios*

Hollywood gravitated toward Amazon's billionaire founder and vice versa. At Amazon's Golden Globes party at the Beverly Hilton Hotel in January 2018, Bezos partied with A-listers Matt Damon, Taika Waititi, and Chris Hemsworth. *Alberto E. Rodriguez/Getty Images*

(*Left*) Worldwide Consumer CEO Jeff Wilke championed the more humane elements of Amazon's hard-edged culture. "He is simply one of those people without whom Amazon would be completely unrecognizable," Bezos wrote when Wilke announced his departure in 2020. *Joe Buglewicz/Bloomberg*

(*Right*) Amazon Web Services CEO Andy Jassy lobbied to conceal the stellar financial performance of his division, which now accounts for more than 60 percent of Amazon's operating profits, for as long as possible. In 2021, Bezos announced Jassy would succeed him as CEO of all of Amazon. *David Paul Morris/Bloomberg*

(*Left*) Beth Galetti, the only woman on the executive S-team for more than three years, took over Amazon HR shortly after a devastating article about the company's culture appeared in the *New York Times* in 2015. She was asked to "radically simplify" its performance review system. *Holly Andres*

(*Right*) Dave Clark has run Amazon's vast operations division since 2012. He spearheaded the acquisition of robot firm Kiva and the expansion into delivering packages, amid criticism of Amazon's safety record. He replaced Jeff Wilke as consumer CEO in 2021. *Kyle Johnson*

(*Above Left*) During his presidency, Donald Trump railed against Amazon, accusing it of tax avoidance and defrauding the U.S. Postal Service. In June 2017, Bezos, Microsoft CEO Satya Nadella, and other tech leaders made a largely peaceful pilgrimage to the White House. *Jabin Botsford/The Washington Post/Getty Images*

(*Above Right*) In July 2017, Bezos attended the exclusive Allen & Company Conference in Sun Valley, Idaho. A widely circulated photo revealed the CEO's heightened workout regimen, spawned countless internet memes, and popularized the phrase "swole Bezos." *Drew Angerer/ Getty Images*

(*Below*) In November 2015, Blue Origin launched and landed both a crew capsule and its reusable booster rocket, a historic feat. "Welcome to the club," Bezos tweeted at Elon Musk when SpaceX did it one month later. But Blue's advantage wouldn't last. *Blue Origin/ZUMA Press*

After the *National Enquirer* made their relationship public, Bezos and Lauren Sanchez started moving openly through elite society. In February 2020, they attended a fashion show in Los Angeles with Jennifer Lopez and legendary *Vogue* editor Anna Wintour. *Calla Kessler/The New York Times/Redux*

Bezos returned to India in January 2020 for a much different visit than the one in 2014. This time, small merchants protested the CEO's arrival, while Bezos and Lauren Sanchez dressed up and took a photo in front of the Taj Mahal. *PAWAN SHARMA/AFP/Getty Images*

By the January 2018 opening of The Spheres, three interlinked glass conservatories at its headquarters in Seattle, Amazon occupied a fifth of all premium office space in the city and relations with the progressive city council were frosty. *Jack Young – Places/Alamy*

Vociferous opposition greeted Amazon's decision to locate half of its second headquarters in Long Island City, Queens, New York. Protesters unfurled anti-Amazon banners and jeered at an HQ2 city council hearing in January 2019. Amazon cancelled its plans to build new offices there only days later. *Drew Angerer/ Getty Images*

At the start of the Covid-19 pandemic, criticism flooded in from Amazon's hourly workforce. Despite instituting temperature checks, social distancing guidelines, and other safety measures, some employees were still getting sick and workers protested that the company was prioritizing sales over safety. *Leandro Justen*

After it resisted making Bezos available to testify before Congress, Amazon was forced to relent. On July 29, 2020, the CEO appeared virtually, along with Facebook's Mark Zuckerberg, Google's Sundar Pichai, and Apple's Tim Cook, during the House Judiciary Subcommittee's hearing on online platforms and market power. *Mandel Ngan*

"My life is based on a large series of mistakes," Bezos said in November 2019 at the Smithsonian's American Portrait Gala in Washington D.C. He was introduced by his oldest son, Preston. *Joy Asico/AP for National Portrait Gallery*

Bezos sorted through binders of artists before choosing the photo-realistic painter Robert McCurdy. He was looking for "someone who would paint me hyper-realistically, with every flaw, every imperfection, every piece of scar tissue that I have."

lawyers restricted the practice, particularly as European antitrust authorities investigated Google for the similar practice of privileging its own services in search results, private-label executives felt sheepish about it. "For a lot of people on the team, it was not an Amazonian thing to do," said JT Meng, a former manager in the consumables division. "Just putting our badges on those products when we didn't necessarily earn them seemed a little bit against the customer, as well as anti-competitive."

Amazon's search results had evolved from a straightforward, algorithmically ordered taxonomy of products into an over-merchandised display of sponsored ads, Amazon Choice endorsements, editorial recommendations from third-party websites, and the company's own private brands. In some product categories, only two organic search results appeared on an entire page of results. Since brands and sellers could no longer count on customers finding their products the old-fashioned way, through the site's search engine, they were even further inclined to open their wallets and spend more money on search ads. A bipartisan report by the U.S. House antitrust subcommittee would later disapprovingly conclude that Amazon "may require sellers to purchase their advertising services as a condition of making sales" on the site, since consumers only tend to look at the first page of search results.

By 2017, revenues from sponsored products had eclipsed those from display advertising like banner ads and would soon after leave them in the dust. That year, sales in the "other" category on Amazon's income statement (the former home of AWS revenues), where the company parked advertising revenues, hit $4.65 billion—a 58 percent jump from the year before. Amazon had discovered a veritable gold mine in its own backyard.

———

But first Bezos had to prevent the consumer retail business from looting the sponsored ad business. By insisting during the OP1 reviews in the fall of 2017 that Amazon's oldest business must stand on its own merits, without the camouflage of advertising, Bezos forced a reversal in the company's longtime operating posture. An all-encompassing pursuit of revenue and market share growth was replaced by the quest for profit. A mandate to plant seeds in all corners of the business was replaced by a sense that only the largest trees mattered—often ones sowed by Bezos himself—while other expensive bets should be pruned back.

Over the next few months, Amazon did something rare in its history: it retreated. Websites set up to sell tickets to concerts and other events were shuttered in the U.S. and UK. The company slowed down the introduction of a service called Amazon Restaurants into new cities, where it was meant to compete with startups like Grubhub, DoorDash, and, in the UK, Deliveroo, and two years later closed it altogether. It also cut the investment in its beleaguered Chinese marketplace, which was hopelessly behind Alibaba and JD.com and would also close for good in 2019.

Amazon also froze hiring in the retail division almost entirely. For years there had been few constraints on recruiting talented employees. Amazon's headcount in Seattle had ballooned to forty thousand employees in 2017 from five thousand in 2010. Over the next year, it was basically flat. "We just decided that after years of rapid fixed cost investment, it made sense for us to slow it down at least for a year and digest the growth and make sure we were being efficient," said Jeff Wilke.

Profitability, a foreign concept for years, was tried on for the first time, like a new suit. Retail executives were ordered to revisit relationships with major brands, like Coca-Cola and Unilever, to extract more favorable terms on products, like bottled water, that were costly to ship. They turned again to their search engine to advance the company's commercial priorities, experimenting with factoring the profitability of items into the algorithmic equation that determined which products received an "Amazon's Choice" badge. The ongoing "hands off the wheel initiative," which replaced retail managers with software, also kicked into higher gear, with brands directed to tools on the Amazon website to run their promotions and manage their sales, instead of working with Amazon employees. The company still offered white glove service to its largest vendors but now would charge them for it.

In the midst of this realignment, Bezos found another way to reduce fixed costs, flatten his organizational chart, and avoid a specter that he dreaded: that Amazon might become a stodgy "Day 2 company." He issued a company-wide mandate ("He's doing that all the time, of course, and people scramble like ants being pounded with a rubber mallet whenever it happens," wrote former Amazon engineer Steve Yegge in a 2011 blog post). From henceforth, all Amazon managers—whose direct reports consisted primarily of other managers—would have to have a minimum of six employees reporting to them.

Though it sounded innocuous, the directive, dubbed "span of control," set off the equivalent of a neutron bomb inside the company. Senior managers with only three, four, or five direct reports had to reach into their organizations and appropriate employees from a subordinate to get to six direct reports, leaving the underling without the necessary number. These actions had a cascading effect, and executives who had steadily climbed Amazon's ranks in pursuit of management responsibility now found the path upward was sealed off.

To many Amazon employees, the organizational rearrangement revived the feeling that an informal cruelty was present in the corporate culture, reminiscent from the days of stack ranking. While some divisions, like AWS, got a reprieve from the directive, others were hit hard. Executives in retail say that 10 to 20 percent of their colleagues (stripped of their direct reports and roles as managers) departed amid these shake-ups, moving either to high-growth divisions like AWS and Alexa or leaving Amazon altogether.

"From the standpoint of organizational morale, they couldn't possibly have handled it more poorly," said Stan Friedlander, a former chief merchant in Amazon's shoe and apparel category who otherwise enjoyed his ten years at the company. "When most big companies go through this, they usually announce they are going to have layoffs," he said. "You can stick around or get a severance. But Amazon to this day never announced how many people they were trying to get rid of, so it created a culture of fear, which they probably prefer."

The informal, musical chairs–style reorganization allowed Amazon to avoid the internal and external stigma of announcing layoffs. And it accomplished it under the mantle of attacking organizational complexity and hewing to Bezos's goal of fighting "Day 2" stasis. It was a typical Bezos move—brilliant, and rather cruel. At the same time as he issued the directive, he also ordered S-team members to watch a nineteen-minute video on YouTube, produced by Bain & Company, called "Founder's Mentality." It was all about eliminating bureaucracy, maintaining the voice of customers in everyday decision-making, and preserving the mindset and motivation of an insurgent startup. "One of the paradoxes of growth is that growth creates complexity and complexity is the silent killer of growth," said Bain director James Allen in the video.

Many executives figured there must be something more to the disruptive moves and tried to get inside Bezos's head. Some speculated that he liked being the sole risk-taker at the company and felt that his deputies were investing too much in random areas. One longtime executive, who left after the shake-up, said that his "best thesis" was that Bezos simply "wants to be the king of L.A." and that the march toward profitability was an attempt to finance the expanding bet on Amazon Studios and original TV shows and films. Others opined that Bezos might have been concerned about the impact of a stagnating share price on Amazon's stock-heavy compensation plans and understood that generating a profit would wow Wall Street.

If that was the gambit, it worked magnificently. After the contentious OP1 reviews and the "span of control" directive over the fall of 2017, headcount growth slowed and Amazon's retail margins expanded, just as Prime's global membership rolls surpassed 100 million and AWS continued its fervid expansion. As a result, Amazon's net income—its annual profit—jumped from $3 billion in 2017 to $10 billion in 2018, sending investors into a defibrillated frenzy. Amazon's stock price levitated. Its market capitalization soared past $550 billion by the end of 2017, to $730 billion at the end of 2018.

And that, of course, had profound repercussions. Veteran employees who had enjoyed years of accumulated stock grants saw their net worth skyrocket. Long-term Amazon investors were richly rewarded for their fealty. And in the fall of 2017, Jeff Bezos finally overcame Bill Gates in the race for the title of world's wealthiest person. Adjusting for inflation, he would soon be richer than Gates at the height of the Microsoft Windows monopoly and richer than Sam Walton during the period of Walmart's iron grip over U.S. retail.

Even for Bezos, who had been in the public eye for two decades, the designation brought an entirely new level of admiration from peers and scrutiny from the media. "The day that Jeff was declared the richest person in the world was the day that the phrase entered the first paragraph of any story about Amazon, no matter the subject," said Jay Carney. Added Josh Weinstein, the high school friend who had accompanied Bezos to his childhood home in Miami, "The business of being the richest person in the world changed the way other people look at him. It became a different world for him."

Bezos himself was the architect of that shift. By discovering the gold mine of search advertising, then insisting his company avoid turning ads into a crutch while battling to contain the growth of his own bureaucracy, he unlocked perhaps the most fertile period of growth in Amazon's history. In the terrestrial world of business, at least, he had established absolute dominance over most of his peers in retail and technology.

CHAPTER 11

Gradatim Ferociter

A year before Jeff Bezos went to war against the bureaucracy at Amazon, an unusual set of meetings transpired on the sixth floor of newly opened Day 1 tower. Over the course of several weeks in the fall of 2016, executives from Bezos's other company, Blue Origin, which he owned and operated independently of Amazon, took turns hailing Ubers from their offices in Kent, Washington, for the half-hour midday drive to downtown Seattle. The occasion? A rare one-on-one lunch with their founder to discuss what ailed the sixteen-year-old space startup.

Amid the resplendent success of Amazon and the striking revival of the *Washington Post*, Blue Origin was the straggler in Bezos's expanding empire of accomplishment. A program to fly tourists to suborbital space on a reusable rocket called *New Shepard* had suffered numerous delays and lost two unmanned vehicles to fiery explosions—or "rapid unscheduled disassemblies," in the macabre lexicon of the rocket scientists. An even more ambitious project to take tourists and cargo into orbit on a much bulkier rocket, *New Glenn*, was years away from completion.

Meanwhile, SpaceX, the private space company that Tesla cofounder Elon Musk founded two years after Blue Origin, was making significant headway as well as history. Its steadfast *Falcon 9* rocket was regularly sending commercial and military satellites into orbit and had just been designated to resupply the International Space Station. That April 2016, the firm landed a *Falcon 9* booster on a drone platform floating in the Atlantic Ocean. It was an extraordinary technical achievement, one that offered a sharp contrast between the two space firms and their billionaire backers.

Now Bezos was spending part of his Amazon workday trying to understand the problems at Blue Origin. Over the course of a series of lunches, some which lasted as long as two hours, Blue executives tried to enlighten their owner. They complained about poor internal communication, time-consuming meetings, and inexplicable spending decisions. One engineer described the company as a Potemkin village—its dysfunctional culture concealed beneath an industrious façade. Another executive threatened to quit if problems weren't promptly addressed.

Many of the Blue employees who lunched with Bezos were circumspect when it came to the root of these problems. They danced around the way Bezos constrained the company's headcount while expanding its ambitions. Figuring Bezos might share their accounts, they were also reticent to discuss the person who ran the firm on his behalf: president Rob Meyerson, a thirteen-year Blue veteran.

Nevertheless, Bezos listened carefully, took notes, and seemed to get the message. After the lunches, he informed Meyerson that he wanted to begin to look for something Blue Origin had never had in its history: a CEO. Susan Harker, Amazon's vice president of recruiting, led the search for Bezos. The process included an entreaty to Gwynne Shotwell, SpaceX's dynamic chief operating officer and president, who quickly rebuffed it, saying that it "wouldn't look right," according to a person privy to the discussion.

Blue Origin's CEO search stretched on for over a year. Meyerson helped to interview candidates and his colleagues wondered if he might be proceeding slowly to protect his job, or whether Bezos was having trouble making up his mind. Finally, talks intensified with Bob Smith, president of the mechanical systems and components division of Honeywell Aerospace and a former executive director at United

Space Alliance, a company that supported NASA's retired space shuttle program.

Smith, like Bezos, was "an Apollo kid" who had spent part of his childhood in Texas watching American astronauts walk on the moon. He interviewed with Blue Origin executives more than two dozen times over the course of a twelve-month courtship and later recalled asking in jest, "Do you want my dental records too?"

Just as Bezos was surpassing Bill Gates as the wealthiest person in the world, and a year after his meetings with Blue staff at the Day 1 tower, Smith finally got the job in August 2017. There was no formal announcement and little fanfare in the press. But Bezos's mandate to Smith was clear: turn an underachieving research and development organization into a mature business that justified the backing and bravado of the world's richest person. Blue Origin "had really hit a severe inflection point" is how Bob Smith later put it in an interview. It was time "to step through some much bigger doors."

———

Jeff Bezos's passion for space travel was etched into the public's earliest understanding of his illustrious biography. As a child, his parents sent him every summer to the South Texas ranch of his retired grandfather, Lawrence Preston Gise, who had worked on space technology and missile defense systems in the fifties and sixties for the Atomic Energy Commission. Gise passed on a passion for space to his grandson. Bezos spent his summer vacations watching the Apollo launches, devouring the extensive science fiction collection at the local library, and dreaming of humanity's manifest destiny in space. He often said that his grandfather, whom everyone called "Pop," taught him the value of self-reliance. Together they fixed windmills, rebuilt an old bulldozer, and vaccinated cattle. In his valedictorian speech at Miami Palmetto Senior High School, Bezos ruminated on solving the problems of overpopulation and pollution by putting millions of people into orbiting space stations.

In 2000, Bezos deployed the bounteous resources from his success at Amazon to pursue those dreams. He founded Blue Origin—the name refers to humanity's birthplace, Earth—with a hypothesis that quickly proved incorrect: that significant advancements in space would require alternatives to liquid-fueled rockets. For the first few years, Blue resembled "a club more than a company," as journalist Steven Levy later wrote in *Wired*, a think tank that included a dozen aficionados, like novelist Neal Stephenson and science historian George Dyson, who brainstormed radical and unproven ways to travel into space.

By 2003, Bezos had changed course, acknowledging the unrivaled efficiency of conventional liquid propulsion. Instead of trying to reinvent rockets, the firm would focus on lowering the cost of building them, by making them reusable. That year, he hired Meyerson, a NASA veteran coming off six years at the failed space startup Kistler Aerospace. An introverted engineer with a plaintive demeanor and no executive-level management experience, Meyerson started as a senior systems engineer on *New Shepard*. But Bezos, who already had an all-consuming day job, couldn't approve every decision and wanted Blue to move faster. Soon after he hired him, he made Meyerson the program manager and president of the small firm.

While Bezos couldn't supervise every detail at Blue Origin, he could devise the mechanisms—a system of invention—to guide how employees set priorities and conducted their work. In June 2004, he wrote an eight-hundred-word memo, informally dubbed "The Welcome Letter," which to this day is given to new Blue employees as part of their hiring packet and has never before been publicly revealed.

"We are a small team committed to seeding an enduring human presence in space," Bezos began, reflecting his original desire to keep the company under seventy employees. "Blue will pursue this long-term objective patiently, step by step." He described releasing new versions of its rockets at six-month intervals with "metronome-like regularity," and predicted the company would eventually shift its focus to a crewed orbital vehicle program that "will stretch Blue's organization and capabilities." He drew a distinction between those plans and more hypothetical longer-term scenarios, like building a spacecraft to visit the moon, and cautioned employees to focus on the task at hand and work methodically.

"We've been dropped off on an unexplored mountain without maps and the visibility is poor," he wrote. "You don't start and stop. Keep climbing at a steady pace. Be the tortoise and not the hare. Keep expenditures at sustainable levels. Assume spending will be flat to monotonically increasing." He reassured employees that he understood that funding Blue personally would be expensive. "I accept that Blue Origin will not meet a reasonable investor's expectation for return on investment over a typical investing horizon," he wrote. "It's important to the peace of mind to those at Blue to know I won't be surprised or disappointed when this prediction proves true."

The document, signed by Bezos, took on the same sacred inviolability inside Blue as Amazon's inaugural letter to shareholders, with employees returning to it each year at all-hands meetings. He condensed its central idea into the company's Latin motto, *Gradatim Ferociter*, or "Step by Step, Ferociously." He also devised an elaborate coat of arms that depicted two tortoises standing on the Earth and appealing to the stars, over an hourglass with wings, a symbol of fleeting time.

The Welcome Letter and its subsequent representations served as a sort of beacon in the dark, quietly speaking to other enthusiasts at the company who dreamed of opening the space frontier, while Bezos kept Blue Origin enveloped in secrecy. New employees were all required to read the memo and reflect on it; prospective job candidates were even asked to write essays reflecting on the depth of their passion for the Blue mission, and were turned down if their yearnings were seen as not devotional enough.

In the mid-2000s, Bezos's interests in space attracted the attention of another prominent devotee: Elon Musk, who founded SpaceX in 2002 with the same goal of making more economical, reusable rockets and opening the space frontier. Bezos and Musk met privately twice to discuss their mutual obsession, once in San Francisco and soon afterward in Seattle with their spouses at the time, MacKenzie and Justine Musk. The couples had dinner at a restaurant downtown, and then Jeff and MacKenzie gave Musk and his wife a tour of Blue's original warehouse office, which a colleague recalled he had curiously cleared ahead of time of employees and any revealing indications of their work.

In many ways, SpaceX back then was the antithesis of Blue Origin. Financed with seed investments by Musk and an array of venture capitalists, it desperately pursued profitability from the outset by bidding against established aerospace giants for government contracts to launch commercial satellites and military hardware into orbit. With Blue, Bezos was thinking more long-term. He intended to finance the firm himself and wanted to develop technologies with *New Shepard* that could later be integrated into more ambitious missions into orbit and beyond. "Don't just build a space vehicle, build a company that builds space vehicles," Bezos had written in the Welcome Letter.

Musk later told me that he "thought it was cool that Jeff created Blue Origin and that there was someone else with similar philanthropic goals with regard to space, and a lot of resources." He recalled their early meetings as friendly and remembered getting into a technical debate with Bezos over the merits of Blue Origin's planned fuel mix, which used peroxide, a compound known to decompose rapidly when exposed to sunlight. "Peroxide is great until you come back one weekend and your vehicle is gone and your test site is gone," Musk said. But Bezos was operating on the advice of his chief propulsion officer at the time, William Kruse, a former engineer for the aerospace corporation TRW. Kruse favored peroxide's non-cryogenic properties and the fact that it could be used with an existing turbo pump, which required little extra engineering effort.

Bezos felt that working with such existing components would

allow Blue Origin to keep its engineering teams small and move fast—principles laid out in the Welcome Letter. He believed that constraints drove innovation, and he wanted to develop space vehicles with the cadence of a software project, incorporating new ideas into frequent iterations, using as many standard technologies as possible. The method worked well at internet companies like Amazon, where bugs could be easily fixed. But at an aerospace firm perpetually stretched for resources, it was a recipe for errors to sneak into systems that needed to be strenuously tested and mission hardened.

In 2011, Blue Origin was launching a test vehicle on Bezos's three-hundred-thousand-acre ranch in West Texas. That August, a simple software error drew the rocket off course, forcing an onboard safety system to terminate the flight at forty-five thousand feet. Residents of the town of Van Horn, thirty miles away, saw a "rapid unscheduled disassembly." The company ensured that no video was made public and only acknowledged the incident when the media started to investigate. "Not the outcome any of us wanted, but we're signed up for this to be hard," Bezos wrote in a blog post on the Blue Origin website.

By then Blue was already redeveloping *New Shepard*, acceding to Musk's advice on the volatility of peroxide by shifting to a higher-performance rocket fuel mixture of liquid oxygen and liquid hydrogen. The company also started to tentatively apply for government contracts, receiving $25 million in awards for the initial two phases of CCDev, an Obama-era program to solicit proposals from private companies to ferry astronauts to the International Space Station. But the more stringent requirements of Phase 3, conducted over the winter of 2012, called for participating companies to build a complete orbital spacecraft in three years.

Competing in this crucial phase would require Bezos to radically depart from some of the principles of the Welcome Letter—his desire for the company to stay lean, for example, and operate "step by step." Blue was still largely focused on *New Shepard*, and so decided to pass. SpaceX won the contract, along with Boeing, and earned an initial haul of $440 million. Years later, after the Office of Inspector General published an audit of the program that revealed SpaceX had ended up receiving a total of $7.7 billion for the project, Bezos would forget those early conversations and wonder aloud, according to a colleague's recollection, "Why did we decide not to bid on that?" Asked about the comment, Blue said Bezos never questioned the decision not to bid.

As a result of these divergent approaches, SpaceX quickly grew much larger and faster. By the time Blue hired its 250th employee in 2013, SpaceX had 2,750 workers and was already sending unmanned spacecraft to the International Space Station. Blue was consumed with *New Shepard*, but SpaceX had entirely skipped the intermediate stage of building suborbital rockets to take tourists to space, which Bezos felt was necessary in part to acclimate people to the idea of space travel, to achieve his ultimate goal of creating a future where millions of humans are living and working in space.

While Bezos and Musk seemed like-minded in their respective space ambitions, they had philosophical differences driving their companies. Musk's oft-stated goal was to colonize Mars and make humans a "multi-planetary species" as an insurance policy against calamity on Earth. Bezos believed "that of all the planets in the solar system, Earth is by far the best one," and that lowering the cost of access to space was the path to putting large, vibrant populations onto space stations, where they could harvest solar energy and mine the abundant metals and other resources from the surface of the moon. Bezos hypothesized that at the current rate of population growth and energy use, humanity would have to start rationing resources within several generations, leading to a society of stasis. "We go to space to save the Earth," he declared on Twitter.

Nevertheless, Blue Origin and SpaceX were, inevitably, headed for conflict. They would end up competing not just for government contracts, talent, and resources but for the adulation and attention of the space-enthusiast public and press. By 2013, the amiability of the early meetings between Musk and Bezos was gone, and in its place was a budding rivalry between two successful, strong-willed, and ego-tistical entrepreneurs.

That September, in a transparent attempt to slow down its rival, Blue Origin protested SpaceX's plan to lease NASA's historic 39A launch complex at Kennedy Space Center in Cape Canaveral, the original home of the Apollo program. Responding to Blue's legal chal-lenge in an email to *SpaceNews*, Musk wrote, "We are more likely to discover unicorns dancing in the flame duct" than see Blue Ori-gin produce a rocket qualified to dock with the ISS over the next five years. Blue's protest failed, and it later secured the smaller Launch Complex 36, which required a more expensive rehabilitation. In 2014, the companies also dueled over a flimsy Blue Origin patent for land-ing a rocket on a sea barge. SpaceX challenged the patent in court and prevailed.

But Bezos was studying SpaceX and the reasons for its mount-ing success. Musk's company was funding its rapid growth by sell-ing its launch services; perhaps Blue could do something similar, while remaining focused on its "step by step" path to getting to space. After Russia invaded Crimea in 2014, an opportunity presented it-self: the United Launch Alliance (ULA)—a partnership between the aerospace divisions of Lockheed Martin and Boeing, and the premier launch provider for the U.S. military at the time—announced it would search for a U.S. engine supplier in case it was forced not to buy any more rocket engines from Russia. Blue executives offered to sell ULA its new BE-4 liquefied natural gas engine it was developing for the *New Glenn* orbital booster.

ULA's parent organizations wanted to be sure they weren't helping a future rival, like SpaceX, that would end up competing for lucrative satellite launches. Bezos got on the phone with executives from both companies and was apparently persuasive. Competing against ULA's main engine vendor, Aerojet Rocketdyne, Blue won the deal, which was announced on September 17, 2014. But Blue Origin would prove itself to be an inconsistent partner.

In April the following year, for the first time, Blue launched a prototype of the *New Shepard* crew capsule from Bezos's ranch. The capsule, stuffed with employee memorabilia like toys, business cards, and jewelry as part of an internal program called "fly your stuff," reached the Kármán line, the zero-gravity environment at a hundred kilometers above sea level, separated from the rocket, and floated down to Earth on its three parachutes. But instead of returning gently to the ground, the reusable booster suffered a hydraulic failure and another "rapid unscheduled disassembly" as it made a fiery landing.

"We always learned more from failure than we did success," said longtime Blue Origin executive Gary Lai. "In hindsight, with the proper ground testing, the failure that occurred during M1 could have been avoided." Other colleagues recalled Bezos sounding frustrated. "Are we making sophisticated errors or embarrassingly stupid errors?" he asked during an analysis of the mishap.

But that November, in perhaps its shining moment, Blue Origin finally pulled off the feat. The test vehicle reached into space, and the booster, its rockets pounding the desert floor, settled back to the launchpad amid a cloud of dust and remained upright. In the control center, everyone erupted in cheers and "all sense of decorum was lost," Gary Lai said.

After the capsule returned safely via parachute, an ebullient Bezos, wearing a cowboy hat, brought out what Lai described as "the largest bottle of champagne I have ever seen," and then, instead of pulling out the cork, took out a large knife and sabered the bottle's stem clean off. "I had tears in my eyes. It really was one of the most magnificent things I have ever seen," Bezos said as employees toasted. "This is a huge milestone, but it isn't the end, it is the beginning. This is the start of something amazing. This is truly a great day not just for Blue Origin, but for all of civilization. I think what we have done today is going to be remembered for thousands of years and you should be so proud of yourselves."

SpaceX, meanwhile, had started with an expendable low-tech

system and backed into reusability. When it landed its own reusable booster for the first time a month later, Bezos tweeted a wry "Welcome to the club" at Musk.

But the genetic difference between the two companies ensured that Blue's advantage would be fleeting. At the time of the successful launch, Blue had about 400 employees with their attentions mainly focused on *New Shepard*, along with some long-term planning for the fledgling New Glenn program and the BE-4 engine.

Meanwhile, SpaceX had 4,500 employees and was growing quickly, with a sole focus on orbital missions. Blue was reliant on funding from Bezos, while Uncle Sam, taxpayers, and other customers were paying most of SpaceX's bills.

In other words, this wasn't a fable: the tortoise was racing an actual hare, and not surprisingly, the hare was winning.

———

Despite these battles, Blue Origin employees, like their counterparts at Amazon, were almost religiously indoctrinated to ignore the prospect of competition and stay focused on the task at hand. Working amid the resplendence of Bezos's expanding wealth, it wasn't difficult to do so. From the outside, their headquarters in an industrial neighborhood of Kent looked unremarkable: a sprawling, 300,000-square-foot former factory where Boeing once manufactured drill bits for the Chunnel. But on the inside, the offices had been converted into a space enthusiast's playground, filled with artifacts and science fiction curios purchased over the years by Bezos himself.

The personal collection spanned the arc of humanity's journey into space. There was a Mercury-era NASA hard hat, a pressure suit worn by Soyuz astronauts, and a heat shield tile from a space shuttle. In a second-floor atrium was the model of the *Starship Enterprise* used in the original *Star Trek* films. Next to it was a two-story replica of the steampunk spacecraft depicted in the Jules Verne novel *From the Earth to the Moon*. A quote attributed to Leonardo da Vinci adorned a wall nearby: "Once you have tasted flight, you will forever walk the earth with your eyes turned skyward. For there you have been, and there you will always long to return."

For employees, respite could be found on the building's northwest side, in an outdoor space dubbed "the secret garden," after the Frances Hodgson Burnett novel. A koi pond, a walking path, an outdoor kitchen, and a smoker were nestled amid fruit trees and blueberry bushes that blocked out the concrete jungle beyond. A bench in the park had a memorial plaque on it that displayed the name Elizabeth Korrell—Bezos's late business manager and personal attorney, who died of cancer in 2010 at the age of forty-two.

Korrell had stayed out of the limelight aside from one brush with notoriety: on March 6, 2003, she and Bezos were scouting property near Cathedral Mountain in West Texas when their helicopter crashed into a shallow creek, trying to take off amid high winds. Korrell suffered a broken vertebra; Bezos walked away with minor scratches. The biggest lesson, he told an interviewer afterward, was to "avoid helicopters whenever possible."

Bezos and Korrell eventually found suitable land near the town of Van Horn and made a series of purchases through holding companies bearing names of famous explorers. Bezos wanted the same kind of Texas retreat that his grandfather had owned, where he spent so many formative summers. It would double as a Blue Origin facility and launchpad.

A decade later, the ranch offered Blue engineers another escape of wealth and fun. The property included a pool and patio, an outdoor firepit, and a domed high-powered telescope where they could peer at the stars on cloudless Texas nights. During the day, they occasionally rode dune buggies on the property; at night, Bezos hosted dinners and served expensive liquor from an outdoor saloon that he ceremonially named Parpie's Bar, after the nickname all the grandkids called his father, Mike Bezos. Whenever they finished a premium bottle of scotch, he'd have everyone sign it.

After these interludes, they would return to reality and to an organization that felt vexingly bipolar. Bezos set increasingly lofty goals while allocating the minimum of resources to accomplish them. For long periods, he limited the time he spent with the company, coming in only on the occasional Saturday for deeply technical program reviews where he would impress employees by sparring with the company's rocket scientists and aerodynamicists. He enjoyed interacting with engineers and wanted a visible role in the firm's most important architectural and design decisions. But he preferred to manage many of the details of daily operations invisibly, via email with Rob Meyerson.

This style of oversight put the company's president in a difficult position. Meyerson was acting as a conduit for Bezos but had none of his imposing authority; he also struggled to follow Bezos's inconsistent directives, embracing constraints while hiring rapidly to accommodate the company's growing ambitions. He held confrontational Monday meetings with his direct reports, which he often used to criticize them for not moving fast enough, leaving them demoralized and unproductive. They viewed him skeptically, according to numerous accounts, believing that he took copious notes for the purpose of sending Bezos frequent reports and acted as a distorting filter between them and their real boss.

All these frictions inside Blue Origin culminated in a series of acrimonious clashes in 2016. Morale was low, and Bezos, frustrated by the lack of progress, was allowing some of the edgier management habits and notorious outbursts that he had suppressed at Amazon to reemerge at Blue Origin. In a technology review meeting that February, he directed a withering stream of invective at *New Shepard* systems architect Greg Seymour, who had been with the company for twelve years. Seymour, who had already been unhappy, quit via text message at 3 a.m. the following morning.

Later that summer, Bezos also castigated Meyerson and other senior executives when they surprised him with a proposed budget of well over $500 million, which far exceeded his expectations. They were trying to forecast the cost of capital projects like the rocket and engine factories for New Glenn. Bezos, worth some $45 billion at the time, had sticker shock. "I'm not spending that," he complained. "If it was this big, you should have called me in the middle of the night to tell me about it!"

In the Welcome Letter, Bezos had vowed that he wouldn't be surprised or disappointed if the company didn't immediately provide a return on his investment. But now it seemed like he was both. Employees said that after a long absence from visiting the Kent headquarters on Wednesdays, the usual day he spent at Blue Origin, Bezos started coming in for a few hours each week to talk to department heads to better understand the mounting expenses and incessant dysfunction. Believing that Blue was hindered by slow decision-making, he also began appearing at the company cafeteria at lunchtime. Anyone could approach him to get a rapid decision on a problem or idea, as long as they came prepared with a one-page document that outlined the challenge and potential solutions.

Everything came to an awkward denouement in the fall of '16. The American Astronomical Society named Meyerson a recipient of its Space Flight Award, given annually to "the person whose outstanding efforts and achievements have contributed most significantly to the advancement" of space exploration. When Bezos announced the accolade at a management meeting, no one applauded; almost in unison, Blue executives cast their eyes downward. "Okay, maybe I need to say this again, it's a very prestigious award," Bezos said. The room remained silent. Everyone was furious over their internal battles, the yawning gap between their resources and ambitions and the pummeling now being administered on a regular basis to their collective dignity by SpaceX.

That's when Bezos started inviting executives one by one to his Amazon office for lunch.

———

As Blue Origin initiated its search for a CEO who could introduce "Amazon-like operational excellence" to the company, Bezos appeared to change his mind about how he operated Blue, discarding some of the guiding principles that had constrained the firm's growth. He backed away from the "metronome-like incrementalism" he had described in the Welcome Letter and committed Blue fully to a set of ambitious parallel programs. He also abandoned the notion that the company's expenditures should be "flat to monotonically increasing," and authorized a major budget expansion. When he announced at the April 2017 Space Symposium in Colorado Springs that he was selling $1 billion a year of Amazon stock to fund Blue Origin, employees were stunned—that was the first they had heard of it.

As happened with so many of Bezos's reversals at Amazon, like his demand later that year that the retail unit show profitability without advertising, Blue employees strained to understand his sudden change of mind. The only plausible answer was the one staring them in the face: the hare had outraced the tortoise. Bezos recognized the need to change strategies if Blue was ever going to start winning commercial and government contracts to fund its own growth and catch up with Elon Musk and SpaceX.

For more than a decade, Blue's attention had been fixed on giving paying customers an eleven-minute thrill ride to the edge of space. But after a fifth successful *New Shepard* test flight in October 2016, the suborbital spacecraft wouldn't fly again for more than a year. Instead, focus and resources shifted to what Bezos dubbed *New Shepard*'s bigger brother.

That fall, the company unveiled *New Glenn* to the public, pledging a maiden flight by the end of the decade—a goal it would fail to meet. Designs for *New Glenn* showed that it would have more boosting capacity than SpaceX's *Falcon 9* and its bulkier twin, the *Falcon Heavy*. It was also equipped to take payloads like commercial and military satellites into a high-altitude geosynchronous orbit—precisely the market United Launch Alliance officials had believed that Blue Origin was not interested in.

"ULA executives felt like they were betrayed and lied to," said George Sowers, the former chief scientist and vice president at ULA. Executives from the two companies stopped talking; tensions were so high that they walked past one another in the halls of the annual Space Symposium that year without acknowledging one another. Blue later disputed the notion that its execs stopped talking to counterparts at ULA. Nevertheless, the story ULA execs eventually heard from employees at Blue, Sowers said, was that Bezos was frustrated that the government was funding Elon Musk's space dreams and wanted to get in on the action.

To compete for those lucrative contracts and to "get paid to practice," as Bezos put it to colleagues, Blue would eventually reach *New Glenn* launch contracts with satellite operators like France's Eutelsat, Canada's Telesat, and UK's OneWeb. And when the U.S. Air Force announced the next phase of a competition to spur development of launch systems to put national security satellites into orbit, Bezos was clear: he wanted Blue Origin to be a prime competitor, not just an engine supplier to other participants. Blue ended up winning a $500 million launch service agreement, alongside Northrop Grumman and ULA.

Blue Origin was now nakedly opportunistic. After Donald Trump won the presidency and announced the goal of returning Americans to the moon by 2024, Blue executives quickly put together a seven-page proposal outlining a lunar service to the Shackleton crater on the moon's south pole, paving the way for human colonies there. "It is time for America to return to the Moon—this time to stay," Bezos emailed the *Washington Post*, after it obtained a copy of the proposal. The idea would evolve into another massive undertaking, called Blue Moon.

As Blue Origin's scope expanded, Bezos became a more prominent evangelist for its mission, and for his own vision for human space travel. Gone entirely was his old conviction that Blue should discuss its goals in public only after it had accomplished them. That August, at the EAA AirVenture show in Oshkosh, Wisconsin, an annual gathering for aviation and space enthusiasts, he showed off the finished *New Shepard* capsule. It had six reclining chairs, each perched before a large forty-three-inch-high shatterproof window to better take in the curvature of the planet and the vastness of space. "Space changes people," Bezos said to the assembled crowd, as the surviving Apollo astronauts toured the capsule. "Every time you talk to . . . somebody who has been to space, they will tell you that when you look back at the Earth and see how beautiful it is, and how fragile it is, with that thin limb of the Earth's atmosphere, it makes you really appreciate home."

A company executive told the assembled crowd they planned to start sending paying customers up in the next year or two. Blue Origin would fail to meet that timeline as well.

To pursue these parallel objectives, Blue's headcount soared past a thousand people in 2017 and doubled in 2018. A portion of those employees came from Musk's company, and the damning refrain in the industry—that "Blue was the country club you go to after toiling at SpaceX"—would have infuriated Bezos if he heard it. Blue Origin also broke ground on rocket production facilities in Cape Canaveral and Huntsville, Alabama. It would fall to new CEO Bob Smith to digest all this growth and professionalize the company.

Smith hired veteran executives from Raytheon, the aerospace division of Rolls-Royce, Boeing, Lockheed Martin, Northrop Grumman, and other legacy companies. SpaceX executives were openly contemptuous of such firms, viewing them as complicit in decades of stagnation in space innovation. But no such compunction existed at the new Blue Origin, which needed "to do things that all businesses need to do, which is have good financials, a good HR process, and [leaders] that know how to lead and develop and have large teams," said Bob Smith. "All those things were necessary steps we needed to take to make the routine flying of people possible."

With the influx of professional managers, many of the longtime employees who had strolled in the secret garden and celebrated their triumphs at Parpie's Bar in Texas felt displaced and left Blue Origin. Rob Meyerson remained, nominally in charge of "advanced development programs," but without authority or direct reports. As Bezos transferred his attention to Smith and withdrew once again from regular appearances at the company, Meyerson felt sidelined. He left Blue Origin in late 2018, reasoning that the new CEO no longer wanted him there.

———

In the Welcome Letter, Bezos had predicted that Blue Origin would eventually create a return on his massive investment. "I do expect that over a very long-term horizon, perhaps even decades from now, Blue will be self-sustaining, operationally profitable and will yield returns," he wrote. "It will just take an unusually long time."

But as he continued to evangelize in public for Blue Origin, Bezos began to frame the operation less as a hobby or business pursuit and more as a kind of long-term philanthropy. "I get increasing conviction with every passing year that Blue Origin, the space company, is the most important work that I'm doing," he said in a May 2018 onstage interview with Mathias Döpfner, CEO of media giant Axel Springer. "I'm pursuing this work, because I believe if we don't, we will eventually end up with a civilization of stasis, which I find very demoralizing. I don't want my great-grandchildren's great-grandchildren to live in a civilization of stasis."

His generation's destiny, he explained, was to lower the cost of access to space and unleash the same forces of creativity that had unlocked the golden age of innovation on the internet. The goal was a trillion humans one day living and working throughout the solar system on space stations that operated on the plentiful power of the sun.

This soaring objective was inspired by one of Bezos's favorite space theorists, the late physicist Gerard K. O'Neill. It was also a useful one for the world's wealthiest person, whose charitable contributions were now the subject of constant scrutiny and criticism. Instead of an e-commerce kingpin with an expensive hobby, Bezos was a great industrialist making a grand gift to humanity.

The philanthropic message was a new one to many of his longtime colleagues at Blue Origin. It also helped to obscure the more evident reality that Blue was still struggling twenty years into its existence. By the spring of 2021, it still hadn't brought a tourist past the Kármán line or ever flown to orbit. These were inconvenient facts that Bezos's rival, Elon Musk, who also framed his efforts in space as a way to inspire humanity and potentially save it from extinction, took every opportunity to point out.

"I have a lot of respect for anyone who has flown a rocket to orbit," Musk said at the unveiling of SpaceX's next generation rocket prototype, the fifty-meter-tall *Starship*, in September 2019, taking a subtle dig at Blue. At an interview at a financial conference a few weeks later, Gwynne Shotwell was more explicit. "They're two years older than us, and they have yet to reach orbit," she said. "They have a billion dollars of free money every year."

On its website, Blue Origin insisted, "We are not in a race, and there will be many players in this human endeavor to go to space to benefit Earth." Yet the contrast between the two companies was never starker. In 2020, SpaceX would fly its one hundredth mission, bring humans to the International Space Station, and establish itself as the world's dominant rocket company. Musk, who vaulted temporarily past Bezos to become the world's richest person during the run-up of Tesla's stock price in 2021, was industrializing space first and didn't shy away from viewing it as a contest. "Competition I think is a good thing not a bad thing," he told me. "The Olympics would be pretty boring if everyone just linked arms and crossed the finish line."

Blue remained secretive, struggling with the dysfunction encoded into its genetic makeup by Bezos, who had otherwise succeeded in nearly everything else he had created. Still, the entertaining exchange of barbs between the tycoons continued—about their plans for the moon, for Mars, whether Amazon was copying SpaceX with its plans to launch a constellation of low Earth satellites in space, and over Amazon's purchase of Zoox, an autonomous vehicle company that might one day compete with Tesla.

Musk and Bezos were a lot alike—relentless, competitive, and absorbed with their self-images. But Musk eagerly sought the spotlight and cultivated a kind of cultlike adoration at his companies and among his fans, preening on stage at Tesla events and extemporaneously (and often recklessly) riffing on Twitter. He also seemed entirely comfortable sharing the salacious details of his personal life, like his relationship with the musician Grimes.

Bezos, on the other hand, was more guarded. He always followed a meticulous and well-rehearsed script in public and endeavored to put systems and values at the center of Blue Origin, instead of the heavily regulated resources of his own time and reputation. And he was far more circumspect than Musk with the details of his private life.

But those details were going to prove difficult to suppress for much longer. In July 2018, Blue Origin conducted the ninth test flight of *New Shepard* on Bezos's ranch in Texas. After the successful launch, *New Shepard* managers had to contend with an additional expense on their budget—charges for the services of a company called Black Ops Aviation, which Bezos had hired to record aerial footage for an uncharacteristic promotional stunt: a Super Bowl commercial for Blue Origin.

The founder of Black Ops was by Bezos's side at the launch: an attractive former TV anchor named Lauren Sanchez. It was another unfathomable shift to contemplate because, as they all knew, Jeff Bezos hated helicopters.

PART III

INVINCIBILITY

Amazon, December 31, 2018

Annual net sales:	$232.89 billion
Full- and part-time employees:	647,500
End-of-year market capitalization:	$734.41 billion

Jeff Bezos end-of-year net worth:	$124.93 billion

CHAPTER 12

License to Operate

B y the start of 2018, the disparate threads from Jeff Bezos's private pursuits and Amazon's business triumphs were finally converging to create the picture of a company and its founder in brilliant ascent. Millions of people around the world owned an Amazon Echo, moving Amazon from their doorstep into their homes with the virtual assistant Alexa promising to usher in an age of seamless voice computing. The cashierless Amazon Go store had finally opened to the public in Seattle and would soon start appearing in major cities around the U.S. In the costly race for e-commerce supremacy in India, the company was dueling on equal footing with the Walmart-owned Flipkart. In Hollywood, hits like *The Marvelous Mrs. Maisel* and *Fleabag* had established the company as part of a disruptive new wave, and streaming video as another doorway into the prosperous Prime ecosystem.

In its original e-commerce business, Amazon had harnessed the chaotic force of Chinese capitalism to boost its third-party marketplace, completed its acquisition of Whole Foods Market, and developed a last-mile transportation network that supported its growth and mitigated its dependency on package delivery companies and national postal services. AWS remained the company's primary engine of cash flow and profit, but Amazon had also developed a secondary source: a lucrative online advertising business.

Even with an employee base nearing six hundred thousand—with almost two-thirds of its workers in the FCs—Amazon in early 2018 remained inventive and demonstrated considerable leverage over its fixed costs. For that unique combination, and for seemingly being unbound from the laws of organizational gravity that inhibited most large enterprises, investors that June awarded it with a market capitalization that surpassed $800 billion for the first time. And the stock price continued heading up.

Bezos let all those plates spin on their own, returning to them only occasionally and usually without warning to generate provocative new ideas, clamp down on costs, and whack at the gathering bureaucracy. On his own time, he tinkered with the business and technology of the *Washington Post*, supervised the new management at Blue Origin, and exulted in launching test flights of the *New Shepard* rocket from his ranch in West Texas. He also considered plans for charitable work in the wake of public pressure to give away a fortune that had surpassed $100 billion. And as always, he contemplated Amazon's long-term future—not just the dramatic new things it could do, but where it would do them.

On January 29, 2018, Bezos hosted journalists, political luminaries like Washington governor Jay Inslee, and other guests on Amazon's corporate campus in downtown Seattle for the opening of the Spheres, three interlinked glass-and-steel conservatories that housed a lush profusion of tropical plants, artificial creeks, and aquariums. It marked the culmination of an eight-year-long journey, starting when Amazon leased eleven low-rise buildings in the South Lake Union neighborhood from Microsoft cofounder Paul Allen's Vulcan Inc. in the belief that they would accommodate its growth for the foreseeable future. Bezos felt that a dynamic urban campus could help Amazon attract and maintain coveted young technical employees. But headcount, expected to increase gradually, started to grow between 30 to 60 percent annually, along with the brisk expansion of Amazon's business, and the six-story buildings in South Lake Union bulged with people.

In 2012, Amazon bought the entire campus from Vulcan, along

with an additional three-block site nearby, and started planning a high-rise office complex. In October of that year, Bezos happened to tour the Ferrari headquarters in Maranello, Italy. Always a collector of other companies' quirks and customs, he may have been inspired by the indoor gardens that lined the luxury carmaker's tranquil factory floor and soon after had a radical idea for Amazon's new headquarters.

"Alexa, open the Spheres," Bezos said at the unveiling, standing at a podium facing the assembled crowd. "Okay, Jeff," responded the disembodied voice of Alexa, Boulder singer Nina Rolle, as a circular ring affixed to the domed ceiling illuminated with blue light and misters began to spray water onto thousands of exotic plants and trees. Employees and guests applauded, while Bezos reared back with his inimitable, barking laugh.

But not everybody was celebrating. By the opening of the Spheres that January in 2018, forty-five thousand Amazon employees worked in Seattle, and the company occupied about a fifth of all the premium office space in the city. New hotels, restaurants, and construction sprouted in an already dense downtown core. Amazon had altered the quirky character of its hometown, once known as an industrial city and as the source of alternative trends like grunge music and fashion.

All of the downsides of twenty-first-century urbanism had accompanied these rapid changes. Historic neighborhoods with rich cultural histories, like the largely Black Central District three miles east of Amazon's offices, had gentrified at an alarming rate. The average rent for a one-bedroom apartment in Seattle increased by 67 percent between the years of 2013 and 2017, according to the National Low Income Housing Coalition. Traffic on the I-5 freeway into the city, and over the bridges to West Seattle and to the eastern suburbs, crawled to a standstill during rush hour. With restrictive land use regulations and neighborhood opposition limiting the construction of new housing, low-income families were displaced and homelessness on Seattle streets became sickeningly ubiquitous.

Most public officials agree that the city was unprepared for these changes and didn't move swiftly enough to counter them. "What was surprising to us in government was the depth and breadth and acceleration of Amazon's growth," said Tim Burgess, a city councilman who was briefly Seattle's mayor in 2017. "In many ways, the city wasn't ready for it." Maud Daudon, the former CEO of the Seattle Metropolitan Chamber of Commerce, said that Seattle was "inevitably caught a bit flat-footed as a community" by Amazon's rise. "It was just so transformational."

The same dynamic was playing out eight hundred miles south in Silicon Valley, where the recoil from longtime residents to the changes wrought by companies like Google and Facebook came to be known colloquially as the "techlash." In Seattle, it was very specifically an "Amazonlash."

Absorbed with the mechanics of its relentless growth, Amazon executives and employees were easy to vilify. Unlike its older peers Microsoft and Boeing, the company donated almost nothing to local philanthropies like the county chapter of the United Way, and didn't even match the charitable contributions of its workers. (Amazon disputed this characterization and said it "has long supported local Seattle initiatives.") Bezos appeared to prefer to funnel every available nickel into new product lines or reducing prices for customers. Communication between Amazon and its hometown amounted to genteel emails between John Schoettler, Amazon's longtime real estate chief, and city planning officials. Unlike other local luminaries such as Bill and Melinda Gates or Pearl Jam front man Eddie Vedder, Jeff Bezos was largely invisible and a relative cipher in the community.

Sensitive to criticism from the *Seattle Times* and other local media that it was absent in hometown philanthropy, the company began to look for ways to contribute in 2016. Schoettler spearheaded the donation of a former Travelodge Hotel on company property to a local nonprofit called Mary's Place, which served homeless women and children. When the hotel was demolished, Amazon moved the shelter to a nearby Days Inn, then reserved eight floors for it in one of its new office buildings. That year, Amazon also backed a coalition that proposed a successful $54 billion ballot initiative to expand light rail and other public transit in the region.

Bezos was aware of these initiatives, said Amazon employees who worked on them. He supported them, several felt, because they boosted Amazon's image and required a relatively minor investment of dollars and his own time. He was characteristically focused on the business and largely transactional when discussing community involvement. Internal documents at the company advocated that Amazon do enough to maintain its "social license to operate"—the business concept that refers to the public's acceptance of a company, its employees, and business practices.

For decades, that long-standing contract between companies and their communities had remained relatively stable. A business could create jobs, pay its taxes, and perform a modicum of public service, then quietly go about its way. But in the twenty-first century, the relationship between cities and the sprawling global conglomerates in their midst was the subject of probing questions. What was the public cost when cities enticed corporations with tax breaks and property giveaways? How could companies become good faith partners with their communities? And as governments failed to solve the intractable problems of income disparity and poverty, what responsibility did corporations have to step in and confront them?

In Seattle, the corporate responsibility movement was embodied by the election of Kshama Sawant, a self-styled Marxist socialist who joined Seattle's city council in 2014. Sawant and her allies proposed a litany of additional taxes aimed at forcing Amazon to pay for the negative effects of its growth. Former mayor Tim Burgess says, "Her election was seminal in terms of changing the mood and the quality of public discourse."

In June 2017, Sawant cosponsored a bill proposing a 2.25 percent increase on income tax for individuals making more than $250,000 a year. Amazon employees said the measure, which passed the council unanimously but was successfully challenged in court and never implemented, caught the attention of Bezos, who paid little attention to local politics. Later that year, Sawant also floated a "head tax" that would impose a new tariff on companies based on their number of local employees. The idea was defeated but would return again and again over the coming years. As a result, Amazon executives came to feel unappreciated by a city that was long beset by boom and bust cycles, a condition neatly summarized by a famous 1970s billboard: "Will the last person leaving SEATTLE—Turn out the lights."

At the same time, another factor weighed heavily on Bezos's long-term plans: even as Amazon built new offices, it was running out of space in Seattle. By 2018, thousands of new hires were joining the company each month. Employees working in office buildings like Doppler and Day 1 recalled that the offices were so cramped, coworkers were sometimes given desks in hallways. Company events were packed, and that year was the first that Amazon wasn't able to hold the annual summer picnic at CenturyLink Field. Now there were simply too many employees.

Recruiting was also becoming more difficult. The company was exhausting the number of people—engineers, but also lawyers, economists, and human resource executives—it could convince to move to the escarpment of fog and rain clouds that hung over the Pacific Northwest. For its next phase of growth, Amazon was going to have to look elsewhere.

A white paper produced in August 2016 had considered this inevitability. The paper, with the verbose title "Real Estate Site Selection Initiative Update, Site Selection for Amazon North America Campus," was written by executives on Amazon's economic development team. It outlined the relative merits and available tech talent of twenty-five cities, including Dallas, New York, and Washington, D.C., where Amazon might locate around twenty thousand employees and enjoy the efficiencies of a large satellite office.

The document and subsequent S-team discussion were the first step down a provocative new path—mitigating Amazon's dependence on its hometown. A year later, in September 2017, stunned Seattle officials would learn about Amazon's quest to develop a second headquarters in the media, along with everybody else.

———

By all accounts, the process that would come to be known as HQ2 was Bezos's brainchild. Amazon's founder had noticed when Washington State authorized a package of incentives worth $8.7 billion to entice Boeing to build its wide-body 777X aircraft in the state. He observed when Elon Musk magically dubbed Tesla's planned lithium-ion battery plant a "Gigafactory," then pitted seven states against one another before selecting a site east of Reno, Nevada, and receiving a tax relief package worth $1.3 billion. Musk was personally involved in the search, deploying his singular charisma in meetings with governors and tours of prospective sites. By the end of the process, Nevada had offered Tesla the biggest tax relief package in the state's history and allowed it to operate there practically tax-free for a decade.

To its credit, Amazon never asked for or received tax relief from Seattle or the state of Washington. But now Bezos concluded that Amazon, with its high-paying jobs and reputation as an innovator, should also be able to secure a large incentive package from a similarly business-friendly region. Amazon's economic development team was instructed to "find us a durable advantage"—not just cash grants that the company might burn through quickly, but a city that might be willing to offer them exclusive and enduring tax relief.

As usual, Bezos's standards were high and patience was thin. When Amazon secured $40 million in tax incentives in January 2017, for example, to lease an air hub at Cincinnati/Northern Kentucky International Airport for fifty years, Bezos fired off a disappointed email wondering why Musk had a special "superpower" of amassing tax breaks. And as the *Wall Street Journal* later reported, Amazon's economic development team was assigned an S-team goal that year to amass $1 billion in annual tax incentives.

The boldest idea for how to attract such tax relief ended up coming from Bezos himself. Over the summer of 2017, he processed the conclusions of the previous year's white paper from the economic development team, the shifting political sentiment in Seattle, and the outsized success that Tesla, Boeing, and Taiwanese manufacturer Foxconn were having in securing tax breaks from state and local governments. And he produced a very Bezosian idea—novel in its complete inversion of the traditional ways that corporations courted localities.

Instead of developing numerous offices in multiple cities, or negotiating privately with one location for a satellite office, Amazon would announce its intention to create a second headquarters—an equal to its home in Seattle. It would then open the site selection process to all cities in North America and allow them to compete for a prize of some fifty thousand jobs and $5 billion in capital investments over a span of fifteen years. Such a process, Bezos argued, could highlight what communities coveted from the company instead of what its critics feared about it. "Part of it was a cheerleading exercise," said a member of the HQ2 team, who like many others involved, declined to speak on the record for fear of retribution. "Who wanted us? That would come through in the process itself."

To kick off the project, members of the public affairs and economic development teams drafted a six-page document, much of which was reflected in the press release and HQ2 RFP (request for proposal) that Amazon made public on September 7, 2017. In addition to outlining the company's preference for a metropolitan area of more than 1 million residents, with a business-friendly environment and access to strong talent and transportation networks, the RFP pointedly described what it would take to win the competition: it used the word "incentive" or "incentives" twenty-one times and said that forms of tax relief "will be significant factors in the decision-making process" and that a competitive offer might even require regions to pass special legislation.

The direct language struck some as distasteful. After its release, Mike Grella, a D.C.-based member of Amazon's economic development team who worked on securing locations for AWS data centers, started fielding calls from city officials he knew around the country. They were alarmed by the RFP and the very notion of a private process that Amazon was going to conduct out in the open, where it would be subject to unpredictable political forces and public opinion.

But then a funny thing happened. "They were all outraged," Grella said. "And then they fell into line."

The announcement of Amazon's HQ2 initiative sparked a media frenzy. In the two weeks after the announcement, media outlets disgorged more than eight hundred articles and opinion pieces on the contest, according to the database LexisNexis. Local newspapers handicapped their city's chances and veteran Amazon watchers placed bets. The *New York Times* predicted Denver would win, citing "the city's lifestyle and affordability, coupled with the supply of tech talent from nearby universities." The *Wall Street Journal* picked Dallas. Amazon execs favored Boston, *Bloomberg News* reported.

There were a few dissenting voices. Silicon Valley congressman Ro Khanna tweeted that tech companies shouldn't "be asking for tax breaks from cities within my district or those outside. They should be investing in communities." A *Los Angeles Times* columnist called the process "arrogant, naive and more than a teensy bit cynical." But as Bezos had hoped, the overall response was positive and clarifying. While tech-industry critics in Seattle and Silicon Valley were questioning the tech giants' role in accelerating gentrification and homelessness, other cities were desperate to host them. The result was an unprecedented public scrum for a once-in-a-generation bounty of high-paying jobs and much needed economic activity.

In all, 238 proposals were submitted by the October 19, 2017, deadline. Cities like Detroit, Boston, and Pittsburgh added videos to their applications, touting their charms with soaring music and iMovie-quality special effects. A video produced by the Tampa–St. Petersburg region featured a shot of beach volleyball players frolicking in the sand; Dallas flaunted, among other things, its "flavor," "vibe," and "margaritas." Unphotogenic city officials wearing suits and ties sidled up to the camera and spoke directly to Amazon in submissive tones.

A few cities resorted to more peculiar measures. Birmingham, Alabama, staged three giant cardboard boxes around town and asked residents to take selfies with them and post the photos to social media. Kansas City's mayor bought a thousand products on Amazon.com and had each reviewed using superlatives about the town. Calgary, Canada, tagged the sidewalks in Seattle with graffiti and hung a two-hundred-foot-long red banner near Amazon's offices that read, "Not saying we'd fight a bear for you ... but we totally would." Stonecrest, Georgia, a suburb twenty miles east of Atlanta, offered to rename itself "Amazon." Tucson, Arizona (2019 population: 545,000), tried to send a twenty-one-foot saguaro cactus to the company, which donated it to a museum. And on and on.

Many city officials said they had no choice but to show their constituents they were vying for such a lucrative prize. "In my personal opinion, the future of work is all about technology and if you are not a participant in some way, your economy will be completely left behind," said Ryan Smith, a director in the Nevada Governor's Office of Economic Development, who worked on Las Vegas's futile bid.

The applications were routed to a small team of about half a dozen HR, PR, public policy, and economic development executives in Amazon's Seattle and Washington, D.C., offices. For years Amazon's presence in the nation's capital had been negligible. The policy team once occupied a single floor in a run-down D.C. row house, over an office occupied by a pair of lobbyists for the Cherokee Nation. Employees shared a single bathroom and had to use a VPN to access Amazon's network. Such was the extent of Amazon's commitment to government relations that Jay Carney, when he worked for the Obama administration, said he "never met anybody from Amazon, not once, even when we went out to Seattle to do fundraisers."

After Carney joined Amazon as senior vice president of global corporate affairs in 2015, the D.C. team started reporting directly to him and getting more resources. Amazon had just moved to a modern office building at 601 New Jersey Avenue, across the street from the Georgetown University Law Center. The company was now attracting plenty of government attention; it could no longer hide in plain sight.

While Carney was based in D.C., he traveled frequently to Seattle, so the office was run by Brian Huseman, a vice president of public policy and former Department of Justice prosecutor. Huseman, a native Oklahoman, was a polarizing figure in the office, known by colleagues as an adept player of internal politics. In the fall of 2017, as the HQ2 process started, he carefully planned Amazon's presence at a black-tie ceremony in D.C., where Bezos received the National Equality Award from the Human Rights Campaign. Huseman also designed the interior of Amazon's ninth-floor offices, so that the elevators opened to a reception area framed by a wall of old door desks—a symbol of Amazon frugality. Down one hallway was a public event space adorned with a Kiva robot, a prototype package-delivery drone, and video screens that rotated clips from Amazon Studios productions. Down another and behind a set of turnstiles were the spare, Amazon-style offices. One of those rooms required a special key to open and was reserved for the HQ2 team to conduct their secretive work. Newspapers covered the windows; if anybody was caught peeking inside, they were reported to security.

In the weeks after the initial HQ2 bids were submitted, the D.C. team put in twelve-hour days, six to seven days a week, reviewing the inundation of applications. At one point, the process risked turning dangerously arbitrary, until a member of the group reminded his colleagues that they needed to develop objective criteria and deliver all available data to the S-team. They returned to the RFP and created spreadsheets weighing different factors, like population, the number of local STEM graduates, employment rates, and regional GDP.

Idealism largely pervaded the effort. Members of the HQ2 team earnestly believed that any city had an opportunity to win. At one point, they put their predictions for the finalist cities on pieces of paper and sealed them in an envelope. Holly Sullivan, Amazon's eloquent and well-connected economic development director, came closest to guessing the outcome. "We genuinely thought we were working on the most important economic development project in a generation and were going to change the lives of hundreds of thousands of people," said one of the HQ2 employees.

In early January, Sullivan and finance director Bill Crow presented all of the data and applications to the S-team. Colleagues say Bezos, cognizant of the responsibility of giving every candidate a sincere look, read through the applications of all 238 regions. The review lasted for hours.

As they prepared to announce the twenty finalists on January 18, 2018, employees working on the HQ2 project submitted various proposals for how to unveil the short list. One idea from the public relations team was to amplify the suspense by revealing a new city every hour, but Bezos vetoed that idea. Perhaps he recognized that Amazon didn't need to do anything more to augment the considerable public relations exposure that HQ2 was generating all on its own—or that the political winds gusting around the process were already too unpredictable.

In the days before the finalists were announced, the HQ2 team divided the list of more than two hundred cities that hadn't made the cut and placed phone calls to local officials, alerting them to the bad news. Most asked why, while expressing disappointment with the amount of time and resources they had put into the failed effort. Amazon employees responded with blasts of data. *"Your metro area only has 375,000 people and of those only 10 percent have advanced degrees,"* went a typical explanation. *"Sorry, that's not enough of a labor pipeline."* City officials mostly agreed that Amazon's outreach was conscientious, and that Holly Sullivan in particular spent more time than she needed answering questions and preserving relationships that might be helpful to the company in the future.

After Amazon announced the short list, generating another fourteen hundred news stories that week alone, the HQ2 team hit the road. A group of a dozen employees led by Sullivan and John Schoettler, the real estate chief, traveled nearly nonstop from February to the end of April, barnstorming cities in three separate trips to the West Coast, the South, and the East Coast, with only a few weeks of downtime between outings. They traveled, Amazon-style, in coach on commercial airplanes or on buses, starting early in the morning and ending late at night.

Cities were alerted to their visits a few days beforehand and given little guidance, other than that Amazon wanted to tour their proposed sites and hear about the city's talent pool and education systems. Some did a better job preparing than others. L.A. mayor Eric Garcetti impressed the Amazon entourage with a dynamic presentation and breakfast with the presidents of local universities. In Nashville, Amazon execs met with local musicians. In Dallas, city officials took the group on the scenic M-Line trolley downtown and to dinner at a country western restaurant in the hip Uptown neighborhood. "The Amazon team was very genuine" in their interest, said Mike Rosa, senior vice president at the Dallas Regional Chamber. "Some of the people writing the articles about 'it was all a sham' weren't in the room I was in. They were as genuine as any project I've ever worked on."

From Seattle, Bezos stayed interested and involved, though unlike Elon Musk with the Gigafactory, he remained well behind the front lines. HQ2 was stirring a media tempest all on its own, and he didn't want his own visibility—and the optics of his enormous wealth—to divert from the preferred focus on job creation and community investment. Colleagues said that Sullivan would get frequent emails from Bezos and other S-team members, asking for details of site visits and city proposals. On one trip to Seattle, she sat with Bezos on the sixth floor of Day 1 tower, waiting in tense silence to answer his questions while he flipped through binders of applications.

For Bezos, the HQ2 search was not only the subject of pressing interest for the future of his company but a PR spectacle that was now casting a large shadow over most of his public appearances. That April, he traveled to Dallas to speak at the George W. Bush Presidential Center's Forum on Leadership at Southern Methodist University. At the cocktail party afterward, Dallas mayor Mike Rawlings walked up to him and went for it, saying, "Look, we're the right place for you." Bezos was coy and said only that he had heard great things about the city from friends who lived there. "I felt a shyness from him that didn't make me feel great," Rawlings later told me.

The team completed their visits that month and prepared a six-page paper for the S-team with their results and recommendations. I viewed that paper, along with two other key HQ2 documents, during the course of my research. Prepared in June 2018, this first paper broke the twenty finalists into three groups: "not viable," "hotly debated," and "top tier."

Austin, Columbus, Denver, Indianapolis, Miami, Montgomery County in Maryland, Newark, and Pittsburgh were all cast in the first category and dismissed, largely because they were too small and did not have the required infrastructure and talent. In addition, the team had concluded from their visits and from analyzing public sentiment that Austin and Denver might be hostile to Amazon's presence. "It was clear from our visits that Austin and Denver were not as supportive of the project as other sites," they wrote. Pittsburgh was "still recovering from economic hardships." Newark was flatly rejected because talented engineers from New York City "would not want to work there."

Atlanta, Boston, Los Angeles, Nashville, Toronto, and Washington, D.C., were listed in the "hotly debated" category. The HQ2 group cited high costs and high taxes as negatives for Boston and Toronto. They described the traffic congestion of Atlanta as problematic, as well as a recent move by the Georgia legislature to kill a tax exemption for Delta Air Lines' jet fuel purchases because of the airline's controversial decision to end discounts for National Rifle Association members after the school shooting in Parkland, Florida. To Amazon, the state's move to penalize a company for its political values was troubling.

The document also stated: "We all had high expectations of Nashville, but the city isn't ready for an investment of our size." Of Los Angeles, it opined: "It is the world's most congested city, does not provide geographic diversity and California is not a business-friendly state."

The "top-tier" locations were Chicago, Dallas, New York City, Northern Virginia, Philadelphia, and Raleigh. Despite recommending these cities the most, the HQ2 team still expressed concerns about them. They worried that choosing geographically isolated Dallas would make it more challenging to recruit top-notch talent. New York City was the costliest location in terms of local taxes, employee compensation rates, and real estate prices, and with so many other major employers, "we would not be able to leverage our presence in a positive way as we could in other locations." Northern Virginia was business-friendly but not a hotbed of engineering talent, or particularly inexpensive.

In closing, the HQ2 committee recommended that the S-team settle on a smaller final round of cities so that the company could start talking to elected officials and secure the best real estate. It suggested they announce the winner on September 7, the one-year anniversary of the search announcement. "Our goal with this next HQ2 milestone is to continue driving positive press and fortifying our corporate reputation, while not giving our critics unnecessary ammunition or feeding the perception that this is an over-the-top reality show," the document stated, before recommending three, surprising finalists from months of travel, meals, speculation, and negotiation:

Chicago, Philadelphia, and Raleigh. "The locations do not have the largest concentration of existing tech talent but we believe they have the foundation for talent growth across our many businesses," the paper concluded.

———

Yet such documents at Amazon present only options and recommendations; they are the beginning of the deliberative process at the company, not the end. Bezos and the S-team met with the HQ2 leaders that month in Seattle, read the document in silence, and then engaged in a multi-hour discussion that changed the course of the entire project.

Raleigh, North Carolina, was business-friendly, had a low cost of living and little traffic, but was too small for Amazon's expanding needs. Chicago's governmental institutions were often in conflict with one another, and the city and state were consistently rated by credit agencies as financially unstable. Philadelphia was not a hotbed of engineering talent, and in the meeting, AWS chief Andy Jassy, according to one person's recollection, opined that he disliked the city, which was the bitter rival of his favorite football team, the New York Giants, and suggested that he and his employees would never want to live there. Jassy was apparently joking, but some members of the HQ2 team, coming off months of detailed, quantitative work, later expressed exasperation that the process was now exposed to the arbitrary personal preferences of senior executives.

HQ2 managers emerged from the meeting with a radically different short list than the one they had proposed. In the second document I reviewed, produced in August, the team reflected that they had left the June session with a decision to follow up on five locations: Dallas, Los Angeles, New York City, Northern Virginia, and Nashville. That eliminated the three top contenders the HQ2 team had recommended, though the paper suggested they revisit Chicago, but only "to minimize potential negative reaction if Chicago does not move forward in the process."

The priorities in the HQ2 search had changed. The hunt for the most robust incentives package had been replaced by an interest in the largest cities, the best opportunities for recruitment, and the friendliest political environment. That was no accident. For at the same time as executives were honing their shortlist, Amazon's relations with its hometown were rapidly deteriorating.

Back in Seattle, Kshama Sawant and the leftward-careening city council had again proposed a head tax—dubbed the Employee Hours Tax—that would charge large employers up to $500 per employee and raise up to $86 million to counter problems like homelessness and the lack of affordable housing. It was a draconian measure: by comparison, Chicago had a measly $4 per employee head tax for nearly thirty years before mayor Rahm Emanuel demonstrated that it was responsible for jobs losses and convinced the city council to phase it out.

Under the proposal, raised in April 2018, Amazon's local tax bill would increase by an additional $22.5 million annually, on top of the $250 million in state and local taxes it paid. That would be a fraction of Amazon's $10 billion profit in 2018, but it was the antagonistic thought that counted. Seattle was moving to double-tax both corporate income and headcount, a situation necessitated in part because Washington is one of seven states with no personal income tax (a fact that had neatly benefited Bezos and other Amazon execs over the years). Amazon believed the company already paid plenty in municipal taxes, and if the city wasn't spending its money in the right ways and to address the most pressing problems, that was hardly their fault.

After the head-tax proposal, Bezos contacted John Schoettler and ordered the real estate division to stop construction on "Block 18," a seventeen-story tower near Day 1, and to sublease most of the

800,000-square-foot building that Amazon had completed at nearby Rainier Square rather than occupy it. The real estate team predicted that the move would cost the company more than $100 million, according to a person familiar with its calculations (although this person said the company later broke even on the transaction). But Bezos said he didn't care: Amazon wasn't going to grow in a city that didn't want it.

At the same time, Bezos instituted another internal edict: he capped Amazon's Seattle headcount at around fifty thousand employees. Amazon, which already occupied more than 19 percent of prime office space in the city, was due to hit that number within twelve months. After that point, managers inside the company would have to funnel their headcount growth to Amazon offices in other cities. Schoettler and the real estate team scrambled to accommodate the new demand. Since Amazon employed around seven hundred people only fifteen minutes away, across Lake Washington in Bellevue—an affluent Seattle bedroom suburb that at the time was opportunistically running promotional campaigns targeting local corporations—Amazon execs decided that the Seattle overflow could go there, and established a target of moving twenty thousand employees. That fall, Amazon would sign a lease in Bellevue for the twenty-story former headquarters of online travel company Expedia.

While the cap was never publicly revealed, Amazon loudly publicized the move to stop construction on Block 18 and to sublease Rainier Square Tower. This was a power play, a muscular showing of Amazon's influence in its hometown and of the business maxim "Capital goes where it is welcome and stays where it is well treated." "I saw it as an unusually strong move by a company that doesn't do that lightly," said Maud Daudon, the former head of the Seattle Metropolitan Chamber of Commerce.

But city officials heard the message loud and clear. In May, the $480-per-employee head tax was downgraded to a $275-per-employee levy, a compromise that they mistakenly believed was acceptable to

Amazon. The tax unanimously passed the city council, and then Amazon promptly contributed $25,000 to a committee to put a repeal on the November ballot. Other local firms, like Starbucks and Vulcan, as well as family-owned favorites like the fast-food chain Dick's Drive-In, also contributed and aligned against the new tax.

With that, the public turned against the city council in voter polling and sided with their local companies and largest employers; stunned council members were now outmaneuvered. When it became evident that the referendum against the tax would amass enough signatures to get on the ballot and likely pass, the council ignominiously changed course and repealed their own tax with a 7-to-2 vote. Seattle mayor Jenny Durkan, who had signed the head-tax bill, now signed its repeal.

But these weren't the only miscalculations at play. Bezos and other Amazon executives saw only a city council captured by leftist legislators hostile to business. They didn't seem to recognize or care that shifting public sentiment in Seattle also represented something broader: resistance to tech companies and to the dizzying changes they were bringing to their communities. That was the so-called techlash, unfolding outside the visible spectrum of Amazon's well-compensated senior leadership. Their failure to recognize these forces was about to have serious repercussions.

In addition to identifying Bellevue as an immediate alternative for headcount growth, some Amazon executives concluded that HQ2 would now have to be bigger than previously planned and most likely ramp up faster than initially expected. By the time the seventeen-page August document was written, the HQ2 and S-teams were homing in on New York City and Crystal City in Northern Virginia—regions they believed could accommodate the coming expansion. "If costs and business climate are primary factors, we recommend Northern Virginia as the top site. If existing talent is primary driver, we recommend New York City," the paper read.

The HQ2 team predicted that both cities would be politically welcoming—even if Amazon selected Long Island City in Queens, just

outside the Manhattan business core, a once gritty industrial community that over the last fifteen years had gentrified at disorienting
speed. "We have support from the state and have worked closely with
New York State's economic development director, who is a close con-
fidant of governor [Andrew] Cuomo's," the document read. "Mayor
[Bill] de Blasio will not be an outspoken champion for the project
and is generally critical of big business, but we believe he is supportive of New York City being selected."

———

As before, the document was only the starting point for an S-team
discussion. And when HQ2 managers emerged from the meeting that
September, they stunned their colleagues with the leadership group's
decision. Bezos and the S-team had opted to split HQ2 between New
York City and Northern Virginia and to establish a smaller "Operations Center of Excellence" in Nashville. Amazon had spent an entire
year hunting for a single location, but considering the company's talent needs, as well as Bezos's edict that Amazon expand primarily outside Seattle, one site would no longer be enough. Said an employee on
the HQ2 project: "I couldn't believe it, but at the same time, I could.
It's Amazon, and shit is weird."

The decision put Amazon's corporate spinmeisters in an uncomfortable spot. For more than a year, they had aggressively refuted the
most cynical interpretations of the HQ2 process and any intimations
that the fix was in for one of the dual centers of power on the East
Coast. Now Amazon was about to validate that pessimism: one of the
richest companies in the world, led by the world's richest person, was
expanding its presence in the political and financial capitals—cities
where Jeff Bezos owned lavish homes. Adding to the awkwardness, on
the morning of Tuesday, September 4, Amazon's shares were worth as
much as $2,050—briefly tipping the company's market capitalization
over the momentous threshold of a trillion dollars, before the stock
price retreated.

The third HQ2 document that I reviewed, dated October 2018, addressed this challenge and outlined options for how to announce the decision and circumnavigate a potential hurricane of negative reaction. It acknowledged that "the announcement is going to dominate the national news cycle no matter what we do" and contemplated "well-funded critics" who might accuse Amazon of going back on its word to select a single city equal to Seattle.

Listing these likely critics, the paper cited the advocacy organization Good Jobs First, which promoted corporate and government accountability in economic development, and the Institute for Local Self-Reliance, which supported the interests of communities and small businesses against chain stores and conglomerates. It also mentioned by name NYU professor Scott Galloway, who had charged that HQ2 was a "hunger games beauty contest" preordained to land "where Jeff wants to spend more time. My bet is the NYC metro area," as well as Lina Khan, who had authored an article for the *Yale Law Journal* accusing Amazon of anticompetitive behavior and the nation's antitrust laws of being woefully out of date.

Ominously, the paper neglected to mention the progressive politicians on the New York City Council, or the charismatic Democratic candidate for the House of Representatives running that fall in New York's 14th Congressional District—Alexandria Ocasio-Cortez. "Given that we see this announcement as an opportunity to demonstrate that Amazon is a positive investor in the economy and job creator and good community partner, we think it's important to minimize the airtime of our critics ... who we believe are champing at the bit to use our announcement to further their own agendas," the document read.

The company revealed the winners a few weeks later, on the morning of Tuesday, November 13. "Amazon Selects New York City and Northern Virginia for New Headquarters," trumpeted the press release. Curiously absent from the announcement, and from the talking points of Amazon spokespeople, was any mention of the abbreviation "HQ2." For a company and CEO who agonized over each word in every document, that could not have been accidental; Amazon was trying to obfuscate some of its very own messaging from the last fourteen months.

As expected, there was a dust storm of disappointment from the other finalists. They now recognized that Amazon chose the largest population centers' corridors of power and technical talent over other aspects highlighted in the original RFP, such as cost of living, geographic diversity, and the size of incentive packages. Holly Sullivan called Dallas mayor Mike Rawlings to deliver the bad news. The financial incentives from Dallas and the state of Texas had totaled $1.1 billion, considerably higher than the $573 million in cash grants offered by Arlington County and Virginia, though not quite as much as the city and state of New York's enticement of $2.5 billion in tax credits and rebates. It was also about 40 percent cheaper to build in Dallas than on the East Coast—but in the end, that hadn't mattered at all. "Help me here, why did you put us through all of that if this is where you were going all along!" an exasperated Rawlings asked Sullivan.

Officials in the losing cities had other reasons to be cynical. At a conference for economic development executives held in Salt Lake City in March 2019, some three hundred attendees would hear Holly Sullivan mention offhand that she had spoken regularly throughout the process to Stephen Moret, CEO of the Virginia Economic Development Partnership. "I appreciated that she was so candid about having regular discussions with him about the project," said one of several people in the audience who heard the comment. But it "really opened up questions about the true sincerity of that exercise."

In Arlington County, Moret and other officials were jubilant over their victory. But in New York, and in the borough of Queens, an immediate outpouring of dissent mounted among local officials who were out of the loop and taken by surprise by the news. City council speaker Corey Johnson issued a statement condemning Amazon, the governor, and the mayor for bypassing community input and cutting the city council out of the negotiations. Jimmy Van Bramer, deputy

leader of the city council, issued a joint statement with state senator Michael Gianaris, proclaiming inaccurately that the tax incentives
being dangled before Amazon were unparalleled. "We are witness to a
cynical game in which Amazon duped New York into offering unprecedented amounts of tax dollars to one of the wealthiest companies on
Earth," they wrote, neglecting the larger hauls in other states delivered to Boeing, Foxconn, and others.

The newly elected Ocasio-Cortez jumped into the conversation:
"We've been getting calls and outreach from Queens residents all day
about this," she tweeted. "Amazon is a billion-dollar company. The
idea that it will receive hundreds of millions of dollars in tax breaks
at a time when our subway is crumbling and our communities need
MORE investment, not less, is extremely concerning to residents
here."

As they prepared to respond to this criticism, Amazon's HQ2
team was hit with another unpleasant surprise. Their counterparts on
the real estate team, they learned, had at the very last minute inserted
into the "memorandum of understanding" with both cities a provision requiring them to help secure the necessary air rights and permit
approvals for the development and operation of a helipad.

It should be ideally "onsite," but if not, "in reasonable proximity"
to the company's offices, according to an email that an Amazon attorney had sent earlier that month to the head of the Empire State
Development Corporation. Amazon would cover all the costs. Both
cities, accustomed to indulging the tech giant's whims during the
fourteen-month HQ2 bakeoff, had agreed to accommodate yet another one.

Local media quickly reported and ridiculed this new stipulation
("Queens Ransom," shouted the November 14 *New York Post*, with
an illustration of Bezos hanging out of a helicopter and holding bags
of money). Members of the Amazon HQ2 team were confused: the
company did not own any helicopters. The optics of well-heeled internet executives zooming over gridlocked city streets and packed

subway cars were awful. Even the idea itself was *un-Amazonian*. Frugality—and the humility it conveyed—was one of the company's prized fourteen leadership principles.

Several employees argued that the helipads were a terrible idea but were told the request came right from the top and wasn't going to be rescinded. "The helipad was the worst thing they could have ever asked for," mourned Mitchell Taylor, bishop of Center of Hope International church in Long Island City and a supporter of HQ2. "Why do you have to put that front and center? They could have had a helipad after the fact."

Amazon employees were now just as perplexed as their counterparts at Blue Origin were when a company called Black Ops Aviation and its cofounder, former television personality Lauren Sanchez, started appearing at *New Shepard* launches in West Texas to record promotional videos for the secretive space firm. Unless something significant had changed, making a grand aerial entrance into a company office was hardly Jeff Bezos's style.

———

In the wake of the awkward HQ2 announcement and the uproar over the helipad, grassroots opposition to Amazon's proposed expansion into Long Island City exploded. Grassroots organizers, energized by Alexandria Ocasio-Cortez's election victory, pivoted to this new cause. Protests were organized at local churches; volunteers walked the streets handing out fliers warning residents that the same forces of gentrification and displacement that had overwhelmed Seattle were going to alter Queens as well.

Amazon was caught flat-footed. The company had opted for secrecy instead of on-the-ground preparation and for autonomy over hiring experienced public affairs and lobbying firms to counter any negative reaction. Newcomers to New York's bare-knuckle style of politics, Amazon executives had incorrectly calculated that support from Cuomo, de Blasio, and other allies would carry the day. "New

York was lost from the moment they announced it," said Tom Stringer, head of site selection for the business consulting firm BDO.

After the initial shock, Amazon scrambled to develop a ground game. It hired the political consulting and communications firm SKDK, as well as lobbyist Mark Weprin, a former city councilman representing Queens. They had a perfectly optimistic message to convey—that Amazon would bring up to forty thousand jobs to a previously blighted area of the waterfront over the course of fifteen years; that the tax incentives were merely rebates on the public revenues that Amazon would generate; and that many of those incentives were in fact required under a city program meant to encourage commercial development in the outer boroughs.

But those were rational arguments, and the battle for New York was shaping up to be an emotional one—pitting a populace that felt like their city and its housing and transportation networks were already bursting at the seams, and who were exasperated by the growing wealth gap, against the specter of a distant monopoly and the world's richest person.

Amazon would get its first chance to face its critics at a city council hearing that December. At least one consultant wanted Jay Carney to testify, figuring that as a former member of the Obama administration, he'd be appealing to local Democrats. But Amazon rejected that, determining that it would amplify the spectacle. Instead, VP of public policy Brian Huseman would appear, along with Holly Sullivan.

The pair prepared for the hearing from Amazon's office in D.C. Sullivan was dynamic and fast on her feet, but the consultants worried that Huseman sounded cagey and arrogant. He insisted on writing his own opening remarks, which included the well-worn Amazon phrase: "We are proud to be Earth's most customer-centric company." The consultants begged him to strike it—the city council wanted to know what Amazon was going to do for the neighborhood, not the planet. But he insisted.

The hearing on December 12, 2018, was a catastrophe. Over the course of three hours, city council members took turns grilling the pair over everything from why the wealthy tech giant needed tax incentives, to AWS's sale of facial recognition technology to the Immigration and Customs Enforcement agency. They faced a few curveballs too. "Why do you need a helipad?" Corey Johnson, speaker of the city council, asked at one point. After Huseman answered evasively, Johnson thundered, "Do you realize how out of touch that seems for the average New Yorker?!" Meanwhile, angry protesters in the mezzanine unfurled anti-Amazon banners ("Amazon Delivers Lies") and jeered.

After the disastrous session, Amazon refocused on old-fashioned retail politics. Holly Sullivan and her longtime D.C. colleague, Braden Cox, the soft-spoken and introverted director of public policy, traveled through Queens, meeting with community groups and local officials. Schoettler invited twenty small business owners to dinner at a local Italian restaurant in Long Island City. The company marshaled its supporters into counterprotests and promoted polls that showed the majority of the community supported the plan. Fliers appeared in the mailboxes of Queens residents, declaring "Happy New Year from your Future Neighbors at Amazon" and highlighting the coming jobs, career training, and tax revenues Amazon would generate.

But as the debate stretched into the new year, it started to coalesce around a different and potentially dangerous topic: organized labor. New York City was a union town, plain and simple. Amazon had fiercely defended against all unionization attempts in its FCs, and Bezos had told human resources VP David Niekerk said that a disgruntled and entrenched hourly workforce posed one of the greatest dangers to the company.

Amazon actually had some union support in the city: the influential building and labor trades, which also backed the company in Seattle and whose members would construct the new buildings. But other unions, which over the previous decade had failed to organize workers in Whole Foods supermarkets and Amazon fulfillment centers, saw an opening. Amazon was on their turf now.

Though none of this had much to do with the white-collar workers who would fill Amazon's new offices, that hardly mattered. A kinetic political fight was gathering energy and feeding on itself.

A second city council hearing devoted to Amazon's plans in Queens took place on January 30, 2019. Huseman, looking impatient and annoyed, did most of the talking and delivered a veiled threat. "We want to invest in a community that wants us," he told the council. Then, for another three hours, Huseman and Sullivan endured withering questions and offhand anecdotes about the historic importance of labor unions to New York City.

Finally, Corey Johnson, the council speaker, asked pointedly: Would Amazon commit to neutrality if its New York City workers wanted to organize?

"We respect the right for all employees under federal and state law to organize if that is what they so choose" was the legal boilerplate that Huseman should have recited—but didn't.

Instead, he blundered with "No we would not agree to that," and the battle was lost. Asked about the issue later that day at a news conference, Mayor Bill de Blasio offered: "Welcome to New York City. We're a union town." He added, "There is going to be tremendous pressure on Amazon to allow unionization and I will be one of the people bringing that pressure."

On February 8, the *Washington Post* reported the company was rethinking its New York plans. "The question is whether it's worth it if the politicians in New York don't want the project, especially with how people in Virginia and Nashville have been so welcoming," an anonymous source who was almost certainly a member of the Amazon public relations department told the paper.

On the ground in Queens, Amazon's HQ2 staff and their lobbyists were kept in the dark and believed a deal was close. On February 13, Huseman, Sullivan, and Braden Cox met in the governor's office with officials from several unions to hash out the basis of an agreement that would allow Amazon workers in New York City to hold "fair elections" about whether to unionize. Mayor de Blasio would later say that it appeared things were "moving forward."

Then, on the morning of Valentine's Day, February 14, Cox and other Amazon employees delivered a presentation and answered questions from members of the largely supportive HQ2 community advisory committee at the Brewster building in Queens. Senior staffers from the mayor's and governor's offices, also oblivious, were there as well. On the subway back to Manhattan afterward, members of Amazon's entourage received text messages informing them that the company had just dismissed its PR firm, SKDK. That was odd. About fifteen minutes later, their phones started blowing up. Amazon had announced it was canceling the plan to build an office complex in Long Island City.

Jay Carney called both de Blasio and Cuomo to deliver the news. Their reactions diverged both on the phone and later in public: the mayor raged in disappointment, while the governor tried to bargain for a second chance. On the 15th, an apoplectic de Blasio appeared on local radio station WNYC and complained that Amazon's move was "disrespectful to the people of New York City.... To get a call out of the blue saying 'see you . . . we're taking our ball and we're going home'—it's absolutely inappropriate. I've never experienced anything like this."

Though Carney tried to discourage it, Cuomo angled to rescue the deal. Eighty business officials, union leaders, and politicians signed a full-page letter to the company, a docile apology begging for a second chance, which was published as an advertisement in the *New York Times*. "We know the public debate that followed the announcement of the Long Island City project was rough and not very welcoming," it read. "Opinions are strong in New York—sometimes strident. We consider it part of the New York charm!" Cuomo also reportedly spoke on the phone with Bezos, but he wasn't changing his mind.

There was plenty of blame to go around. The mayor and governor had enticed Amazon to Queens without securing the backing of its local politicians. Those leaders were also at fault; they assembled the opposition atop the falsehood that Amazon was getting an indecorous $2.5 billion handout, rather than a rebate on the sizable tax contributions it would make over the course of two decades. They also played on innate fears that the character of a cherished community and its surrounding neighborhoods would change. Yet much of Long Island City had gentrified years ago, and most of the lower-income housing in the area and surrounding neighborhoods was either rent-stabilized or belonged to large public housing complexes whose residents were protected from rising rents. And the alternative to rising home prices and an increased cost of living is rarely stasis; usually, it's falling home prices, a lower cost of living, and hopelessness. By rejecting Amazon, an outer borough undergoing its own dramatic transformation was robbed of an economic injection that may have tangentially benefited its poorer residents.

But Amazon executives deserved censure for the debacle as well. Inexperienced in the martial art of New York City politics, they counted on the backing of two public officials who normally never got along, including a mayor whose support for the deal "almost de facto meant that the rest of the city council would oppose it," as Carney later admitted.

Moreover, their synapses were molded by fifteen months of supplication—from cities and their own colleagues—during the HQ2 process. Bezos and his S-team figured they'd be viewed as conquering heroes and blithely stumbled into New York's complex terrain of regulation, union politics, and community activism. They seemed to care little about what it took to earn a "social license to operate" in New York City. And unlike Elon Musk, who had personally led the Gigafactory site selection, Bezos had remained invisible from the public process and tried to keep his intentions private—even as he micromanaged things from afar and journalists guessed at his personal preferences anyway, with stunts like tracking his private plane to see which HQ2 candidate cities he might be visiting.

In characteristic style, Amazon was also vague about the reasons it pulled out, citing resistance from local politicians and their constituents. "The decision to pivot away from New York for this specific project was really based upon, 'Did we have that political support for the long term?'" said Holly Sullivan at the conference in 2019. "We were increasingly getting the feeling that we didn't."

But one of the specific breaking points, of course, was the talk of unions, which had triggered the same reaction from Jeff Bezos and his colleagues that they had exhibited across the entire arc of Amazon history—at a Seattle call center in 2000, at German fulfillment centers in 2013, and soon, in France, at the start of the deadly Covid-19 pandemic. In all those cases, when talk of unionization and worker strikes came up, Amazon either tamped down on growth plans in the region, temporarily shut things down, or walked away from a site altogether. Nevertheless, Amazon later insisted that unionization concerns had nothing to do with its withdrawal from New York.

Inside Amazon, little self-reflection followed the New York City fiasco. The D.C. team did not author a "correction of error" or COE report—which is often the case when Bezos himself is partly responsible for some mistake. Brian Huseman somehow evaded blame for his bungling of the ground game in Queens and remained in his role. Holly Sullivan, by consensus the hero of the process, was promoted to head of worldwide development and later to vice president. Only mild-mannered Braden Cox seemed to pay a price; he promptly lost most of his direct reports in a reorganization and left the company soon after. Many of his colleagues felt that he had been unfairly scapegoated.

In the ensuing years, Amazon would expand its offices in the Hudson Yards area of Midtown Manhattan and announce plans to hire an additional two thousand workers in New York City, considerably fewer than the forty thousand employees once slated for Long Island City. It also grew in cities like Bellevue, Austin, Dallas, Denver, Phoenix, and San Diego—but not in Seattle, or in Queens. After navigating a disaster of its own making, the company barely missed a step. Online purchases, cloud computing contracts, and Prime video streams appeared totally impervious to the unanticipated flavors of controversy that were suddenly coming Amazon's way. This was the true lesson of the HQ2 saga: Amazon was getting perilously close to invincible.

CHAPTER 13

Complexifiers

Jeff Bezos was late. It was February 14, 2019, and the S-team was meeting for the first time since the shocking revelations had ricocheted around the globe—the world's richest man was romantically involved with a married former television host and getting divorced from his wife of twenty-five years. Just that morning, Amazon had publicly canceled its plans to build part of its second headquarters in Long Island City. As executives waited for their tardy boss in the early afternoon, the large conference room on the sixth floor of Day 1 tower in downtown Seattle vibrated with even more anxiety than usual.

Finally, Bezos strode in and took his seat at the center of the main table. He picked up the six-pager that had been placed in front of his chair, looked up, and surveyed the assembled group. "Raise your hand if you think you've had a harder week than I've had," he said, momentarily cutting through the tension by leading the group in a hearty laugh. Then his colleagues settled back into an expectant silence. Bezos was a master compartmentalizer; his ability to keep the intricate threads of his personal and professional lives separate was unrivaled. But now those threads had gotten tangled up. He needed to address the elephant in the room.

"Just to set the record straight," he started slowly, according to two people who heard the comments, "I did have a relationship with this woman. But the story is completely wrong and out of order. Mac-Kenzie and I have had good, healthy adult conversations about it. She is fine. The kids are fine. The media is having a field day. All of this is very distracting, so thank you for being focused on the business."

With that, Bezos picked up the document that outlined a new set of headcount goals across the company, indicating it was time to get back to work. Colleagues would remember his short speech as remarkable—a moment when Bezos came short of apologizing for a scandal he had brought to the gates of Amazon but still managed to express a sense of humility and gratitude.

Still, many Amazon execs and alums would have a hard time moving on so easily. Bezos had always demanded that Amazonians comport themselves with discretion and impeccable judgment. He ripped documents in half and walked out of rooms when employees fell short of expectations. By conducting an extramarital relationship so carelessly that it became fodder for a salacious spread in the *National Enquirer* and then a high-profile media free-for-all, he had failed to meet his own high standards. Dozens of current and former executives would later say that they were surprised and disappointed by Bezos's affair. Their infallible and righteous leader was, after all, a flawed human.

The revelations also might have explained some of the more curious changes in his recent behavior. Bezos had been increasingly hard to find in the Seattle offices over the past year; OP1 meetings had been delayed or postponed, and longtime deputies were finding it difficult to get time on his calendar. He was spending more time traveling, colleagues had noticed, and that November had popped up with only a few hours' notice in the Santa Monica offices of Ring, the connected doorbell startup Amazon had acquired in February 2018.

There were also those inexplicable helipads that Amazon requested for the new headquarters in Long Island City and Northern Virginia. Amazon's PR representatives claimed that having helipads in New York City would have been "useful for certain events, like receiving dignitaries." But it was also true that Bezos's new girlfriend, Lauren Sanchez, was a helicopter pilot, and he had taken flying lessons himself. His personal holding company, Poplar Glen LLC, had even purchased at least one helicopter from the Bell Textron company around this time, according to the FAA Aircraft Registration database.

News of Bezos's impending divorce seemed relevant to another nagging mystery as well. A few weeks before Jeff and MacKenzie made their announcement, Amazon's legal and finance departments began canvassing the company's largest institutional shareholders asking whether they would support the creation of a second class of Amazon stock that carried a lower share price and reduced voting rights. Such dual-class stock structures, employed at Facebook and Google's parent company, Alphabet, can end up concentrating voting power with their founders, giving them ultimate sway over matters of corporate governance even when they own only a small percentage of the stock. Amazon had gone public a decade before most of its Silicon Valley brethren, before such A- and B-class stock formulations were in vogue.

When Amazon made this request, some shareholders were perplexed. Why would such a venerated CEO need to secure greater control over his own company? His influence stemmed not from his 16 percent ownership stake but from twenty-five years of prophetic invention, strategic foresight, and disciplined management. There was little chance an activist investor could gobble up Amazon shares and then win over other big investors to support major changes—like splitting apart the AWS and retail units—as they had done so successfully at companies like eBay and Whole Foods Market.

Amazon said it began studying this arrangement in early 2018 and explained that it was exploring the change to be able to give stock to fulfillment center workers, who often had to sell the shares they received to cover their tax obligations. Amazon also said it could use a second class of stock to pursue acquisitions, in much the same way as Warren Buffett's Berkshire Hathaway. But according to some investors who heard the pitch at the end of 2018, the argument was strange and unpersuasive. Amazon had just announced it would no longer grant stock to warehouse workers after the wage hike to $15 an hour; and a tough regulatory environment meant that it probably wasn't going to be doing any massive acquisitions anytime soon. "Compared to the typical Amazon argument, it was thin and not aggressively supported," said an investor who received the pitch and joined others in opposing it. "It left all of us feeling confused."

After Bezos tweeted news of his divorce though, some of the people who had heard about the stock plan felt their confusion clearing up. Though Amazon disputed this interpretation and called it misleading, they felt that the plan wasn't about trying to furnish workers with stock at all, but about Bezos remaining firmly in control of the company in the face of a costly divorce settlement that would end up reducing his stake in the company to 12 percent.

Control—that was precisely the thing that had eluded Bezos over these stormy past few months. For the first time in his career, he was cornered by adversaries and the consequences of his own behavior. Amid the seemingly overlapping dissolution of his marriage and the start of a new relationship, Bezos faced a scheming Hollywood manager looking to peddle his most intimate text messages, a trashy supermarket tabloid bent on humiliating him, and a zealous media ready to lap up the whole drama and tear down the planet's richest person. And on the other side of the world, there was Mohammed bin Salman—the crown prince of Saudi Arabia, who was embittered at Bezos for the *Washington Post*'s coverage of the murder of dissident Jamal Khashoggi, and who some cybersecurity experts would come to believe had hacked Bezos's cell phone.

The entire episode—prurient, tawdry, and completely uncharacteristic of a man who had extolled the virtues of his wife and family for twenty years—belonged more to the pages of a trashy novel than the business tomes that Amazon inspired. It was also Bezos's biggest challenge to date: a test not only of his company's well-honed ability to mold a media narrative but of his personal character, and his extraordinary ability to navigate out of a jam.

Back in Seattle, the planning meeting stretched into the early evening. Harried finance execs scurried in and out of the room distributing spreadsheets. Bezos might not be able to control the scrum of tabloid press gleefully chronicling his sybaritic escapades with Lauren Sanchez, but he could control headcount growth across all of Amazon's divisions.

As the sun set over the Olympic mountains, casting a golden glow into the conference room, executives started furtively glancing at their phones and responding to texts from their significant others. Finally, at 7:30 p.m., senior vice president Jeff Blackburn spoke up and said what everyone else was thinking: "Hey Jeff, how long do you think this meeting is going to go? A lot of us have plans." It was, after all, Valentine's Day.

"Oh, that's right," said Bezos, laughing. "I forgot about that."

———

For years, Bezos wove the story of his courtship and marriage to MacKenzie Bezos (née Tuttle) into his public persona. In speeches, he routinely joked about his bachelorhood quest to find a woman resourceful enough to "get me out of a third-world prison," as if the bookish MacKenzie, a novelist and English graduate from Princeton University, might one day rappel down from the roof of a Venezuelan jail with a lock pick in her teeth. In an interview in 2014, he said "my wife still claims to like me. I don't question her aggressively on that," and celebrated the virtues of doing the dishes every night, which he said was "the sexiest thing I do." In the onstage conversation with his brother Mark at the 2017 Summit LA conference, they showed a photograph of the young couple in 1994, as they prepared for their historic drive to Seattle that led to the founding of Amazon.com.

While Bezos and his handlers crafted the image of a doting husband and family man, he and his wife were developing different interests and diverging appetites for public attention. In the years following the creation of Amazon Studios, Bezos was visibly drawn to the energy and dynamism of Hollywood, attending the Golden Globes and Academy Awards, showing up at Hollywood movie premieres and hosting an annual holiday party every December at the family's palatial property in Beverly Hills, high above the Sunset Strip.

He also frequently traveled to Washington, D.C., alone, where he attended meetings of the Alfalfa Club, a gathering of powerful business people and politicians, and hosted salon dinners for *Washington Post* executives, government officials, and other luminaries. These took place in the private dining rooms of hip D.C. eateries, while his 27,000-square-foot Kalorama-neighborhood mansion, the former Textile Museum, underwent an extensive renovation. As he became ever more successful, the gravity in all of these star-studded rooms bent toward him; at parties, associates often had to intercept or gently pry away any unwelcome interlopers.

By all accounts, Bezos relished the limelight. He was emerging from a chrysalis, no longer the spindly tech nerd from Seattle with a boisterous laugh but a fashionable dresser with the physique of a private trainer and the kind of exorbitant wealth and fame that drew awed consideration even in the upper echelons of the cosmopolitan elite.

MacKenzie accompanied her husband to some of these events but by her own admission was not a social person. "Cocktail parties for me can be nerve-racking," she told *Vogue* magazine. "The brevity of conversations, the number of them—it's not my sweet spot." Friends said both parents were committed to their four children and to keeping them as far away as possible from the corrosive impact of celebrity and garish wealth.

Back then, even her efforts to shout about important causes ended up as more of an unintended whisper. In 2013, she started a charitable LLC called Bystander Revolution, a website "offering practical, crowdsourced advice about simple things individuals can do to defuse bullying." The site featured videos from celebrities like Monica Lewinsky, Demi Lovato, Michael J. Fox, and Dr. Ruth Westheimer. Gavin de Becker, a noted security consultant, bestselling author, and close Bezos family friend, added a number of his own testimonials, including one outlining the universal warning signs of kids who might become mass shooters. To launch the project, MacKenzie enlisted the help of one of Amazon's Silicon Valley PR firms, the Outcast Agency.

People who worked on the campaign recalled MacKenzie as humble and laid-back but also zealously protective of her privacy. She wanted to put as little of herself and of her husband's widening fame into the launch as possible. Perhaps as a result, Bystander Revolution was barely mentioned in the press when it debuted in 2014 and never gained much momentum. The organization sent out its last tweet two years later, and its website has barely been updated since. Journalists who set out to profile her over the years had to resort to analyzing "the public-facing introvert" in each of her two novels, as the *New Yorker* once put it, as well as her account in a 2013 TV interview of falling in love with Bezos's booming laugh as a twenty-three-year-old research associate at D. E. Shaw ("It was love at first listen") and getting engaged to him within three months of dating.

By 2018, Bezos was already seeing Lauren Sanchez, legal documents later showed, while keeping up the appearance of an intact marriage. That April, the Bezos family went to Norway for MacKenzie's birthday and stayed in an ice hotel; he posted a short video to Twitter on a dogsled, giggling gleefully. "It really was an incredible vacation," he later told an onstage interviewer. "We got it all done in three and a half days. It was amazing." A few months later, the couple launched the $2 billion Bezos Day One Fund, a philanthropy to address homelessness and build preschools in low-income neighborhoods.

In October, they hosted another edition of Campfire, the annual family camp/conference at the Four Seasons Resort in Santa Barbara—the event that Bezos liked to call "the highlight of his year." Once again, guests and their families flew in on private planes, all paid for by Amazon, and were festooned with extravagant gifts in their hotel rooms. That year, author Michael Lewis spoke about his new book about the Trump presidency, *The Fifth Risk*, Jane Goodall talked about climate change, and Justice Ruth Bader Ginsburg appeared via satellite. Maria Toorpakai Wazir, a Pakistani athlete, won over attendees with her experience of having to impersonate a boy for sixteen years so she could play competitive squash. On the last night, Jeff Tweedy, Dave Matthews, Jon Bon Jovi, St. Vincent, and others attending the event got on stage and jammed.

To the guests who knew them personally, Bezos and MacKenzie seemed normal and affectionate that weekend. But who can really know what happens within the private confines of a marriage? Two months later, MacKenzie was absent at the annual Amazon Studios Christmas party at Bezos's home in Beverly Hills. By his side instead was Lauren Sanchez, as well as her older brother, Michael.

Sanchez, then forty-eight, was an exuberant extrovert. The wife of Patrick Whitesell, the powerful chairman of the Endeavor talent agency, she personally knew most of the two hundred or so assembled guests at the party, including Matt Damon, Brad Pitt, Barbra Streisand, Katy Perry, Jennifer Lopez, and Alex Rodriguez. Some had attended her star-studded 2005 wedding to Whitesell.

Ebullient and curvaceous, with a penchant for walking into a room and embracing everybody in it, Sanchez was supremely comfortable under the high-wattage lights in cities like Los Angeles, New York, and Washington, D.C. In many ways, she was the opposite of MacKenzie. If Bezos was ever imprisoned in Venezuela, she would likely march into the jail, beguile all the guards, and persuade at least one into unlocking the cell door voluntarily.

Like Bezos, Sanchez was born in Albuquerque, New Mexico. Their families didn't know one another, but the couple would later chart all the coincidental overlap among their relatives at places such as the Bank of New Mexico, where Jackie and Mike Bezos first met and where her cousin had once worked. Sanchez's father, Ray, ran a local flight school, Golden Airways, and owned ten planes. Her mother, Eleanor, also had a pilot's license, and when Sanchez was young was seriously injured in a plane crash after she was practicing stalls with a flight instructor and the engine wouldn't restart.

Her parents divorced when Sanchez was eight years old, ending a contentious marriage wracked by mutual recriminations of infidelity. Sanchez and her older brothers, Paul and Michael, went to live with their mom, who remarried three more times and started a peripatetic career that would lead her to become an assistant deputy mayor of Los Angeles and later an administration executive at Columbia University. While Sanchez was dyslexic and struggled academically in school, she won attention as a model and was crowned Miss Junior America New Mexico in 1987. After high school, she attended the University of Southern California and then dropped out to start a career in local broadcast news.

In the late nineties, Sanchez became a correspondent on the syndicated gossip magazine program *Extra* and then a morning anchor on Fox's *Good Day LA*. She later hosted the first season of the popular reality TV show *So You Think You Can Dance* and cameoed in major films (that's her playing a news reporter, ninety-one minutes into *Fight Club*). She broke off at least three engagements over the years and had a son with NFL player Tony Gonzalez before marrying Whitesell, the Hollywood superagent, and having a son and a daughter.

Bezos reportedly met Sanchez through Whitesell and reconnected with her at his 2016 Amazon Studios party in L.A. for *Manchester by the Sea*. After her marriage faltered, she bonded with Bezos over their shared love of flying. The exact origin of the romance is unknown, though by the beginning of 2018, her helicopter company, Black Ops Aviation, was filming documentary videos for Blue Origin and posting them to YouTube.

In March 2018, Bezos invited Sanchez to Palm Springs to attend the third annual MARS conference, his invite-only symposium for luminaries in space travel, artificial intelligence, and robotics. MacKenzie didn't attend, while Sanchez's voice can be heard in the background of a video clip of Bezos playing table tennis at the event against a Japanese robot.

A few weeks later, Sanchez told her brother, Michael, that she wanted to introduce him to her new beau. In April, they had dinner at the Hearth & Hound, a hip West Hollywood restaurant, accompanied by Michael Sanchez's husband and two other friends. Michael sat across from Bezos and hit it off with Amazon's CEO. He also emerged alarmed about how the couple openly expressed their affections for each other, potentially within sight of the local paparazzi while both were still married to their respective spouses.

In retrospect, Bezos did carry on the relationship with curious disregard for public reaction. He also brought Sanchez to Seattle with her mother and brother, where they got a VIP tour of the Spheres, and to Washington, D.C., where he showed her the *Washington Post* printing presses. She attended the ninth launch of *New Shepard* that summer and helped produce an inspirational two-minute video for Blue Origin featuring aerial shots of the rocket, accompanied by a rare voice-over by Bezos himself, waxing philosophically about Blue's mission as the song "Your Blue Room" by U2 and Brian Eno plays in the background. "The human need to explore is deep within all of us," he intones at the start of the video.

By late summer of 2018, Michael Sanchez was growing even more anxious about the couple's brazenness. A handsome, gay Trump supporter and skilled amateur tennis player with a predilection for double-bridged Gucci eyeglasses, his career had taken a much different path than his sister's. After working at the Hollywood talent agency ICM Partners and then in sales and marketing for MTV, he started Axis Management, a talent and PR agency that represented a slate of right-wing cable news pundits and reality television stars. In 2007, he cofounded Dead of Winter Productions and produced the horror film *Killer Movie* (with a Rotten Tomatoes score of 19 percent). The film included a small role for his sister as a TV reporter named "Margo Moorhead." After the movie bombed, one of the film's financiers sued him, claiming he was owed money. To protect his assets, Michael Sanchez declared bankruptcy in 2010; his public filings showed that he owed his sister $165,000.

Sanchez bickered with his sister over the years over financial issues and they were frequently estranged. But Michael was also a groomsman at his sister's wedding to Whitesell and godfather to their son. When she started a secret exchange of text messages and intimate photographs with Bezos, she frequently forwarded his messages to Michael. The sibling relationship was, to put it mildly, unusual.

But all of that was happening well outside Bezos's line of sight. He was enthralled by the adventurous Sanchez and by nature was not predisposed to be paranoid or immediately skeptical of anyone—especially not the brother of his new paramour. "It's better to assume trust and find out that you are wrong than to always assume people are trying to screw you over," was essentially his philosophy, according to a friend.

———

Over the summer of 2018, as the romance between Bezos and Sanchez intensified, the editors of the *National Enquirer* started investigating Bezos's personal life. The famously voyeuristic tabloid, which had paid sources for sensationalist gossip since the 1950s, was coming off a catastrophic few years. In addition to declining newsstand sales, its publisher, the unfortunately named David Pecker, had directed the paper to "catch and kill" stories about his friend Donald Trump's marital infidelity, a practice that had drawn the *Enquirer*'s parent company, American Media Inc., into the bottomless pit of Trumpworld scandal. Pecker's deputy, chief content officer Dylan Howard, who oversaw all forty of AMI's media properties, including *RadarOnline*, *Men's Journal*, and *Us Weekly*, had also been outed by the *New Yorker* writer Ronan Farrow for trying to discredit accusers of disgraced movie mogul Harvey Weinstein.

Howard was a short and stout thirty-six-year-old Australian and an acid-penned chronicler of the hypocrisies and indiscretions of American celebrities. The journalistic force behind such tabloid supernovas as Mel Gibson's recorded anti-Semitic rants and Arnold Schwarzenegger's love child, Howard was by nature protective of his work and combative toward perceived rivals. When the *Washington Post* aggressively covered AMI's catch-and-kill problems, a bristling Howard enthusiastically authorized a tough look at its wealthy owner's life.

One line of inquiry, according to an email that went out to AMI reporters from the company's news desk in late summer, was to examine Bezos's relationship with the family of his biological father, Ted Jorgensen, and why the CEO hadn't contacted them as Jorgensen was dying in 2015. The memo didn't mention anything about an extramarital affair.

What happened the very next day is difficult to dismiss as simply a coincidence. But however you interpret the unlikely events that transpired over the next year, such coincidences abound in the volumes of interview transcripts, email and text message records, and other evidence that would later accumulate in the myriad of civil and criminal cases that were the primary legacy of the entire saga.

On Monday, September 10, Michael Sanchez wrote an email to Andrea Simpson, an L.A.-based reporter for AMI. Sanchez and Simpson were close friends; he regularly sent her news about his clients, like his sister's one-day return to host *Extra* that month, and they had once gotten tattoos together on a whim. (His, on his forearm, read "*Je suis la tempête*.")

In his email, Michael Sanchez said he had a hot tip for Simpson. A friend, he wrote, worked for a well-known "Bill Gates type" who was married and having an affair with "a B-list married actress." The friend, Sanchez wrote, had compromising photos of the couple but wanted a six-figure payout for the scoop. Sanchez claimed to be working as the middleman.

Simpson and her editors in New York could only guess at the identities of the mystery lovers. In emails later made public as part of a lawsuit Michael Sanchez filed against AMI in L.A. district court, the journalists speculated about figures like Evan Spiegel, Mark Zuckerberg, and Michael Dell. For weeks, Sanchez kept them guessing and tried to bump up his asking price by hinting at the possibility that the story could end up with a British tabloid. In early October, he teased the matter further, meeting with Simpson and showing her text messages and photos with the faces obscured. But the gossip reporter suspected anyway. "Just doing a look around and by the body, I think it may be Jeff Bezos," she wrote to her New York bosses.

Finally, on October 18, Sanchez called up Dylan Howard and revealed that the "Bill Gates type" was in fact Amazon's CEO. Sanchez and AMI then signed a contract, entitling him to a payout of around $200,000—the most the *National Enquirer* had ever paid for a story. The contract stipulated that the *Enquirer* would make every effort to safeguard Sanchez's anonymity and withhold his identity as the source of the scoop.

Sanchez didn't yet reveal the name of the "B-list married actress," but it didn't take long for *Enquirer* editors to figure it out. Dylan Howard dispatched photographers to track Bezos's jet and was at the MIPCOM entertainment industry festival in Cannes, France, when he received photos of Amazon's CEO and Lauren Sanchez disembarking from his Gulfstream G650ER.

On October 23, Michael Sanchez flew to New York and had dinner with Howard and James Robertson, another *Enquirer* editor, and corroborated what they now already knew. He also showed them a flash drive containing a collection of texts from Bezos to his sister, as well as a handful of personal photographs that the couple had exchanged; and he intimated that at a later date he could show them a more explicit "selfie" that Bezos had sent to Lauren Sanchez. Howard, Robertson, and Simpson would all later submit in federal court, under the penalty of perjury, that Michael Sanchez was the sole source of all the compromising material they received during the investigation.

Inside AMI's drab offices on the southern tip of Manhattan, a windowless warren of open desks enveloped in a toxic atmosphere caused by years of downsizing and scandal, the Bezos story was met with excitement. Dylan Howard believed it could revive the publication's battered reputation, which had once evoked grudging admiration

from prestige media rivals after world-beating scoops on the pecca-
dillos of figures like Tiger Woods and John Edwards. "This is a great
story. It's an *Enquirer* story," Howard told a colleague, when asked
why they were pursuing a business figure who was likely of limited interest to the tabloid's celebrity-obsessed readers. "This is peeling back
the gilded façade of the famous and extraordinarily rich, it's exactly
what we should stand for."

But as the paper worked on the Bezos story, David Pecker was nervous. The company had filed for bankruptcy protection in 2010 and
was loaded with debt from acquiring magazines such as *In Touch* and
Life & Style. An effort to secure an investment from the Kingdom of
Saudi Arabia to finance a bid to buy *Time* magazine wasn't panning
out, and Anthony Melchiorre, the seldom-photographed chief of the
company's principal owner, New Jersey hedge fund Chatham Asset
Management, was anxious about anything that might land the media
company in fresh legal peril.

That September, AMI had signed a non-prosecution agreement
with the Department of Justice over allegations that it tried to buy
and bury negative stories about Donald Trump. The deal required its
executives to cooperate with the federal investigation of Trump lawyer Michael Cohen and to operate in the future with unimpeachable
honesty. It also ensured the company would remain under the watch-
ful eye of prosecutors for years. Breaking the agreement could mean
financial ruin for AMI.

Pecker, a temperamental boss who conducted much of his work
from his cell phone while driving between his homes and offices in
Connecticut and New York City, was alternatively energized about
and fearful of the Bezos story. He called one draft of the article "the
best piece of journalism the *Enquirer* has ever done," and opined in
an email to editors that "each page of a story should be another death
blow for Bezos," according to a person with knowledge of the subsequent criminal investigations. But Pecker was also terrified of getting
sued by the world's richest person, particularly over a story of little in-

terest to the paper's Hollywood-obsessed readers. He demanded the story be "100 percent bullet proof" and vacillated about when and even if they should publish it at all.

In early November, Pecker grew even more agitated when he learned that Dylan Howard and Cameron Stracher, AMI's general counsel, had inserted an unusual provision into Michael Sanchez's contract delineating that he would receive his payment up front, before the story was published. Now Pecker was hemmed in; if they didn't run the story, or if it broke elsewhere, they would have wasted the large sum and exposed the company to another possible "catch and kill" allegation. After Pecker exploded in anger at Stracher over lunch at Cipriani Wall Street in lower Manhattan, the veteran lawyer walked out of the restaurant, essentially quitting on the spot. That elevated his recently hired deputy: Jon Fine, who—another unlikely coincidence—had previously worked at Amazon for nine years.

For the rest of that fall, the *Enquirer* worked on the story with Michael Sanchez's help. He emailed the paper a selection of the couple's personal photographs and text messages and reassured Dylan Howard that they knew nothing of the investigation, when the editor wondered whether Bezos and Lauren Sanchez were deliberately planting the story. Sanchez also tipped the paper off to the couple's travel plans; and when he had dinner with them at the Felix Trattoria restaurant in Venice, California, on November 30, two reporters were stationed at tables nearby and the tabloid's photographers were clicking away surreptitiously.

On the promised explicit selfie of Bezos though, Sanchez seemed to equivocate. He arranged to share it with Howard in L.A. in early November, then canceled the meeting. A few weeks later, on November 21, after *Enquirer* editors kept hounding him, he finally agreed to show it to Andrea Simpson while Howard and James Robertson watched via FaceTime from New York.

The media, most observers, and even his own extended family would later condemn Sanchez for this astonishing act of betrayal. But in his own mind, at least—distorted by bitter resentments, years of feuds with his sister, and the dysfunctional dynamics of a complex family—Michael Sanchez believed he was cleverly manipulating the *Enquirer*.

His sister and Bezos were conducting their relationship out in the open and it was only a matter of time before their families and the larger world discovered it. He was trying to "bring the 747 in for a soft landing," as he later put it, referring to the delicate process of allowing the couple to inform their respective spouses, initiate divorce proceedings, and then introduce their relationship to the public. "Everything I did protected Jeff, Lauren, and my family," Sanchez later emailed me. "I would never sell out anyone." He also believed his source agreement with AMI precluded the media company from using the most embarrassing material he had provided them.

That justification would ring hollow to many. But on one issue, at least, Sanchez appeared to tell a straightforward truth. He later told FBI investigators for the Southern District of New York that he never actually had an explicit photograph of Bezos in his possession. In the meeting with *Enquirer* reporter Andrea Simpson on November 21, with Dylan Howard and James Robertson watching via FaceTime from New York and recording the transaction, Sanchez didn't show them a picture of Bezos at all, but an anonymous photograph of male genitalia that he had captured from the gay escort website Rent.men.

———

On Monday January 7, 2019, *Enquirer* editors sent a pair of text messages to Jeff Bezos and Lauren Sanchez that started with a single, incendiary sentence: *"I write to request an interview with you about your love affair."* The entire ordeal, unfolding at the very same time as the HQ2 saga approached its fateful denouement in New York, was now nearing its own conclusion, fueled by a half-dozen people each with their own interlocking relationships and complex agendas.

With what must have been substantial alarm, the couple moved swiftly in response. Lauren Sanchez turned to the person closest to her who best knew the brazen byways of the tabloid industry: her brother. In the midst of the crisis, Michael Sanchez innocently suggested he could exploit his relationships with editors at the *Enquirer* to find out what materials they had. After signing a $25,000-a-month contract with his sister to help her navigate the descending insanity, he called Dylan Howard to announce that he was acting as his sister's representative and suggested that he come to New York to review the paper's reporting (which, of course, he had provided). Confident in the promise of confidentiality from AMI, Michael Sanchez was now playing both sides.

Bezos, meanwhile, involved his longtime security consultant, Gavin de Becker, as well as de Becker's longtime L.A.-based entertainment attorney, Marty Singer. Early on Wednesday, January 9, racing to get ahead of the story, Bezos instructed the shocked employees in Amazon's public relations department to release the news of his marital breakup from his official Twitter account. "We want to make people aware of a development in our lives," the statement began. "As our family and close friends know, after a long period of loving exploration and trial separation, we have decided to divorce and continue our shared lives as friends."

In New York, Dylan Howard was watching the scoop of his career wriggle from his grasp. Even though the *Enquirer* published on Mondays, he convinced David Pecker to authorize a special eleven-page print run and posted the paper's first story online that evening. "Married Amazon Boss Jeff Bezos Getting Divorced Over Fling With Movie Mogul's Wife," screamed the headline. That night, Michael Sanchez surreptitiously texted Howard, apologizing for Bezos's tweet and a subsequent story in the *New York Post*, adding "thanks for trying to work with me, even if those fucks wouldn't."

The *Enquirer*'s story was designed not only to expose Bezos's extramarital relationship but to humiliate him as well. In addition to skirting the confidentiality provision in its contract with Michael Sanchez by quoting from the private text messages and describing a few of the intimate photos, it also bizarrely quoted "Aunt Kathy"—the ex-wife of his biological father's brother—who had last seen Jeff Bezos when he was two years old. And the story utilized every insult in the tabloid arsenal, such as "billionaire love cheat," "brazen backdoor man," and so on.

The article's ferocity and tone led Gavin de Becker and other observers to naturally question whether presidential politics might sit behind the investigation. Donald Trump, Pecker's friend and ally before the prosecution of Michael Cohen, regularly railed on Twitter against the *Washington Post* and accused Amazon of not paying its fair share of taxes and weakening the U.S. Postal Service. The thrice-married Trump also piled onto Bezos's latest predicament on Twitter:

Donald J. Trump
@realDonaldTrump

So sorry to hear the news about Jeff Bozo being taken down by a competitor whose reporting, I understand, is far more accurate than the reporting in his lobbyist newspaper, the Amazon Washington Post.

 5:45 PM · Jan 13, 2019

Despite suspicions that its motives might be political, the *Enquirer* continued to play its hand, pushing out additional stories across its media properties with more details about Bezos and Sanchez and their private text exchanges. Eventually, Michael Sanchez brokered a temporary cease-fire: it called for AMI to stop publishing new articles in exchange for exclusive paparazzi access to Lauren Sanchez, walking with two friends at the Santa Monica airport. The article ran on January 14 in *Us Weekly*, along with canned quotes and the gentle headline "First Photos Show Jeff Bezos' Girlfriend Lauren Sanchez Carefree After Scandal."

After the story ran, Michael Sanchez privately texted Dylan Howard to thank him. "The level of cooperation that you and I have built in 14 days will be written about in textbooks," he wrote. The next week, Howard emailed Michael Sanchez and reassured him that his anonymity as the original leaker was secure. "The untold story—if you will—has not been told," he wrote. "I'm saving it for my tombstone."

But this was an unstable peace. Bezos had given de Becker "whatever budget he needed to pursue the facts" of how the paper obtained his private exchanges with Lauren Sanchez. The Hawaii-based de Becker had served on two presidential advisory boards, written four books about the psychology of violence, and consulted for a litany of high-profile political and entertainment figures. Bezos had selected his 1997 book, *The Gift of Fear*, as one of the first topics of discussion for the S-team reading club and had personally ensured that it was featured in the new Amazon Books stores.

In other words, de Becker was a savvy and experienced judge of character. After a series of phone calls and text messages with Michael Sanchez, the veteran investigator sensed something was amiss. The brother of Bezos's new paramour boasted about his ability to control *Enquirer* editors, shared conspiracy theories about cyber espionage, and referenced a passing acquaintanceship with Trumpworld characters like disgraced conservative political consultant Roger Stone. With no obvious evidence that Bezos's phone had been hacked, it didn't take much to convince de Becker that there was a mole in Camp Bezos, and that it might in fact be the person most ardently claiming that he could help.

To publicize his suspicions, de Becker turned to a friendly outlet: the *Daily Beast*, the media company run by Barry Diller, a friend of Bezos's. In an article on January 31, the *Daily Beast* revealed that de Becker had identified Michael Sanchez as a possible culprit. But perhaps overly invested in positioning the embarrassment of his client as part of a larger conspiracy, de Becker also tied the *Enquirer*'s investigation to President Trump and his campaign against the *Washington Post*, opining in the article that "strong leads point to political motives."

The saga here reached an even higher orbit of absurdity. De Becker's insinuation that a political conspiracy was behind the tabloid drama—which was frankly all too believable in the gilded age of Trump—increased the pressure on the *National Enquirer*. AMI's boss, David Pecker, fretted that even the rumor of the paper's involvement in such a plot might undermine its non-prosecution agreement with the Southern District of New York. AMI's chief financial backer, the shadowy Anthony Melchiorre of Chatham Asset Management, was terrified Bezos might sue AMI and that his own investors, which included drama-shy state pension funds, might withdraw their money from the hedge fund after yet another whiff of scandal.

Pecker and Melchiorre implored Dylan Howard to *fix* it—to settle the feud with Bezos's camp and to secure an acknowledgment that the investigation wasn't politically motivated and that the *Enquirer* hadn't used illegal means in scoring the story. Fortunately, Dylan Howard had a personal relationship with Marty Singer, one of the attorneys who was representing Bezos in the matter. The two were known to attend sporting events together and were frequent sparring partners over the litany of revelations the *Enquirer* often published about Singer's famous clients. Howard was actually at dinner with Singer and film director Brett Ratner in New York City when the attorney got the call to help represent Bezos in the unfolding drama.

But in a way, their casual friendship would help contribute to the tabloid editor's undoing. Over the first week in February, Howard and Singer engaged in their familiar dance, trying to negotiate an end to the media hostilities between the *Enquirer* and the Bezos camp. Howard asked the lawyer to get Bezos and de Becker to accept that it wasn't a political hit job and promised he would cease publication of damaging stories. Singer wanted to know exactly what unpublished text messages and photos the paper possessed. Howard was dubious; he suspected the lawyer was hunting for confirmation of the identity of his anonymous source.

Contributing further tensions to the discussion was the prospect that the *Washington Post* was preparing to publish an article on the scandal that would question whether the exposé was "just juicy gossip or a political hit job." David Pecker feared that another such insinuation in one of the world's most respected papers could doom his non-prosecution agreement. He again urged Howard to resolve the matter. So Howard finally relented and started showing his cards.

In an email he sent to Singer on the afternoon of February 5, AMI's chief content officer wrote, "with the *Washington Post* poised to publish unsubstantiated rumors of the *National Enquirer's* initial report, I wanted to describe to you the photos obtained during our newsgathering." Howard then listed the nine personal photos that Bezos and Lauren Sanchez had exchanged. These were the pictures that she had shared with her brother, and which her brother had passed to the *Enquirer*.

With an abundance of misplaced swagger and burning with injured pride that his tabloid triumph was being maligned, Howard also referenced another photo: the "below-the-belt selfie" that he'd captured via FaceTime from the meeting between Michael Sanchez and reporter Andrea Simpson. Unbeknownst to Howard, he was bragging about the anonymous image that Michael Sanchez had lifted from Rentmen. "It would give no editor pleasure to send this email," Howard concluded. "I hope common sense can prevail—and quickly."

But common sense was in short supply. The *Post* published its article that night; in it, de Becker once again identified Sanchez as a possible culprit and charged that the leak was "politically motivated." Michael Sanchez also spoke to the *Post* reporters, and battling charges of his own culpability, indiscriminately interjected another round of disinformation into the public domain. He suggested incorrectly that de Becker might have leaked news of the affair himself and also convinced the *Post* (and later, other papers) to report that the *Enquirer* had started investigating the affair over the summer of 2018—months before his initial outreach (there's no evidence to suggest that was the case).

After the article was published, Pecker called Dylan Howard to say that Melchiorre, the hedge fund manager, was "ballistic," and again pressured Howard to stop the madness. Howard then started negotiating directly over the phone with Bezos's representative, the savvy de Becker. Suspicious and wary, they both recorded the phone calls.

Howard had good reason to be cautious. "I suggest clients compel the extortionist to commit to his sleaziness, which puts him on the defensive," de Becker had written in his bestselling book, *The Gift of Fear*. "I ask victims to repeat, 'I don't understand what you're getting at,' until the extortionist states it clearly." In the phone calls, according to transcripts of the conversations that were later described to me, de Becker seemed to be trying to do exactly that: "So you guys will publish these photos unless we do a written acknowledgment?" he asked Howard.

Howard tried to avoid making such an explicit threat but approached the abyss anyway by continuing to reserve the paper's rights to publish the materials. "This is not in any way to be construed as some form of blackmail or anything like that!" he told the veteran investigator at one point. "It's in both parties' interest to come to terms, given the specter of legal claims that are flying around."

Howard and de Becker appeared to make progress. On February 6, AMI's new deputy general counsel Jon Fine—the hasty replacement for Cameron Stracher and a relative stranger to the Machiavellian hellscape of tabloid lawyering—sent the proposed terms of an agreement via email to Marty Singer. AMI would agree not to publish or share any of the unpublished photos or texts if Bezos and his reps join the company in publicly rejecting the notion that the *Enquirer*'s "reporting was instigated, dictated or influenced in any manner by external forces, political or otherwise."

The email was easily viewed as extortive. On February 7, Bezos told his advisors that he knew exactly what he was going to do. He wrote a thousand-word-plus essay titled "No thank you, Mr. Pecker," and handed it off to Jay Carney at Amazon, whose brow furrowed in surprise as he read it for the first time while on a Chime video conference with colleagues. Then he had it uploaded to the publishing site Medium.

In the post, Bezos included the entirety of the emails from Jon Fine and Dylan Howard and wrote:

> Something unusual happened to me yesterday. Actually, for me it wasn't just unusual—it was a first. I was made an offer I couldn't refuse. Or at least that's what the top people at the National Enquirer thought. I'm glad they thought that, because it emboldened them to put it all in writing.

Bezos then recounted AMI's legal entanglements with the Trump administration and its failed attempts to win an investment from the government of Saudi Arabia—another government hostile to the *Washington Post's* reporting. His ownership of the paper, Bezos wrote, "is a complexifier for me. It's unavoidable that certain powerful people who experience Washington Post news coverage will wrongly conclude I am their enemy." He also added that he didn't regret owning the paper, "a critical institution with a critical mission" and "something I will be most proud of when I'm 90 and reviewing my life, if I'm lucky enough to live that long . . ."

This noble sentiment, of course, had little to do with his yearlong open conduct of an extramarital relationship, the calculated perfidy of his girlfriend's brother, or the desperate attempts of AMI to escape a cloud of political suspicion. But like the "Reynolds Pamphlet," which Alexander Hamilton penned in the 1790s, accusing his opponents of extortion when he was confronted with charges of an adulterous affair, the *Medium* post was a public relations master stroke. Bezos cast himself as a sympathetic defender of the press and an opponent of "AMI's long-earned reputation for weaponizing journalistic privileges, hiding behind important protections, and ignoring the tenets and purpose of true journalism."

Whether or not Bezos knew or even suspected that the *Enquirer's* threat to publish an explicit photograph was hollow is unclear. To interested readers blissfully unaware of the behind-the-scenes shenanigans, Bezos was taking a brave stand against the devious tactics of Donald Trump's tabloid allies while vulnerably offering his own embarrassing photographs as collateral. "Bezos Exposes Pecker," declared the *New York Post* memorably, as public sympathies in the imbroglio immediately shifted to his side.

As the *Medium* post was being published on the afternoon of February 7, Gavin de Becker stalled Dylan Howard, who was pressing him via text messages for an update on the Bezos camp's response to AMI's offer. Finally, the famed security consultant delivered the coup de grâce, texting the tabloid editor: "As you can likely see, I ran into resistance to your proposal."

———

Dylan Howard was also getting dunked on closer to home. Shifting into damage control mode and trying to preserve his company's precarious legal and financial position, David Pecker blamed his chief content officer for the entire debacle. He removed Howard from his position and gave him the largely ceremonial role of senior vice president of corporate development, where he had few editorial responsibilities. Howard left AMI when his contract expired a year later.

"I paid the ultimate sacrifice for a story that was 100 percent true," Howard said when I contacted him for his recollections of the saga, before noting that the ongoing litigation prevented him from addressing it further. "I was tarred with the unfounded allegation that I did it with political motivations."

In addition to sinking Howard's career at AMI, Bezos's essay took the already muddled question of how the paper obtained his private text messages and photographs and confused it further. Bezos artfully suggested in his post that AMI's apoplexy over the investigation into the story's origins was "still to be better understood" and that "the Saudi angle seems to hit a particularly sensitive nerve."

Gavin de Becker followed up those assertions in March by writing an article for the *Daily Beast*. He pointed to AMI's frantic attempts to defend itself from the charge of engaging in a political conspiracy and suggested that there must be another layer of hidden truth in the whole ordeal. "Our investigators and several experts concluded with high confidence that the Saudis had access to Bezos' phone and gained private information," he wrote. "As of today, it is unclear to what degree, if any, AMI was aware of the details."

Pecker and his colleagues had first faced the allegation that they were operating on behalf of Donald Trump; now they confronted the insinuation that they were in league with the Saudis. With Howard sidelined and on vacation in Mexico, the company decided that it need not honor its confidentiality promise to Michael Sanchez. "The fact of the matter is, it was Michael Sanchez who tipped the National Enquirer off to the affair on September 10, 2018, and over the course of four months provided all of the materials for our investigation," the company said in a statement. "His continued efforts to discuss and falsely represent our reporting, and his role in it, has waived any source confidentiality."

But AMI's disclosures carried little weight, particularly since its executives had lied so flagrantly about the "catch and kill" allegations related to Trump. Hints of an international conspiracy endured—in large part because of the improbable truth in the idea that the government of Saudi Arabia was out to get Jeff Bezos.

Like other U.S. business leaders, Bezos had cultivated a personal relationship with Mohammed bin Salman, or MBS, back in early 2018, when the young crown prince of Saudi Arabia appeared committed to liberalizing the religiously conservative country and weaning it off its dependence on oil revenues. Bezos met MBS on the prince's spring tour of the U.S. that year, and they exchanged WhatsApp numbers. Over the next few months, they kept in touch over WhatsApp and discussed Amazon's plans to spend as much as $2 billion putting AWS data centers in the country. That May, the crown prince sent Bezos an encrypted video file that appeared to contain a promotional video, touting the country's low broadband prices. Bezos was befuddled by the message, which was in Arabic. "Impressive numbers and video," he eventually replied.

A few months later, on October 2, Bezos was in Washington, D.C., accepting the Samuel J. Heyman Spirit of Service Award and sitting with *Washington Post* colleagues. In the middle of the event, publisher Fred Ryan leaned over and whispered that he had news to share, then wrote it down on a piece of paper: earlier that day, Jamal Khashoggi, a contributing *Post* columnist who had written columns criticizing MBS's vicious turn to authoritarianism, had walked into the Saudi Arabian consulate in Istanbul to obtain a marriage license and hadn't come out. Bezos read the note and whispered back, "Let me know what I can do to help."

Over the next few weeks, the *Post* doggedly investigated Khashoggi's grisly murder while its opinion writers condemned the Saudi government and called for U.S. companies to sever ties with Saudi business interests. Like other business leaders, Bezos canceled plans to attend bin Salman's Future Investment Initiative, the annual event known as "Davos in the Desert." But curiously, MBS continued to text Bezos, including sending a WhatsApp message that appeared to allude to Bezos's marital problems, which were still secret in the fall of 2018. "Arguing with a woman is like reading the Software License agreement," MBS wrote, alongside an image of a brunette who bore a vague resemblance to Lauren Sanchez. "In the end you have to ignore everything and click I agree."

Meanwhile, an ad hoc Twitter army organized by MBS's regime hit at Bezos online, posting graphics and videos that labeled him a racist enemy of Saudi Arabia and called for a boycott of Amazon and its subsidiary, Souq.com.

عادل جابر
@aadelljaber

We as Saudis will never accept to be attacked by The Washington Post in the morning, only to buy products from Amazon and Souq.com by night! Strange that all three companies are owned by the same Jew who attacks us by day and sells us products by night!

🐦 12:20 PM · Nov 4, 2018

In early 2019, as his battle with the *Enquirer* burst into the open, Bezos (who is not Jewish) would have additional reasons to believe his smartphone was compromised. On February 16, after Bezos had aired his suspicions about Saudi Arabia's involvement in the entire affair, MBS again texted Bezos, writing a message in English replete with typos: "Jeff all what you hear or told to it's not true and it's matter of time tell you know the truth. There is nothing against you or amazon from me or Saudi Arabia."

De Becker then commissioned an examination of Bezos's iPhone X. The eventual report by Anthony Ferrante, a longtime colleague of de Becker's and the former director for cyber incident response for the U.S. National Security Council, concluded that the promotional video about broadband prices that MBS had sent Bezos the previous year likely contained a copy of Pegasus, a piece of nearly invisible malware created by an Israeli company called NSO Group. Once the program was activated, Ferrante found, the volume of data leaving Bezos's smartphone increased by about 3,000 percent.

Some prominent cybersecurity experts questioned Ferrante's conclusions amid an absence of more concrete forensic evidence. The massive "exfiltration of data" from the phone that Ferrante documented also happened to coincide with Bezos's exchange of text messages and personal videos with Lauren Sanchez. Nevertheless, the

Wall Street Journal reported that Saudi officials close to the crown prince were aware of a plan to attack Bezos's phone. In 2020, a report produced by United Nations human rights investigators Agnes Callamard and David Kaye confirmed with "medium to high confidence" that the Saudis had hacked the phones of Bezos and other political and press figures, part of a broad attempt to try to control media coverage of its government.

Had MBS's regime learned of Bezos's relationship with Lauren Sanchez and tipped off the *National Enquirer* or even supplemented the information it received from Michael Sanchez? That possibility might make certain logical sense if you squinted hard enough. David Pecker had once unsuccessfully courted Saudi investors to finance AMI's purchase of *Time*. To boost their prospects, AMI executives had even produced a sycophantic ninety-seven-page glossy magazine, called *The New Kingdom*, on the eve of the crown prince's U.S. tour. But at least from my vantage point, at this particular moment in time, there is not any conclusive evidence to support the hypothesis that the Saudis alerted the tabloid paper to Bezos's affair—only a fog of overlapping events, weak ties between disparate figures, and more strange coincidences.

For Bezos and his advisors though, who were still trying to positively spin the embarrassing events surrounding his divorce, such a cloud of uncertainty was at the very least distracting from the more unsavory and complicated truth.

———

As the entire mêlée quieted over the course of 2019, Bezos and Lauren Sanchez started appearing together in public. In July, they attended the Allen & Company conference in Sun Valley, Idaho, mingling with the likes of Warren Buffett, Tim Cook, and Mark Zuckerberg. A few days later, they watched the Wimbledon men's finals from the Royal Box, three rows behind Prince William and Kate Middleton. In August, they gamboled in the western Mediterranean Sea on the super yacht of mogul David Geffen. There were also trips to Solomeo, Italy, for a summit organized by luxury designer Brunello Cucinelli and to Venice, aboard the mega yacht of Barry Diller and Diane von Furstenberg. During these trips, Bezos was repeatedly photographed wearing a pair of stylish octopus-print multicolor swim trunks, inadvertently igniting a fashion trend.

For two decades, Bezos had remained singularly focused on Amazon and his family, with Blue Origin and space travel capturing his only scraps of time left. But his extraordinary wealth, insatiable curiosity about interesting people, and thirst for new experiences, as well as his relationship with Lauren Sanchez, had clearly changed him. It turned out that he relished the trappings of his extraordinary success. To those who had spent an inordinate amount of time observing him, he looked vibrant and happy.

His divorce from MacKenzie was finalized in July 2019. She received 19.7 million shares of Amazon stock, worth about $38 billion. As part of the settlement, he retained voting rights over her stock, though not after she sold it or gave it away—one of the reasons, investors had speculated, that Amazon might have explored the creation of a second class of stock the year before.

She also retained their Seattle and L.A. homes and signed the Giving Pledge, a commitment to give away more than half her wealth. Over the course of 2020, she would donate almost $6 billion to organizations like food banks, community groups, and historically Black colleges, while posting a personal essay about her motivations—a departure from her reticent approach to promoting Bystander Revolution years before. She also changed her name to MacKenzie Scott—the middle name she had grown up with.

Michael Sanchez, meanwhile, moved to San Francisco with his husband. His entire family stopped speaking to him, save for his mother, Eleanor. In two separate defamation lawsuits in L.A. district court, he sued AMI, and Bezos and Gavin de Becker, and lost nearly every subsequent legal decision as the facts dribbled out. In early 2021, Bezos asked the court to compel Sanchez to pay $1.7 million in attorney fees, though the judge later lowered that amount to $218,400. And in the Southern District of New York, federal prosecutors investigated Bezos's allegation, leveled in his *Medium* essay, that he was extorted by AMI after it published the *National Enquirer* article. The evidence must have been lacking though, because prosecutors appeared to quietly drop the matter without ever bringing a case.

For his part, Bezos quickly moved on. In October, he turned up unexpectedly outside the former Saudi consulate in Istanbul to commemorate the one-year anniversary of the murder of Jamal Khashoggi. Gavin de Becker handled the intricate security arrangements. Bezos sat next to Hatice Cengiz, Khashoggi's fiancée, and embraced her during the ceremony. "Right here where you are, you faced that street for hours, pacing and waiting, and he never came out. It is unimaginable," he said. "And you need to know that you are in our hearts. We are here."

The trip into potentially dangerous territory was another sign to employees of the *Washington Post* that their owner would stand up for their journalism, whatever the personal cost. It was also an arrow aimed directly at Bezos's enemy, MBS.

As such dramatic gestures replaced the scandal in the collective memory, Bezos's colleagues at Amazon could only watch and wonder: Did their CEO still belong to them, or to some alternate dimension of wealth, glamour, and international intrigue? He seemed to show up just as frequently in the press as in the office, buying historic works of art, and snapping up David Geffen's nine-acre Beverly Hills estate for $165 million, a California real estate record. And there he was talking climate change with Emmanuel Macron in February 2020, with Lauren Sanchez by his side, and cavorting with her and other celebrities at the Super Bowl in Miami—even taking a turn in the DJ booth of a popular night club. What did the future hold for their founder?

One clue to that question could be found in the shipyards of the Dutch custom yacht builder Oceanco. There, outside Rotterdam, a new creation was secretly taking shape: a 127-meter long, three-mast schooner about which practically nothing was known, even in the whispering confines of the luxury yacht industry—except that upon completion, it would be one of the finest sailing yachts in existence. Oceanco was also building for the same high-end clients an accompanying support yacht, which had been expressly commissioned and designed to include—you guessed it—a helipad.

Despite everything that had happened, Bezos's armor of invincibility was only slightly dented. And now the greatest challenges to Amazon in its twenty-five-year history loomed: an opening salvo from its foes in the U.S. and European Union, who sought to curb the company's formidable market power, as well as the Covid-19 pandemic, which was about to bring the entire global economy to the brink of whimpering collapse.

CHAPTER 14

Reckoning

I n the year after the Bezos-Sanchez tabloid melee, Amazon continued its dazzling ascent. With its market value drifting ever closer to the $1 trillion troposphere, the company announced that it would upgrade its shipping guarantee for U.S. members from two days to one, further strengthening the case for shopping online. Following the finalization of his divorce from MacKenzie in July 2019, Bezos's personal net worth had dropped from $170 billion to $110 billion. Yet such was the buoyancy of Amazon's stock price that he retained the title of richest person alive and recovered all of that surrendered ground within twelve months. His personal wealth was larger than the gross domestic product of Hungary; larger than even the market capitalization of General Motors.

In the midst of this ascendency, a reckoning was finally at hand. Americans and Europeans tend to lionize the business triumphs of their shrewdest entrepreneurs. But they are also inherently skeptical of large, distant corporations and can be downright vituperative toward the exceedingly wealthy, particularly at a time of grotesquely widening income inequality.

And so the dual rise of Jeff Bezos's fortune and his company's market cap generated not just plaudits for a historic business accomplishment but also an incongruous amount of anger. In the final years of the company's most prosperous decade, there was a dawning sense that the system was rigged, that consumers and smaller firms were caught in Amazon's merciless grip, and that it and other tech giants were swallowing the economy whole. Emboldened politicians across the spectrum on both sides of the Atlantic Ocean started to investigate the power of Amazon and its big tech brethren, Google, Facebook, and Apple, initiating several campaigns to curb their rampant growth. If not yet the conclusive battle over the tech giants and their far-reaching influence, it was, at the very least, the opening salvo in a coming war.

Jeff Bezos said he welcomed this scrutiny, even if he did nothing to blunt the sharper edges of Amazon's business tactics. "All big institutions of any kind are going to be and should be examined, scrutinized, inspected," he told the private equity billionaire David Rubinstein during an onstage interview at the Economic Club in Washington, D.C., in 2018. "It's not personal, it's kind of what we as a society want to have happen." He sounded almost resigned toward whatever outcome might result: "We are so inventive that whatever regulations are promulgated or however it works, that will not stop us from serving customers."

In private though, Bezos prepared to take a less accommodating approach toward the intensifying techlash. In the fall of 2019, the S-team and Amazon's board of directors read *The Great A&P and the Struggle for Small Business in America*, by the economic historian Marc Levinson. The book traces the rise and fall of the first American grocery chain of the twentieth century, as well as its strategic drift after the death of its founders and the decades-long crusade against it by populist politicians and determined trustbusters. The campaign against A&P, the book concludes, was mostly political, propelled by the cumulative complaints of thousands of sympathetic mom-and-pop stores and their suppliers, and by a company that exhibited unusual passivity in the face of early criticism.

Though A&P was known for strong-arming suppliers and undercutting rivals with predatory prices, the idea that the company actually doomed itself by failing to properly answer its critics, and then to plan for succession after the death of its founders, seemed to res- onate with Bezos and other Amazon executives. "The takeaway was, we really can't ourselves get distracted by all the noise out there. This is going to happen. It's inevitable," said David Zapolsky, senior vice president and general counsel. "This is kind of how our society reacts to large institutions."

Amazon could not ignore what was coming. As public and politi- cal sentiment around big tech began to perceptibly shift, the company faced a set of largely antagonistic candidates for the 2020 Democratic nomination for the U.S. presidency. It also confronted a campaign to increase wages for workers in its fulfillment centers and a controversy over the minuscule amount of corporate taxes it paid in the U.S. and Europe. President Donald Trump, an avowed enemy of Bezos and his newspaper, the *Washington Post*, leveled fresh accusations that Ama- zon's deal with the U.S. Postal Service was inequitable, while allegedly interfering with AWS's pursuit of the so-called JEDI contract, a lu- crative deal to host the U.S. Department of Defense's computer oper- ations in the cloud.

To cap it all off, after a sixteen-month-long investigation into the state of competition in the digital economy, the U.S. House Judiciary Subcommittee on Antitrust delivered a scathing, 450-page report on the abuses of Amazon and other tech companies. Among other things, the report charged that Amazon enjoyed a dominant position in online retail, engaged in anticompetitive acquisitions, and bullied small sellers in its third-party marketplace. It recommended that Amazon be broken up like the railroad and telecommunication trusts of yesteryear.

Defending the company with his usual combativeness, senior vice president Jay Carney said of the subcommittee's report, "There was very little that I see that has a lot of credibility to it." But Lina Khan, who had helped steer the report as counsel to the subcommittee and whose *Yale Law Journal* paper on revitalizing antitrust statutes had provided the intellectual foundation for Congress's investigation, rejected the notion that the proceedings were political. Only thirty-one years old and already one of Amazon's most credible adversaries, she told me in an interview that Amazon "can dictate terms to everyone dependent on its platform and increasingly enjoys the power to pick winners and losers throughout the economy. When information advantages and bargaining power are so skewed towards a single player that unilaterally sets all the rules, it's no longer a 'market' in any meaningful sense."

———

As politicians and pundits lobbed such rhetorical grenades at Amazon, the size of its global communications and policy department exploded. In 2015—the time of the infamous *New York Times* exposé—the global PR and policy group numbered 250; by the end of 2019, it had grown along with the company to nearly a thousand. The expanded division included a "rapid response team," set up to monitor coverage and triage inbound inquiries at all hours of the day. "We are both brand ambassadors and brand protectors," read one of the department's sacred tenets, the principles forged in conjunction with the S-team that guided employee decision-making. "Although at times we are willing to be misunderstood, we respond quickly, forcefully, and publicly to correct the record when false or misleading information about Amazon appears in the press, analyst reports, or among policy makers."

The source of this obsessive sensitivity to the way Amazon was portrayed was of course Bezos himself. Employees shuddered at his ability to find and circulate any article or piece of analysis he viewed as inaccurate, then ask his PR team why they hadn't pushed back on it more strenuously. Bezos's longtime PR deputy, Drew Herdener, urged the communications staff to consider "every blade of grass," to never overlook even minor facts and subtle insinuations if they were perceived as incorrect and merited a response. So when the zeitgeist around big technology companies shifted, and Amazon became a frequent subject of political discourse, the company was prepared to respond vehemently—if not always sensibly—to many of the criticisms directed its way.

One of the company's earliest adversaries was Massachusetts senator Elizabeth Warren, the former Harvard professor and Wall Street nemesis who had successfully advocated for and helped set up the Consumer Financial Protection Bureau after the great recession. In 2016, Warren delivered a clarion call at New America, a left-leaning think tank in Washington, D.C., declaring that "competition is dying" in the U.S. economy and that big tech companies like Amazon and Google exploited their status as dominant platforms to steer customers to their own products and services.

Warren resumed this cause after entering the race for the Democratic Party's presidential nomination, authoring an aggressively titled article on the publishing site *Medium* in March 2019, "Here's How We Can Break Up Big Tech." It argued that tech companies were too powerful and advised forcing them to surrender their largest acquisitions—in Amazon's case, Whole Foods Market and Zappos.

In the article and in a subsequent town hall discussion on CNN, Warren also charged that Amazon had a monopolistic stranglehold on e-commerce and that it undermined third-party sellers by introducing its own private-label versions of their most popular products. (As we have seen, employees in Amazon's private-label group had, in fact, violated a loosely enforced internal policy restricting them from viewing sales data from independent merchants.) "You can be the umpire in the baseball game and you can run an honest platform, or you can be a player," Warren said on CNN. "That is, you can have a business or you can have a team in the game. But you don't get to be the umpire and have a team in the game."

The day after Warren's CNN town hall, Amazon punched back from its corporate Twitter account. It claimed that it controlled only a small share of overall retail (online *and* off-line) and denied that its private-label business was exploitive while minimizing its size:

Amazon News
@amazonnews

We don't use individual sellers' data to launch private label products (which account for only about 1% of sales). And sellers aren't being "knocked out" – they're seeing record sales every year. Also, Walmart is much larger; Amazon is less than 4% of U.S. retail.

Warren and other Democratic presidential candidates also seized on a report from the Institute on Taxation and Economic Policy, which revealed that Amazon had received a $129 million tax *rebate* from the federal government in 2018, despite recording $11.2 billion in profit. An especially adept navigator of tax law, Amazon was the benefactor of tax benefits attributable to its growing number of fulfillment centers and rising stock price. It had effectively offset its federal income tax obligation by deducting the cost of equipment in its supply chain and the value of its employee stock grants, as well as by taking advantage of tax credits arising from its vast R&D budget.

The maneuverings, which were entirely legal, set off another wave of anti-Amazon attacks. "I have nothing against Amazon," tweeted Joe Biden, the future president, on June 13, "but no company pulling in billions of dollars of profits should pay a lower tax rate than firefighters and teachers. We need to reward work, not just wealth."

The guardians of Amazon's reputation tweeted back that same day:

Amazon News
@amazonnews

We've paid $2.6B in corporate taxes since 2016. We pay every penny we owe. Congress designed tax laws to encourage

companies to reinvest in the American economy. We have.
$200B in investments since 2011 & 300K US jobs. Assume VP
Biden's complaint is w/ the tax code, not Amazon.

At the same time as he instilled this type of combativeness in his communications teams, Bezos also advised that they should consider backpedaling on some battles. "What I teach and preach inside Amazon is [that] when you're criticized, first look in a mirror and decide, are your critics right?" he said in an onstage interview in Berlin in 2018. "If they're right, change. Don't resist."

Amazon employed this strategy in late 2018, when another of its loudest critics, Vermont senator Bernie Sanders, extended his ongoing criticism of Bezos's wealth by unleashing a blistering critique of Amazon's compensation of its warehouse workers. He then unveiled what he theatrically called the "Stop BEZOS" bill (for "Stop Bad Employers by Zeroing Out Subsidies"), which proposed a new tax on companies based on the number of their employees that relied on public assistance programs such as food stamps.

Instead of going into another protective crouch or ignoring the bill, which was destined to go nowhere in a GOP-controlled Senate, Bezos convened an S-team meeting to reconsider the issue of worker pay. Earnings in Amazon fulfillment centers varied by state, but some employees were making as little as $10.00 an hour, which was above the $7.25 federal minimum wage. The S-team weighed a number of proposals from operations chief Dave Clark, including incrementally raising wages to $12 or $13 an hour. Instead, Bezos opted for the most aggressive plan, raising the entry-level U.S. hourly rate across the board to $15. At the same time, he compensated for at least part of the additional expense by discarding supplemental sources of worker income, such as stock grants and collective bonuses that were awarded to employees based on the performance of their facility.

The move was tactically brilliant. Amazon had surveyed its warehouse workers over the years and found a large majority were living paycheck to paycheck and would rather have the instant gratification of up-front pay than stock grants. By getting rid of the grants, Bezos not only helped to partially offset the pay increase but eliminated another incentive for unproductive or disgruntled low-level workers to stay at the company for more than a few years.

The wage hike also satisfied many of Amazon's critics, made arduous fulfillment center work more appealing to job candidates, and put the company in a position to lobby for raising the federal minimum wage, which its less affluent retail competitors could ill afford. But Amazon's subsequent virtue-signaling of the pay raise also struck some executives as disingenuous. "We decided it was time to lead—to offer wages that went beyond competitive," Bezos wrote in his shareholder letter that year. His colleagues knew all too well though that Bezos wasn't really leading but *reading*—in this case, the rising criticism of the company by politicians and the press over what they characterized as penurious wages for warehouse workers. Bezos's habit of only responding on an issue when public protests mounted would soon repeat itself.

After the pay raise was announced, Bernie Sanders tried to get Bezos on the phone to thank him. When the senator was routed to Carney instead ("a frequent disappointment, I'm afraid," Carney said), he thanked the S-team member and quizzed him on reports that some tenured workers might end up making less in the new compensation scheme. Carney assured him that no employees would emerge worse off.

The explanation seemed to satisfy Sanders, who then held off on criticizing Amazon for a generous two months before returning to Twitter to harangue the company for paying nothing in federal income tax. This was the new reality for Amazon as it inched ever closer to $1 trillion in market value: an unceasing assault from both sides of the political aisle.

———

During his lone, four-year term, Donald Trump could barely conceal a raging, indiscriminate contempt for Amazon, Jeff Bezos, and for the newspaper he privately owned, the *Washington Post*. He ranted regularly on Twitter and in interviews about Amazon's tax practices ("Amazon is getting away with murder tax-wise"), how it killed Main Street retail ("Towns, cities and states throughout the U.S. are being hurt—many jobs being lost!"), and implausibly, how it used the *Post* to further its own political agenda ("In my opinion the Washington Post is nothing more than an expensive [the paper loses a fortune] lobbyist for Amazon"). The cause of Trump's animus toward Bezos was widely speculated upon; most armchair observers calculated that it lay not only in Bezos's ownership of a media entity but in his wealth, which far exceeded the president's.

Ever since his 2015 tweet offering to "#sendDonaldtospace," Bezos had listened to his advisors and restrained himself from responding to attacks from the White House. Jay Carney later said that there was no need to return fire, because most neutral reporters understood that Trump's arguments were baseless and motivated by his fury over the *Post*'s journalism. "The fact that we were attacked episodically by the President had almost nothing to do with Amazon and everything to do with the fact that Jeff owns an independent newspaper," he said.

But several vectors of the president's attack did get Amazon's attention. In late 2017, Trump began regularly condemning Amazon's contract with the U.S. Postal Service and charging that it underpaid for package deliveries and was responsible for the agency losing taxpayer money.

> **Donald J. Trump**
> @realDonaldTrump
>
> Why is the United States Post Office, which is losing many billions of dollars a year, while charging Amazon and others so little to deliver their packages, making Amazon richer and the Post Office dumber and poorer? Should be charging MUCH MORE!

As with many Trump charges, locating any truth in the miasma of misinformation was difficult. The Postal Service covered its own expenses by charging for postage and other delivery services. But the agency had lost money for years in large part because of congressional mandates to prefund its workers' pensions and retirement healthcare accounts. Moreover, the post office's contract with Amazon, like similar deals to deliver packages for UPS and FedEx, was required by law to be profitable.

Despite these facts, Trump believed that the U.S. Postal Service could recover if it charged Amazon more. In several meetings over the course of 2017 and 2018, he demanded that postmaster general Megan Brennan double Amazon's rates, the *Washington Post* reported. Brennan pointed out that postal rates were set by an independent commission and that package delivery was the fastest growing part of its business. The president's logic also neglected the critical fact that if the agency raised prices beyond reasonable market rates, Amazon would simply accelerate the shift in deliveries to its own growing logistics service and leave the Postal Service in an even worse predicament.

Trump finally commissioned a task force to review package delivery prices, which in late 2018 recommended a modest increase in rates, though a far less substantial one than he had hoped for. In this respect, Amazon largely escaped the president's wrath. But in another, Trump's vendetta against Jeff Bezos and the *Washington Post* would exact a significant toll.

After Trump took office in 2017, leaders in the U.S. military arrived at an urgent conclusion: the Defense Department's sprawling, fragmented technology infrastructure needed a massive overhaul. Trump's then secretary of defense, Jim Mattis, embarked on a West Coast tour that summer to solicit advice from CEOs at big tech companies, meeting with Sundar Pichai and Sergey Brin of Google. He also met with Jeff Bezos, who tweeted a photo of himself and the defense secretary walking and talking in a Day 1 hallway.

Mattis returned from the trip convinced that modern technologies were changing the nature of war and that the Defense Department needed to shift its war-fighting technologies into the cloud. He convened a steering group to pursue that goal, which after extensive consideration decided to select a single cloud provider for security reasons and to make data more accessible to troops in the field, instead of the usual matrix of multiple contractors and middlemen that service most government needs.

An RFP for this contract, evocatively dubbed JEDI—for Joint Enterprise Defense Infrastructure—was issued in July 2018 and promised to be worth $10 billion over ten years. Such a lucrative, publicly validating reward in the hotly competitive field of enterprise computing immediately turned JEDI into the subject of one of the most bitterly contested battles in the history of government procurements. "I never in my mind even dreamed of the political interference that would take place," said Teresa Carlson, the Kentucky-born former speech pathologist and vice president of AWS's public sector business, who steered Amazon's bid. "I was not prepared to see the behavior that occurred."

Rancor dogged the process almost from the start. After previewing the specifications of JEDI, many tech companies concluded that it was positioned exclusively for AWS, which controlled a commanding 47.8 percent share of the cloud market in 2018 and which had possessed a high level of security clearance ever since winning a 2013 cloud contract with the CIA. At least nine tech companies, including

Microsoft, IBM, and SAP America, banded together to protest that the process was biased in Amazon's favor and to lobby Congress and the Pentagon to split the contract into multiple parts.

One of those companies, Oracle, then went even further. Acting in the flamboyant and antagonistic style of its founder, Larry Ellison, Oracle sued the Department of Defense, challenging the legality of a single-winner award and sowing doubts about the sanctity of the process. Its complaint alleged that several Defense Department officials had either worked for or advised Amazon in the past and had improperly influenced JEDI. Separately, a mysterious thirty-three-page dossier started circulating in Washington, claiming that a web of inappropriate personal and professional relationships that existed between several Defense Department officials and executives at Amazon had undermined the integrity of the process. The dossier was traced back to RosettiStarr, a D.C.-based private investigation firm. But most observers saw the unmistakable fingerprints of Oracle on it.

In its review of Oracle's lawsuit, the General Accountability Office acknowledged a few minor improprieties but ruled that they were insignificant and tossed out Oracle's complaint. Oracle escalated its case to federal court and would subsequently receive an undignified stream of legal defeats over the next few years. But in one respect, its crusade succeeded. The JEDI process was now mired in highly publicized controversy and was about to capture the attention of a more formidable figure—Trump himself.

On April 3, 2018, venture capitalist Peter Thiel brought Oracle's co-CEO Safra Catz to dinner at the White House. Catz, a registered Republican who had served on Trump's transition team in 2016 and was a major donor to his reelection campaign, complained to Trump that the contract seemed designed for Amazon. Trump listened and said he wanted the competition to be fair, according to a *Bloomberg News* report at the time.

That October, as final bids were due, Alphabet dropped out of the competition, saying that it didn't have proper security certifications for some aspects of the work and that the project conflicted with its corporate values. Leading up to its decision, Google employees had publicly protested their company furnishing powerful artificial intelligence technologies to the U.S. government.

If Amazonians had the same concerns, they were more circumspect about expressing them in the face of Bezos's outright advocacy for defense work. "If big tech companies are going to turn their back on the U.S. Department of Defense, this country is going to be in trouble," Bezos said in a speech at the defense forum at the Reagan Library in Simi Valley, California.

Four companies eventually submitted bids. Two of them, Oracle and IBM, were promptly eliminated from the competition in April of 2019, leaving Amazon and Microsoft. As Trump tweeted at Bezos that spring over everything from the post office to tax avoidance, Amazon Web Services employees toiled over provisioning the necessary resources in case they won. But they couldn't help but wonder if their efforts were doomed. "It came up more than once that Trump is not going to let this happen," said a high-level AWS executive who spoke on condition of anonymity.

In July of 2019, Trump was asked at a joint press conference with the Dutch prime minister about the contentious JEDI contest. "Which one is that, the Amazon?" he replied. "So, I'm getting tremendous complaints about the contract with the Pentagon and with Amazon. They're saying it wasn't competitively bid. . . . Some of the greatest companies in the world are complaining about it . . . different companies like Microsoft and Oracle and IBM."

A few hours later, Donald Trump Jr., the president's son, magnified the unseemly optics of injecting politics into the procurement process by tweeting, "Looks like the shady and potentially corrupt practices from @Amazon and No Bid Bezos may come back to bite them."

The contract was supposed to be awarded in August, but after

Trump's comment, his new secretary of defense, Mark Esper, suspended the process to examine the growing conflict-of-interest complaints. The contract then remained in limbo for another eighty-five days. In the midst of that delay, Esper recused himself because his son worked for IBM, adding yet another element of farce to the situation.

Finally, on October 25, 2019, the Pentagon announced a winner, effectively crowning a new leader in the burgeoning field of public sector cloud computing: Microsoft. The enterprise technology sector was stunned by the outcome, and most media outlets treated it as a major upset. AWS's Teresa Carlson said she had girded for such a result, but several AWS employees later admitted to being disappointed. "The amount of work we put into the bid process was massive," said the anonymous AWS senior executive, echoing the complaints so recently articulated by losing cities in the HQ2 contest. "We toiled endlessly, nights and weekends. It was devastating."

Even Microsoft CEO Satya Nadella seemed to concede that political calculations played a role in his unexpected victory. "To me, it goes back to, if anything, Microsoft staying out of politics and staying focused on what the customer's needs are," he told the tech news site *GeekWire*.

Amazon promptly sued in federal court, setting off yet another sequence of complex litigation that is unresolved even as of this writing more than a year later. In its defense, the Pentagon claimed that Microsoft had submitted the more economical bid. But executives at AWS were such ardent believers in the superiority of their technology that they couldn't possibly broach the possibility that Microsoft had won on the merits; there simply had to be political interference. These were the same hardcore devotees, after all, who in 2019 declared a rousing success a sparsely attended, and somewhat disastrous, music festival dubbed Intersect, which accompanied the annual AWS re:Invent conference. In other words, the corporate Kool-Aid at AWS was potent.

"We are the best partner," Jassy told me after the JEDI loss. "If you really evaluate the options, it's very clear-cut that we have a lot more capability for them and a lot more experience having done what we've done in the intelligence community."

Left unsaid was the way that Amazon's sprawling lines of business and Bezos's own empire of personal holdings were starting to create artificial limits to the opportunities for Amazon's fastest growing and most profitable division. Just as competing retailers Walmart and Target avoided AWS and Walmart asked its suppliers to do the same, it was easy to believe that Trump had nudged the Pentagon away from delivering a consequential government contract to an avowed political enemy. By purchasing one of the most prominent political newspapers in the U.S., Bezos had alienated an impetuous and vindictive man who, for four tumultuous years, was the most powerful person on the planet. Here finally was the true purchase price of the *Washington Post*: in the end, it likely cost Amazon $10 billion.

———

In the late 1990s, the legal departments inside many technology companies drew important lessons from the U.S. government's antitrust case against Microsoft and the damning emails, deposition transcripts, and meeting notes that were entered into evidence. At Amazon, executives were put through rigorous compliance and competition training, where they were instructed how to properly react to various scenarios and avoid the same mistakes that Microsoft made. If they ever heard colleagues talking about setting prices or colluding with partners, for example, they were instructed to "knock over the closest cup of coffee in the room," stand up, and vocally object, according to Amazonians who recounted details of internal sessions.

For David Zapolsky, a former Brooklyn prosecutor turned forceful and protective corporate attorney, preparation for potential legal scrutiny went even further. Zapolsky felt that "language matters in law," and after being appointed Amazon's general counsel in 2012, he started keeping a list on his office wall of certain indelicate words that he never wanted used in internal documents or discussions. Employees shouldn't use the word "market" unless they specified exactly what market they meant, or "platform," which loosely suggested a kind of distant, all-powerful authority over other firms. Other phrases on the wall included "dominating," "big data," and business jargon he found annoying such as "drill down" and "level set."

Words mattered, Zapolsky preached constantly; they had power, and the wrong ones could be used against Amazon. "Those terms aren't helpful, and they are particularly unhelpful when regulators start using them as buzzwords," Zapolsky said, "because they can actually do damage."

That advice, it turned out, was prescient. As pressure on the company mounted from Trump and the 2020 Democratic candidates, Amazon was also the subject of a separate strain of scrutiny from legal theorists, lawmakers, and regulators. They aimed to prove that Amazon was engaged in illegal, anticompetitive conduct and should be treated the same way as the fearsome monopolists of the past, such as the Standard Oil Company, U.S. Steel, and AT&T.

The person most responsible for initiating this argument was Lina Khan, who in her last year of Yale Law School in January 2017 published a ninety-three-page article in the *Yale Law Journal* titled "Amazon's Antitrust Paradox." The paper challenged the recent history of lax antitrust enforcement in the U.S. and invited authorities to take a harder look at the e-commerce giant, which she believed uniquely demonstrated how current laws had failed "to capture the architecture of market power in the twenty-first century marketplace." Coinciding with mounting criticism over Amazon's tax avoidance and its treatment of independent sellers—as well as newfound skepticism of big tech—the article not only struck a nerve; it arguably started a movement.

Khan was an unlikely figure to challenge decades of conventional wisdom on antitrust. The oldest child of Pakistani parents who immigrated to the U.S. when she was eleven, she majored in political theory at Williams College and wrote her thesis on the philosopher

Hannah Arendt's 1958 book *The Human Condition*, which examines how modern technologies affected democracy.

After graduation in 2010, Khan joined New America, where Elizabeth Warren would deliver her original anti-tech stem-winder, and worked with Barry Lynn, a senior fellow and a prolific author of books and articles that advanced a critical view of modern monopoly power. For one of her first tasks, Lynn assigned Khan to write a report on the history of Amazon's first and most dominant market, the book industry.

A few years later, Khan applied the same skeptical, journalistic approach to her article for the *Yale Law Journal*. Her paper took its name from a seminal 1978 book by Robert Bork, *The Antitrust Paradox*, which argued that regulators should curb market power only when it might result in higher prices for consumers. Khan soberly countered that the so-called "consumer welfare standard" was ill-suited to the consolidating effects of the internet and to a company like Amazon, which ruthlessly *lowered* prices to bleed out competitors and amass market share—a perpetually money-losing strategy that was nevertheless endorsed by its patient investors.

The paper challenged not just Amazon but an entire regulatory status quo. Set against the rapid growth of Amazon and the other tech giants, it became essential reading in policy circles in D.C. and Brussels. Politicians started referencing it in interviews and urging a "reconsideration of antitrust" to examine not only price effects but the impact that dominant companies have on workers, wages, and small companies. One critic of Khan's paper derisively called it "hipster antitrust." The moniker, not necessarily pejorative, stuck.

Khan's article also drew attention in Seattle. Six months after it was published, David Zapolsky called Barry Lynn at New America out of the blue and said he was in Washington with an Amazon policy team and wanted to meet. Lynn invited Khan, who was in town that summer, as well as Jonathan Kanter, an antitrust lawyer and former FTC staff attorney.

The hour-long meeting at New America's offices was cordial. Zapolsky asserted that Amazon wasn't a monopoly because it controlled only a small portion of the $24 trillion global retail industry and argued that its impact on competition and smaller companies was positive. He asked his critics what they believed Amazon should be doing differently and invited them to contact him if they heard about any problems caused by its conduct—presumably instead of writing acrimonious law review articles or giving hostile interviews to the press. "It was just this sort of surreal moment between folks who were going to be looking down the barrel of each other's guns for a long time," said Kanter.

It turned out that Zapolsky was withholding a piece of information that his adversaries would find especially ominous. The next day, on January 16, 2017, Amazon announced the acquisition of Whole Foods Market. In a sign that regulators were yet to be swayed by Khan's article or by Barry Lynn's relentless commentary on big tech, the FTC approved the merger in a swift sixty-eight days.

But Khan and Lynn's provocative ideas about curbing tech's power were slowly seeping into the regulatory firmament. A year later, Margrethe Vestager, the European Union's dynamic competition commissioner, opened an investigation into whether Amazon improperly exploited data from its independent sellers to bolster its private-label products. A year after that, in May of 2019, Makan Delrahim, the assistant attorney general for antitrust at the Department of Justice, and Joseph Simons, the chair of the FTC, followed her example and began investigating the four big tech companies. The DOJ would examine Google and Apple while the FTC looked at Facebook and Amazon.

Lionized only a few years before for their innovative prowess and wealth creation, the big tech companies were now facing an extraordinary groundswell of government scrutiny. In the midst of this wave, Rhode Island Democratic representative David N. Cicilline, a former criminal defense attorney who had called on the House Subcommittee on Antitrust, Commercial and Administrative Law to scrutinize

Amazon's acquisition of Whole Foods, approached Lina Khan. He had just taken over as chairman of the subcommittee, issuing a call to "hold big tech companies accountable." Khan had finished law school and a stint as a legal fellow at the FTC; would she be interested in serving as counsel in the most prominent government investigation yet of big tech's unassailable economic might?

Khan jumped at the opportunity. Announced in June 2019, the bipartisan examination of competition in digital markets would last a grueling sixteen months. The investigation, steered in large part by Cicilline and Khan, had to navigate a host of improbable obstacles: the impeachment of President Trump by the full House Judiciary Committee; the withdrawal from the Judiciary Committee of the ranking Republican, Doug Collins, after he decided to run for Senate; and the chaos that was generated by his replacement, Ohio's Jim Jordan, who was obsessed with examining not just monopoly power but anti-conservative bias by the social networks. Then there was the onset of the Covid-19 pandemic in early 2020, which upended the world and forced congressional investigators to work remotely for months.

Against these formidable odds, the subcommittee managed a wide-ranging and provocative examination of the way the tech giants accumulated and preserved power. From Amazon, it requested all internal communications related to acquisitions, product pricing, and the rules that governed its third-party marketplace. It later published a trove of these documents, which revealed Amazon execs strategizing back in 2009 to run the company's diapers business at a loss to combat the company that operated Diapers.com, and to buy the internet doorbell company Ring in 2018—not for its technology, but to gain a dominant position in the market.

In January 2020, the subcommittee convened a hearing in Boulder, Colorado, and heard firsthand why many brands and sellers have such a strained relationship with the e-commerce giant. David Barnett, founder of a company called PopSockets, which made decorated grips for the backs of smartphones, testified that Amazon allowed knockoffs to proliferate on the site and sold his products below their mutually agreed-upon price. When he tried to control his prices by moving away from a wholesale relationship with Amazon and establishing himself as an independent seller on the marketplace, the company wouldn't let him—and effectively booted PopSockets off the site. "Jeff Bezos can't possibly know that this is how this unit is behaving," Barnett later told me. "If he did, he would step in and stop it."

One of Cicilline's goals throughout the investigation was clear: to get Bezos and the other tech chiefs to testify before Congress under oath. But Amazon's policy executives clearly didn't want to subject their CEO to the same public drubbing that Facebook's Mark Zuckerberg had repeatedly endured. They answered the subcommittee's invitation to Bezos not with a reply signed by the CEO but with one from Brian Huseman, the public policy vice president who had presided over the HQ2 fiasco. "We remain prepared to make the appropriate Amazon executive available to the Committee to address these important issues," Huseman wrote evasively.

Behind the scenes, Lanny Breuer, the former head of the Justice Department's criminal division under Barack Obama and a partner at a law firm that conducted work for Amazon, Covington & Burling, tried to influence Democratic committee members and keep Bezos out of the limelight. Lina Khan later told me they viewed Amazon's posture as "ruthlessly aggressive and, frankly, rude to lawmakers," and compared it unfavorably to Google's more decorous approach, which had been forged by a decade of previous experience with government scrutiny.

Finally, a bipartisan group of lawmakers threatened to subpoena Bezos, citing the *Wall Street Journal* article that quoted private-label employees on how they used internal data from third-party merchants to launch Amazon-branded products. An Amazon lawyer, Nate Sutton, had previously vowed under oath before the committee that such practices did not occur, so the lawmakers demanded that Bezos address this conduct and the question of whether Sutton had perjured himself. He and the company couldn't avoid it anymore: for the first time, Bezos would have to testify before Congress.

With the pandemic raging, Amazon's policy and communications executives emerged from their respective quarantines to help prepare Bezos in his Day 1 office. Jay Carney later called the prep sessions "one of the high points of my year, work-wise," both because he got to see colleagues in person and because Bezos was characteristically curious and willing to learn how best to navigate the challenge at hand. In one respect, he would have it easy on this maiden voyage: the four CEOs being called to testify didn't have to be physically present on Capitol Hill, confined in a packed hearing room amid swarming photographers, but would instead present their testimony remotely, via live video conference.

The hearing, on July 29, 2020, was avidly watched on both coasts and in the capitals of Europe. "Our founders would not bow before a king, nor should we bow before the emperors of the online economy," said Cicilline in his introductory remarks, with Lina Khan hovering over his right shoulder in a sky-blue blazer and mask. Bezos appeared on camera from his desk in Seattle, wearing a dark navy suit and tie, and used his opening statement to deliver an elegant tribute to his parents and to the trust that customers place in Amazon while stipulating that the size of the retail industry left room for many competitors.

From there, the hearing grew chaotic. Over more than five hours, representatives directed questions at Bezos, Sundar Pichai, Mark Zuckerberg, and Tim Cook, boomeranging between the unique issues related to each of their companies. Committee members frequently interrupted the CEOs, rushing to insert theatrical political statements into their constrained time limits instead of listening to fuller answers and any corporate boilerplate. Several Republicans also trampled over the topic with allegations of anti-conservative bias in tech. And to cap it all off, after his opening remarks, a technical glitch with the video conferencing software sidelined Bezos during the first hour of questioning.

But when the technical issues were ironed out, committee members homed in on Bezos. He was assailed on topics that he had never before been forced to address publicly, such as counterfeit goods, and revelations from *The Everything Store* about Amazon's furious price war with Diapers.com and its private attitude toward small book publishers, which it had once revealed by declaring itself a cheetah and naming an internal negotiation program "the gazelle project." As Amazon's legal department had long feared, the indiscriminate use of words and phrases was now being weaponized against the company.

Mostly though, policymakers lasered in on the most accessible illustration of Amazon's potentially anticompetitive behavior: its third-party marketplace and the torrent of complaints they had received from aggrieved independent sellers. Bezos earnestly answered these questions, but also seemed somewhat ill-prepared and unable (or unwilling) to respond with anything other than defensive corporate aphorisms. Former Amazon executives later compared his performance to that of countless employees who had worked hard, prepared for weeks, and still gotten their butts kicked when peppered with probing questions by the demanding and bellicose S-team.

Pramila Jayapal, the Seattle congresswoman and an avowed Amazon critic, was the first to ask Bezos the central question: Did Amazon employees snoop on the private sales data of sellers? "It's a candy shop. Anyone can have access to anything they want," she quoted a former employee who had talked to the subcommittee.

"We do have certain safeguards in place. We train people on the policy. We expect people to follow that policy the same way we would any other," Bezos told Jayapal. He almost certainly knew that the policy was poorly enforced and had been regularly trampled upon by desperate employees striving to meet aggressive internal benchmarks. But he vaguely asserted that he couldn't "guarantee you that the policy has never been violated" and insisted that an internal investigation into the matter was still ongoing. "The fact that we have such a policy is voluntary," he added. "I think no other retailer even has such a policy."

Cicilline then asked why a small apparel seller had compared selling on Amazon to a drug habit. "Sir, I have great respect for you and this committee," Bezos said, "but I completely disagree with that characterization. . . . It was a very controversial decision inside the company to invite third-party sellers to come into what is really our most valuable retail real estate, our product detail pages. We did that because we were convinced it would be better for the consumers, it would be better for the customer to have all of that selection."

Representative Lucy McBath from Georgia posed the question this way: "If Amazon didn't have monopoly power over these sellers, do you think they would stay in a relationship that is characterized by bullying, fear, and panic?"

"With all respect, Congresswoman," Bezos replied, in the moments before he was interrupted again. "I do not accept the premise of that question. That is not how we operate the business. In fact, we work very hard to provide fantastic tools for sellers and that's why they've been successful."

———

As Lina Khan and other congressional staffers drafted their final report over the summer of 2020, I wondered about Amazon's true popularity among the tens of thousands of sellers on its crowded marketplace. According to the evidence presented to the subcommittee by disgruntled merchants, Amazon appeared to be an almost cartoonish villain, bullying sellers, stealing their data, booting them from the site indiscriminately, and hurting their lives and livelihoods.

In response, Amazon executives argued that the case for widespread discord was based on nothing more than anecdotes and that most of the independent merchants who sold 60 percent of the phys-

ical products on Amazon were thriving. "Anytime you have a population of a million, it's not going to be too hard to find some folks
who are unhappy," said David Zapolsky. While he conceded that some
of those anecdotes arise from Amazon's mistakes, he said that most
come from disgruntled sellers who "are not winning as much as they
think they should be winning."

In lieu of some magical, all-encompassing poll to gauge the real
sentiment of Amazon sellers, I decided to canvass not the vocal band
of familiar antagonists in the seller community but the company's
own allies—the merchants who had previously lobbied for Amazon or
spoken out on its behalf. As Congress deliberated the real character of
Bezos's empire, what did they think of Amazon's always-evolving retail frontier and whether the company was fulfilling its duties as a fair
and principled marshal?

Paul Saunders had testified twice on Capitol Hill, in 2017 and
2018, as part of Amazon's campaign to demonstrate it was helping
small business. Saunders, a veteran of the U.S. Marine Corps, exem-
plified the Marine motto of *Semper fidelis*, or "always loyal," by repeatedly praising Amazon to lawmakers for abetting the extraordinary
growth of his Evansville, Indiana–based business, eLuxury, which
sells high-quality housewares. "Amazon is vilified so often," he once
told a group of high-ranking public officials, during a private meeting
about Amazon's economic impact. "If it wasn't for Amazon, I may not
have been able to build a business that employs seventy-five people,
pays millions in local and federal taxes, and invests significantly in
employee benefits."

But when I reached him in 2020, Saunders's views had evolved.
Rising fees and the increasingly expensive requirements of advertising on Amazon had gutted his profits; AmazonBasics products
directly competed next to his listings in search results; and foreign
sellers with lower costs, unenforced tax obligations, questionable reviews, and the fruits of other seemingly nefarious business practices
had made it almost impossible to compete. Loyal to the bone, Saun-

ders was extremely hesitant to share his concerns on the record at first and continued to reach out to Amazon executives in an attempt to enlist help. When he finally agreed, he sent me excerpts of a six-page, Amazon-style document he had presented personally to company executives, including senior vice president Doug Herrington.

The paper exhibited the raw feelings of a frustrated partner. It suggested numerous ways for Amazon to support the welfare of the sellers who had played a role in its success, concluding: "I have gone 'beyond the call of duty' to be a trusted and impactful partner to Amazon and your customers. Unfortunately, and increasingly, it appears that Amazon may not share in this philosophy, specifically as it relates to third-party sellers."

A few months after those meetings, when nothing had significantly changed, Saunders moved much of eLuxury off Amazon in favor of more trusted partners like Walmart, Target, Wayfair, and Overstock, where he was seeing continued growth. He was disappointed and surprised that Amazon would not act promptly to penalize bad actors and protect their mutual customers. "I truly believe, and I know firsthand that numerous Amazonians agree, that Amazon understands the marketplace is a mess, but they just don't know how to fix it," he told me.

Wendell Morris largely agreed with that sentiment. The founder of the Santa Monica–based YogaRat was one of the first sellers on Amazon to hawk yoga mats and yoga towels; he later expanded into beach towels and microfiber blankets, all sourced from China. In 2014, he became one of the few Amazon sellers that Jeff Bezos touted by name in his widely read annual letters to shareholders. "The beauty of Amazon is that someone can say, 'I want to start a business,' and they can go on Amazon and really start a business," Bezos had quoted Morris as saying that year. "You don't have to get a lease on a building or even have any employees at first. You can just do it on your own. And that's what I did."

But by the time I talked to him, Morris, like Saunders, had changed his opinion. In 2016, when YogaRat employed seven people, he found that his listings were inexplicably disappearing from Amazon's search results. He spent hours on the phone with an Amazon customer support staffer in India and wrote pleading emails to Bezos's public email address. His listings were finally restored, though they never returned to their previous positions at the top of search results. A year later, his seller account was suspended altogether because some of the images on his listings violated Amazon's guidelines against depicting groups of people in product photos. Morris conceded the error while bitterly showing me how countless other sellers violated the same rules without penalty. Someone—probably a competitor—had singled him out to Amazon's enforcement team.

While Morris scrambled to reinstate his account, other sellers of the same merchandise replaced him atop search results. Yoga-Rat never recovered. He now runs what's left of his firm alone with his wife, and the challenges are daunting. He is constantly fighting overseas knockoffs of his designs and reviews of his products that mysteriously show up on rival listings. When he calls Amazon customer service, he suspects the reps' primary metric for success is how quickly they can get off the phone. Once a devoted yogi, Morris can barely stand to look at a yoga mat anymore.

"I'm all for competition, but I did not start my business and go sell on Amazon so that I could eventually become fertilizer for Amazon's growth as I am buried and destroyed," he told me. "It's apparent this is happening to a lot of sellers, and I don't believe it's right. What Amazon does is analogous to being invited over for Thanksgiving dinner, then finding out as you sit down to dine that you're the turkey."

Stephan Aarstol and his firm Tower Paddle Boards made Bezos's shareholder letter published in April 2016 (with his name misspelled there and in *Invent & Wander*, Bezos's subsequent collection of writings, as Stephen). An entrepreneur with a memorable turn on the TV show *Shark Tank*, Aarstol employed ten people at the height of his company's success and was selling more than $11,000 in inflatable paddle boards every day. Over the years he was a reliable guinea pig for Amazon, entering into a new program for Amazon-exclusive brands that agreed not to sell anywhere else and borrowing money from Amazon to fund his expansion, using the merchandise he stored in its warehouses as collateral. "His business has become one of the fastest-growing companies in San Diego, in part with a little help from Amazon Lending," Bezos wrote.

For Aarstol, the turning point came soon after. Hundreds of stand-up paddleboard sellers, with generic names like XYLove and FunWater, flooded onto the site, mainly from China, and jockeyed with Tower for sales. Some of these sellers competed by fraudulently generating one of the site's most valuable commodities, positive customer reviews, which helped to determine the position of products in search results.

Aarstol tried to advertise on Amazon to boost his visibility but that gutted his profits. In the years after he was mentioned in Bezos's letter, he went from employing ten people to three and from recording $4 million in annual sales to less than $1.5 million. "Amazon doesn't give a shit about brands," said Aarstol, who by 2020 was almost completely off Amazon and focusing on sales over his own website. "They don't care whether you live or die."

In the same investor letter, Bezos had also touted Bernie Thompson's company, Plugable Technologies, quoting him as saying that shipping products in bulk to Amazon warehouses in Europe and Asia "changes the paradigm." Thompson had competed with Chinese vendors for years; he was the seller who was once told, "Bernie, I'm sorry, but I'm going to run you over," by Steven Yang, the otherwise genteel founder of the Chinese consumer electronics seller Anker.

Despite that vow, and unlike the other former Amazon allies I talked to, Plugable was still thriving. Thompson had overcome identical products from AmazonBasics by keeping prices low and quality high, and he constantly launched new gadgets as the old ones became commoditized. But Thompson still harbored the sneaking fear that

Amazon might suspend his listings at any time. In mid-2019, like Paul
Saunders, Thompson capitalized on his goodwill with the company to
get an audience in Seattle and delivered a twenty-page PowerPoint
presentation outlining his dependence on the company and the danger he faced when products disappeared from the site arbitrarily. The
solution was "no surprises," and "less uncertainty," one slide implored.

But Thompson's plea wasn't heeded. With the arrival of thousands
of new sellers onto the marketplace every month, Amazon's enforcement staff was badly outgunned and the automated systems they set
up were often gamed by bad actors. Just a few months after he delivered his presentation, on a Sunday in July, Thompson's top-selling
product, a laptop docking station that accounted for 40 percent of his
sales, disappeared off the site.

The listing finally returned after four days and $100,000 in lost
sales—and only then because Thompson paid Amazon $60,000
a year for a premium service to engage the attention of an account
manager, which "feels a bit like a protection racket," he said. He never
found out exactly why the laptop dock was suspended.

The stories of these erstwhile Amazon allies underscored the
problems that were laid out to the congressional subcommittee. Years
ago, Jeff Bezos had given his marketplace team a few simple instructions: remove all friction to selling on Amazon; eliminate the barriers
to cross-border trade; address any problems with innovative technology and automated systems, not costly manpower. One result was an
explosion of low-priced selection that fueled the historic growth of
Amazon's e-commerce business. But another was the disintermedi-
ating forces of globalization that crushed Western sellers and created
a dynamic that made it exceedingly difficult to protect intellectual
property, prevent fraud, and fairly adjudicate disputes.

Amazon knew about these problems but disguised them with its
unrelenting corporate communications machine, which insisted that
the company was a friend to entrepreneurs. "Third party sellers are
kicking our first party butt. Badly," Bezos wrote in the shareholder

letter that was published in 2019, explaining how the marketplace was so successful that it was eclipsing Amazon's retail business. A TV commercial that flooded U.S. airwaves in 2020, titled "Supporting Small Business," depicted a woodworking shop opening up for the day. But as many Amazon sellers surely knew, those kinds of artisanal crafts makers could thrive on the bohemian enclave of Etsy, not on Amazon's brutal and bloody capitalist frontier.

Bezos was far removed from this battlefield. "The company has become so complex that it makes no sense for him to be aware of all the details of these things," said James Thomson, a former Amazon Marketplace employee and chief strategy officer for the e-commerce consultancy Buy Box Experts. "But he should know that some of the things that Amazon works hard to tell a good story about are wildly broken."

The final report from the antitrust subcommittee was published on October 6, 2020, and contained 450 pages of allegations and damning conclusions about the abusive practices of Amazon, Google, Facebook, and Apple. Lina Khan and her colleagues made a persuasive case: that the big tech platforms arbitrarily and self-interestedly controlled our political discourse, our financial lives, and the health of countless smaller companies—and that the failure to regulate them was a dangerous abdication of government responsibility.

"Our investigation leaves no doubt that there is a clear and compelling need for Congress and the antitrust enforcement agencies to take action that restores competition . . ." wrote Cicilline in a joint statement with Judiciary Committee chairman Jerry Nadler. Among the report's proposed remedies was splitting up Amazon and the other tech companies to eliminate conflicts of interest between their disparate lines of business, such as Amazon's retail store and third-party marketplace, and its e-commerce and AWS divisions.

While neutral lawmakers and antitrust academics without a stake in the bitter political dogfight agreed with some of these principles, others believed such remedies sounded excessive. Splitting the company apart wouldn't help Amazon's sellers, partners, or customers, and there was little legal basis for shutting down private-label lines like AmazonBasics. After all, retailers as far back as the Great A&P had studied what sold well, cultivated house brands at lower prices, and provided customers an additional choice on their shelves.

The report also struggled to establish that Amazon even had the kind of monopoly power that might make certain conduct illegal under U.S. law. The industry's most widely cited data gatherer, eMarketer, put Amazon's share of U.S. e-commerce sales at 38.7 percent. The success of Walmart and Target's websites, as well as the Canadian company Shopify, which developed sites for brands to sell directly to customers, also belied the notion that Amazon had any kind of hammerlock on the industry. (Only Amazon's utter dominance in the U.S. in books and e-books, estimated at 42 percent and up to 89 percent respectively in 2018, might merit a deeper look.) "While there is no single seller online that can match Amazon, it's pretty hard under conventional antitrust to find someplace where Amazon has monopoly power," said Jay Himes, a former antitrust bureau chief in the New York Attorney General's Office.

But the report also suggested plenty of ways that the government could address Amazon's market might without resorting to the kind of drawn-out antitrust lawsuit that was directed at AT&T in the 1970s and Microsoft in the 1990s. For example, regulators could examine Amazon's contracts with sellers and prevent it from penalizing them if they listed a cheaper price elsewhere. They could also restore the ability of sellers to engage in class action lawsuits against Amazon and block the current provisions that force them into a lengthy and secretive arbitration process. The report also proposed that Congress elevate the requirements for big tech companies to get approvals for mergers, so that dominant firms would have to disclose even smaller acquisitions and show how they are "necessary for serving the public interest."

Not mentioned in the report, to quell the chaos of the Amazon

Marketplace, lawmakers could also reform the notorious Section 230 of the Communications Decency Act, which currently holds that internet providers like Amazon are not liable for the legal infractions of their users. Changes to Section 230 could force Amazon to be accountable for fraudulent or unsafe products sold on its site by third-party sellers. Regulators could also compel Amazon to verify sellers with a tax ID number or require them to put down a security deposit, which they'd forfeit with any signs of fraud (Alibaba's Tmall website does this). Adding significant friction to the process of becoming an Amazon seller would restore balance to a competitive playing field that currently favors sellers in China.

But those remedies only address the most obvious part of the alleged misconduct. The subcommittee also charged Amazon with something more significant: using profits from AWS and advertising to subsidize its retail operation, to undercut rivals on prices, and to finance entry into unrelated markets, and gobble up even more digital real estate. But the report couldn't prove that charge; it complained that Amazon "failed to produce the financial data that would have enabled Subcommittee staff to make an independent assessment."

And that's the most formidable challenge facing the trustbusters. To make a credible case for breaking up Amazon, they will have to answer questions that the company goes to remarkable lengths to obscure. How do its various components interlock? How do you gauge the true profitability of the individual business units when some costs are covered by the subscription fees of services like Amazon Prime? Is it anticompetitive when Amazon increases those fees or seeks to improve its market position by dropping them altogether, as it did in the fall of 2019 when it waived a separate $15 a month charge for grocery delivery?

"There is no company in the world that is more complex and difficult for outsiders to understand than Amazon," said Kurt Zumwalt, Amazon's treasurer for fifteen years, before he left in 2019. "This is not a typical corporate conglomerate like Berkshire Hathaway or General Electric. Almost every aspect of Amazon is built around subtly increasing its connection to customers. The power of the business model is the combination of the sum of its self-reinforcing businesses and services, enabled by world-class technology, operational excellence, and a rigorous review and measurement process."

For now, the highest profile investigation yet into Amazon's power was over, though troubles certainly lay ahead. "When corporate executives' emails tell one story and they publicly try to spin another, historically those efforts to deny reality have rarely worked out for the corporation," said Lina Khan, who President Biden prepared to appoint as one of five FTC commissioners in early 2021. And in Europe, competition chief Margrethe Vestager charged Amazon with damaging retail competition by unfairly using sensitive internal data from third-party sellers to privilege its own products. That case could stretch on for years and result in the kind of large fines that the EU once levied against Google.

Bezos seemed to welcome whatever came next, even hinting that it might actually burnish Amazon's standing. "One of the unintended consequences often of regulation is that it really favors the incumbents," he said during an event in Berlin. "Now, Amazon at this point is an incumbent, so maybe I should be happy about that. But I wouldn't be because I think for society, you really want to see continued progress." He added, "These are very challenging questions. And we're not going to answer them, even in a few years. I think it's going to be an ongoing thing for quite a while."

That uncertain future hinged on many factors: shifting party control of the U.S. Congress, the relative urgency of addressing the conduct of other technology companies like Google and Facebook first, and the public's overall sentiment toward Amazon and Bezos. For despite the heightened suspicion of big tech and of Amazon's tightening grip over Western economies, the company had become a salvation of sorts in the year 2020—a life preserver, thrown to millions of households around the world, as they quarantined amid the relentless assault of the Covid-19 pandemic.

CHAPTER 15

Pandemic

Amazon's recent challenges seemed like mere speed bumps. The HQ2 misadventure, the drama in Bezos's personal life, the loss of the JEDI contract, and battles with Donald Trump and antitrust regulators—they barely slowed Amazon's inexorable rise. Jeff Bezos and his global empire appeared, at least in the moment, totally unbound from the laws of corporate gravity that slowed the growth of large enterprises, inhibited their agility, and clouded the judgment of senior leaders with exorbitant wealth.

New obstacles appeared, of course, but Amazon swiftly navigated those as well. On September 20, 2019, thousands of Amazon employees left their desks to join technology workers and students from around the world in a general climate strike organized by the teenage activist Greta Thunberg. In Seattle, they gathered in front of the Spheres at 11:30 a.m., holding signs that read, "Amazon, Let's Raise the Bar, Not the Temperature," and "No AWS for Oil and Gas," while arguing that the company had to rethink its devotion to greater selection, faster shipping, and delighting customers, regardless of the environmental cost.

It was the day after Jeff Bezos had introduced the Climate Pledge at a press conference in Washington, D.C., promising that Amazon would reach net zero in its carbon emissions by 2040, ten years before the most ambitious goals set by the Paris climate accord. Companies such as Verizon, Microsoft, and Mercedes-Benz would sign on to the initiative, and Amazon would purchase the naming rights to a new sports coliseum in Seattle and call it "Climate Pledge Arena."

The media around the world covered the employee protests, and in a far more sympathetic way than the hazy and ambitious promises of Amazon's Climate Pledge. The contrast heralded the emergence of a new kind of political power, one wielded by tech company employees instead of their omnipotent corporate masters. Guarding against this dangerous dissension from within its own ranks would be one of Amazon's greatest tests during the unexpected trials of the coming year. But attention quickly drifted away from Amazon's significant carbon output. The company had reassured the world it had a plan.

Bezos himself hovered well above any emerging critique of Amazon and its impact on society and the planet. In November, the political and media elite gathered for the black-tie affair at the Smithsonian's National Portrait Gallery in Washington, D.C., to celebrate the new portraits added to its collection of distinguished Americans. Bezos, one of the six honorees, brought along a large contingent of supporters, including Amazon board members, executives from the *Washington Post*, his parents, children, and his girlfriend, Lauren Sanchez.

In his speech, Bezos deployed a few of his well-worn routines, such as ridiculing the Fire Phone and recalling his realization, in Amazon's earliest years, that they should buy packing tables rather than kneeling on the floor to prepare books for shipment. The audience laughed along. But it was the rare introduction from his oldest son, nineteen-year-old Preston Bezos, that described a dimension to the billionaire that was arguably unknown to the public:

I remember sitting in the kitchen when I was eight years old, watching him slowly wind a piece of wire around a nail. I remember him taking the ends of that wire and touching them to a battery. I remember when he brought that nail close to a piece of metal and they stuck together. I remember the absolute awe in my eyes when he dragged a white board from the basement and tried to explain to me as best you can, to an eight-year-old, the absolute magic that can imbue that nail with magnetic force.... And the reason that memory is so special for me is because he had shown me how to do that maybe a dozen times before. But that was the time that it stuck.... It was that caring compassion, that gleeful pursuit of knowledge, and that patient perseverance, that made it possible. Those are the things that I love about my dad. Those are the things I think are so special about him. And it's what I hope, at the end of the day, he is remembered by.

Bezos appeared genuinely moved. "I have to recover for a little bit after that," he said as he took over the lectern. "I did not know what Preston was going to say. He did not want to tell me in advance. He wanted it to be a surprise for me." It was an impromptu moment for a father, and business titan, who usually sought to script and rehearse every public appearance.

Two months later, Bezos would have another opportunity to cultivate a public profile that was evolving in interesting and unexpected ways. In mid-January, 2020, he visited India, his first trip to the country since his publicity stunt back in 2014 featuring the oversized check on top of a truck. So much had changed since then. On this tour, Bezos and Lauren Sanchez posed for photographs in front of the Taj Mahal, paid their respects at Mahatma Gandhi's tomb, and dressed in fashionable Indian evening wear to attend a Prime Video premiere in Mumbai. Amazon had been operating in the country for more than half a decade, but Bezos asserted that the company was only getting started. "This country has something special," Bezos told his senior vice president and former technical advisor, Amit Agarwal, on stage at an Amazon summit for independent merchants. "This is going to be the Indian century."

But now his brand of techno-optimism and "patient perseverance," as Preston Bezos had put it, wasn't nearly as welcome. Coalitions of local merchants protested his arrival, calling him an "economic terrorist," and waving signs that read: "Jeff Bezos, go back!" Two days before he arrived, the country's Competition Commission announced a new probe into anticompetitive discounting on Amazon and its chief rival, the Walmart-owned Flipkart, while government ministers attacked Bezos for articles in his newspaper, the *Washington Post*, about the country's persecution of religious and ethnic minorities. Prime Minister Narendra Modi declined to meet with Bezos altogether, and many observers believed the government was tacitly backing the e-commerce efforts of Mukesh Ambani, India's wealthiest person and the chief of the sprawling telecom and retail conglomerate Reliance Industries.

Still, none of the perennial challenges in India or elsewhere seemed to impede Amazon's overall business performance. On January 30, after Bezos returned to the U.S., the company announced a gangbuster holiday financial report. The move to deliver packages to Prime members the day after they ordered, instead of two days, had turbocharged sales, and the continued strength of AWS and durable bounty of advertising, the gold mine in the backyard, had minted $3.3 billion in profit, well above Wall Street's expectations. Amazon also announced that there were 150 million Prime members worldwide, up from 100 million two years before, and that it employed around eight hundred thousand people, solidifying its position as the second largest private employer in the U.S., behind only Walmart.

In the wake of the quarterly earnings announcement, investors bid up Amazon's stock; its market capitalization leapt over the magical threshold of a trillion dollars and a few weeks later, finally remained there for good. It almost felt like the whole story could have ended right here, with Jeff Bezos worth an astounding $124 billion and Amazon's aura of invincibility looking more impervious than ever. But it was at this exact moment executives got their first glimpse of the mythological black swan—the rare and unforeseen calamity—spreading its wings over the charred landscape that would soon describe the year 2020.

———

Dr. Ian Lipkin, the Columbia University epidemiologist known as the "master virus hunter" for tracking the West Nile virus outbreak in the late nineties and the SARS epidemic in 2003, had seen enough to be disturbed. On a trip to China in January, the streets of Beijing and Guangzhou were deserted, stores vacant, and hospitals overflowing with ill patients. The highly contagious novel coronavirus, which caused the disease Covid-19, was thought to have emerged from an open-air meat and seafood market in the western city of Wuhan and spread across the country in weeks.

On February 5—the day after he returned on the last direct flight from Beijing to Newark and began a two-week quarantine in his apartment on Manhattan's Upper West Side—Lipkin received a phone call from Katie Hughes, a longtime health and safety manager at Amazon. Like other U.S. companies, Amazon had restricted employee travel to and from China, but it was starting to see the virus spread around Italy, where it had a dozen warehouses and transportation hubs. Hughes asked Lipkin if he could help Amazon analyze its risks and navigate the coming storm.

Lipkin was a Prime member and an admirer of the company, though he lamented its impact on smaller merchants and whenever possible tried to buy from local stores. He also knew enough about the new contagion to recognize that if his worst fears came true, Amazon's workers faced a serious risk. Other companies could shutter their doors and send employees home. Amazon's hundreds of densely packed fulfillment centers around the world had the potential to be petri dishes for an infectious virus, while its delivery staff interacted with the public every day. Lipkin agreed to sign on as an advisor.

In regular virtual conversations with Amazon's HR and operations teams that February, Lipkin doled out advice on everything from how to clean surfaces in the warehouses thoroughly and scrub the air with so-called MERV-13 filters to imposing mask and glove requirements and installing temperature check stations at each site. "These guys are driven by math and technology, and if you make a suggestion that is rigorous and scientific and evidence-based, they will implement it," Lipkin said. "Cost never came into it, and I can't say that for every other group I've worked with."

On February 27, Lipkin spoke via video to the full S-team. He told Bezos and other senior executives about his recent travels in China and laid out the risks Amazon employees could face. Though it was several weeks before the Trump administration declared a national state of emergency and the epidemiological lexicon officially entered the vocabulary of many Americans, Amazon executives already seemed knowledgeable. They asked him pointed questions about the virus's incubation period and its R0 or "R naught" potential, the number of people who can be infected by a single individual. Lipkin didn't recall what Bezos asked, but said, "I remember looking at the guy. He looked pretty fit."

The day after the S-team meeting with Lipkin, Amazon stopped all nonessential employee travel. On March 4, after a Seattle corporate employee was diagnosed with the virus, the company ordered office workers to work from home for two weeks, then extended the deadline to return in increments, before finally instructing them to stay at home for the rest of the year. A week after that, Amazon canceled all in-person interviews and moved to virtual conversations with most job candidates using its in-house video conferencing software, Amazon Chime. The moves underscored a sharp divide and one of Amazon's biggest challenges; it was allowing white-collar workers to transition to safe, remote work, while deeming its warehouse employees essential to the business and exposing them to greater risk.

By early March, a subgroup of the S-team was gathering virtually every afternoon at 4 p.m. Seattle time to discuss their response to the crisis. The meetings were run by human resources head Beth Galetti and included Jeff Wilke, Andy Jassy, operations chief Dave Clark, and Bezos. Amazon's CEO normally spent much of his time on projects whose potential was years in the future. Now he locked his gaze firmly onto the urgent present. He asked questions, made observations, and led brainstorming sessions on new ways to use technology to protect employees while meeting surging demand from quarantined customers.

He also boosted his own visibility. "Dear Amazonians," he wrote in a letter to the whole company on March 21. "This isn't business as usual, and it's a time of great stress and uncertainty. It's also a moment in time when the work we're doing is its most critical.... People are depending on us." The letter outlined a few of Amazon's early preventative health measures, such as increasing the frequency of cleanings, and the attempts to buy masks for employees amid an overall shortage. It also announced that Amazon would hire one hundred thousand employees in the warehouses and temporarily increase pay by two dollars an hour, along with increasing overtime wages and giving employees unlimited unpaid time off. "My own time and thinking is now wholly focused on COVID-19 and on how Amazon can best play its role," he wrote.

After years of keeping many of his daily activities at Amazon private, Bezos was now heavily promoting them. On March 26, he posted a photo of himself to Instagram from his ranch in West Texas, video chatting with Tedros Adhanom Ghebreyesus, the director-general of the World Health Organization. The following day, he posted a picture of himself talking with Washington governor Jay Inslee. On April 8, Amazon tweeted a video of the CEO walking through a fulfillment center and Whole Foods near Dallas, wearing a mask and with his sleeves rolled up—the first time he had toured a warehouse in years, said several operations employees. Meanwhile, he skipped his Wednesday meetings at the *Washington Post* and Blue Origin. Executives there said they didn't speak to him for weeks during the early stages of the pandemic.

The increase in Bezos's public prominence was partly the work of a CEO trying to demonstrate leadership at a challenging time. As the virus spread, anxiety followed. Absenteeism in the fulfillment centers soared; by some estimates, 30 percent of Amazon workers failed to show up as they got sick with Covid or heard about colleagues, friends, or family contracting the disease, fearing that they might be next. This time, the long-term goals of the Climate Pledge weren't going to cut it. Amazon needed to add fresh workers amid the overlapping challenges of high absenteeism and exploding customer demand while changing, on the fly, many of the deeply ingrained processes in the vast Amazon supply chain.

In this respect, Amazon was in an enviable position. Dave Clark, the bespectacled former middle school band teacher, had proven himself uniquely capable of developing large, complex systems, like the network of warehouses using Kiva robots and the in-house transportation division, Amazon Logistics, which was now responsible for approximately half of all Amazon deliveries globally and two-thirds in the U.S. If supply chains win wars, as the old military proverb went, Bezos had one of the most accomplished generals in the world by his side.

By April 4, as Lipkin had advised, Clark and his team introduced temperature checks inside fulfillment centers, sortation centers, and transportation hubs. Instead of widespread use of handheld infrared thermometers, which would require PPE-clad temperature takers to stand in close physical proximity to workers as they entered a building, Amazon spent millions to acquire thermal cameras, and then stationed them at entryways to remotely scan employees for fevers. Executives also put in a massive order for masks, sorting through hundreds of emails from entrepreneurs who were all trying to exploit the corporate world's sudden needs. "It seemed like everybody had a cousin, uncle, aunt, or family friend who had a manufacturing site in China that made masks," Clark recalled.

To complement its supplies, Amazon also looked inward, redeploying the 3D printers in its Prime Air drone lab to make plastic face shields. By early April, Amazon said it had distributed millions of masks to employees and was donating N95 masks to frontline health-care workers. "It was a crazy environment," Clark said. "Every day lasted at least a week."

Amid the tumult, the company was forced to act in ways that were contrary to its well-honed instincts for growth. It withdrew Mother's and Father's Day promotions and the recommendations on its web-site that showed customers what others with similar purchase histo-ries had bought. It also postponed Prime Day until the fall to relieve pressure on the warehouses, and it announced that for several critical weeks over the spring, it would only accept "household staples, med-ical supplies and other high-demand products" from independent sellers who participated in Amazon's third-party shipping program, Fulfillment by Amazon.

The prohibition alienated some sellers who depended on FBA and elicited charges the company was unfairly advantaging itself by con-tinuing to sell its own stock of nonessential items, like hammocks and fish tanks. (Amazon later conceded to the Judiciary Antitrust sub-committee that selling those items was a mistake.) The ban lasted until mid-April, when Amazon announced it was hiring yet another seventy-five thousand workers to help satisfy the additional demand.

Clark's biggest challenge was preventing workers from clustering in the FCs, which were built for maximum efficiency, not rigorous so-cial distancing. Teams charged with enforcing the new guidelines to stay six feet apart wandered the warehouses, monitoring for distanc-ing and mask compliance, while hazmat-suit-wearing cleaners in the FCs sprayed hospital-grade misting disinfectant. But most of Ama-zon's solutions were technological. The robotics group built a system called "Proxemics" to analyze security camera footage inside facilities and track the distance between employees. The system used AI algo-rithms to identify problem areas and generate data-rich reports for general managers about how well their buildings were responding. With another program, Distance Assistant, Amazon deployed additional cameras and TV screens to warehouses to monitor employees as they passed by. If workers were walking too close together, their images on the screen were overlaid with red circles.

Not everything that Amazon's operations division tried ended up working. An autonomous cart designed to roam the aisles of Whole Foods supermarkets and blast shelves with disinfecting UV light, for example, was discontinued after public health officials concluded that surface transmission of the virus on grocery items wasn't a serious risk. Another project to regularly test the oxygen levels of FC workers with pulse oximeters didn't meaningfully identify anyone with Covid-19 and was also abandoned, as was a trial to track the location of employees inside warehouses using their personal cell phones and their facility's Wi-Fi network.

Dr. Ian Lipkin had talked to the S-team about the urgent need for rapid testing, to address the issue of asymptomatic people who are infected and come to work, unknowingly spreading the disease. With the U.S. grappling with a critical shortage of Covid-19 tests and Amazon unable to procure a supply of its own, Bezos decreed that Amazon should make tests itself—even though it had no previous experience in the area. He was "dealing in the real world, which was, there is no vaccine and there's certainly not going to be one in the immediate near term," said Jay Carney.

The resulting project was dubbed Ultraviolet. With Jeff Wilke leading the initiative, sections of Amazon's Lab126 offices in Sunnyvale, California, and operations hub in Louisville, Kentucky, were converted into impromptu medical labs. A team of health experts, research scientists, and procurement specialists left their regular jobs and set about building a large-scale in-house testing capacity. By the fall, thousands of employees in Amazon warehouses in twenty-three states were volunteering to swab each nostril for ten seconds and send it to one of the two labs. The company said it was conducting thousands of tests a day across 650 sites.

"If you're a shareowner in Amazon, you may want to take a seat, because we're not thinking small," Bezos wrote in the first quarter earnings release in April, predicting that the company would spend billions over the summer in Covid-related expenses. "Providing for customers and protecting employees as this crisis continues for more months is going to take skill, humility, invention, and money." Amazon would point to this large investment, and to its wide-ranging attempts to manage the pandemic's risk, amid the unending criticism that was coming its way. "We did everything we could, taking all of the guidance that we had," said HR chief Beth Galetti.

Jay Carney added, "I am confident that when both the early and long-term histories are written, no company of our scale will have done more, faster and better, than Amazon did.

"Did we do it perfectly? No, absolutely not."

———

As Covid-19 rampaged across the U.S. and Europe, many physical retailers shut their doors while essential items like toilet paper and disinfectant disappeared from the shelves of stores that remained open. Paradoxically, Amazon and other online retailers were buoyed by this tidal wave of uncertainty and fear. It was now safer for someone at home to click and buy from the comfortable and comparatively sterile confines of their living room. Online orders skyrocketed, and even the lagging parts of the Amazon empire, such as Amazon Fresh and its Whole Foods grocery delivery service, saw huge spikes in volume. One analyst said that Covid-19 had been akin to "injecting Amazon with a growth hormone."

Once again, Amazon's achievements were accompanied hand-in-hand by criticism. The company could roll out as many protective initiatives as executives could conceive of, raise entry level wages for a few months, and temporarily boost overtime pay. But to continue to serve customers, it was going to be putting its employees at risk, even if part of the danger came with commuting to and from Amazon buildings.

This was clear by March, when at least five Amazon workers in Italy and Spain contracted the virus. Over the ensuing weeks, cases popped up in Amazon facilities across the U.S. I asked Dave Clark if there was ever any discussion of resolving this deadly trade-off by shutting down facilities or suspending service altogether. "We looked at certain buildings and different parts of the world," he said. "But people needed a way to get these items, particularly in the early days."

That angered many warehouse workers, as well as labor unions, which had long viewed Amazon as an avowed enemy. In mid-April, the French trade union Solidaires Unitaires Démocratiques sued Amazon in a Parisian court, calling for the company to shut its six fulfillment centers in the country. A judge ruled that Amazon had to limit sales to essential items such as health and food products or face a $1.1 million fine for each violation.

That was easier said than done, since workers in the sprawling network could easily err and ship products that didn't conform to the new rules. Amazon's French operations team calculated that the liabilities could add up to more than a billion dollars. The directive then came from Seattle to shut down the French FCs. The judge's ruling, along with the specter of massive liabilities, "made it not a hard choice," said Clark.

The French FCs would stay closed for a month and generate plenty of acrimony. Anne Hidalgo, mayor of Paris, called for a boycott of Amazon in favor of local shops while France's culture minister inveighed, "Amazon is gorging itself. It's up to us to not feed it."

The battle also took a toll inside the company. The European operations teams had labored for years to establish Amazon as a trusted employer; some executives now felt that insular, centralized decision-making from their colleagues thousands of miles away in Seattle was undermining that work. In the midst of the fight in France, Roy Perticucci, the longtime vice president of Amazon's EU operations, abruptly left the company and was soon followed out the door by several other senior members of his team.

Criticisms also flooded in from the hourly workforce in the U.S. Despite the company's attempts at mandating social distancing, its work floors and break rooms were still packed with people, according to the photographs and videos that employees posted on social media. The company's solutions were ineffectual, they charged, and it was prioritizing sales over safety. Workers at an FC in Southern California's Riverside County grumbled they were only told about infections days after they were reported in the local press, and that hand sanitizer dispensers were often empty. Workers in other FCs and transportation hubs complained that they were given a single disinfectant wipe at the start of their shifts to clean their workstations or vans.

These harrowing charges were anecdotal but raised the possibility that Amazon's attempts at containing the risks to workers during the pandemic's early days were more haphazard than executives might like to admit. At IND9, a 600,000-square-foot facility south of Indianapolis, workers complained that plastic shower curtains, prone to rips, were initially hung between tightly spaced inbound receiving stations as makeshift dividers (and only a few weeks later replaced by Plexiglas barriers). In a breakroom at CMH1, an 855,000-square-foot FC east of Columbus, Ohio, managers removed several of the dozens of microwaves in a well-meaning effort to increase distance between them. That simply resulted in crowding around the remaining units, workers said. At DEN3, a hulking warehouse alongside Colorado's I-25 freeway, cleaning supplies like disinfectant and hand sanitizer were scarce well into May; employees were directed to scrounge for substitutes from what they called "damage land"—an area for discarded items that were unfit to ship.

As many employees took advantage of Amazon's offer of unlimited unpaid time off, workers at the SDF9 fulfillment center in Shepherdsville, Kentucky, said the building felt emptier than usual during the early weeks of the pandemic. But when that temporary perk expired on May 1, even though the growth in cases in the U.S. wasn't slowing down, the building became more crowded as adherence to social-distancing policies, such as the floor markings that directed movement through the facility, decreased. "It's been kind of scary," said one SDF9 worker. "Associates aren't following the guidelines that have been put in place."

No one did more to highlight these concerns than an assistant manager named Chris Smalls from the Staten Island fulfillment center, JFK8. Employees at JFK8 had already demonstrated a penchant for speaking out and organizing, in conjunction with the same unions that had opposed Amazon's HQ2 campus in Long Island City. In early March, workers at JFK8 returned from a training trip to Seattle, an early virus hotspot, and began to show symptoms of infection, Smalls claimed. Seemingly indifferent, the facility's managers sponsored an indoor event for staff on March 12, complete with a DJ and raffle, to encourage them to sign up for various Amazon affinity groups.

Social-distancing measures went into effect soon after, but workers were initially told to keep only three feet apart, per the guidelines from the Centers for Disease Control at the time. Smalls also felt that other requirements, like congregating in groups no larger than ten, were impossible to comply with given the nature of the warehouse's team-based work. A five-year veteran of JFK8, he started taking time off and lobbying his superiors to temporarily close the fulfillment center for a thorough cleaning.

On March 24, Smalls returned to work and attended a regular standing meeting. Senior managers informed the group of JFK8's first confirmed Covid-19 case, an employee who hadn't been in the building for more than two weeks. Smalls argued that the warehouse needed to be shut down and sanitized, and all workers sent home with pay. His superiors resisted. Smalls disagreed and brazenly "told as many people as possible as I was making my exit towards the door," he said.

In the days that followed, Chris Smalls filed complaints with the city, the state, and the CDC. Though he conceded that he had been in contact with an infected colleague, he returned to the warehouse and staged breakroom sit-ins. On Saturday, March 28, a supervisor told

Smalls he was being placed on paid "quarantine leave" and to stay at home. Nevertheless, the following Monday, he organized a demonstration outside the warehouse—timed to a lunch break—and tipped off the press. Protesters, some clustered together with their masks tucked under their chins, held up signs that read, "Jeff Bezos, can you hear us?" and "Alexa, send us home!" Amazon workers and reporters live-streamed the protest.

"I was trying to scare people," said Smalls. "More and more people were realizing that this is a scary situation, that we don't know what we're dealing with." A few hours later, he was fired—ostensibly for violating the stay-at-home order, but in his view, for trying "to stand up for something that's right."

Compounding the unfolding public relations problem for Amazon, a few days later *Vice News* published a leaked memo from an S-team meeting, where senior executives discussed how to handle Smalls, who is Black, and whose objections to Amazon's safety precautions were receiving plenty of media attention. "He's not smart, or articulate, and to the extent the press wants to focus on us versus him, we will be in a much stronger PR position than simply explaining for the umpteenth time how we're trying to protect workers," said David Zapolsky, Amazon's language-conscious general counsel, according to the meeting notes. "Make him the most interesting part of the story, and if possible, make him the face of the entire union/organizing movement."

Zapolsky, who said he didn't know Smalls's race at the time, later went to considerable lengths to apologize publicly for the remark, including sending out an email to his staff expressing support for the Black Lives Matter movement that gained momentum from the murder of George Floyd that May. "I should never have let my emotions get to me," he told me. "I shouldn't have used that characterization for any Amazon employee. It was incredibly regrettable."

But the company's opposition to anything that even whiffed of union organizing was now cast starkly into the open, in cynical and arguably prejudicial terms. In the months ahead, additional news reports would expose a pair of Amazon job listings for intelligence analysts to identify "labor organizing threats" within the fulfillment centers, as well as the existence of heat maps at Whole Foods Markets that scored each store on variables like employee turnover, racial diversity, and safety violations to gauge potential pro-union sentiment.

Central to the dissension in the FCs was how Amazon alerted staff to infections in their facilities. In the early days of the pandemic, the company's internal communications department was overwhelmed and struggled to develop a protocol for informing associates of infections. Debate within the comms team centered around what degree of certainty about an infection—a suspected case, or one confirmed by a test result—should trigger a mass alert to employees. It wasn't a trivial question, since documentation might take a couple days to obtain, delaying the start of quarantine leave for the individual and notification to his or her coworkers. But sharing suspected cases might raise undue alarm and trigger panic.

Eventually, the team settled on a plan that called for notifying all employees in a building, via text messages and robocalls, only after a case had been confirmed through testing. There was further handwringing over how much to reveal about the positive individual's job and shift in the facility, without violating their privacy or fueling rumors and speculation on social media. The team instituted a plan that involved using warehouse video footage to perform contact tracing. Workers who had been in close contact with the infected individual then received follow-up instructions from HR to quarantine at home, with pay.

It was a reasonable solution amid challenging circumstances, but the sheer volume of cases among Amazon workers that spring bred further confusion and frustration among employees. They complained that they weren't specifically told how many infections there were or given enough detail to gauge their own exposure. One employee involved in the conversations around notification guidelines compared it to "building an entire fleet of ships while you're trying to get across the Atlantic."

The absence of reliable data about cases inspired some employees, in classic Amazon style, to try to fill the breach themselves. Jana Jumpp, a fifty-nine-year-old associate at SDF8 fulfillment center in south Indiana, left work at the start of the pandemic and spent her time poring over unofficial Facebook groups for Amazon fulfillment center workers and collating unreported cases and rumors to try to keep her colleagues apprised.

In May, Jumpp gave an interview to CBS's *60 Minutes* about her efforts to track and report case data that Amazon declined to share. The piece, which included an interview with Chris Smalls, was punishing, particularly about the company's reluctance to release any information about infection rates in the FCs. Dave Clark was trotted out alone to face the formidable Lesley Stahl; he affably maintained that the number of overall Covid-19 cases wasn't a useful figure, since Amazon believed most employees were infected in their communities, not at work.

But by the fall, Amazon had reversed course amid growing pressure. It reported that around twenty thousand of its 1.3 million frontline employees had tested or been presumed positive for Covid-19. The company argued that its preventative measures had made that figure far lower than could be predicted based on the infection rates in local communities. It also noted that not a single competitor had released similar data, or for that matter come under commensurate criticism from public officials and the media.

Nevertheless, Jana Jumpp, like Chris Smalls and the founders of Amazon Employees for Climate Justice, was fired. Amazon also dismissed Katie Doan, a Whole Foods employee who tracked coronavirus cases across its supermarkets; Bashir Mohamed, a Somali FC worker in Minnesota, who had agitated for greater safety protections; and Courtney Bowden, a Pennsylvania worker who passed out buttons advocating for paid leave for part-time employees.

The company insisted that it was not retaliating against these employees for speaking out. In each case, Amazon spokespeople described an internal policy that had been violated, such as social distancing or the guidelines against talking to the media without the company's authorization. But that was difficult to believe. While Jeff Bezos and his colleagues had bristled at external criticism over the years, they seemed to find it completely intolerable when it came from inside the company. It was as if they feared that an incendiary spark from within their own ranks might finally ignite the long-feared inferno of a disgruntled and activist workforce.

———

Tim Bray could no longer stay at Amazon in good conscience. For five years, Bray, a fedora-wearing software developer and one of the creators of the influential web programming language XML, had worked at AWS as a vice president and distinguished engineer, a member of the company's technical high priesthood that parachuted into troubled projects. Bray was getting assailed by his friends on the progressive left; how could he remain at a company that fired whistleblowers with impunity and was portrayed as having a reckless disregard for the safety of its workforce?

It turned out, he couldn't. In early May, Bray quit his job and wrote a stinging rejoinder on his personal website, arguing that the firings were unjust and that Amazon's careless view toward its workers reflected a flaw in the company's genetic makeup. "Firing whistleblowers isn't just a side-effect of macroeconomic forces, nor is it intrinsic to the function of free markets," he wrote. "It's evidence of a vein of toxicity running through the company culture. I choose neither to serve nor drink that poison."

I caught up with Bray a few months later via video conference from the home office he had been working from on his motorboat in Vancouver. He was sheepish about the good job and haul of unvested stock he had left behind but took at face value the flood of social media posts by workers alleging unsafe conditions. He said the firings of activist employees had affected him deeply. "Firing whistleblowers was just a different level," he said. "It felt ethically so far beyond the pale. It's just not something you can explain away as a company playing hard by the rules. It's not something I could live with."

During the brief media fracas over Bray's blog post, Amazon's PR department had discreetly reached out to reporters and pointed them to a rebuttal, posted on LinkedIn by another distinguished engineer at Amazon named Brad Porter. Porter disputed Bray's insinuation that the company was slow in rolling out safety precautions and objected to his claim that the company treated its workers as commodities to be used up and discarded. "If we want people to choose to work for Amazon helping deliver packages to customers, job number one is to convince those valuable employees that you are doing everything you can every day to keep them safe," he wrote.

Still, Porter's retort, as well as Amazon's reaction to the criticism of its Covid-19 plans, missed the substantive elements of Bray's conscientious objection. Bray believed the testimonials of the activist employees reflected understandable anxiety at a harrowing time. But Amazon, in its reflexive defensiveness, didn't see regular people with genuine concerns but the invisible hand of its opposition, such as organized labor groups. "Sometimes in the noise, it's hard to tell when it's our employees talking and when there are some of these paid third-party groups that are, you know, amplifying things," Dave Clark told me. "There's a group of people who love us no matter what we do, and there's a group of people who really don't like us, no matter what we do."

Bray was also making an important argument not just about Amazon but about the U.S. and how it fails to protect its most vulnerable workers. He had come to believe that employees and contractors at Amazon and other companies badly needed enhanced legal protections from the federal government.

In many European countries, for example, workplaces of a certain size have legally mandated Works Councils, which are independent of labor unions but give employees a voice in major developments at their facilities. There is no such thing in the U.S., where dramatic changes to workers' lives can be made thousands of miles away—and if they don't like it, they have no recourse except to quit and find another job, or speak up publicly and risk getting fired.

Other prosperous countries have livable minimum wages and government-mandated benefits such as paid sick leave and parental leave, equal treatment protections for part-time workers, and restrictions on working hours. In the U.S., where the federal minimum wage remained at a trifling $7.25 an hour, those were viewed by many lawmakers and some business executives as unaffordable luxuries and a tax on the competitiveness of U.S. companies. As a result, many workers were left to drift in the Covid-19 crisis, clinging to their paychecks and employer-based health insurance if they had it, fearing for their jobs, and with no choice but to put their lives and the safety of their families at risk.

"Amazon is a symptom of a larger problem," said Bray from his motorboat. "I'd like to talk to companies the way I talk to my kids. 'Play nice!' But that's not going to work. What you need are regulatory frameworks. If you dislike the way the warehouse people are treated, there should be regulations that rule that out.

"We are in a situation where it is perfectly legal to treat line employees like shit," he continued. "So that is going to happen. Because if you don't, your competitor will."

———

By the end of 2020, as Covid-19 continued to inflict a deadly toll across the world and in the U.S. in particular, a new kind of normalcy was reestablished inside Amazon. It was time to take stock.

Amid the general misfortune of that year, almost perversely, Amazon had flourished. Despite its significant investment in Covid-19 testing and safety measures, the company recorded its most profitable year ever, and its annual revenues surged 37 percent to over $380 billion. In the fall, with a new wave of infections spreading across the U.S. and Europe and the fulfillment centers ingesting more workers than ever, Amazon employed one million full- and part-time workers for the first time.

With teleconferencing and distance learning substituting for business travel and in-person interaction, usage of AWS, a key part of the internet's unseen infrastructure, soared. Homebound customers interacted more often with Alexa and turned to the voice-activated assistant for solace amid the unending isolation. Prime Video thrived, with hits like the violent superhero drama *The Boys* and the comedy *Borat Subsequent Moviefilm* further establishing Amazon Studios at the forefront of the Hollywood vanguard, along with Netflix and rising competitors such as Disney+.

By the end of the year, Amazon boasted a $1.6 trillion market cap and Jeff Bezos was worth more than $190 billion. His wealth had increased by more than 70 percent during the pandemic. It was both a breathtaking achievement and a startling juxtaposition with the economic devastation and strife in Amazon's fulfillment workforce wrought by the virus. The playing field of global business, already slanted toward Amazon and the other technology giants, had tilted even further in their favor as smaller and local companies perished in droves.

At Day 1 tower in Seattle, an era was ending. In January, Jeff Wilke, the fifty-three-year-old CEO of Amazon's consumer business, had told Bezos he wanted to retire over the next year. But as the pandemic intensified, he asked his boss not to worry about his departure for the time being. "I'm going to be here until we are really confident that the company is stable and that we understand the world that we're operating in," he said. By August, he was comfortable that Amazon had endured the worst, and decided to announce his departure.

Wilke had architected the fulfillment network during the dot-com bust, the lowest ebb in Amazon's history, then oversaw the disparate services in its sprawling e-commerce division. He was also widely viewed as a champion of the more humane elements in its hard-edged culture. "Jeff's legacy and impact will live on long after he departs," Bezos wrote to the company. "He is simply one of those people without whom Amazon would be completely unrecognizable."

Unsurprisingly, Wilke nominated Dave Clark to take over his role. After the triumphs of building Amazon Logistics and navigating the coronavirus crisis, Clark became the retail CEO under Bezos and in January 2021 would write a letter to the new presidential administration of Joe Biden, offering Amazon's help in vaccine distribution. It would be up to Clark's successors in operations, whose instincts had not been similarly forged in the chaotic trenches of the fulfillment centers during Amazon's formative years, to manage its sprawling operations with a mix of dispassionate proficiency and empathy for the struggles of the frontline workforce.

Many other longtime execs also stepped away quietly—either because they were exhausted by the ride, already inordinately wealthy, or because they sought the more energizing confines of a smaller company. Among the departures was twenty-three-year veteran Charlie Bell, a senior vice president at Amazon Web Services and one of the technical gurus behind the profitable division. In their place was a new guard, which included several inductees to the S-team, among them Christine Beauchamp of Amazon Fashion, Colleen Aubrey from advertising, and Alicia Boler Davis from operations. They joined Beth Galetti in finally beginning to change the contours of an expanded twenty-five-person leadership group that for years had been marked by a conspicuous lack of gender and racial diversity.

As for Bezos, with Amazon's pandemic response largely set, he could finally set into motion a new set of plans. In February of 2020, he had pledged to donate $10 billion in grants to scientists, activists, and climate groups, as part of a new philanthropic effort he called the Bezos Earth Fund. The Covid-19 crisis delayed that, and in the meantime, MacKenzie Scott surprised the world, first by speedily committing nearly $6 billion in unrestricted grants to various Black colleges and women's and LGBTQ rights groups, and then by getting remarried to Seattle chemistry teacher Dan Jewett, who also signed the Giving Pledge. The juxtaposition with her ex-husband's incipient philanthropic efforts was stark.

Over the fall of 2020, Bezos and Lauren Sanchez started video-conferencing with climate and conservation groups. Executives at these organizations said that the couple asked insightful questions and earnestly solicited advice about how they could make a difference. After they reached out to a wider cohort of nonprofits, including smaller grassroots organizations that worked on causes such as protecting low-income neighborhoods from pollution, they may have been surprised by the reception: some of these groups were distrustful of Bezos's money and cautious of affiliating too closely with the CEO of a company that had a reputation for mistreating workers.

One recipient, the NDN Collective, an organization devoted to creating sustainable solutions that empowered indigenous people, would receive $12 million from the Bezos Earth Fund, and afterward release an extraordinary statement that read in part: "We will not tiptoe around the fact that Amazon and Jeff Bezos in particular have been rightfully criticized for unjust working conditions, corporate bailouts, and for directly contributing to climate change in the world." Other grassroots groups insisted they be treated as relative equals to the large environmental groups that were slated to receive $100 million grants, like the Environmental Defense Fund and World Resources Institute. Five such environmental justice organizations would receive a total of $151 million.

But a few groups went further and demanded that Bezos contribute to climate organizations that also advocate for fair labor standards. With some of these talks growing more complex and contentious than perhaps he had expected, Bezos asked Patty Stonesifer, a longtime Amazon board member and former CEO of the Bill and Melinda Gates Foundation, to intercede. Environmental groups recalled how she took over the process that fall, helping to add organizations like the Climate and Clean Energy Equity Fund and the Hive Fund for Climate and Gender Justice to the list of grantees receiving Bezos's largesse. She also gently ended the dialogue with groups like the NAACP Environmental and Climate Justice Program that adamantly viewed labor rights as an integral component of climate justice.

The announcement of the first $791 million in grants from his Earth Fund, on November 16, 2020, showed that Bezos was finally turning his legendary intellect and colossal fortune toward the greatest challenge of his generation. Even though skepticism from environmental groups had dogged his best intentions, he wasn't going to change the way he operated after a lifetime of remarkable success.

This attitude applied to how he closely managed the newest and most promising endeavors inside Amazon, even as his stature continued to grow. Just as he had nurtured the projects that became Alexa and the Amazon Go stores, he helped to develop Project Kuiper, an ambitious plan to launch satellites that would provide high-speed internet connectivity to people around the world. Amazon's $10 billion project directly challenged the Starlink satellite system already deployed by Elon Musk's SpaceX. The two companies battled before regulators over portions of the radio spectrum and lower Earth altitudes where signals are strongest; once again, it pitted two of the wealthiest people in the world against each other in another high-profile competition.

Similarly, Bezos continued to oversee Amazon's play in the roughly $4 trillion U.S. healthcare market. This included Amazon Pharmacy, a long-gestating service that allowed Amazon customers to order prescriptions online, which the company introduced publicly that November as Covid-19 raged on in the U.S. Other elements of their health efforts were the Fitbit-like Halo smart band, unveiled in August of 2020, and Amazon Care, a smartphone app-based service that offered Amazon employees in Washington State virtual consultations with physicians, and which Amazon was just beginning to roll out to other companies. Bezos believed there was significant potential for disruption and innovation in healthcare and met regularly with a secretive group inside the company, dubbed the "grand challenge," whose purpose was to generate and pursue ideas in the field.

Bezos remained consumed with identifying promising new business opportunities that could significantly improve his company's already robust fortunes. He also continued to cede more authority over the older divisions to key deputies, like Andy Jassy and Dave Clark. And on February 2, 2021, in a historic announcement, Amazon disclosed that he would also cede something else: his job as CEO. Atop its quarterly financial report, the company announced that later in the year, Bezos would transition to executive chairman and hand over the chief executive role to Jassy, the longtime leader of AWS, who long ago was his first full-time technical advisor.

The move heralded a formal changing of the guard at Amazon and the evident end of one of the most epic runs in modern business history. Over the course of two and a half decades, Bezos had taken an idea to sell books on a new medium called the Web, and through invention, the unencumbered embrace of technology, and the ruthless pursuit of leverage, spun it into a global empire worth more than one and a half trillion dollars.

Few current or former colleagues seemed all that surprised by the news. Bezos had been drifting away gradually for years, spreading his time over his many priorities outside Amazon. They also wondered about his girlfriend, and whether he might be more inclined to a life of extravagant leisure with Lauren Sanchez in their lavish homes and soon, on their grand sailing yacht.

Bezos had another reason to elevate himself out of the top role: being Amazon CEO was about to get a lot less fun. There were complicated, maturing businesses to oversee, like the Amazon Marketplace, with its bevy of dissatisfied merchants who consistently complained of fraud and unfair competition; and the Amazon fulfillment network, with more than a million blue-collar workers, a vocal portion of them agitating for higher pay and better working conditions. Those parties tended to train their ire on Amazon's top executive and to hold him personally responsible for problems. Related regulatory challenges also loomed in Washington and Brussels. With Jassy, fifty-three, Bezos was anointing a disciplined leader he had meticulously trained in his unusual way of managing, who performed well in the spotlight and presented a somewhat humbler target for Amazon's political opponents. His former technical advisor had amply proven himself by building and running the most profitable part of Amazon, and had the bandwidth for an increasingly engrossing job.

"Being the CEO of Amazon is a deep responsibility, and it's consuming. When you have a responsibility like that, it's hard to put attention on anything else," Bezos wrote in an email to employees. "As Exec Chair, I will stay engaged in important Amazon initiatives but also have the time and energy I need to focus on the Day 1 Fund, the Bezos Earth Fund, Blue Origin, the *Washington Post*, and my other passions. I've never had more energy, and this isn't about retiring."

Jeff Bezos's mission had been to stave off stasis and to keep Amazon a "Day 1" company with an inventive culture and durable customs that would outlast him. "Amazon is not too big to fail," he once warned employees at an all-hands meeting. "In fact, I predict one day Amazon will fail. Amazon will go bankrupt. If you look at large companies, their lifespans tend to be thirty-plus years, not a hundred-plus years."

It would now largely fall to Andy Jassy to prevent that dark possibility. Among the new CEO's greatest challenges will be retaining the company's deep bench of experienced senior leaders, even if Amazon's stock price stagnates; keeping the ever-growing warehouse workforce motivated and happy; and navigating the impending regulatory scrutiny inside and outside the U.S. That climactic battle, which might one day culminate in an antitrust lawsuit against Amazon by the U.S. government, was still largely ahead.

But with its fourteen sacrosanct leadership principles, interlocking business units, and overwhelming momentum, Bezos had seemingly set up Jassy and the company to flourish well after he stepped aside. In this respect, his life's work, at Amazon at least, was arguably done.

Still looming, of course, was a definitive answer to a perennial question that even now is almost impossible to resolve: Is the world better off with Amazon in it?

Or perhaps, in the wake of Amazon's evolution into a trillion-dollar empire and Jeff Bezos's graduation into the annals of business history, it simply no longer makes sense to ask. The company is now woven inextricably into our lives and communities, hooking customers on the convenience of ordering from home and posing insurmountable challenges for all but the nimblest local retailers. It calls to mind Bezos's old saying about one-way and two-way doors, and "type one" irreversible decisions. Long ago, we stepped through a one-way door and into the technological society conceived of and built in large part by Jeff Bezos and his colleagues. Whatever you think about the company—and the man—that controls so much of our economic reality in the third decade of the twenty-first century, there is no turning back now.

Epilogue

On a perfect, balmy Saturday night in August 2021, celebrities, business luminaries and relatives of Jeff Bezos and Lauren Sanchez gathered at a palatial estate in the tony L.A. neighborhood of Bel Air to revel in a celestial achievement: Bezos's 10-minute rocket ride to the edge of space. "Out of this World," was the theme of the party, planned by Sanchez, and the mood that evening was ebullient, even amid the ongoing Covid-19 pandemic and its rampaging Delta variant.

The couple's children and parents were there, along with Bezos's parents and his younger brother Mark, who had accompanied him on the maiden crewed voyage of Blue Origin's New Shepard space craft. Microsoft co-founder Bill Gates, I heard from an attendee who dared to break the rigorous NDA guests were asked to sign, did a breakdancing jig on the dance floor. But the star of the event and the center of attention, naturally, was Bezos, who had fulfilled his childhood dream: traveling to space, frolicking in zero gravity, and peering down from above at our blue planet. "Every astronaut, everybody's who's been up into space, they say that it changes them," Bezos had said after the launch. "I can vouch for that."

Over the course of the evening, Bezos and Sanchez were inseparable, dancing and canoodling, exulting in his space success while putting their romance on flamboyant display. Before the launch, he told partygoers, he had written private personal letters to Sanchez, his parents and four children, just in case he and his crewmates unexpectedly perished on the journey. It was an astronaut tradition going back to the Apollo missions of the 1960s. But on the morning of the launch, he said, he had been unable to resist and gave his letter for Sanchez to her. Party guests cooed with endearment as they heard about the gesture and inundated Bezos and Sanchez with compliments.

Which was strange, because at that very moment, beyond the cocooned and unmasked bubble at the party, the space trip was being widely criticized and even mocked. Lawmakers in both political parties panned Bezos for what they perceived as an expensive joyride and contrasted it with Amazon's strained relationship with its employees and the communities where it operated. "Maybe—and I'm just spitballing here—if Amazon and other companies paid their fair share in taxes, we could lift all kids—if not into space—at least out of poverty," wrote Democratic congressman Adam Schiff in a typical Tweet. The late-night talk show hosts were merciless. "He looks like a mash-up between Buzz Lightyear and Woody," Jimmy Fallon joked on *The Tonight Show* about Bezos's pairing of a blue space jumpsuit with a cowboy hat. On *The Late Show*, Stephen Colbert roasted, "If something is really important, it doesn't need a big wet celebration. You'll remember Buzz Aldrin didn't douse Neil Armstrong with Gatorade."

I had attended the July 20th space launch at Bezos's sprawling ranch in west Texas and observed the recently retired Amazon CEO trying to reconcile the obviously bad optics of the mission with his lifelong commitment to seeing it through. The buildup that morning was intense. The press corps was told to gather, somewhat regrettably, at 2:30 a.m. at a community center in the three-restaurant highway town of Van Horn, Texas. Then we were bussed an hour through the dark to a hangar a few miles from Launch Site One, the spaceport Bezos had constructed on his 165,000-acre ranch for the New Shepard rocket. As the sun rose over the dusty Texas plains, Blue Origin started broadcasting to an audience on television and the web that would reach some 13 million people. A frisson of nervous tension drifted over the assembled guests, which included correspondents from all the major broadcast networks. Were we about to watch the world's richest man get blown to smithereens in an arguably frivolous and somewhat inexplicable pursuit?

But then, mercifully, it all went as planned. Bezos, his brother Mark (sporting his own cowboy hat), the garrulous 82-year-old Wally Funk, a pioneering female Mercury-era astronaut who NASA had never allowed to fly to space, and 18-year-old Dutch college student Oliver Daemen, whose father had paid for the seat in an auction, took an early morning ride to the launchpad in an electric truck proto-type made by Rivian, an Amazon-backed Tesla rival. Bezos and his crew boarded the New Shepard crew capsule at around 7:30 a.m. and blasted off atop a billow of rocket fire and exhaust smoke a little after 9:00 a.m. Outside the press hangar, we held our breaths, eyes fixed skyward, and listened to audio over the loudspeakers of Bezos and his crewmates marveling at their view and enjoying zero-G. A sonic boom rolled over us a few minutes later as the booster returned to earth, its four jets pounding the asphalt of the landing pad as it settled upright. A few minutes later, the capsule floated back down to earth underneath three parachutes, and Bezos—still wearing that cowboy hat—burst from the door, embraced his visibly relieved mom, Jackie, oldest son, Preston, and Sanchez.

Afterward, the press corps was bussed to The Barn, a makeshift auditorium with an elevated stage perched in the shadow of a tower-ing New Shepard prototype. We waited more than hour. Lauren San-chez walked in a few minutes before the proceedings began, wearing a slender black dress, cowboy boots and cowboy hat. Bezos and his crew emerged after that, pumping their fists as family members and Blue employees erupted in raucous celebration.

The gathering was billed as a press conference, but Bezos had other plans. He introduced the daughters of Apollo astronaut Alan Shepard, talked about keepsakes he had taken on the ride, like Ame-lia Earhart's old aviator goggles, and suggested improbably that the short space jaunt had deepened his conviction about fighting climate change. "The most profound piece is looking out at the earth, looking at the earth's atmosphere," he said. "When you get up above what you see is the atmosphere is this incredible thing... and we are damaging it. That is profound. It's one thing to recognize it intellectually, it's another to see it with your own eyes, how fragile it actually is."

Then he changed the topic altogether and unveiled what he called the Courage and Civility Awards—financial grants to leaders who were countering a polarized political environment. Bezos announced that he would give celebrity chef José Andrés and commentator Van Jones $100 million each. They could donate the money in any way they saw fit. "We need unifiers, not vilifiers," he said on stage, with the pair on hand to emotionally accept his largesse. It was a perfectly noble sentiment but incongruous for the setting. And it spoke to another mission that the former Amazon chief was on that day: to try to change his public image, from that of an exorbitantly wealthy and unempathetic technology chieftain into a philanthropist, magnanimously bent on solving humanity's most pressing problems.

By this point, the day was arguably veering off course. Maybe it was the overt orchestration of the morning's events, or the fact that his suborbital space jaunt was dwarfed by the much more impressive *orbital* launches that Elon Musk's SpaceX was now pulling off nearly every week. Maybe it was that cowboy hat. Or perhaps it was the sentiment that Bezos relayed at the start of his talk, after expressing gratitude toward his family, Blue Origin engineers and the town of Van Horn: "I also want to thank every Amazon employee and every Amazon customer, because you guys paid for all this. Seriously."

Bezos would get flambéed for that. Amazon's warehouse employees and drivers were putting their lives at risk during a ceaseless pandemic. The notion that their efforts had gone to finance a billionaire's ten-minute space excursion with a tenuous public benefit played poorly inside and outside the auditorium. Heavily promoted trips on New Shepard later in the year, by the actor William Shatner and football player-turned-TV-anchor Michael Strahan, would do little to change the prevailing negativity. Leaving the CEO role at Amazon and improving his own image was going to be more difficult than Bezos ever imagined.

———

Bezos spent much of 2021 engaged in this delicate balancing act—pursuing his private passions while amplifying his philanthropy and trying to change the public narrative. In April, he gave $200 million to the Smithsonian's National Air and Space Museum, the same institution that had inducted his portrait into the National Portrait Gallery more than a year before. In September, he earmarked another billion to the Bezos Earth Fund, designating it for conservation of rain forests and indigenous cultures in places like the Congo Basin and tropical Andes, as well as $150 million for groups helping the disadvantaged communities bearing the brunt of climate change. "We must conserve what we still have, we must restore what we've lost, and we must grow what we need to live without degrading the planet for future generations to come," Bezos said at the United Nations' COP26 conference in Glasgow, where he hobnobbed with VIPs like Prince Charles and British premier Boris Johnson.

Two months later, he gave $96.2 million in grants through the Bezos Day One Fund to groups fighting family homelessness, and $100 million to the Obama Foundation. It was the largest ever contribution to the organization headed by the former President, which nevertheless felt the need to mark the moment by mentioning their support of organized labor. "President Obama is strongly supportive of unions," executive director Valerie Jarrett, the former White House advisor, told the *New York Times*, but "appreciates the fact that Jeff is being philanthropic and helping not just us but many other organizations do what they couldn't do but for his generosity."

If Bezos moved somewhat meticulously in his new career as a philanthropist, it was primarily because he was trying not only to give money away but to build a sustainable charitable foundation. Like he had at Amazon with projects like Alexa and AWS, he preferred to put people he trusted in charge of new projects, then build around them. In March, after a long search, he hired Andrew Steer, executive director of the World Resources Institute, to run the Bezos Earth Fund. "Lauren and I are thrilled to have Andrew aboard and very energized about what lies ahead for the Fund and our partners," Bezos wrote on his suddenly prolific Instagram account. Sanchez, the fund's new website revealed at the same time, was vice chair of the organization.

Even as Bezos accelerated his charitable giving, it still suffered in the most obvious comparison: to the philanthropy of his ex-wife, MacKenzie Scott. She was on her own furious mission—to give away her money as quickly as possible. Scott donated $5.7 billion in 2020 and another $2.7 billion in 2021—mostly in unrestricted, no-strings-attached donations to small and overlooked nonprofits on the frontlines of helping disadvantaged and impoverished groups. She accompanied these grants with several posts on the blogging site Medium that suggested she believed the $60 billion fortune she had taken in the divorce was the result not of her ex-husband's cleverness, but of a rigged system. Scott, her new husband Dan Jewett and their philanthropic advisors "are all attempting to give away a fortune that was enabled by systems in need of change," she wrote in a June 15th essay. "In this effort, we are governed by a humbling belief that it would be better if disproportionate wealth were not concentrated in a small number of hands."

Bezos had always joked that MacKenzie was smart enough to get him out of jail. Now here she was effectively relegating him to one—a PR prison built on her speedy and substantial donations, as well as her insinuation that the money she had taken from the divorce was morally compromised.

There were other obstacles to Bezos's attempted reinvention. While he talked about and donated to climate solutions and for equitable treatment of underprivileged communities, he continued to live in staggering opulence with Sanchez. Tabloid publications avidly followed their jaunts to Cabo, Greece, Bora Bora and Hawaii in 2021 alone, where they met up with celebrities like Tom Hanks and Rita Wilson, Barry Diller and Diane von Furstenberg, and Leonardo DiCaprio and his model girlfriend Camila Morrone.

At the same time, Bezos was expanding his already extensive real estate holdings. In April, he paid $23 million to add a fourth condo to his spread of three connected residences in a high-rise in New York's flatiron district. In November, the couple paid $78 million for a 14-acre estate on the south shore of the Hawaiian island of Maui, on a private bay nestled amid a dormant lava field. This was on top of palatial homes they already owned in Beverly Hills, Seattle, Washington, D.C. and the ranch in Texas—making Bezos one of the largest private landowners in the U.S. And in October, Y721, the code-name for Bezos's extravagant sailing yacht, emerged from an Oceanco shipyard in Zwijndrecht and made its way through the Dutch canals for its final fitting. Onlookers photographed the ship and the media made endless hay out of a particular detail—that the forthcoming luxury yacht would have its own accompanying support yacht for the couple's helicopters.

If it was getting easy to dunk on Bezos, no one took more advantage of it than his bitter rival, Elon Musk. The pair continued to duel in lawsuits and public statements over various NASA contracts, their competing satellite networks, SpaceX's Starlink and Amazon's proposed Project Kuiper, and their conflicting visions for space exploration (Musk wants humans to go to Mars; Bezos to permanent orbiting habitats.) But as Bezos drifted further from Amazon and toward the intersecting worlds of philanthropy and celebrity, Musk was moving in the opposite direction. During his own eventful year, he broke up with his girlfriend, the artist Grimes, and sold his homes in Bell-Air and the Bay Area to move to a tiny prefabricated house in Boca Chica, Texas, which he rented from SpaceX. The goal, he announced on twitter, was to devote himself fully to "working on sustainable energy for Earth with Tesla" and "making life multiplanetary with SpaceX."

For investors, the hard work was paying off. In September, with Tesla stock price and SpaceX's private valuation soaring, Musk displaced Bezos as the world's wealthiest person. He was not shy about marking the occasion. "I'm sending a giant statue of the digit '2' to Jeffrey B., along with a silver medal," he emailed a reporter.

On stage in Texas after his trip to space, Bezos was asked about his departure from the all-consuming job of being Amazon CEO. "I'm going to split my time between Blue Origin and the Bezos Earth Fund," he replied. "There's going to be a third thing and a fourth thing, but I don't know what those are yet. I'm not good at doing just a few things."

At the time, I wondered if we were supposed to take his ongoing commitment to Amazon for granted. After all, Bezos remained executive chairman, mentor and putative boss of new chief executive Andy Jassy, and he had promised employees in February that he wasn't going far. "As Exec Chair I will stay engaged in important Amazon initiatives," he wrote in a email to the company. "I've never had more energy, and this isn't about retiring."

But as the year progressed, it seemed that Bezos, amid his space pursuits and personal travels, was perfectly happy to give his successor the independence to put his own imprint on the company and to repair its own moldering public image. For even amid its business triumph, with a rough $1.5 trillion dollar valuation, Amazon remained a company under constant attack—accused in the press and by its critics of deliberately churning through employees in its fulfillment centers, tolerating widespread fraud and counterfeiting in its vast marketplace, and putting a fleet of harried contract drivers on the road to fulfill its Prime delivery promise to customers.

Jassy's challenge was to change the company's narrative, just as Bezos was struggling to fix his own. That his tenure would be marked by a fresh approach was evident several days before he officially became CEO, when Amazon added to its sacred list of 14 leadership principles two new entries: "Strive to be Earth's Best Employer," and "Success and Scale Bring Broad Responsibility." Bezos spearheaded the new edicts and hashed them out with Jassy and other Steam members before his departure, a person close to the company told me. But the idea that Amazon had an obligation to cultivate a diverse workforce that felt empowered, productive, and safe, and that it must be "humble and thoughtful about even the secondary effects of our actions" on its communities and the planet was a remarkable departure from how Amazon had historically operated. For its first 27 years, satisfying the almighty customer was the company's first and only north star.

In Jassy, Amazon had a humbler and more empathetic leader than Bezos. The new boss was often described as "nice," and an active member of the Seattle community and contributor to causes like getting underprivileged kids into college and combatting Seattle's homeless problem. Jassy and his family also lived modestly—at least compared to Bezos. They lived in a 10,000 square foot home in a Seattle residential neighborhood, and he drove the same vehicle that he owned on the first day he started at Amazon: a 1998 Jeep Cherokee Sport. Jassy was also the primary author of one of the company's greatest business successes—Amazon Web Services, which in 2021 generated more than $60 billion in sales and as a standalone entity would almost certainly sport its own trillion-dollar valuation.

But as leader of the entire company, Jassy faced a wider and more significant set of challenges. Despite years of Bezos's personal involvement, Amazon Studios, its entertainment arm, still lagged Netflix, Hulu and arguably Disney Plus and the race to define the next wave of home entertainment. In May, Amazon announced its intent to acquire MGM, home to the James Bond, *Rocky* and *Robocop* films, for $8.4 billion. The deal would give Prime Video a vast catalog of mainstream intellectual property and another way to broaden the appeal of its Prime membership program. But first, in a highly politicized environment where regulators were wary of tech companies consolidating their influence, Jassy and his colleagues would have to convince regulators like Lina Khan, its longtime critic and now the chairman of the Federal Trade Commission, that the deal posed no competitive threat.

More seriously, Covid-19 quarantine had super-charged Amazon's retail growth, and to keep up, the company had gone on a spending spree, doubling the size of its warehouse network and hiring more than half a million workers. It had also finished its air hub in northern Kentucky, increased the size of its air freight fleet by about a third, and now delivered more than half of its own packages, according to Nielsen Consumer LLC. But keeping all those workers and drivers happy, particularly amid low unemployment and the Great Resignation—a record number of people leaving their jobs as the pandemic eased—was going to be costly. In September, the company raised its starting hourly wage for new hires to $18 an hour, announced it was giving signing bonuses of up to $3,000 and expanded benefits to parents and caregivers

As a result, Amazon's expenses soared and investors were unsettled by $2 billion in unexpected costs. Empathy, it turned out, was expensive. During the infamous supply chain squeeze that holiday season, Amazon also spent a few more billion more to stockpile products and reroute them around backlogs at major ports. Jassy called it "the right prioritization for our customers and partners" in the earnings report, but for the first time in awhile, Amazon stock lost ground over the second half of the year. Inevitably, that increased the company's already robust turnover rate, as many employees left to pursue higher compensation and better opportunities elsewhere. One departing AWS exec told me he was seeing 20 percent attrition in his division.

If all this unsettled Amazon's new CEO, he didn't show it. In November, Jassy addressed the company in the bi-annual all-hands meeting, his first as chief executive. In previous sessions, which are broadcast internally to all employees, Bezos hosted the event and handed off specific questions to his various deputies. This time, in a video of the meeting I obtained afterward, the founder was nowhere to be seen. Jassy handled it all himself, looking newly svelte, wearing a blue blazer and jeans, and speaking casually without notes before a bank of three video cameras. "I can't explain it," he said, answering a question about his pandemic pastimes by revealing that he and his wife had watched virtually every episode of *Law and Order*. "For some reason they're fascinating to us."

He also talked about major new initiatives like the Amazon Astro, an Alexa-equipped home robot the company had been developing for years, crowed about the early success of Amazon's online fantasy game *New World*, and touted the company's various health care initiatives. "We're going to look back 10 years from now and we're going to think it was crazy" that people waited in line at doctor's offices and pharmacies, instead of using the internet, Jassy said.

But in the most interesting part of the all-hands meeting, he addressed the near constant scrutiny and criticism of the company. "I would not be sheepish about educating whether it's people, you know, or the press or politicians or whoever, even ourselves, how much good this collective team is doing," he said, with customary Amazonian defensiveness. Then in nearly the same breath, he acknowledged that some things had to change. "We should take any criticism we get and listen to it and evaluate whether there's any truth to it and where there is improve." The company, he added, can have "high standards while also leading and caring for our employees with empathy."

———

As 2021 ended, Amazon stood at a crossroads. The intoxicating gold-rush days of online shopping and cloud computing were inevitably coming to an end. Upstart competitors like Canada's Shopify, social commerce on sites like Instagram and TikTok, and Microsoft and Google's incursions in cloud computing, were carving away market share. Regulators seemed eager to stymie the tech giant at every opportunity.

Bezos had managed through such fraught moments in the company's history with ingenuity. Amazon had been his science project, a grand experiment into the exploration of the possible. Now it would fall to Jassy, the disciple, to find the dramatic new inventions and opportunities while containing costs, courting finicky employees, and atoning for the sins of the past.

Amazon was once seen as practically unbound—impervious to the laws of gravity that beset large institutions of every kind. Now, at the end of one epic business story and the start of possibly another, that no longer appeared to be the case. The sun was setting on Day 1. After almost three decades, just like everything else in this world—rockets, the reputations of celebrities, and the evolving stories that we tell about the most important figures in human history—Jeff Bezos and the company he started in his garage were floating back down to earth.

Acknowledgments

I started reporting this book in early 2018 and wrote it over the course of 2020 during the Covid-19 pandemic. Like so many other things during that challenging time, successfully completing it was only possible with the support and wisdom of friends, family, and colleagues to whom I am deeply indebted.

At Simon & Schuster, Stephanie Frerich was a graceful editor who never shied away from asking difficult questions, rearranging clunky prose, and keeping the larger narrative from veering off course. She made the book immeasurably better. Emily Simonson, Elisa Rivlin, Jackie Seow, Matthew Monahan, Samantha Hoback, and Lisa Erwin helped to get it across the finish line during an accelerated publication schedule. Jonathan Karp, Dana Canedy, Richard Rhorer, Kimberly Goldstein, Stephen Bedford, Marie Florio, Larry Hughes, and the late Carolyn Reidy were believers in this book and proponents of an unrestrained examination of its powerful subject.

My agent, Pilar Queen at UTA, was a relentless advocate and advisor. She patiently urged me to return to the rapidly evolving topic of Amazon and Jeff Bezos, then became an avid champion and an early reader. I owe her many thanks.

Lindsay Gellman provided valuable research assistance, in addition to fact-checking help alongside the meticulous and fast-working team of Lindsay Muscato, Rima Parikh, and Jeremy Gantz. Diana Suryakusuma assisted with photographs. All errors are solely my own. Thanks also to Chris Oster and Halle Gordon at Amazon for facilitating multiple interviews and herding innumerable facts.

At *Bloomberg News*, I'm grateful to John Micklethwait, Reto Gregori, and Heather Harris, who were enthusiastic backers of this project and indulgent of my periodic retreat from our daily work. I'm enormously proud to be part of *Bloomberg*'s Global Technology team; Tom Giles, Jillian Ward, Mark Milian, Peter Elstrom, Edwin Chan, Giles Turner, Molly Schuetz, Alistair Barr, and Andy Martin are tremendous partners who lead a group of sixty-five talented technology journalists around the world. Joel Weber, Kristin Powers, and Jim Aley at *Bloomberg Businessweek* were steadfast allies; Max Chafkin offered plenty of sound counsel and dark humor during the writing process.

My *Bloomberg* colleagues Mark Gurman, Austin Carr, Ellen Huet, Josh Brustein, Dina Bass, Priya Anand, Ian King, Nico Grant, Kartikay Mehrotra, Anne Vandermey, Naomi Nix, Tom Metcalf, Jack Witzig, Brody Ford, and Devon Pendleton all answered my periodic pleas for assistance. Sarah Frier and Emily Chang were always ready with motivation and encouragement. Saritha Rai helped me unravel the story of Amazon in India, and Chapter 3 is based in part on a cover story we jointly wrote for *Bloomberg Businessweek*. Ashlee Vance was an unfaltering friend and co-conspirator.

I owe special thanks to *Bloomberg* reporters Spencer Soper and Matt Day and editor Robin Ajello, whose work is heavily endnoted in these pages. They provided indispensable feedback and a reservoir of deep knowledge about Amazon. Together we're working on an audio version of Amazon's story, as part of Bloomberg Technology's podcast series, *Foundering*, produced by Shawn Wen. Please keep an eye out for it.

Anne Kornblut, Matt Mosk, Adam Piore, Sean Meshorer, Ethan Watters, Michael Jordan, Fred Sharples, Ruzwana Bashir, Adam Rogers, Daniel McGinn, and Charles Duhigg all offered friendship and assistance at various moments of need. Nick and Chrysta Bilton generously hosted me on several trips to Los Angeles; Nick and Emily Wingfield offered the same hospitality in Seattle. Steven Levy has provided wise counsel and invaluable friendship over many years.

I'm extremely fortunate to have a large and supportive family, including my brothers, Brian Stone and Eric Stone, Dita Papraniku Stone and Becca Zoller Stone, Luanne Stone, Maté Schissler and Andrew Iorgulescu, and Jon and Monica Stone. My father, Robert Stone, is my closest reader and was a sounding board for the ideas in this book; my mother, Carol Glick, offered unconditional love, advice, and the appropriate level of concern over the magnitude of the undertaking. My grandmother, Bernice Yaspan, remains an avid reader at 103 years old, and one of my personal goals was to place this volume in her hands.

My daughters, Isabella Stone, Calista Stone, and Harper Fox, make me exceedingly proud every day. Set against their resilience during the pandemic, writing another book seemed relatively easy. But of course, it wouldn't have been remotely possible without the love, patience, and infinite encouragement of my wife, Tiffany Fox.

Endnotes

INTRODUCTION

3 *No concrete way existed to achieve this goal*: Matt Day, "Amazon Tries to Make the Climate Its Prime Directive," *Bloomberg*, September 21, 2020, https://www .bloomberg.com/news/features/2020-09-21/amazon-made-a-climate-promise -without-a-plan-to-cut-emissions (January 16, 2021).

4 *"Amazon Employees for Climate Justice"*: Amazon Employees for Climate Justice, "Open Letter to Jeff Bezos and the Amazon Board of Directors," *Medium*, April 10, 2019, https://amazonemployees4climatejustice.medium.com/public -letter-to-jeff-bezos-and-the-amazon-board-of-directors-82a8405f5e38 (January 18, 2021).

7 *the grudge-holding CEO hid an acronym,* milliravi: "Meaningful Innovation Leads, Launches, Inspires Relentless Amazon Visitor Improvements" was the basis for the acronym *milliravi*, a word that an Amazon executive coined to mean "a significant mathematical error of a million dollars or more." See Brad Stone, *The Everything Store: Jeff Bezos and the Age of Amazon* (Boston: Little, Brown and Company, 2013), 135.

11 *Bezos was the thirtieth richest person in the world, with an $18.1 billion net worth*: Jeff Bezos profile, "Billionaires: March 2011," *Forbes*, March 9, 2011, retrieved from https://web.archive.org/web/20110313201303if_/http://www.forbes.com /profile/jeff-bezos (January 17, 2021).

12 *In early 2012, anonymous fliers taped around South Lake Union found a derogatory name*: Nicole Brodeur, "Neighbors Talking About Amazon," *Seattle Times*, January 12, 2012, https://www.seattletimes.com/seattle-news/neighbors -talking-about-amazon/ (January 17, 2021).

14 *"Today's big tech companies" . . . Zappos and Whole Food Market and be stamped into smaller parts*: Senator Elizabeth Warren, "Here's How We Can Break Up Big Tech," *Medium*, March 8, 2019, https://medium.com/@teamwarren/heres-how -we-can-break-up-big-tech-9ad9e0da324c (January 17, 2021).

CHAPTER 1: THE ÜBER PRODUCT MANAGER

29 *the Ivona founders then had to renegotiate the actor's contract*: Katarzyna Nied-
urny, *"Kariera Głosu Ivony. 'Wsiadam do windy i słyszę jak mówię"piętro pier-
wsze'"* ("Ivona's Voice Career. 'I get in the elevator and hear me say "first floor"'")
January 4, 2019, https://wiadomosci.onet.pl/tylko-w-onecie/jacek-labijak-o
-karierze-glosu-jacek-w-syntezatorze-mowy-ivona/kyht0wl (January 19, 2021).

31 *he asked it to play one of his favorite songs: the theme to the classic TV show* Battlestar Galactica: Eugene Kim, "The Inside Story of How Amazon Created Echo,
the Next Billion-Dollar Business No One Saw Coming," *Business Insider*, April 2,
2016, https://www.businessinsider.com/the-inside-story-of-how-amazon-created
-echo-2016-4 (January 19, 2021).

34 *Users could ask it questions . . . almost crashed the company's servers*: David
Baker, "William Tunstall-Pedoe: The Brit Taking on Apple's Siri with 'Evi,'"
Wired UK, May 8, 2012, https://www.wired.co.uk/article/the-brit-taking-on-siri
(January 19, 2021).

34 *with a rumored $26 million deal*: Mike Butcher, "Sources Say Amazon Acquired
Siri-Like Evi App For $26M—Is A Smartphone Coming?" *TechCrunch*, April 17,
2013, https://techcrunch.com/2013/04/17/sources-say-amazon-acquired-siri
-like-evi-app-for-26m-is-a-smartphone-coming/ (January 19, 2021).

34 *"giant treelike structure"*: James Vlahos, "Amazon Alexa and the Search for the
One Perfect Answer," *Wired*, February 18, 2018, https://www.wired.com/story
/amazon-alexa-search-for-the-one-perfect-answer/ (January 19, 2021).

37 *harness a large number of high-powered computer processors to train its speech
models*: Nikko Ström, "Nikko Ström at AI Frontiers: Deep Learning in Alexa,"
Slideshare, January 14, 2017, https://www.slideshare.net/AIFrontiers/nikko
-strm-deep-learning-in-alexa (January 19, 2021).

39 *a patent on the idea was filed*: Amazon. Techniques for mobile deceive charging
using robotic devices. U.S. Patent 9711985, filed March 30, 2015. https://www
.freepatentsonline.com/9711985.html (January 19, 2021).

39 *"The biggest needle movers . . . inner imagination about what's possible"*: Jeff Bezos,
"2018 Letter to Shareholders," Amazon, April 11, 2018, https://www.aboutamazon
.com/news/company-news/2018-letter-to-shareholders (January 19, 2021).

40 *tried to get the 3D display to work . . . owl-themed code name, Duke*: Austin Carr,
"The Inside Story of Jeff Bezos's Fire Phone Debacle," *Fast Company*, January 6,
2015, https://www.fastcompany.com/3039887/under-fire (January 19, 2021).

41 *Freed said that Bezos told him afterward, "You can't . . . lose a minute of sleep"*:
Charles Duhigg, "Is Amazon Unstoppable?" *New Yorker*, October 10, 2019,
https://www.newyorker.com/magazine/2019/10/21/is-amazon-unstoppable
(January 19, 2021).

43 *army of workers manually reviewed the recordings*: Matt Day, Giles Turner, and

Natalia Drozdiak, "Amazon Workers Are Listening to What You Tell Alexa," *Bloomberg*, April 10, 2019, https://www.bloomberg.com/news/articles/2019 -04-10/is-anyone-listening-to-you-on-alexa-a-global-team-reviews-audio?sref =dJuchiL5 (January 19, 2021).

44 *lobbied to include a remote control . . . to see if customers would use it*: Joshua Brustein, "The Real Story of How Amazon Built the Echo," *Bloomberg*, April 19, 2016, https://www.bloomberg.com/features/2016-amazon-echo/ (January 19, 2021).

46 *"I just spoke to the future and it listened"*: Mario Aguilar, "Amazon Echo Review: I Just Spoke to the Future and It Listened," *Gizmodo*, June 25, 2015, https://gizmodo.com/amazon-echo-review-i-just-spoke-to-the-future-and-it -1672926712 (January 19, 2021).

46 *"it's the most innovative device Amazon's made in years"*: Kelsey Campbell-Dollaghan, "Amazon's Echo Might Be Its Most Important Product in Years," *Gizmodo*, November 6, 2014, https://gizmodo.com/amazons-echo-might-be-its -most-important-product-in-yea-1655513291 (January 19, 2021).

48 *2015 holiday season, Amazon sold a million Echo devices*: Brustein, "The Real Story."

50 *"like something you might plant a succulent in"*: David Pierce, "Review: Google Home," *Wired*, November 11, 2016, https://www.wired.com/2016/11/review -google-home/ (January 19, 2021).

50 *sell Alexa in eighty new countries*: Todd Bishop, "Amazon Bringing Echo and Alexa to 80 Additional Countries in Major Global Expansion," *GeekWire*, December 8, 2017, https://www.geekwire.com/2017/amazon-bringing-echo-alexa -80-additional-countries-major-global-expansion/ (January 19, 2021).

51 *March 2018, a bug caused Alexas . . . unprompted laughter*: Shannon Liao, "Amazon Has a Fix for Alexa's Creepy Laughs," *Verge*, March 7, 2018, https:// www.theverge.com/circuitbreaker/2018/3/7/17092334/amazon-alexa-devices -strange-laughter (January 19, 2021).

51 *"extremely rare occurrence" . . . "as unlikely as this string of events is"*: Matt Day, "Amazon's Alexa recorded and shared a conversation without consent, report says," *Seattle Times,* March 24, 2018, https://www.seattletimes.com/business /amazon/amazons-alexa-recorded-and-shared-a-conversation-without-consent -report-says (February 12, 2021).

52 *errantly informed a child that Santa was a myth*: James Vincent, "Inside Amazon's $3.5 Million Competition to Make Alexa Chat Like a Human," *Verge*, June 13, 2018, https://www.theverge.com/2018/6/13/17453994/amazon-alexa -prize-2018-competition-conversational-ai-chatbots (February 12, 2018).

CHAPTER 2: A NAME TOO BORING TO NOTICE

54 *"Only if we can have a truly differentiated idea . . . we would love to"*: Jeff Bezos interviewed by Charlie Rose, *Charlie Rose*, 34:40, November 16, 2012, https://charlierose.com/videos/17252 (January 19, 2021).

54 *an article in the* New York Times *that . . . recognize cats*: John Markoff, "How Many Computers to Identify a Cat? 16,000," *New York Times*, June 25, 2012, https://www.nytimes.com/2012/06/26/technology/in-a-big-network-of -computers-evidence-of-machine-learning.html (January 19, 2021).

64 *used a pole with a camera attached to it to peek inside*: Jacob Demmitt, "Amazon's Bookstore Revealed? Blueprints Provide New Clues About Mysterious Seattle Site," *GeekWire*, October 12, 2015, https://www.geekwire.com/2015/amazons -bookstore-revealed-blueprints-provide-new-clues-about-mysterious-seattle -site/ (January 19, 2021).

65 *to serve as a model for kitchens . . . as part of a massive rollout of Go stores*: Brad Stone and Matt Day, "Amazon's Most Ambitious Research Project Is a Convenience Store," *Bloomberg*, July 18, 2019, https://www.bloomberg.com /news/features/2019-07-18/amazon-s-most-ambitious-research-project-is-a -convenience-store?sref=dJuchiL5 (January 19, 2021).

66 *ended up being delayed a year*: Laura Stevens, "Amazon Delays Opening of Cashier-less Store to Work Out Kinks," *Wall Street Journal*, March 27, 2017, https://www .wsj.com/articles/amazon-delays-convenience-store-opening-to-work-out-kinks -1490616133 (January 19, 2021); Olivia Zaleski and Spencer Soper, "Amazon's Ca-shierless Store Is Almost Ready for Prime Time," *Bloomberg*, November 15, 2017, https://www.bloomberg.com/news/articles/2017-11-15/amazon-s-cashierless -store-is-almost-ready-for-prime-time?sref=dJuchiL5 (January 19, 2021).

66 *"The whole process . . . items weren't free"*: Shara Tibken and Ben Fox Rubin, "What It's Like Inside Amazon's Futuristic, Automated Store," *CNET*, January 21, 2018, https://www.cnet.com/news/amazon-go-futuristic-automated-store -seattle-no-cashiers-cashless/ (January 19, 2021).

67 *In 2017, Amazon spent $22.6 billion on R&D*: Amazon includes the costs of operating AWS as part of its R&D expenses. See Rani Molla, "Amazon Spent Nearly $23 Billion on R&D Last Year—More Than Any Other U.S. Company," *Vox*, April 9, 2018, https://www.vox.com/2018/4/9/17204004/amazon-research -development-rd (January 19, 2021).

67 *Bezos had envisioned thousands of Amazon Go stores*: Spencer Soper, "Amazon Will Consider Opening Up to 3,000 Cashierless Stores by 2021," *Bloomberg*, September 19, 2018, https://www.bloomberg.com/news/articles/2018-09 -19/amazon-is-said-to-plan-up-to-3-000-cashierless-stores-by-2021?sref =dJuchiL5 (January 19, 2021).

68 *"We've learned a lot . . . ten times as big"*: Sebastian Herrera and Aaron Til-

ley, "Amazon Opens Cashierless Supermarket in Latest Push to Sell Food," *Wall Street Journal*, February 25, 2020, https://www.wsj.com/articles/amazon -opens-cashierless-supermarket-in-latest-push-to-sell-food-11582617660?mod =hp_lead_pos10 (January 19, 2021).

68 *"We all know if you swing for the fences . . . important to be bold"*: Jeff Bezos, "2015 Letter to Shareholders," https://www.sec.gov/Archives/edgar/data /1018724/000119312515144741/d895323dex991.htm (January 19, 2021).

69 *Amazon Dash Carts, which allowed shoppers to scan items*: Robin Ajello and Spencer Soper, "Amazon Develops Smart Shopping Cart for Cashierless Check-out," *Bloomberg*, July 14, 2020, https://www.bloomberg.com/news/articles /2020-07-14/amazon-develops-smart-shopping-cart-for-cashierless-checkout ?sref=dJuchiL5 (January 19, 2021).

CHAPTER 3: COWBOYS AND KILLERS

I visited Amazon.in and Flipkart in Bangalore, India, in September 2018 with my colleague Saritha Rai. This chapter is based in part on our story, "Amazon Wants India to Shop Online, and It's Battling Walmart for Supremacy," *Bloomberg Businessweek*, October 18, 2018, https://www.bloomberg.com/news/features/2018 -10-18/amazon-battles-walmart-in-indian-e-commerce-market-it-created (January 19, 2021). I also relied in part on *Big Billion Startup: The Untold Flipkart Story* by Mihir Dalal (New Delhi: Pan Macmillan India, 2019). I interviewed Juan Carlos Garcia, the former CEO of Amazon Mexico, on August 3, 2019—before he became a fugitive from justice.

72 *CCTV, drew attention to counterfeit goods, such as fake brand-name cosmetics, on Amazon's marketplace*: Nicholas Wadhams, "Amazon China Unit Closes Vendor After Report of Fake Cosmetics," *Business of Fashion*, March 20, 2014, https://www.businessoffashion.com/articles/technology/amazon-china-unit -closes-vendor-report-fake-cosmetics (January 19, 2021).

73 *Between 2011 and 2016, Amazon's market share in China fell from 15 percent to less than 1 percent*: Arjun Kharpal, "Amazon Is Shutting Down Its China Marketplace Business. Here's Why It Has Struggled," CNBC, April 18, 2019, https://www.cnbc.com/2019/04/18/amazon-china-marketplace-closing-down -heres-why.html (January 19, 2021), and Felix Richter, "Amazon Has Yet to Crack the Chinese Market," *Stastista*, February 22, 2017, https://www.statista .com/chart/8230/china-e-commerce-market-share/ (January 19, 2021).

74 *the Bansals asked for $1 billion*: Dalal, *Big Billion Startup*, 101.

75 *A shaky handheld video of the launch*: "Amazon.in Goes Live—5th June 2013," YouTube video, 2:38, posted by Amit Deshpande, March 11, 2016, https:// www.youtube.com/watch?v=TFUw6OyugfQ&feature=youtu.be&ab_channel =AmitDeshpande (January 19, 2021).

76 *"You guys are going to fail . . . need cowboys"*: Jay Green, "Amazon Takes Cowboy Tactics to 'Wild, Wild East' of India," *Seattle Times*, October 3, 2015, https://www .seattletimes.com/business/amazon/amazon-takes-cowboy-tactics-to-wild-wild -east-of-india/ (January 19, 2021).

77 *responsible for around 40 percent of sales*: Mihir Dalal and Shrutika Verma, "Amazon's JV Cloudtail Is Its Biggest Seller in India," *Mint*, October 29, 2015, https://www.livemint.com/Companies/RjEDJkA3QyBSTsMDdaXbCN /Amazons-JV-Cloudtail-is-its-biggest-seller-in-India.html (January 19, 2021).

77 *("Test the Boundaries of what is allowed by law")*: Aditya Kalra, "Amazon documents reveal company's secret strategy to dodge India's regulators," Reuters, February 17, 2021, https://www.reuters.com/investigates/special-report/amazon -india-operation (February 23, 2021).

78 *Flipkart announced a fresh infusion of $1 billion in venture capital*: Dalal, *Big Billion Startup*, 163.

78 *"My own view . . . thinking about their customers"*: Sunny Sen and Josey Puliyenthuruthel, "Knock on Wood, India Is Shaping Up Like Our Businesses in Japan, Germany, the UK and the US," *Business Today*, October 26, 2014, https://www.businesstoday.in/magazine/features/amazon-ceo-jeff-bezos -sachin-bansal-binny-bansal/story/211027.html (January 19, 2021).

79 *"I am completely at his disposal"*: "Amazon CEO Jeff Bezos Meets PM Narendra Modi," *India TV*, October 4, 2014, https://www.indiatvnews.com/business/india /narendra-modi-jeff-bezos-amazon-ceo-flipkart-e-commerce-14744.html (January 20, 2021).

80 *the country represented less than 7 percent of its total sales in Latin America*: Carolina Ruiz, *"MercadoLibre busca alianzas con minoristas en México"* ("MercadoLibre Seeks Alliances with Businesses in Mexico"), *El Financiero*, OctOBER 11, 2014, https://www.elfinanciero.com.mx/tech/mercadolibre-busca-alianzas-con -competidores-en-mexico (January 20, 2021).

81 *"all weak-kneed around entrepreneurs"*: James Quinn, "Jeff Bezos . . . Amazon Man in the Prime of His Life," *Irish Independent*, August 19, 2015, https://www .independent.ie/business/technology/news/jeff-bezos-amazon-man-in-the -prime-of-his-life-31463414.html (January 20, 2021).

82 *$3-4 billion a year for search ads*: Estimate for Amazon's 2015 Google search spend provided by Andy Taylor, director of research at Tinuiti.

85 *leading player in the country's $7 billion ecommerce market—slightly ahead of MercadoLibre and Walmart*: Daina Beth Solomon, "Amazon Becomes Mexico's Top Online Retailer in 2017: Report," Reuters, December 15, 2017, https://www .reuters.com/article/us-mexico-retail/amazon-becomes-mexicos-top-online -retailer-in-2017-report-idUSKBN1E92ID (January 20, 2021).

85 *"Ex-Amazon Mexico CEO on the run"*: Jon Lockett, "Ex-Amazon Mexico CEO on the Run in the US After Wife's Mysterious Murder . . . Months After 'Battering

Her,'" *The Sun*, December 12, 2019, https://www.thesun.co.uk/news/10538850 /amazon-boss-shooting-mexico-fugitive/ (January 20, 2021).

86 *Chai Carts*: Aditi Shrivastava, "How Amazon Is Wooing Small Merchants With Its 'Chai Cart' Programme," *Economic Times*, August 21, 2015, https://economictimes .indiatimes.com/small-biz/entrepreneurship/how-amazon-is-wooing-small -merchants-with-its-chai-cart-programme/articleshow/48565449.cms (January 20, 2021).

87 *"much more than a market"*: "Modi in US: 10 Things PM Said at US-India Business Council," *Financial Express*, June 8, 2016, https://www.financialexpress .com/india-news/modi-in-us-10-things-pm-said-at-us-india-business-council /277037/ (January 20, 2021).

87 *"reliable partner"*: Ibid.

88 *"for making Amazon.in the most visited e-commerce site in the country"*: Malavika Velayanikal, "It's Official: Flipkart's App-Only Experiment with Myntra Was a Disaster," *Tech in Asia*, March 28, 2016, https://www.techinasia.com/flipkart -myntra-app-only-disaster (January 20, 2021).

88 *proposed a new set of rules . . . brokering more than 25 percent of the site's total sales*: Jon Russell, "New E-commerce Restrictions in India Just Ruined Christmas for Amazon and Walmart," *TechCrunch*, December 27, 2018, https://techcrunch.com/2018/12/27/amazon-walmart-india-e-commerce -restrictions/ (January 20, 2021).

91 *Binny Bansal was promptly ousted*: Saritha Rai and Matthew Boyle, "How Walmart Decided to Oust an Icon of India's Tech Industry," *Bloomberg*, November 15, 2018, https://www.bloomberg.com/news/articles/2018-11-15/how -walmart-decided-to-oust-an-icon-of-india-s-tech-industry?sref=dJuchiL5 (January 20, 2021); Saritha Rai, "Flipkart Billionaire Breaks His Silence After Walmart Ouster," *Bloomberg*, February 4, 2019, https://www.bloomberg .com/news/articles/2019-02-05/flipkart-billionaire-breaks-his-silence-after -walmart-ouster?sref=dJuchiL5 (January 20, 2021).

91 *And in 2020, ugly divorce proceedings*: "Flipkart Founder Sachin Bansal's Wife Files Dowry Harassment Case," *Tribune*, March 5, 2020, https://www .tribuneindia.com/news/nation/flipkart-founder-sachin-bansals-wife-files -dowry-harassment-case-51345 (January 20, 2021).

92 *it tightened foreign investment laws*: Vindu Goel, "Amazon Users in India Will Get Less Choice and Pay More Under New Selling Rules," *New York Times*, January 30, 2019, https://www.nytimes.com/2019/01/30/technology/amazon -walmart-flipkart-india.html (January 20, 2021).

93 *"collectively launch a new movement against data colonization"*: Manish Singh, "India's Richest Man Is Ready to Take On Amazon and Walmart's Flipkart," *TechCrunch*, December 31, 2019, https://techcrunch.com/2019/12/30/reliance -retail-jiomart-launch/ (January 20, 2021).

CHAPTER 4: A YEAR FOR EATING CROW

94 *"I don't know what to say about Amazon . . . until you make some money"*: Steve Ballmer interviewed by Charlie Rose, *Charlie Rose*, 48:43, October 21, 2014, https://charlierose.com/videos/28129 (January 20, 2021).

97 *DynamoDB*: Werner Vogels, "A Decade of Dynamo: Powering the Next Wave of High-Performance, Internet Scale Applications," *All Things Distributed*, October 2, 2017, https://www.allthingsdistributed.com/2017/10/a-decade-of -dynamo.html (January 20, 2021); "Dynamo: Amazon's Highly Available Key -Value Store," https://www.allthingsdistributed.com/files/amazon-dynamo -sosp2007.pdf (January 20, 2021).

99 *a 2006* Businessweek *story*: "Jeff Bezos' Risky Bet," *Bloomberg Businessweek*, November 13, 2006, https://www.bloomberg.com/news/articles/2006-11-12/jeff -bezos-risky-bet (January 20, 2021).

100 *"good intentions don't work, only mechanisms do"*: "Maintaining a Culture of Builders and Innovators at Amazon," Gallup, February 26, 2018, https://www.gallup.com/workplace/231635/maintaining-culture-builders -innovators-amazon.aspx (January 20, 2021).

103 *70 percent growth rate and 19.2 percent operating margin*: "2015 Amazon.com Annual Report," https://ir.aboutamazon.com/annual-reportsproxies-andshare holder-letters/default.aspx (March 10, 2021).

103 *"one of the technology industry's biggest and most important IPOs"*: Ben Thompson, "The AWS IPO," *Stratechery*, May 6, 2015, https://stratechery.com/2015 /the-aws-ipo/ (January 20, 2021).

104 *generated more than $9 billion in sales*: Jon Russell, "Alibaba Smashes Its Record on China's Singles' Day with $9.3B in Sales," *TechCrunch*, November 10, 2014, https://techcrunch.com/2014/11/10/alibaba-makes-strong-start-to-singles-day -shopping-bonanza-with-2b-of-goods-sold-in-first-hour/ (January 20, 2021).

105 *"Don't make this convoluted . . . we have to do it really well"*: Karen Weise, "The Decade Tech Lost Its Way," *New York Times*, December 15, 2019, https://www.nytimes .com/interactive/2019/12/15/technology/decade-in-tech.html (January 20, 2021).

105 *he highlighted a section that targeted ten thousand deals for Prime Day*: Ibid.

108 *an article in* Fast Company *suggested that Prime Day cynically manipulated shoppers*: Mark Wilson, "You're Getting Screwed on Amazon Prime Day," *Fast Company*, July 12, 2019, https://www.fastcompany.com/90374625/youre -getting-screwed-on-amazon-prime-day (January 20, 2021).

109 *Amazon's market capitalization surpassed Walmart's*: Matt Krantz, "Amazon Just Surpassed Walmart in Market Cap," *USA Today*, July 23, 2015, https://www.usatoday.com/story/money/markets/2015/07/23/amazon-worth -more-walmart/30588783/ (January 20, 2021).

109 *employees flooded into Seattle's CenturyLink Field*: Taylor Soper, "A Good

Day: Macklemore Performs for Amazon Employees After Company Crushes Earnings," *GeekWire*, July 24, 2015, https://www.geekwire.com/2015/a-good -day-macklemore-performs-for-amazon-employees-after-company-crushes -earnings/ (January 20, 2021).

109 *a 5,800-word gut punch of an article*: Jodi Kantor and David Streitfeld, "Inside Amazon: Wrestling Big Ideas in a Bruising Workplace," *New York Times*, August 15, 2015, https://www.nytimes.com/2015/08/16/technology/inside-amazon-wrest ling-big-ideas-in-a-bruising-workplace.html (January 20, 2021).

110 *"misrepresented Amazon"*: Jay Carney, "What the New York Times Didn't Tell You," *Medium*, October 19, 2015, https://medium.com/@jaycarney/what-the -new-york-times-didn-t-tell-you-a1128aa78931 (January 20, 2021).

110 *"doesn't describe the Amazon I know or the caring Amazonians I work with every day"*: John Cook, "Full Memo: Jeff Bezos Responds to Brutal NYT Story, Says It Doesn't Represent the Amazon He Leads," *GeekWire*, August 16, 2015, https://www .geekwire.com/2015/full-memo-jeff-bezos-responds-to-cutting-nyt-expose-says -tolerance-for-lack-of-empathy-needs-to-be-zero/ (January 20, 2021).

111 *"It seems to me you are all just a bunch of barnacles"*: Diego Piacentini in con-versation with the author, and Georges Guyon de Chemilly in conversation with the author.

113 *Amazon would soon become a mainstay of those lists*: Amazon Staff, "Amazon Ranks #2 on Forbes World's Best Employers List," Amazon, October 20, 2020, https://www.aboutamazon.com/news/workplace/amazon-ranks-2-on-forbes -worlds-best-employers-list (January 20, 2021).

114 *Amazon also instituted an internal appeal process*: Spencer Soper, "Am-azon Workers Facing Firing Can Appeal to a Jury of Their Co-Workers," *Bloomberg*, June 25, 2018, https://www.bloomberg.com/news/articles/2018-06 -25/amazon-workers-facing-firing-can-appeal-to-a-jury-of-their-co-workers ?sref=dJuchiL5 (January 20, 2021).

CHAPTER 5: DEMOCRACY DIES IN DARKNESS

117 *"I predicted Osama bin Laden . . . a good location in real estate"*: Glenn Kes-sler, "Trump's Claim That He 'Predicted Osama bin Laden,'" *Washington Post*, December 7, 2015, https://www.washingtonpost.com/news/fact-checker/wp /2015/12/07/trumps-claim-that-he-predicted-osama-bin-laden/ (January 20, 2021).

121 *"going to have such problems"*: Tim Stenovic, "Donald Trump Just Said If He's Elected President Amazon Will Have Problems," *Business Insider*, Feruary 26, 2016, https://www.businessinsider.com/donald-trump-says-amazon-will-have -such-problems-2016-2 (January 20, 2021).

121 *The* Post *would expand and fortify Bezos' reputation*: See Jill Abramson, *Mer-*

chants of Truth (New York: Simon & Schuster, 2019), for more on the challenges at the *Washington Post* before Jeff Bezos's purchase of the newspaper and the changes he made afterward.

121 *"focus the mind"*: Ibid., 256.

123 *Fred Hiatt, editor of the opinion page, offered to resign*: Matthew Cooper, "Fred Hiatt Offered to Quit Jeff Bezos's Washington Post," *Yahoo News*, November 5, 2013, https://news.yahoo.com/fred-hiatt-offered-quit-jeff-bezoss-washington -post-123233358--politics.html (January 20, 2021).

123 *"it's entirely legitimate for an owner to have an editorial page that reflects his world view"*: Craig Timberg and Paul Farhi, "Jeffrey P. Bezos Visits the Post to Meet with Editors and Others," *Washington Post*, September 3, 2013, https://www.washingtonpost.com/lifestyle/style/jeffrey-p-bezos-visits-the -post-to-meet-with-editors-and-others/2013/09/03/def95cd8-14df-11e3-b182 -1b3bb2eb474c_story.html (January 20, 2021).

123 *lamented the rise of so-called aggregators . . . like the* Huffington Post: Dan Kennedy, "The Bezos Effect: How Amazon's Founder Is Reinventing *The Washington Post*—and What Lessons It Might Hold for the Beleaguered Newspaper Business," Shorenstein Center on Media, Politics and Public Policy, June 8, 2016, https://shorensteincenter.org/bezos-effect-washington-post/ (January 20, 2021).

123 *"You have to accept it and move forward . . . institution like* The Washington Post": Abramson, *Merchants of Truth*, 262.

124 *"It's the most important newspaper . . . I'm eighty that I made that decision"*: Mathias Döpfner, "Jeff Bezos Reveals What It's Like to Build An Empire . . . ," *Business Insider*, April 28, 2018, https://www.businessinsider.com/jeff-bezos -interview-axel-springer-ceo-amazon-trump-blue-origin-family-regulation -washington-post-2018-4 (January 20, 2021).

125 *subscribers of other newspapers free online access*: Justin Ellis, "By Building Partnerships with Other Newspapers, the Washington Post Is Opening Up Revenue Opportunities," Nieman Lab, April 7, 2015, https://www.niemanlab.org /2015/04/congratulations-toledo-blade-reader-on-your-subscription-to-the -washington-post/ (January 20, 2021).

126 *"working on becoming the new paper of record"*: WashPostPR, "CBS: Jeff Bezos Talks Washington Post Growth (VIDEO)," *Washington Post*, November 24, 2015, https://www.washingtonpost.com/pr/wp/2015/11/24/cbs-jeff-bezos-talks -washington-post-growth-video/&freshcontent=1/?outputType=amp&arc404 =true (January 20, 2021).

126 *"Thank you for making* The Washington Post *America's New Publication of Record"*: Ken Doctor, "On the Washington Post and the 'Newspaper of Record' Epithet," *Politico*, December 3, 2015, https://www.politico.com/media /story/2015/12/on-the-washington-post-and-the-newspaper-of-record-epithet -004303/ (January 20, 2021); Frank Pallotta, "WaPo's 'New Publication of

Record' Claim Draws NYT Shots," CNN, November 25, 2015, https://money.cnn.com/2015/11/25/media/washington-post-new-york-times-paper-of-record/ (January 20, 2021).

127 *he froze the* Post's *pension plans*: Steven Mufson, "Washington Post Announces Cuts to Employees' Retirement Benefits," *Washington Post*, September 23, 2014, https://www.washingtonpost.com/business/economy/washington-post-announces-cuts-to-employees-retirement-benefits/2014/09/23/f485981a-436d-11e4-b437-1a7368204804_story.html (January 20, 2021).

129 *boasted that the newspaper had better engineers than many Silicon Valley startups*: Jeff Bezos interviewed by Marty Baron, "Jeff Bezos Explains Why He Bought the Washington Post," *Washington Post* video, 4:00, May 18, 2016, https://www.washingtonpost.com/video/postlive/jeff-bezos-explains-why-he-bought-the-washington-post/2016/05/18/e4bafdae-1d45-11e6-82c2-a7dcb313287d_video.html (January 20, 2021).

129 *"riveting"*: Benjamin Wofford, "Inside Jeff Bezos's DC Life," *Washingtonian*, April 22, 2018, https://www.washingtonian.com/2018/04/22/inside-jeff-bezos-dc-life/ (January 20, 2021).

129 *on a path to generating $100 million in annual revenue*: Gerry Smith, "Bezos's Washington Post Licenses Its Publishing Technology to BP," *Bloomberg*, September 25, 2019, https://www.bloomberg.com/news/articles/2019-09-25/bezos-s-washington-post-licenses-its-publishing-technology-to-bp (January 20, 2021).

130 *exceeding 1.5 million for the first time*: Joshua Benton, "The Wall Street Journal Joins the New York Times in the 2 Million Digital Subscriber Club," Nieman Lab, February 10, 2020, https://www.niemanlab.org/2020/02/the-wall-street-journal-joins-the-new-york-times-in-the-2-million-digital-subscriber-club/ (January 20, 2021).

131 *new $65 million Gulfstream G650ER private jet*: Marissa Perino, "The Most Outrageous Splurges of Tech Billionaires, from Richard Branson's Private Island to Jeff Bezos' $65 Million Private Jet," *Business Insider*, October 15, 2019, https://www.businessinsider.com/elon-musk-bill-gates-jeff-bezos-tech-billionaire-wildest-purchases-2019-10 (January 20, 2021), and Marc Stiles, "Costco Just Sold a $5.5M Boeing Field Hangar to Jeff Bezos," *Puget Sound Business Journal*, October 22, 2015, https://www.bizjournals.com/seattle/blog/techflash/2015/10/costco-just-sold-a-5-5boeing-field-hangar-to-jeff.html (January 20, 2021).

131 *met the recovering Rezaian and his family*: Rick Gladstone, "Jason Rezaian Travels to U.S. on Washington Post Owner's Plane," *New York Times*, January 22, 2016, https://www.nytimes.com/2016/01/23/world/middleeast/rezaian-family-departs-germany-us.html (January 20, 2021).

133 *$12 million renovating the 27,000-square-foot structure, with its eleven bedrooms and twenty-five bathrooms*: Wofford, "Inside Jeff Bezos's DC Life."

CHAPTER 6: BOMBING HOLLYWOOD

135 *Here was a substantial slice of Hollywood's A-list*: Pete Hammond, "Pete Hammond's Notes on the Season: AFI Narrows the Race; 'La La' Hits L.A.; Jeff Bezos Throws a Party 'By The Sea'; Tom Ford Chows Down," *Deadline*, December 8, 2016, https://deadline.com/2016/12/pete-hammonds-notes-on-the-season-afi -narrows-the-race-la-la-hits-l-a-jeff-bezos-throws-a-party-by-the-sea-tom-ford -chows-down-1201867352/ (January 20, 2021), and "Jeff Bezos and Matt Damon's 'Manchester by the Sea' Holiday Party,'" IMDb, www.imdb.com/gallery /rg2480708352/?ref_=rg_mv_sm (January 20, 2021).

136 *"Jeff is the opposite . . . very social guy"*: Rebecca Johnson, "MacKenzie Bezos: Writer, Mother of Four, and High-Profile Wife," *Vogue*, February 20, 2013, https://www .vogue.com/article/a-novel-perspective-mackenzie-bezos (January 20, 2021).

136 *"intent this weekend was clear . . . for both himself and his company"*: Peter Bart, "Peter Bart: Amazon's Jeff Bezos Taking Aim at Hollywood," *Deadline*, December 9, 2016, https://deadline.com/2016/12/jeff-bezos-hollywood-plan-amazon -manchester-by-the-sea-peter-bart-1201867514/ (January 20, 2021).

140 *Comcast did the deal with Netflix instead*: Mathew Ingram, "Here's Why Comcast Decided to Call a Truce with Netflix," *Fortune*, July 5, 2016, https://fortune.com /2016/07/05/comcast-truce-netflix/ (January 20, 2021).

140 *anticompetitive*: Cecilia Kang, "Netflix Opposes Comcast's Merger with Time Warner Cable, Calls It Anticompetitive," *Washington Post*, April 21, 2014, https://www.washingtonpost.com/news/the-switch/wp/2014/04/21/netflix -opposes-comcasts-merger-with-time-warner-cable-calls-it-anticompetitive / (January 20, 2021).

140 *later reached its own agreement with the cable company*: Sarah Perez, "Amazon Prime Video is coming to Comcast's cable boxes," *TechCrunch*, August 2, 2018, https://techcrunch.com/2018/08/02/amazon-prime-video-is-coming-to-com casts-cable-boxes/ February 23, 2021).

141 *Amazon invited anyone to submit screenplays*: Joel Keller, "Inside Amazon's Open-Source Original Content Strategy," *Fast Company*, March 8, 2013, https://www.fastcompany.com/1682510/inside-amazons-open-source-original -content-strategy (January 20, 2021).

143 Transparent *became the first streaming series to win a Golden Globe*: Jenelle Riley, "Amazon, 'Transparent' Make History at Golden Globes," *Variety*, January 11, 2015, https://variety.com/2015/tv/awards/amazon-transparent-make -history-at-golden-globes-1201400485/ (January 20, 2021).

145 *$250 million deal*: Eugene Kim, "Amazon's $250 Million Bet on Jeremy Clarkson's New Show Is Already Starting to Pay Off," *Business Insider*, November 21, 2016, https://www.businessinsider.com/amazon-250-million-bet-on-the-grand -tour-paying-off-2016-11 (January 20, 2021).

146 *Isa Dick Hackett*: Kim Masters, "Amazon TV Producer Goes Public with Harassment Claim Against Top Exec Roy Price (Exclusive)," *Hollywood Reporter*, October 12, 2017, https://www.hollywoodreporter.com/news/amazon -tv-producer-goes-public-harassment-claim-top-exec-roy-price-1048060 (January 20, 2021), and Stacy Perman, "Roy Price, Ousted from Amazon Over Sexual Harassment Claims, Is Ready to Talk," *Los Angeles Times*, November 23, 2020, https://www.latimes.com/entertainment-arts/business /story/2020-11-23/amazon-studios-roy-price-sexual-harassment-responds -me-too (January 20, 2021).

147 *$3.2 billion on Prime Video in 2016*: Michelle Castillo, "Netflix Plans to Spend $6 Billion on New Shows, Blowing Away All But One of Its Rivals," CNBC, October 17, 2016, https://www.cnbc.com/2016/10/17/netflixs-6-billion-content -budget-in-2017-makes-it-one-of-the-top-spenders.html (January 20, 2021).

147 *nearly $4.5 billion in 2017*: Nathan McAlone, "Amazon Will Spend About $4.5 Billion on Its Fight Against Netflix This Year, According to JP Morgan," *Business Insider*, April 7, 2017, https://www.businessinsider.com/amazon-video -budget-in-2017-45-billion-2017-4 (January 20, 2021).

147 *"When we win a Golden Globe, it helps us sell more shoes"*: Mark Bergen, "Amazon Prime Video Doesn't Compete with Netflix Because Viewers Will Just Pick Both," *Vox*, May 31, 2016, https://www.vox.com/2016/5/31/11826166/jeff-bezos -amazon-prime-video-netflix (January 21, 2021).

149 *a reported $250 million*: Lesley Goldberg, "'Lord of the Rings' Adds 20 to Sprawling Cast for Amazon Series," *Hollywood Reporter*, December 3, 2020, https://www.hollywoodreporter.com/live-feed/lord-of-the-rings-adds-20-to -sprawling-cast-for-amazon-series (January 21, 2021).

152 *withdrew from the project*: Brandon Carter, "Djokovic Cancels His Amazon Docuseries," *Baseline*, November 28, 2017, http://baseline.tennis.com/article /70627/novak-djokovic-calls-amazon-documentary (January 21, 2021).

154 *"bit of a gong show"*: Ben Fritz and Joe Flint, "Where Amazon Is Failing to Dominate: Hollywood," *Wall Street Journal*, October 6, 2017, https://www.wsj.com /articles/where-amazon-is-failing-to-dominate-hollywood-1507282205 (January 21, 2021).

154 *"they are in way in over their heads"*: Ibid.

155 *reversed its stance and published her full story:* Masters, "Amazon TV Producer Goes Public."

Chapter 7: The Selection Machine

163 *In 2015, Amazon's domestic retail sales*: Spencer Soper, "Amazon's Clever Machines Are Moving from the Warehouse to Headquarters," *Bloomberg*, June 13, 2018, https://www.bloomberg.com/news/articles/2018-06-13/amazon-s

-clever-machines-are-moving-from-the-warehouse-to-headquarters (January 22, 2021).

171 *In 2010, Peter Szulczewski . . . advertising startup called ContextLogic*: Vidhi Choudary, "Wish, Shopping App for Less Affluent Consumers, Files $1.1B IPO," *TheStreet*, December 7, 2020, https://www.thestreet.com/investing/wish -shopping-app-files-for-1point1-billion-ipo (January 25, 2021).

171 *renamed his company Wish.com . . . to recruit sellers and handle customer service*: Priya Anand, "Wish, the Online Dollar Store, Is Losing Momentum Before IPO," *Bloomberg*, December 15, 2020, https://www.bloomberg.com/news /articles/2020-12-15/wish-the-online-dollar-store-is-losing-momentum-before -ipo (January 25, 2020).

172 *In 2014, Wish raised $69 million from venture capitalists*: Greg Bensinger, "Shopping App Wish Lands $50 Million Financing Round," *Wall Street Journal*, June 27, 2014, https://www.wsj.com/articles/BL-DGB-36173 (January 25, 2021).

172 *They came away with the impression that the Amazon execs were skeptical*: See Priya Anand, "Wish, the Online Dollar Store, Is Losing Momentum Before IPO," *Bloomberg*, December 15, 2020, https://www.bloomberg.com/news /articles/2020-12-15/wish-the-online-dollar-store-is-losing-momentum-before -ipo (January 25, 2020)

172 *By then the Wish CEO . . . canceled and never went*: Author interview with Peter Szulczewski, June 26, 2019. Szulczewski told a very different version of this story to *Forbes* and subsequently to clarify the discrepancy. See Parmy Olson, *Forbes*, "Meet the Billionaire Who Defied Amazon and Built Wish, the World's Most-Downloaded E-Commerce App," March 13, 2019, https://www .forbes.com/sites/parmyolson/2019/03/13/meet-the-billionaire-who-defied -amazon-and-built-wish-the-worlds-most-downloaded-e-commerce-app /#ff927bd70f52 (January 25, 2021).

173 *then shipped them in containers that Amazon reserved at wholesale rates*: Ryan Petersen, "Introducing Ocean Freight by Amazon: Ecommerce Giant Has Registered to Provide Ocean Freight Services," Flexport.com, January 14, 2016, https://www.flexport.com/blog/amazon-ocean-freight-forwarder/ (January 25, 2021).

174 *"The risky downside . . . low-key approach in the import countries"*: See January 22, 2015, email sent by Sebastian Gunningham, released by House Judiciary Subcommittee on Antitrust as submitted testimony, August 6, 2020, https://judiciary.house.gov/uploadedfiles/00185707.pdf (January 25, 2021).

176 *In 2011, a software engineer . . . laptop batteries*: Nick Statt, "How Anker Is Beating Apple and Samsung at Their Own Accessory Game," *The Verge*, May 22, 2017, https://www.theverge.com/2017/5/22/15673712/anker-battery-charger -amazon-empire-steven-yang-interview (January 25, 2021).

176 *heavily subsidized shipping rates . . . within the United States itself*: Dave Bryant, "Why and How China Post and USPS Are Killing Your Private Labeling Business," *EcomCrew*, March 18, 2017, https://www.ecomcrew.com/why-china -post-and-usps-are-killing-your-private-labeling-business/ (January 25, 2021 via https://web.archive.org).

177 *faulty lithium-ion batteries . . . lawsuits against the company*: Alexandra Berzon, "How Amazon Dodges Responsibility for Unsafe Products: The Case of the Hoverboard," *Wall Street Journal*, December 5, 2019, https://www.wsj.com /articles/how-amazon-dodges-responsibility-for-unsafe-products-the-case-of -the-hoverboard-11575563270 (January 25, 2021).

177 *defective batteries . . . and more news coverage*: Alana Semuels, "When Your Amazon Purchase Explodes," *Atlantic*, April 30, 2019, https://www.theatlantic.com /technology/archive/2019/04/lithium-ion-batteries-amazon-are-exploding /587005/ (January 25, 2021).

180 *sandal maker Birkenstock . . . selling its products on the site*: Ari Levy, "Birkenstock Quits Amazon in US After Counterfeit Surge," CNBC, July 20, 2016, https://www.cnbc.com/2016/07/20/birkenstock-quits-amazon-in-us-after -counterfeit-surge.html (January 25, 2021).

181 *just as Amazon became one of the leading apparel retailers*: Pamela N. Danziger, "Amazon, Already the Nation's Top Fashion Retailer, Is Positioned to Grab Even More Market Share," *Forbes*, January 28, 2020, https://www.forbes.com /sites/pamdanziger/2020/01/28/amazon-is-readying-major-disruption-for-the -fashion-industry/?sh=7acace9267f3 (January 25, 2021).

181 *Amazon introduced an initiative called Brand Registry*: Jeffrey Dastin, "Amazon to Expand Counterfeit Removal Program in Overture to Sellers," Reuters, March 21, 2017, https://www.reuters.com/article/us-amazon-com-counterfeit -idUSKBN16S2EU (January 25, 2021).

181 *three hundred and fifty thousand brands would sign up*: John Herrman, "All Your Favorite Brands, from BSTOEM to ZGGCD," *New York Times*, February 11, 2020, https://www.nytimes.com/2020/02/11/style/amazon-trademark-copy right.html (January 25, 2021).

182 *"Third-party sellers are kicking our first-party butt"*: Jeff Bezos, "2018 Letter to Shareowners," AboutAmazon.com, April 11, 2019, https://www.aboutamazon .com/news/company-news/2018-letter-to-shareholders.

183 *In 2019, Amazon spent $500 million . . . 2.5 million accounts*: Charlie Wood, "The Trump Administration Blacklisted 5 Overseas Amazon Websites as 'Notorious Markets' and Amazon Says It's Political Bullying," *Business Insider*, April 30, 2020, https://www.businessinsider.com/us-blacklists-five-amazon-websites -as-notorious-markets-2020-4 (January 25, 2020).

183 *started testing a system aimed at verifying sellers one by one, via video-calls*: Sarah Perez, "To Fight Fraud, Amazon Now Screens Third-Party Sellers

Through Video Calls," *TechCrunch*, April 27, 2020, https://techcrunch.com/2020/04/27/to-fight-fraud-amazon-now-screens-third-party-sellers-through-video-calls/ (January 25, 2020).

183 *top ten thousand largest sellers on Amazon were based in China*: "Chinese Sellers Outnumber US Sellers on Amazon.com," Marketplace Pulse, January 23, 2020, https://www.marketplacepulse.com/articles/chinese-sellers-outnumber-us-sellers-on-amazoncom (January 25, 2021).

183 *the Office of the U.S. Trade Representative . . . administration of Donald Trump*: Jenny Leonard, "Amazon's Foreign Domains Cited by U.S. as Helping Counterfeiters," *Bloomberg*, April 29, 2020, https://www.bloomberg.com/news/articles/2020-04-29/ustr-lists-amazon-s-foreign-domains-in-counterfeiting-report (January 25, 2021).

CHAPTER 8: AMAZON'S FUTURE IS CRaP

184 *the result of osteoarthritis*: Brad Stone, "Whole Foods, Half Off," *Bloomberg*, January 29, 2015, https://www.bloomberg.com/news/articles/2015-01-29/in-shift-whole-foods-to-compete-with-price-cuts-loyalty-app (January 24, 2021).

185 *adopting an alias*: David Kesmodel and John R. Wilke, "Whole Foods Is Hot, Wild Oats a Dud—So Said 'Rahodeb,'" *Wall Street Journal*, July 12, 2007, https://www.nytimes.com/2007/07/12/business/12foods.html (January 24, 2021).

185 *"grounded in an ethical system"*: John Mackey, *Conscious Capitalism* (Boston: Harvard Business Review Press, 2013), 22.

186 *replace longtime board members*: Heather Haddon and David Benoit, "Whole Foods Faces Specter of Long Investor Fight," *Wall Street Journal*, May 12, 2017, https://www.wsj.com/articles/whole-foods-faces-specter-of-long-investor-fight-1494581401 (January 24, 2021).

187 *Amazon executives had recently discussed*: Spencer Soper and Craig Giammona, "Amazon Said to Mull Whole Foods Bid Before Jana Stepped In," *Bloomberg*, April 11, 2017, https://www.bloomberg.com/news/articles/2017-04-11/amazon-said-to-mull-bid-for-whole-foods-before-jana-stepped-in (January 24, 2021).

191 *green Fresh vans for the last-mile delivery:* Greg Bensinger and Laura Stevens, "Amazon, in Threat to UPS, Tries Its Own Deliveries," *Wall Street Journal*, April 24, 2014, https://www.wsj.com/articles/amazon-tests-its-own-delivery-network-1398360018 (January 24, 2021).

192 *Google Shopping Express*: Mark Rogowsky, "Full-Court Express: Google Expands Its Delivery Service, Puts Heat on Amazon," *Forbes*, October 14, 2014, https://www.forbes.com/sites/markrogowsky/2014/10/14/faster-google-expands-its-same-day-delivery-service-into-new-markets-presses-amazon/?sh=1b199d1a5e34 (January 24, 2021).

193 *"Many people think . . . on Amazon"*: "Google: Amazon Is Biggest Search Rival," BBC, October 14, 2014, https://www.bbc.com/news/technology-29609472 (January 24, 2021).

199 *above 40 percent in European countries*: "Private Label Today: Private Label Popular Across Europe," *PLMA International*, 2020, https://www.plmainternational .com/industry-news/private-label-today (January 24, 2021).

200 *With an assortment . . . bizarre names*: Greg Bensinger, "Amazon to Expand Private-Label Offerings—from Food to Diapers," *Wall Street Journal*, May 15, 2016, https://www.wsj.com/articles/amazon-to-expand-private-label-offeringsfrom -food-to-diapers-1463346316 (January 24, 2021).

201 *Amazon's Vine program*: Julie Creswell, "How Amazon Steers Shoppers to Its Own Products," *Wall Street Journal*, June 23, 2018, https://www.nytimes.com /2018/06/23/business/amazon-the-brand-buster.html (January 24, 2021).

203 *"going over the fence"*: Dana Mattioli, "Amazon Scooped Up Data from Its Own Sellers to Launch Competing Products," *Wall Street Journal*, April 23, 2020, https://www.wsj.com/articles/amazon-scooped-up-data-from-its-own-sellers -to-launch-competing-products-11587650015 (January 24, 2021).

206 *"quickly reaching the status . . . Amazon history"*: Todd Bishop, "Amazon's Treasure Truck Launch Message Was a Screw-Up—Another Misstep in Bungled Rollout," *GeekWire*, https://www.geekwire.com/2015/amazon-announces-treasure -trucks-launch-two-months-after-mysterious-delay/ (January 24, 2021).

206 *Treasure Truck burst into flames*: "Amazon Treasure Truck Bursts into Flames in West Philadelphia Parking Lot," CBS Philly, May 3, 2018, https://philadelphia .cbslocal.com/2018/05/03/west-philadelphia-parking-lot-fire-amazon-treasure -truck/amp/ (January 24, 2021).

206 *"would be hard and expensive"*: Roberto A. Ferdman, "I Tried to Figure Out How Many Cows Are in a Single Hamburger. It Was Really Hard," *Washington Post*, August 5, 2015, https://www.washingtonpost.com/news/wonk/wp/2015/08/05 /there-are-a-lot-more-cows-in-a-single-hamburger-than-you-realize/ (January 24, 2021).

206 *sampling an iguana*: Kurt Schlosser, "Hungry for Further Exploration, Jeff Bezos Eats Iguana and Discusses How to Pay for Space Travel," *GeekWire*, March 12, 2018, https://www.geekwire.com/2018/hungry-exploration-jeff-bezos-eats -iguana-discusses-pay-space-travel/ (January 24, 2021).

208 *thirty-three U.S. cities*: Stefany Zaroban and Allison Enright, "A Look Inside Amazon's Massive and Growing Fulfillment Network," *Digital Commerce 360*, August 2, 2017, https://www.digitalcommerce360.com/2017/08/02/amazon-jobs -day-a-look-inside-amazons-massive-and-growing-fulfillment-network/ (January 24, 2021).

209 *"like falling in love . . . meeting was over"*: Ronald Orol, "Whole Foods CEO John Mackey: Meeting Amazon Was Like 'Falling in Love,'" *The Street*, March 5, 2018,

https://www.thestreet.com/investing/stocks/whole-food-ceo-john-mackey-says -meeting-amazon-was-like-falling-in-love-14509074 (January 24, 2021).

210 *"there's the argument that Amazon acquired Whole Foods for free"*: Sinead Carew and David Randall, "Whole Foods Shares Keep Rising in Bidding War Specu- lation," Reuters, June 19, 2017, https://www.reuters.com/article/us-usa-stocks -wholefoods-idUSKBN19A22J (January 24, 2021).

211 *stricter financial terms*: Abha Bhattarchai, "Whole Foods Places New Limits on Suppliers, Upsetting Some Small Vendors," *Washington Post*, January 5, 2018, https://www.washingtonpost.com/business/economy/whole-foods-places-new -limits-on-suppliers-upsetting-some-small-vendors/2018/01/05/7f58b466 -f0a1-11e7-b390-a36dc3fa2842_story.html (January 24, 2021).

211 *eccentric CEOs*: Dana Mattioli, "Amazon's Deal Making Threatened by D.C. Scru- tiny," *Wall Street Journal*, July 3, 2019, https://www.wsj.com/articles/amazons -deal-making-threatened-by-d-c-scrutiny-11562146205 (January 24, 2021).

211 *gave Steve Kessel authority*: Laura Stevens, "Amazon Puts Whole Foods, De- livery Units Under Bezos Lieutenant," *Wall Street Journal*, November 9, 2017, https://www.wsj.com/articles/amazon-puts-whole-foods-rapid-delivery -businesses-under-veteran-executive-1510236001 (January 24, 2021).

CHAPTER 9: THE LAST MILE

213 *Amazon ran around forty fulfillment centers*: "How Amazon's Largest Distribu- tion Center Works," YouTube video, posted by Bloomberg Quicktake, November 26, 2012. https://www.youtube.com/watch?v=bfFsqbIn_3E (January 23, 2021).

214 *"Senator, you have been misinformed"*: Dave Clark, Tweet, posted on Septem- ber 6, 2019, https://twitter.com/davehclark/status/1169986311635079168 (Jan- uary 23, 2021).

220 *The paper reported that the company's warehouse*: Spencer Soper, "Inside Am- azon's Warehouse," *Morning Call*, September 18, 2011, https://www.mcall.com /news/watchdog/mc-allentown-amazon-complaints-20110917-story.html (Jan- uary 23, 2021).

223 *"I only know one way to play poker"*: Spencer Soper, "The Man Who Built Amazon's Delivery Machine," *Bloomberg*, December 17, 2019, https://www .bloomberg.com/news/articles/2019-12-17/amazon-holiday-shopping-the-man -who-makes-it-happen (January 23, 2021).

224 *find a robot that could do a better job*: Chris Welch, "Amazon's Robot Compe- tition Shows Why Human Warehouse Jobs Are Safe for Now," *The Verge*, June 1, 2015, https://www.theverge.com/2015/6/1/8698607/amazon-robot-picking -challenge-results (January 23, 2021).

224 *50 percent more products per square foot*: "Meet Amazon's New Robot Army Shipping Out Your Products," *Bloomberg Technology* video, 2:10, December 1,

2014, https://www.bloomberg.com/news/videos/2014-12-01/meet-amazons-new-robot-army-shipping-out-your-products (January 23, 2021).

224 *employees standing in place and monotonously*: Will Evans, "How Amazon Hid Its Safety Crisis," *Reveal*, September 29, 2020, https://revealnews.org/article/how-amazon-hid-its-safety-crisis/, and United States Department of Labor, "Amazon Fulfillment Center Receives $7k Fine," January 12, 2016, https://www.osha.gov/news/newsreleases/region3/01122016 (January 23, 2021).

225 *casually recalling his old nickname*: Spencer Soper, "The Man Who Built Amazon's Delivery Machine," *Bloomberg*, December 17, 2019, https://www.bloomberg.com/news/articles/2019-12-17/amazon-holiday-shopping-the-man-who-makes-it-happen (January 23, 2021).

226 *choked on the onslaught*: Devin Leonard, "Will Amazon Kill FedEx?" *Bloomberg*, August 31, 2016, https://www.bloomberg.com/features/2016-amazon-delivery/ (January 23, 2021).

226 *Amazon compensate disappointed customers*: Amrita Jayakumar, "Amazon, UPS Offer Refunds for Christmas Delivery Problems," *Washington Post*, December 26, 2013, https://www.washingtonpost.com/business/economy/amazon-ups-offer-refunds-for-christmas-delivery-problems/2013/12/26/c9570254-6e44-11e3-a523-fe73f0ff6b8d_story.html (January 23, 2021).

227 *had found an ingenious solution*: Cecelia Kang, "Amazon to Deliver on Sundays Using Postal Service Fleet," *Washington Post*, November 13, 2013, https://www.washingtonpost.com/business/technology/amazon-to-deliver-on-sundays-using-postal-service-fleet/2013/11/10/e3f5b770-48c1-11e3-a196-3544a03c2351_story.html (January 23, 2021).

228 *Economists called this kind of arrangement*: David Weil, *The Fissured Workplace* (Harvard University Press, 2014). Weil further elucidates these ideas in "Income Inequality, Wage Determination and the Fissured Workplace," in *After Picketty* (Harvard University Press, 2017), 209.

229 *purchased thousands of truck trailers*: Jason Del Rey, "Amazon Buys Thousands of Its Own Truck Trailers as Its Transportation Ambitions Grow," *Vox*, December 4, 2015, https://www.vox.com/2015/12/4/11621148/amazon-buys-thousands-of-its-own-trucks-as-its-transportation (January 24, 2021).

232 *Amazon sued Arthur Valdez*: Ángel González, "Amazon Sues Target-Bound Former Logistics Executive Over 'Confidential' Info," *Seattle Times*, March 22, 2016, https://www.seattletimes.com/business/amazon/amazon-sues-target-bound-former-logistics-executive/ (January 24, 2021).

233 *They used an old internal Microsoft term*: Raymond Chen, "Microspeak: Cookie Licking," Microsoft blog post, December 1, 2009, https://devblogs.microsoft.com/oldnewthing/20091201-00/?p=15843 (January 24, 2021).

235 *On an earnings call with investors*: Mary Schlangenstein, "FedEx CEO Calls Amazon Challenge Reports 'Fantastical,'" *Bloomberg News*, March 17, 2016,

https://www.ttnews.com/articles/fedex-ceo-calls-amazon-challenge-reports -fantastical (January 24, 2021).

235 *Publicly, Clark answered questions*: Alan Boyle, "First Amazon Prime Airplane Debuts in Seattle After Secret Night Flight," *GeekWire*, August 4, 2016, https://www.geekwire.com/2016/amazon-prime-airplane-seafair/ (January 24, 2021).

235 *The Prime Air fleet allowed Amazon*: Jeffrey Dastin, "Amazon Starts Flexing Muscle in New Space: Air Cargo," Reuters, December 23, 2016, https://www.reuters .com/article/us-amazon-com-shipping-insight/amazon-starts-flexing-muscle -in-new-space-air-cargo-idUSKBN14C1K4 (January 24, 2021).

235 *In February 2017, Amazon announced*: Randy Woods, "Amazon to Move Prime Air Cargo Hub to Cincinnati," *Air Cargo World*, February 1, 2017, https://aircargoworld.com/news/airports/amazon-to-move-prime-air-cargo -hub-to-cincinnati/ (January 24, 2021).

235 *Amazon's new air hub*: Jason Del Re, "Amazon Is Building a $1.5 Billion Hub for Its Own Cargo Airline," *Vox*, January 31, 2017, https://www.vox.com/2017/1 /31/14462256/amazon-air-cargo-hub-kentucky-airport-prime-air (January 24, 2021).

236 *belabored public process*: Spencer Soper, "Behind Amazon's HQ2 Fiasco: Jeff Bezos Was Jealous of Elon Musk," *Bloomberg*, February 3, 2020, https://www .bloomberg.com/news/articles/2020-02-03/amazon-s-hq2-fiasco-was-driven -by-bezos-envy-of-elon-musk (January 24, 2021).

237 *Gray was charged with reckless*: Christian Farr, "Former Amazon Driver Acquitted in Death of 84-Year-Old Woman," NBC5, August 1, 2019, https://www .nbcchicago.com/news/local/former-amazon-driver-acquitted-in-death-of-84 -year-old-pedestrian/127151/ (January 24, 2021).

237 *A week before, Amazon had emailed*: Caroline O'Donovan and Ken Bensinger, "Amazon's Next-Day Delivery Has Brought Chaos and Carnage to America's Streets—But the World's Biggest Retailer Has a System to Escape the Blame," *BuzzFeed*, August 31, 2019, https://www.buzzfeednews.com/article /carolineodonovan/amazon-next-day-delivery-deaths (January 24, 2021).

237 *The publications revealed*: Patricia Callahan, Caroline O'Donovan, and Ken Bensinger, "Amazon Cuts Contracts with Delivery Companies Linked to Deaths," *ProPublica/BuzzFeed News*, October 11, 2019, https://www.propublica.org /article/amazon-cuts-contracts-with-delivery-companies-linked-to-deaths (January 24, 2021).

237 *In 2018, a sixty-one-year-old legal secretary*: Patricia Callahan, "His Mother Was Killed by a Van Making Amazon Deliveries. Here's the Letter He Wrote to Jeff Bezos," *ProPublica*, October 11, 2019, https://www.propublica.org/article/his -mother-was-killed-by-a-van-making-amazon-deliveries-heres-the-letter-he -wrote-to-jeff-bezos (January 24. 2021).

238 *Uber-like delivery service called Amazon Flex*: Jacob Demmitt, "Confirmed: Amazon Flex Officially Launches, and It's Like Uber for Package Delivery," *GeekWire*, September 29, 2015, https://www.geekwire.com/2015/confirmed -amazon-flex-officially-launches-and-its-like-uber-for-package-delivery/ (January 24, 2021).

240 *talked to thirteen pilots who worked for Amazon's airlines*: Rachel Premack, "The Family of a Pilot Who Died in This Year's Amazon Air Fatal Crash Is Suing Amazon and Cargo Contractors Claiming Poor Safety Standards," *Business Insider*, September 19, 2019, https://www.businessinsider.com/amazon-atlas-air-fatal -crash-pilots-sue-2019-9 (January 24, 2021).

241 *Sprinter vans from Mercedes-Benz*: Gabrielle Coppola, "Amazon Orders 20,000 Mercedes Vans to Bolster Delivery Program," *Bloomberg*, September 5, 2018, https://www.bloomberg.com/news/articles/2018-09-05/amazon-orders-20 -000-mercedes-vans-to-bolster-delivery-program (January 24, 2021).

241 *And in early 2019, Amazon eclipsed*: Erica Pandey, "Amazon, the New King of Shipping," *Axios*, June 27, 2019, https://www.axios.com/amazon-shipping-chart -fedex-ups-usps-0dc6bab1-2169-42a8-9e56-0e85c590eb89.html (January 24, 2021).

242 *When Donald Trump accused Amazon:* Jim Tankersley, "Trump Said Amazon Was Scamming the Post Office. His Administration Disagrees," *New York Times*, December 4, 2018, https://www.nytimes.com/2018/12/04/us/politics/trump -amazon-post-office.html (January 24, 2021).

242 *UPS had to renegotiate its contract*: Paul Ziobro, "UPS to Start 7-Day Delivery to Juggle Demands of Online Shopping," *Wall Street Journal*, July 23, 2019, https://www.wsj.com/articles/ups-to-start-7-day-delivery-to-juggle-demands -of-online-shopping-11563918759 (January 24, 2021), and Paul Ziobro, "UPS and Teamsters Discuss Two-Tier Wages, Sunday Deliveries," *Wall Street Journal*, May 9, 2018, https://www.wsj.com/articles/ups-and-teamsters-discuss-two-tier -wages-sunday-deliveries-1525860000?mod=article_inline (January 24, 2021).

242 *The cold war between Dave Clark and Fred Smith*: Thomas Black, "FedEx Ends Ground-Delivery Deal with Amazon," *Bloomberg*, August 7, 2019, https://www.bloomberg.com/news/articles/2019-08-07/fedex-deepens -pullback-from-amazon-as-ground-delivery-deal-ends?sref=dJuchiL5 (January 24, 2021).

242 *Smith doubled down*: Paul Ziobro, "Fred Smith Created FedEx. Now He Has to Reinvent It," *Wall Street Journal*, October 17, 2019, https://www.wsj.com/articles /fred-smith-created-fedex-now-he-has-to-reinvent-it-11571324050 (January 24, 2021).

242 *Clark temporarily banned third-party merchants*: Spencer Soper and Thomas Black, "Amazon Cuts Off FedEx Ground for Prime Holiday Shipments," *Bloomberg*, December 16, 2019, https://www.bloomberg.com/news/articles

/2019-12-16/amazon-cuts-off-fedex-ground-for-prime-shipments-this-holiday ?sref=dJuchiL5 (January 24, 2021).

242 *In April 2019, Amazon shifted*: Spencer Soper, "Amazon Will Spend $800 Million to Move to One-Day Delivery," *Bloomberg*, April 25, 2019, https://www .bloomberg.com/news/articles/2019-04-25/amazon-will-spend-800-million-to -move-to-one-day-delivery (January 24, 2021).

242 *Amazon was also able to retire:* Amazon staff, "Ultrafast Grocery Delivery Is Now FREE with Prime," Amazon blog, October 29, 2019, https://www.aboutamazon .com/news/retail/ultrafast-grocery-delivery-is-now-free-with-prime (January 24, 2021).

CHAPTER 10: THE GOLD MINE IN THE BACKYARD

244 *That May, he was trailed by paparazzi*: Chris Spargo, "No Delivery Drones Needed: Amazon Founder Jeff Bezos Flashes His $81bn Smile While Canoodling with His Wife During Some Real-World Shopping at Historic Italian Market," *Daily Mail*, May 11, 2017, https://www.dailymail.co.uk/news/article-4497398 /Amazon-founder-Jeff-Bezos-vacations-Italy.html (January 24, 2021).

244 *tweeting "a request for ideas"*: Nick Wingfield, "Jeff Bezos Wants Ideas for Philanthropy, So He Asked Twitter," *New York Times*, June 15, 2017, https://www .nytimes.com/2017/06/15/technology/jeff-bezos-amazon-twitter-charity.html (January 24, 2021).

244 *In July, he was photographed*: Ian Servantes, "Amazon CEO Jeff Bezos Is Now Buff; Internet Freaks Out," *Men's Health*, July 17, 2017, https://www.menshealth .com/trending-news/a19525957/amazon-jeff-bezos-buff-memes/ (January 24, 2021).

250 *He talked about two hypothetical*: Michael Learmonth, "Advertising Becomes Amazon's Newest Low-Price Weapon," *Ad Age*, October 8, 2012, https://adage .com/article/digital/advertising-amazon-s-newest-low-price-weapon/237630 (January 24, 2012).

252 *No, advertisers couldn't make*: Steve Susi, *Brand Currency: A Former Amazon Exec on Money, Information, Loyalty, and Time* (Lioncrest Publishing, 2019), and interview with the author.

258 *Its meaning was ambiguous:* David Carnoy, "How Is 'Amazon's Choice' Chosen? Amazon Won't Say," *CNET*, March 21, 2018, https://www.cnet.com/news/do -humans-choose-what-products-get-amazons-choice/ (January 24, 2021).

258 *Customers nevertheless flocked*: Monica Nickelsburg, "US Lawmakers Raise Questions About 'Misleading' Amazon's Choice Recommendations," *Geek-Wire*, August 12, 2019, https://www.geekwire.com/2019/us-lawmakers-raise -questions-misleading-amazons-choice-recommendations/ (January 24, 2021).

258 *A* Wall Street Journal *story in 2019 about Amazon's Choice*: Shane Shifflett,

Alexandra Berzon, and Dana Mattioli, "'Amazon's Choice' Isn't the Endorsement It Appears," *Wall Street Journal,* December 22, 2019, https://www.wsj.com/articles/amazons-choice-isnt-the-endorsement-it-appears-11577035151 (January 24, 2021).

259 *In some product categories, only two:* Juozas Kaziukėnas, "Amazon Demotes Organic Results in Search," Marketplace Pulse, October 30, 2019, https://www.marketplacepulse.com/articles/amazon-search-demotes-organic-results (January 24, 2021).

259 *A bipartisan report by the U.S. House*: "Investigation of Competition in Digital Markets: Majority Staff Reports and Recommendations," 2020, https://judiciary.house.gov/uploadedfiles/competition_in_digital_markets.pdf (January 24, 2021).

260 *Amazon did something rare in its history*: Andy Malt, "Amazon Tickets to Close," Amazon blog, February 22, 2018, https://completemusicupdate.com/article/amazon-tickets-to-close/ (January 25, 2021).

260 *It also cut the investment in its beleaguered*: "Amazon Is Preparing to Close a Chinese E-Commerce Store," *Bloomberg,* April 17, 2019, https://www.bloomberg.com/news/articles/2019-04-17/amazon-is-said-to-prepare-closing-of-chinese-e-commerce-store?sref=dJuchiL5 (January 25, 2021).

260 *The company slowed down the introduction*: Mike Rosenberg and Angel González, "Thanks to Amazon, Seattle Is Now America's Biggest Company Town," *Seattle Times,* August 23, 2017, https://www.seattletimes.com/business/amazon/thanks-to-amazon-seattle-is-now-americas-biggest-company-town/ (January 25, 2021).

260 *Retail executives were ordered*: Laura Stevens, Sharon Terlep, and Annie Gasparro, "Amazon Targets Unprofitable Items, with a Sharper Focus on the Bottom Line," *Wall Street Journal,* December 16, 2018, https://www.wsj.com/articles/amazon-targets-unprofitable-items-with-a-sharper-focus-on-the-bottom-line-11544965201 (January 25, 2021).

260 *The ongoing "hands off the wheel initiative"*: Spencer Soper, "Amazon's Clever Machines Are Moving from the Warehouse to Headquarters," *Bloomberg,* June 13, 2018, https://www.bloomberg.com/news/articles/2018-06-13/amazon-s-clever-machines-are-moving-from-the-warehouse-to-headquarters?sref=dJuchiL5 (January 25, 2021).

261 *"He's doing that all the time, of course"*: Staci D. Kramer, "The Biggest Thing Amazon Got Right: The Platform," *Gigaom,* October 12, 2011, https://gigaom.com/2011/10/12/419-the-biggest-thing-amazon-got-right-the-platform/ (January 25, 2021).

262 *At the same time as he issued the directive*: Bain & Company, "Founder's Mentality,SM and the Paths to Sustainable Growth," YouTube, September 10, 2014, https://www.youtube.com/watch?v=Rp4RCIfX66I (January 25, 2021).

263 *And in the fall of 2017, Jeff Bezos finally*: Tom Metcalf, "Jeff Bezos Passes Bill Gates to Become the World's Richest Person," *Bloomberg*, October 27, 2017, https://www.bloomberg.com/news/articles/2017-10-27/bezos-seizes-title-of-world-s-richest-person-after-amazon-soars (January 25, 2021).

CHAPTER 11: *GRADATIM FEROCITER*

Two books were valuable resources for this chapter: Christian Davenport, *The Space Barons: Elon Musk, Jeff Bezos, and the Quest to Colonize the Cosmos* (New York: PublicAffairs, 2018), and Tim Fernholz, *Rocket Billionaires: Elon Musk, Jeff Bezos, and the New Space Race* (New York: Houghton Mifflin Harcourt, 2018).

265 *the firm landed a Falcon 9 booster*: Loren Grush, "SpaceX Successfully Lands Its Rocket on a Floating Drone Ship for the First Time," *The Verge*, April 8, 2016, https://www.theverge.com/2016/4/8/11392138/spacex-landing-success-falcon -9-rocket-barge-at-sea (January 24, 2021).

267 *"a club more than a company"*: Steven Levy, "Jeff Bezos Wants Us All to Leave Earth—for Good," *Wired*, October 15, 2018, https://www.wired.com/story/jeff -bezos-blue-origin/ (January 24, 2021).

270 *Residents of the town of Van Horn*: Clare O'Connor, "Jeff Bezos' Spacecraft Blows Up in Secret Test Flight; Locals Describe 'Challenger-Like' Explosion," *Forbes*, September 2, 2011, https://www.forbes.com/sites/clareoconnor/2011/09/02 /jeff-bezos-spacecraft-blows-up-in-secret-test-flight-locals-describe-challenger -like-explosion/?sh=6cde347836c2 (January 24, 2021).

270 *"Not the outcome any of us wanted"*: Jeff Bezos, "Successful Short Hop, Setback, and Next Vehicle," Blue Origin, September 2, 2011, https://www.blueorigin.com /news/successful-short-hop-setback-and-next-vehicle (January 24, 2021).

271 *SpaceX won the contract*: Jeff Fouse, "NASA Selects Boeing and SpaceX for Commercial Crew Contracts," *SpaceNews*, September 16, 2014, https://spacenews .com/41891nasa-selects-boeing-and-spacex-for-commercial-crew-contracts/ (January 24, 2021).

271 *$7.7 billion for the project*: Nasa Office of Inspector General, "Audit of Commercial Resupply Services to the International Space Station," Report No. IG-18-016, April 26, 2018, pg. 4, https://oig.nasa.gov/docs/IG-18-016.pdf (January 24, 2021).

271 *sending unmanned spacecraft*: Jonathan Amos, "SpaceX Lifts Off with ISS cargo," BBC, October 8, 2012, https://www.bbc.com/news/science-environment -19867358 (January 24, 2021).

271 *"multi-planetary species"*: Elon Musk, "Making Humans a Multi-Planetary Species," Mary Ann Liebert, Inc, *New Space* 5 no. 2 (2017): 46, https://www .liebertpub.com/doi/10.1089/space.2017.29009.emu (January 24, 2021).

271 *"We go to space to save the Earth"*: Jeff Bezos, Tweet, February 3, 2018, 9:30 a.m.,

https://twitter.com/jeffbezos/status/959796196247142400?lang=en (January 24, 2021).

272 *Blue Origin protested SpaceX's plan*: Alan Boyle, "Bezos' Blue Origin Space Venture Loses Protest over NASA's Launch Pad," NBC News, December 12, 2013, https://www.nbcnews.com/science/bezos-blue-origin-rocket-venture-fails-stop-nasas-launch-pad-2D11736708 (January 24, 2021).

272 *"We are more likely to discover unicorns"*: Dan Leone, "Musk Calls Out Blue Origin, ULA for 'Phony Blocking Tactic' on Shuttle Pad Lease," *SpaceNews*, September 25, 2013, https://spacenews.com/37389musk-calls-out-blue-origin-ula-for-phony-blocking-tactic-on-shuttle-pad/ (January 24, 2021).

272 *SpaceX challenged the patent*: Todd Bishop, "Jeff Bezos' Blue Origin Dealt Setback in Patent Dispute with SpaceX over Rocket Landings," *GeekWire*, March 5, 2015, https://www.geekwire.com/2015/jeff-bezos-blue-origin-dealt-setback-in-patent-dispute-with-spacex-over-rocket-landings/ (January 24, 2021); Todd Bishop, "Blue Origin's Rocket-Landing Patent Canceled in Victory for SpaceX," *GeekWire*, September 1, 2015, https://www.geekwire.com/2015/blue-origins-rocket-landing-patent-canceled-in-victory-for-spacex/ (January 24, 2021).

272 *the United Launch Alliance (ULA)*: Armin Rosen, "Elon Musk's Aerospace Argument Just Took a Hit," *Business Insider*, June 17, 2014, https://www.businessinsider.com/ula-wont-buy-rocket-engines-from-russia-anymore-2014-6 (January 24, 2021).

274 *landed its own reusable booster*: Loren Grush, "Spacex Successfully Landed Its Falcon 9 Rocket After Launching It to Space," *The Verge*, December 21, 2015, https://www.theverge.com/2015/12/21/10640306/spacex-elon-musk-rocket-landing-success (January 24, 2021).

274 *Bezos tweeted*: Jeff Bezos, Tweet, December 21, 2015, 8:49 p.m., https://twitter.com/jeffbezos/status/679116636310360067?lang=en (January 24, 2021).

274 *300,000-square-foot former factory*: Eric Berger, "Behind the Curtain: Ars Goes Inside Blue Origin's Secretive Rocket Factory," *Ars Technica*, March 9, 2016, https://arstechnica.com/science/2016/03/behind-the-curtain-ars-goes-inside-blue-origins-secretive-rocket-factory/ (January 24, 2021).

275 *their helicopter crashed into a shallow creek*: Christian Davenport, *The Space Barons: Elon Musk, Jeff Bezos, and the Quest to Colonize the Cosmos* (New York: PublicAffairs, 2018), 11–13

275 *"avoid helicopters whenever possible"*: Alan Deutschman, "Inside the Mind of Jeff Bezos," *Fast Company*, August 1, 2004, https://www.fastcompany.com/50541/inside-mind-jeff-bezos-4 (January 24, 2021).

275 *names of famous explorers*: Mylene Mangalindan, "Buzz in West Texas Is About Jeff Bezos and His Launch Site," *Wall Street Journal*, November 10, 2006, https://www.wsj.com/articles/SB116312683235519444 (January 24, 2021).

278 *selling $1 billion a year of Amazon stock*: Spencer Soper, "Bezos Sells $1 Billion a

Year in Amazon Stock for Space Project," *Bloomberg*, April 5, 2017, https://www
.bloomberg.com/news/articles/2017-04-05/bezos-hopes-big-windows-will-give
-space-tourism-a-boost (January 24, 2021).

278 *unveiled New Glenn*: Chris Bergin and William Graham, "Blue Origin Introduce the New Glenn Orbital LV," NASASpaceFlight.com, September 12, 2016,
https://www.nasaspaceflight.com/2016/09/blue-origin-new-glenn-orbital-lv/
(January 24, 2021).

279 *Blue ended up winning*: Sandra Erwin, "Air Force Awards Launch Vehicle Development Contracts to Blue Origin, Northrop Grumman, ULA," *SpaceNews*, October
10, 2018, https://spacenews.com/air-force-awards-launch-vehicle-development
-contracts-to-blue-origin-northrop-grumman-ula/ (January 24, 2021).

279 *"It is time for America to return to the Moon"*: Christian Davenport, "An Exclusive Look at Jeff Bezos' Plan to Set Up Amazon-Like Delivery for 'Future
Human Settlement' of the Moon," *Washington Post*, March 2, 2017, https://www
.washingtonpost.com/news/the-switch/wp/2017/03/02/an-exclusive-look-at
-jeff-bezos-plan-to-set-up-amazon-like-delivery-for-future-human-settlement
-of-the-moon/ (January 24, 2021).

281 *"I get increasing conviction . . . civilization of stasis"*: Mathias Döpfner, "Jeff
Bezos Reveals What It's Like to Build An Empire . . . ," *Business Insider*, April 28,
2018, https://www.businessinsider.com/jeff-bezos-interview-axel-springer-ceo
-amazon-trump-blue-origin-family-regulation-washington-post-2018-4 (January 20, 2021).

282 *"They're two years . . . every year"*: Michael Sheetz, "SpaceX President Knocks
Bezos' Blue Origin: 'They Have a Billion Dollars of Free Money Every Year,'"
CNBC, October 25, 2019, https://www.cnbc.com/2019/10/25/spacex-shotwell
-calls-out-blue-origin-boeing-lockheed-martin-oneweb.html (January 24, 2021).

CHAPTER 12: LICENSE TO OPERATE

287 *Millions of people around the world owned an Amazon Echo*: Sarah Perez, "39
Million Americans Now Own a Smart Speaker, Report Claims," *TechCrunch*,
January 12, 2018, https://techcrunch.com/2018/01/12/39-million-americans
-now-own-a-smart-speaker-report-claims/ (January 26, 2021).

288 *eight-year-long journey*: Eric Pryne, "Amazon to Make Giant Move to South
Lake Union," *Seattle Times*, December 22, 2007, https://www.seattletimes.com
/business/amazon-to-make-giant-move-to-south-lake-union/ (January 25, 2021).

289 *forty-five thousand Amazon employees*: Matt Day, "Humans of Amazon: Meet
Some of the People Behind Seattle's Tech Juggernaut," *Seattle Times*, March
8, 2018, https://www.seattletimes.com/business/amazon/humans-of-amazon
-meet-some-of-the-people-behind-seattles-tech-juggernaut/ (January 25, 2021);
Rosenberg and González, "Thanks to Amazon."

289 *increased by 67 percent*: Robert McCartney, "Amazon in Seattle: Economic God-send or Self-Centered Behemoth?," *Washington Post*, April 8, 2019, https://www.washingtonpost.com/local/trafficandcommuting/amazon-in-seattle-economic-godsend-or-self-centered-behemoth/2019/04/08/7d29999a-4ce3-11e9-93d0-64dbcf38ba41_story.html (January 25, 2021).

290 *the company donated almost nothing*: Amy Martinez and Kristy Heim, "Amazon a Virtual No-Show in Hometown Philanthropy," *Seattle Times*, March 31, 2012, https://www.seattletimes.com/business/amazon-a-virtual-no-show-in-hometown-philanthropy/ (January 25, 2021).

291 *"license to operate"*: Will Kenton, "Social License to Operate (SLO)," *Investopedia*, August 23, 2019, https://www.investopedia.com/terms/s/social-license-slo.asp (January 25, 2021).

291 *2.25 percent increase on income tax*: Phuong Le, "Seattle Approves New Income Tax for Wealthy Residents," Associated Press, July 10, 2017, https://apnews.com/article/d747b2eef95449c3963bb62f9736ef93 (January 25, 2021).

292 *"head tax"*: "A Close Look at the Proposed Head Tax," *Seattle City Council Insight*, October 30, 2017, https://sccinsight.com/2017/10/30/close-look-proposed-head-tax/ (January 25, 2021).

292 *annual summer picnic*: Taylor Soper, "Amazon Cancels Huge Summer Picnic and Post-Holiday Party as Seattle Employee Count Swells, Plans New Post-Prime Day Concert," *GeekWire*, June 13, 2018, https://www.geekwire.com/2018/amazon-cancels-huge-summer-picnic-holiday-party-seattle-employee-count-swells-plans-new-prime-day-celebration-concert/ (January 25, 2021).

293 *$8.7 billion*: Reid Wilson, "Washington Just Awarded the Largest State Tax Subsidy in U.S. History," *Washington Post*, November 12, 2013, https://www.washingtonpost.com/blogs/govbeat/wp/2013/11/12/washington-just-awarded-the-largest-state-tax-subsidy-in-u-s-history/ (January 25, 2021).

293 *Nevada had offered Tesla*: Jason Hidalgo, "Art of the Tesla Deal: How Nevada Won a Gigafactory," *Reno Gazette Journal*, September 16, 2014, https://www.rgj.com/story/news/2014/09/13/art-tesla-deal-nv-won-gigafactory/15593371/ (January 25, 2021).

294 *$1 billion in annual tax incentives*: Shayndi Raice and Dana Mattioli, "Amazon Sought $1 Billion in Incentives on Top of Lures for HQ2," *Wall Street Journal*, January 16, 2020, https://www.wsj.com/articles/amazon-sought-1-billion-in-incentives-on-top-of-lures-for-hq2-11579179601 (January 25, 2021).

294 *Foxconn*: Watchdog News, "Foxconn Chooses Wisconsin for Manufacturing Plant, Says 13,000 Jobs Will Be Created," *Center Square*, July 26, 2017, https://www.thecentersquare.com/wisconsin/foxconn-chooses-wisconsin-for-manufacturing-plant-says-13-000-jobs-will-be-created/article_9a65242e-869a-5867-9201-4ef7b49fb2aa.html (January 25, 2021).

294 *HQ2 RFP . . . made public on September 7, 2017*: Amazon, September 7, 2017,

https://images-na.ssl-images-amazon.com/images/G/01/Anything/test/images/usa/RFP_3._V516043504_.pdf.

295 *Amazon watchers placed bets*: Spencer Soper, "Amazon Weighs Boston in Search for Second Headquarters," *Bloomberg*, September 12, 2017, https://www.bloomberg.com/news/articles/2017-09-12/amazon-is-said-to-weigh-boston-in-search-for-second-headquarters (January 25, 2021).

295 *"the city's lifestyle . . . universities"*: Emily Badger, Quoctrung Bui, and Claire Cain Miller, "Dear Amazon, We Picked Your New Headquarters for You," *New York Times*, September 9, 2017, https://www.nytimes.com/interactive/2017/09/09/upshot/where-should-amazon-new-headquarters-be.html (January 25, 2021).

295 *Dallas*: Laura Stevens, Sean McDade, and Stephanie Stamm, "Courting a Giant," *Wall Street Journal*, November 14, 2017, https://www.wsj.com/graphics/amazon-headquarters/ (January 25, 2021).

295 *Amazon execs favored Boston*: Soper, "Amazon Weighs Boston."

295 *"be asking for tax breaks . . . communities"*: Tony Romm, "Amazon's Pursuit of Tax Credits to Build a New Corporate Headquarters Is Getting Early Pushback," *Vox*, September 7, 2017, https://www.vox.com/2017/9/7/16268588/amazon-tax-credits-ro-khanna-opposition (January 25, 2021).

295 *"arrogant, naive and more than a teensy bit cynical"*: Michael Hiltzik, "Column: Memo to Civic Leaders: Don't Sell Out Your Cities for Amazon's New Headquarters," *Los Angeles Times*, September 12, 2017, https://www.latimes.com/business/hiltzik/la-fi-hiltzik-amazon-hq-20170911-story.html (January 25, 2021).

296 *Kansas City's mayor*: Natasha Bach, "Kansas City's Mayor Reviewed 1,000 Products on Amazon to Promote His HQ2 Bid," *Fortune*, October 12, 2017, https://fortune.com/2017/10/12/amazon-hq2-kansas-city/ (January 25, 2021).

296 *"not saying we'd fight a bear for you"*: Shannon Liao, "The Eight Most Outrageous Things Cities Did to Lure Amazon for HQ2," *The Verge*, October 19, 2017, https://www.theverge.com/2017/10/19/16504042/amazon-hq2-second-headquarters-most-funny-crazy-pitches-proposals-stonecrest-new-york (January 25, 2021).

299 *tour their proposed sites*: Laura Stevens, Shibani Mahtani, and Shayndi Raice, "Rules of Engagement: How Cities Are Courting Amazon's New Headquarters," *Wall Street Journal*, April 2, 2018, https://www.wsj.com/articles/rules-of-engagement-how-cities-are-courting-amazons-new-headquarters-1522661401?mod=article_inline (January 25, 2021).

301 *end discounts for National Rifle Association*: Richard Fausset, "Georgia Passes Bill That Stings Delta over N.R.A. Position," *New York Times*, March 1, 2018, https://www.nytimes.com/2018/03/01/business/delta-nra-georgia.html (January 25, 2021).

303 *additional $22.5 million annually*: Monica Nickelsburg, "Amazon Suspends

Construction in Seattle While the City Considers a New Tax on Its Biggest Businesses," *GeekWire*, May 2, 2018, https://www.geekwire.com/2018/amazon-suspends-construction-seattle-city-considers-new-tax-biggest-businesses/ (January 25, 2021), and Matt Day, "Amazon Paid $250 Million in Washington State and Local Taxes for 2017, Source Says," *Seattle Times*, May 9, 2018, https://www.seattletimes.com/business/amazon/amazon-paid-250-million-in-washington-state-and-local-taxes-in-2017-source-says/ (January 25, 2021).

303 *stop construction*: Matt Day and Daniel Beekman, "Amazon Issues Threat over Seattle Head-Tax Plan, Halts Tower Construction Planning," *Seattle Times*, May 2, 2018, https://www.seattletimes.com/business/amazon/amazon-pauses-plans-for-seattle-office-towers-while-city-council-considers-business-tax/ (January 25, 2021).

304 *more than 19 percent of prime office space:* Rosenberg and González, "Thanks to Amazon."

304 *sign a lease in Bellevue*: Matt Day, "Amazon Confirms Major Office Lease in Bellevue, Will Occupy Former Expedia Headquarters," *Seattle Times*, August 21, 2018 https://www.seattletimes.com/business/amazon/amazon-confirms-major-office-lease-in-bellevue-will-occupy-former-expedia-headquarters/ (January 25, 2021).

304 *"Capital goes where it is welcome"*: Richard Karlgaard, "Capital Goes Where It's Welcome," *Forbes*, May 18, 2009, https://www.forbes.com/sites/digitalrules/2009/05/18/capital-goes-where-its-welcome/?sh=36ede97353d4 (January 25, 2021).

305 *repealed their own tax*: McCartney, "Amazon in Seattle."

305 *Seattle mayor Jenny Durkan*: Daniel Beekman, "About-Face: Seattle City Council Repeals Head Tax Amid Pressure from Businesses, Referendum Threat," *Seattle Times*, June 12, 2018, https://www.seattletimes.com/seattle-news/politics/about-face-seattle-city-council-repeals-head-tax-amid-pressure-from-big-businesses/ (January 25, 2021).

306 *the company's market capitalization*: Brad Stone, "At $1 Trillion, Amazon Is Still Not Its Stock Price," *Bloomberg*, September 4, 2018, https://www.bloomberg.com/news/articles/2018-09-04/at-1-trillion-amazon-is-still-not-its-stock-price (January 25, 2021).

307 *"hunger games beauty contest"*: Scott Galloway, "Professor Scott Galloway on Amazon HQ2 and Why It's Time to Break Up Big Tech," *SupplyChain 24/7*, January 25, 2018, https://www.supplychain247.com/article/professor_scott_galloway_on_amazon_hq2_break_up_big_tech (January 25, 2021).

307 *"where Jeff wants to spend more time"*: Ibid.

307 *anticompetitive behavior*: Lina M. Khan, "Amazon's Antitrust Paradox," *Yale Law Journal* 126, no. 3 (2017), https://www.yalelawjournal.org/note/amazons-antitrust-paradox (January 25, 2021).

307 *"Amazon selects New York City and Northern Virginia"*: "Amazon Selects New York City and Northern Virginia for New Headquarters," Amazon, November 13, 2018, https://www.aboutamazon.com/news/company-news/amazon-selects-new-york-city-and-northern-virginia-for-new-headquarters (January 25, 2021).

308 *Corey Johnson*: Corey Johnson, Tweet, November 13, 2018, 11:40 a.m., https://twitter.com/CoreyinNYC/status/1062384713535537152 (January 25, 2021).

309 *"we've been getting calls . . . concerning to residents here"*: Alexandria Ocasio-Cortez, Tweet, November 12, 2018, 11:40 p.m., https://twitter.com/AOC/status/1062203458227503104 (January 25, 2021).

309 *"onsite" but if not, "in reasonable proximity"*: Chris Sommerfeldt and Michael Gartland, "NY Officials Went to Great Lengths to Get Amazon a Helicopter Pad in Queens Despite Fear of Local Pushback: Emails," *New York Daily News*, April 16, 2020, https://www.nydailynews.com/news/politics/ny-amazon-queens-heli-pad-emails-20200416-3oi2fwjzpzhmncfzalhqre5aru-story.html (January 25, 2021).

309 *"Queens Ransom"*: Ron Dicker, "Jeff Bezos and Amazon Make Off with Sky-High Perks on New York Post Cover," *HuffPost*, November 14, 2018, https://www.huffpost.com/entry/jeff-bezos-amazon-new-york-post-cover_n_5bec4243e4b044bbb1ab8738 (January 25, 2021).

311 *required under a city program*: "Industrial & Commercial Abatement Program," NYC Department of Finance, https://www1.nyc.gov/site/finance/benefits/benefits-industrial-and-commercial-abatement-program-icap.page (January 25, 2021).

312 *local Italian restaurant in Long Island City*: See J. David Goodman, "Amazon Has a New Strategy to Sway Skeptics in New York," *New York Times*, January 29, 2019, https://www.nytimes.com/2019/01/29/nyregion/amazon-new-york-long-island-city.html (January 25, 2021).

313 *"Welcome to New York . . . bringing that pressure"*: J. David Goodman, "Amazon's New York Charm Offensive Includes a Veiled Threat," *New York Times*, January 30, 2019, https://www.nytimes.com/2019/01/30/nyregion/amazon-queens-nyc-council.html (January 25, 2021).

313 *company was rethinking its New York plans*: Robert McCartney, Jonathan O'Connell, and Patricia Sullivan, "Facing Opposition, Amazon Reconsiders N.Y. Headquarters Site, Two Officials Say," *Washington Post*, February 8, 2019, https://www.washingtonpost.com/local/virginia-politics/facing-opposition-amazon-reconsiders-ny-headquarters-site-two-officials-say/2019/02/08/451ffc52-2a19-11e9-b011-d8500644dc98_story.html (January 25, 2021).

313 *"The question is . . . so welcoming"*: Ibid.

314 *"fair elections"*: Josh Eidelson and Dina Bass, "Amazon Was Holding Talks

Wednesday to Make NYC Deal Happen," *Bloomberg*, February 14, 2019, https://www.bloomberg.com/news/articles/2019-02-14/amazon-was-holding -talks-wednesday-to-make-nyc-deal-happen?sref=dJuchiL5 (January 25, 2021).

314 *"disrespectful to the people . . . anything like this"*: Jillian Jorgensen, "De Blasio Fumes at Amazon and Skeptics of Dashed Deal for HQ2 in Long Island City," *New York Daily News*, February 15, 2019, https://www.nydailynews.com/news /politics/ny-pol-deblasio-amazon-hq2-20190215-story.html (January 25, 2021).

314 *spoke on the phone with Bezos*: J. David Goodman, "Andrew Cuomo Speaks with Jeff Bezos, Hints of 'Other Ways' to Clear Path for Amazon's Return," *New York Times*, February 28, 2019, https://www.nytimes.com/2019/02/28/nyregion /amazon-hq2-nyc.html (January 25, 2021).

315 *tracking his private plane*: Jonathan O'Connell and Andrew Ba Tran, "Where Bezos's Jet Flies Most—and What It Might Say About Amazon's HQ2 Win- ner," *Washington Post*, November 2, 2018, https://www.washingtonpost.com /business/where-bezoss-jet-flies-most--and-what-it-might-say-about-amazons -hq2/2018/11/02/792be19a-de16-11e8-b3f0-62607289efee_story.html (Janu- ary 25, 2021).

316 *Amazon would expand its offices*: See "Amazon Creating 3,500 Jobs in Tech Hubs Across the U.S.," *Business Facilities*, August 21, 2020, https://businessfacilities .com/2020/08/amazon-creating-3500-jobs-in-tech-hubs-across-the-u-s/ (Jan- uary 25, 2021).

CHAPTER 13: COMPLEXIFIERS

322 *"my wife still claims*: Henry Blodget, "I Asked Jeff Bezos the Tough Questions— No Profits, the Book Controversies, the Phone Flop—and He Showed Why Am- azon Is Such a Huge Success," *Business Insider*, December 13, 2014, https://www .businessinsider.com/amazons-jeff-bezos-on-profits-failure-succession-big-bets -2014-12 (January 25, 2021).

322 *"the sexiest thing I do"*: Ibid.

322 *2017 SummitLA conference*: Jeff Bezos in conversation with Mark Bezos, "Amazon CEO Jeff Bezos and Brother Mark Give a Rare Interview About Growing Up and the Secrets to Success," *Summit LA17*, 54:55, November 14, 2017, https://summit .co/videos/amazon-ceo-jeff-bezos-and-brother-mark-give-a-rare-interview -about-growing-up-and-secrets-to-success-3nBiJY03McIIQcgcoe2aUe (Janu- ary 25, 2021).

323 *underwent an extensive renovation*: Benjamin Wofford, "Inside Jeff Bezos's DC Life," *Washingtonian*, April 22, 2018, https://www.washingtonian.com/2018/04 /22/inside-jeff-bezos-dc-life/ (January 25, 2021).

323 *"Cocktail parties . . . not my sweet spot"*: Rebecca Johnson, "MacKenzie Bezos: Writer, Mother of Four, and High-Profile Wife," *Vogue*, February 20, 2013,

https://www.vogue.com/article/a-novel-perspective-mackenzie-bezos (January 25, 2021).

324 *"public-facing introverts"*: Katy Waldman, "The Idealized, Introverted Wives of MacKenzie Bezos's Fiction," *New Yorker*, January 23, 2019, https://www.newyorker .com/books/page-turner/the-idealized-introverted-wives-of-mackenzie-bezos -fiction (January 25, 2021).

324 *2013 TV interview*: Jonah Engel Bromwich and Alexandra Alter, "Who Is Mac-Kenzie Scott?" *New York Times*, January 12, 2019, https://www.nytimes.com /2019/01/12/style/jeff-bezos-mackenzie-divorce.html (January 25, 2021).

324 *on a dogsled*: Jeff Bezos, Twitter video, April 22, 2018, 4:34 p.m., https://twitter .com/JeffBezos/status/988154007813173248 (January 25, 2021).

324 *"It really was an incredible . . . it was amazing"*: Döpfner, "Jeff Bezos Reveals."

324 *Day One Fund*: Sara Salinas, "Amazon's Jeff Bezos Launches a $2 Billion 'Day One Fund' to Help Homeless Families and Create Preschools," CNBC, September 13, 2018, https://www.cnbc.com/2018/09/13/bezos-launches-day-one-fund-to -help-homeless-families-and-create-preschools.html (January 25, 2021).

326 *University of Southern California*: Adrian Gomez, "Celebrity Buzz Centers on 2 ABQ Natives," *Albuquerque Journal*, January 11, 2019, https://www.abqjournal .com/1267508/celebrity-bu-zzcenters-on-2-abq-natives.html (January 25, 2021).

326 *shared love of flying*: Sara Nathan, "Lauren Sanchez's Brother Tells All on Bezos Romance: 'This Was Real,'" *Page Six*, March 30, 2019, https://pagesix.com/2019 /03/30/this-was-real-lauren-sanchezs-brother-tells-all-on-bezos-romance/ (January 25, 2021).

326 *third annual MARS conference*: Daniel Terdiman, "At Amazon's MARS Conference, Jeff Bezos Plots the Future with 200 (Very) Big Brains," *Fast Company*, March 23, 2018, https://www.fastcompany.com/40547902/at-amazons-mars-conference-jeff -bezos-plots-the-future-with-200-very-big-brains (January 25, 2021).

326 *Bezos playing table tennis*: MIT Technology Review, Twitter video, March 20, 2018, 6:57 p.m., https://twitter.com/techreview/status/976231159251324928 ?lang=en (January 25, 2021).

327 *He also brought Sanchez*: Keith Griffith and Jennifer Smith, "Jeff Bezos and Lover Lauren Sanchez 'Made Out Like Teenagers' in Hollywood Hotspot at Table Next to Michael Sanchez 'Just Days After Their Spouses Discovered Affair,'" *Daily Mail*, January 12, 2019, https://www.dailymail.co.uk/news/article-6583895/Jeff -Bezos-lover-reportedly-like-teenagers-Hollywood-restaurant-Felix.html (January 25, 2021).

327 *"The human need to explore"*: "Millions of People Living and Working in Space," YouTube video, 1:57, posted by Blue Origin, October 15, 2018, https://www.youtube.com/watch?v=KMdpdmJshFU&feature=emb_logo&ab _channel=BlueOrigin (January 25, 2021).

327 *he started Axis Management*: David Ng, Stacy Perman, and Richard Winton,

"Who Is Michael Sanchez? Low-Level Hollywood Manager Is a Pivotal Figure in Bezos-Pecker Storm," *Los Angeles Times*, February 13, 2019, https://www.latimes.com/business/hollywood/la-fi-ct-michael-sanchez-20190213-story.html (January 26, 2021).

328 *Dylan Howard*: Gary Baum, "Dylan Howard's Hollywood Reboot: Why Are So Many A-Listers Working with a Tabloid Henchman?" *Hollywood Reporter*, February 3, 2020, https://www.hollywoodreporter.com/features/why-are-a-listers-working-dylan-howard-1275651 (January 26, 2021).

329 *according to an email that went out to AMI reporters*: Lachlan Markay, "Emails Tell the Inside Story of How the Enquirer Got Jeff Bezos' Nudes," *Daily Beast*, July 3, 2020, https://www.thedailybeast.com/emails-tell-the-inside-story-of-how-the-enquirer-got-jeff-bezos-nudes (January 26, 2021).

329 *one-day return to host* Extra: "TV Reunion! Emmy Winner Lauren Sanchez Returns to Host 'Extra' This Thursday," *Radar Online*, September 11, 2018, https://radaronline.com/exclusives/2018/09/tv-reunion-emmy-winner-lauren-sanchez-returns-to-host-extra/ (January 26, 2021).

329 *"Bill Gates type"*: Markay, "Emails."

330 *a payout of around $200,000*: Joe Palazzolo and Michael Rothfeld, *The Fixers: The Bottom-Feeders, Crooked Lawyers, Gossipmongers, and Porn Stars Who Created the 45th President* (New York: Random House, 2020), 351–356.

330 *on October 23*: "Declaration of Dylan Howard, James Robertson and Andrea Simpson in Support of Defendants' Special Motion to Strike," in *Michael Sanchez v. American Media, Inc*, pg. 4, line 19.

331 *financial ruin for AMI and jailtime*: Letter to Charles Stillman and James Mitchell from the U.S. Attorney for the Southern District of New York, September 20, 2018, https://www.justice.gov/usao-sdny/press-release/file/1119501/download (January 26, 2021).

331 *terrified of getting sued*: Michael Rothfeld, Joe Palazzolo, and Alexandra Berzon, "How the National Enquirer Got Bezos' Texts: It Paid $200,000 to His Lover's Brother," *Wall Street Journal*, March 18, 2019, https://www.wsj.com/articles/how-the-national-enquirer-got-bezos-texts-it-paid-200-000-to-his-lovers-brother-11552953981 (January 26, 2021).

332 *Pecker exploded in anger*: Ibid.

333 *"bring the 747 in for a soft landing"*: Evan Real, "Lauren Sanchez's Brother Speaks Out About Involvement in Jeff Bezos Affair Leaking," *Hollywood Reporter*, February 14, 2019, https://www.hollywoodreporter.com/news/lauren-sanchezs-brother-speaks-involvement-jeff-bezos-affair-leaking-1186817 (January 26, 2021).

333 *unfolding at the very same time as the HQ2 saga*: Marc Fisher, Manuel Roig-Franzia, and Sarah Ellison, "Was Tabloid Exposé of Bezos Affair Just Juicy Gossip or a Political Hit Job?" *Washington Post*, February 5, 2019,

https://www.washingtonpost.com/politics/was-tabloid-expose-of-bezos-affair -just-juicy-gossip-or-a-political-hit-job/2019/02/05/03d2f716-2633-11e9 -90cd-dedb0c92dc17_story.html (January 26, 2021).

334 *"We want to make people . . . lives as friends"*: Jeff Bezos, Tweet, January 9, 2019, 9:17 a.m., https://twitter.com/JeffBezos/status/1083004911380393985 (January 26, 2021).

334 *the scoop of his career wriggle from his grasp*: Fisher, Roig-Franzia, and Ellison, "Tabloid Exposé."

335 *Trump also piled onto Bezos's latest predicament*: Matthew Yglesias, "Donald Trump's Twitter Feud with Amazon, Explained," *Vox*, April 4, 2018, https://www .vox.com/policy-and-politics/2018/4/4/17193090/trump-amazon-feud (January 26, 2021).

335 *more details about Bezos and Sanchez*: Dylan Howard, James Robertson, and Andrea Simpson, "Bezos Shared Wife's Pillow Talk with Mistress, Boasted About U2's Bono," *National Enquirer*, January 12, 2019, https://www.nationalenquirer .com/celebrity/jeff-bezos-shared-wifes-pillow-talk-with-mistress-lauren -sanchez/ (January 26, 2021).

335 *"First Photos Show Jeff Bezos's Girlfriend"*: "First Photos Show Jeff Bezos' Girlfriend Lauren Sanchez Carefree After Scandal," *Us Weekly*, January 14, 2019, https://www.usmagazine.com/celebrity-news/pictures/lauren-sanchez-steps -out-after-news-of-jeff-bezos-affair-pics/ (January 26, 2021).

336 *"The untold story . . . tombstone"*: Declaration of Dylan Howard.

336 *"whatever budget is needed"*: Jeff Bezos, "No Thank You, Mr. Pecker," *Medium*, February 7, 2019, https://medium.com/@jeffreypbezos/no-thank-you -mr-pecker-146e3922310f (January 26, 2021).

336 *passing acquaintanceship with Trumpworld characters*: Fisher, Roig-Franzia, and Ellison, "Tabloid Exposé."

336 *de Becker had identified Michael Sanchez*: Lachlan Markay and Asawin Suebsaeng, "Bezos Launches Investigation into Leaked Texts with Lauren Sanchez That Killed His Marriage," *Daily Beast*, January 30, 2019, https://www.thedailybeast .com/bezos-launches-investigation-into-leaked-texts-with-lauren-sanchez-that -killed-his-marriage (January 26, 2021); Lachlan Markay and Asawin Suebsaeng, "Bezos' Investigators Question Michael Sanchez, Brother of Mistress Lauren Sanchez, in National Enquirer Leak Probe," *Daily Beast*, February 13, 2019, https:// www.thedailybeast.com/bezos-investigators-question-the-brother-of-his -mistress-lauren-sanchez-in-national-enquirer-leak-probe (January 26, 2021).

336 *"strong leads point to political motives"*: Markay and Suebsaeng, "Bezos' Investigators."

337 Chatham Asset Management: Gerry Smith and Elise Young, "New Jersey Officials Press National Enquirer's Hedge-Fund Owner over Bezos Feud," *Bloomberg*, February 12, 2019, https://www.bloomberg.com/news/articles/2019

-02-12/n-j-officials-press-enquirer-s-hedge-fund-owner-over-bezos-feud?sref
=dJuchiL5 (January 26, 2021); Katherine Burton, Sridhar Natarajan, and
Shahien Nasiripour, "As N.J. Cuts Hedge Fund Ties, Chatham Shows That Can
Take Years," Bloom-berg, June 11, 2019, https://www.bloomberg.com/news
/articles/2019-06-11/as-n-j-cuts-hedge-fund-ties-chatham-shows-that-can
-take-years?sref=dJuchiL5 (January 26, 2021).

338 *"just juicy gossip or a political hit job"*: Fisher, Roig-Franzia, and Ellison, "Tabloid Exposé."

339 *"reporting . . . external forces, political or otherwise"*: Bezos, "No Thank You."

340 *"Something unusual happened . . . all in writing"*: Ibid.

340 *"AMI's long-earned reputation . . . true journalism"*: Ibid.

342 *"Our investigators . . . AMI was aware of the details"*: Gavin de Becker, "Bezos Investigation Finds the Saudis Obtained His Private Data," *Daily Beast*, March 31,
2019, https://www.thedailybeast.com/jeff-bezos-investigation-finds-the-saudis
-obtained-his-private-information (January 26, 2021).

342 *"His continued efforts . . . source confidentiality"*: See "National Enquirer Says
Saudis Didn't Help on Bezos Story," *Daily Beast*, March 31, 2019, https://www
.thedailybeast.com/national-enquirer-says-saudis-didnt-help-on-bezos-story
(January 26, 2021).

343 *putting AWS data centers in the country*: Katie Paul, "Exclusive: Apple and Amazon in Talks to Set Up in Saudi Arabia—Sources," Reuters, December 28, 2017,
https://www.reuters.com/article/us-saudi-tech-exclusive/exclusive-apple-and
-amazon-in-talks-to-set-up-in-saudi-arabia-sources-idUSKBN1EM0PZ (January 26, 2021); Bradley Hope and Justin Scheck, *Blood and Oil: Mohammed Bin
Salman's Ruthless Quest for Global Power* (New York: Hachette, 2020).

343 *"Davos in the Desert"*: Marc Fisher and Jonathan O'Connell, "The Prince, the
Billionaire and the Amazon Project That Got Frozen in the Desert," *Washington Post*, October 27, 2019, https://www.washingtonpost.com/politics/the
-prince-the-billionaire-and-the-amazon-project-that-got-frozen-in-the-desert
/2019/10/27/71410ef8-eb9c-11e9-85c0-85a098e47b37_story.html (January 26,
2021).

345 *a plan to attack Bezos's phone*: Justin Scheck, Bradley Hope, and Summer Said,
"Saudi Prince Courted Amazon's Bezos Before Bitter Split," *Wall Street Journal*,
January 27, 2020, https://www.wsj.com/articles/saudi-prince-courted-amazons
-bezos-before-bitter-split-11580087674 (January 26, 2021).

345 *"medium to high confidence"*: Marc Fisher, "U.N. Report: Saudi Crown Prince
Was Involved in Alleged Hacking of Bezos Phone," *Washington Post*, January
22, 2020, https://www.washingtonpost.com/politics/un-ties-alleged-phone-hac
king-to-posts-coverage-of-saudi-arabia/2020/01/22/a0bc63ba-3d1f-11ea-b90d
-5652806c3b3a_story.html (January 26, 2021); Jared Malsin, Dustin Volz, and
Justin Scheck, "U.N. Suggests Bezos' Phone Was Hacked Using Saudi Crown

Prince's Account," *Wall Street Journal*, January 22, 2020, https://www.wsj.com /articles/u-n-experts-say-hacking-of-bezoss-phone-suggests-effort-to-influence -news-coverage-11579704647 (January 26, 2021).

345 *they gamboled in the western Mediterranean Sea*: Ben Feuerherd, "Jeff Bezos and Lauren Sanchez Get Cozy on Mega Yacht in Italy," *Page Six*, August 31, 2019, https://pagesix.com/2019/08/31/jeff-bezos-and-lauren-sanchez-get-cozy-on -mega-yacht-in-italy/ (January 26, 2021).

346 *wearing a pair of stylish multicolor swim trunks*: Priya Elan, "Dress Like a Tech Bro in Kaftan, Sliders, Gilet . . . and Jeff Bezos's Shorts," *The Guardian*, November 2, 2019, https://www.theguardian.com/fashion/2019/nov/02/jeff-bezos -shorts-tech-bro-fashion (January 26, 2021).

347 *one-year anniversary of the murder of Jamal Khashoggi*: Bill Bostock, "Jeff Bezos Attended a Vigil at the Saudi Consulate Where Washington Post Writer Jamal Khashoggi Was Murdered One Year Ago," *Business Insider*, October 2, 2019, https://www.businessinsider.com/jeff-bezos-visit-saudi-consulate-istanbul -khashoggi-murder-anniversary-2019-10 (January 26, 2021).

347 *"Right here where you are . . . are here"*: "Washington Post Owner Jeff Bezos Attends Khashoggi Memorial in Istanbul," *Daily Sabah*, October 2, 2019, https://www.dailysabah.com/turkey/2019/10/02/washington-post-owner-jeff -bezos-attends-khashoggi-memorial-in-istanbul (January 26, 2021).

347 *arrow aimed directly at Bezos's enemy*: Ibid.

347 *buying historic works of art*: Eileen Kinsella, "Jeff Bezos Reportedly Spent More Than $70 Million on a Kerry James Marshall and a Record-Shattering Ed Ruscha at Auction Last Fall," *Artnet*, February 6, 2020, https://news.artnet.com /market/jeff-bezos-art-collector-1771410 (January 26, 2021).

347 *David Geffen's nine-acre Beverly Hills estate*: Katy McLaughlin and Katherine Clarke, "Jeff Bezos Buys David Geffen's Los Angeles Mansion for a Record $165 Million," *Wall Street Journal*, February 12, 2020, https://www.wsj.com/articles /jeff-bezos-buys-david-geffens-los-angeles-mansion-for-a-record-165-million -11581542020 (January 26, 2021).

CHAPTER 14: RECKONING

349 *from two days to one*: Spencer Soper, "Amazon Will Spend $800 Million to Move to One-Day Delivery," *Bloomberg*, April 25, 2019," https://www.bloomberg.com /news/articles/2019-04-25/amazon-will-spend-800-million-to-move-to-one -day-delivery?sref=dJuchiL5 (January 25, 2021).

349 *recovered all of that surrendered ground within twelve months*: Jack Witzig, Berber Jin, and *Bloomberg*, "Jeff Bezos's Net Worth Hits a New High After Recovering Losses from Divorce," *Fortune*, July 2, 2020, https://fortune.com/2020/07/02 /jeff-bezos-net-worth-new-high-amazon-shares-divorce/ (January 25, 2021).

350 *"All big institutions of any kind ... that will not stop us from serving custom-ers"*: Transcript of Economic Club of Washington, D.C., interview, September 13, 2018, https://www.economicclub.org/sites/default/files/transcripts/Jeff_Bezos _Edited_Transcript.pdf (January 25, 2021).

350 *The book traces the rise and fall of the first American grocery chain*: Marc Levin-son, *The Great A&P and the Struggle for Small Business in America* (New York: Hill and Wang, 2011).

353 *aggressively titled article*: Elizabeth Warren, "Here's How We Can Break Up Big Tech," *Medium*, March 8, 2019, https://medium.com/@teamwarren/heres-how -we-can-break-up-big-tech-9ad9e0da324c (January 25, 2021).

353 *"You can be the umpire in the baseball game ... have a team in the game"*: "This Is Why Warren Wants to Break Up Big Tech Companies," CNN, April 23, 2019, https://www.cnn.com/videos/politics/2019/04/23/elizabeth-warren-amazon -google-big-tech-break-up-town-hall-vpx.cnn (January 25, 2021).

354 *the benefactor of tax benefits ... vast R&D budget*: Richard Rubin, "Does Ama-zon Really Pay No Taxes? Here's the Complicated Answer," *Wall Street Journal*, June 14, 2019, https://www.wsj.com/articles/does-amazon-really-pay-no-taxes -heres-the-complicated-answer-11560504602 (January 25, 2021).

355 *"What I teach and preach ... Don't resist"*: Döpfner, "Jeff Bezos Reveals."

355 *Earnings in Amazon fulfillment centers varied by state*: Abha Battarai, "Ama-zon Is Doling Out Raises of As Little as 25 Cents an Hour in What Employees Call 'Damage Control,'" *Washington Post*, September 24, 2018, https://www .seattletimes.com/business/amazon/amazon-raises-starting-wage-for-its -workers-to-15-an-hour (January 25, 2021).

356 *"We decided it was time to lead—to offer wages that went beyond competitive"*: Jeff Bezos, "2018 Letter to Shareowners," April 11, 2019, https://www.aboutamazon .com/news/company-news/2018-letter-to-shareholders. (January 25, 2021).

356 *reports that some tenured workers*: Krystal Hu, "Some Amazon Employees Say They Will Make Less After the Raise," *Yahoo! Finance*, October 3, 2018, https://finance.yahoo.com/news/amazon-employees-say-will-make-less-raise -174028353.html (January 25, 2021).

356 *returning to Twitter to harangue the company*: Bernie Sanders, Tweet, Decem-ber 27, 2019, https://twitter.com/BernieSanders/status/1210602974587822080 (January 25, 2021).

357 *"Amazon is getting away with murder tax-wise"*: "Amazon 'Getting Away with Murder on tax', says Donald Trump," Reuters, May 13, 2016, https://www .theguardian.com/us-news/2016/may/13/amazon-getting-away-with-on-tax -says-donald-trump (January 25, 2021).

357 *"Towns, cities and states throughout the U.S. are being hurt—many jobs being lost!"*: Donald Trump, Tweet, August 16, 2017, https://www.thetrumparchive .com/?searchbox=%22many+jobs+being+lost%21%22 (January 26, 2021).

358 *the agency had lost money for years*: "Be Careful What You Assume," United States Postal Service Office of the Inspector General, February 16, 2015, https://www.uspsoig.gov/blog/be-careful-what-you-assume (January 25, 2021).

358 *the post office's contract with Amazon*: Eugene Kiely and D'Angelo Gore, "Trump's Amazon Attack," FactCheck.org, April 5, 2018, https://www.factcheck.org/2018/04/trumps-amazon-attack/ (January 25, 2021).

358 *he harangued postmaster general Megan Brennan*: Damian Paletta and Josh Dawsey, "Trump Personally Pushed Postmaster General to Double Rates on Amazon, Other Firms," *Washington Post*, May 18, 2018, (January 25, 2021).

359 *tweeted a photo of himself and the defense secretary*: Jeff Bezos, Tweet, August 10, 2017, https://twitter.com/JeffBezos/status/895714205822730241 (January 25, 2021).

360 *banded together to protest that the process was biased*: Naomi Nix, "Amazon Has Plenty of Foes in Pentagon Cloud Deal," *Bloomberg*, June 26, 2018, https://www.bloomberg.com/news/articles/2018-06-26/amazon-foes-in-pentagon-cloud-deal-are-said-to-include-sap-csra?sref=dJuchiL5 (January 25, 2021).

360 *most observers saw the unmistakable fingerprints of Oracle*: Naomi Nix, "Inside the Nasty Battle to Stop Amazon from Winning the Pentagon's Cloud Contract," *Bloomberg*, December 20, 2018, https://www.bloomberg.com/news/features/2018-12-20/tech-giants-fight-over-10-billion-pentagon-cloud-contract (January 25, 2021).

360 *was a major donor to his reelection campaign*: Brian Schwarz, "Top CEOs Ramp Up GOP Donations as Biden Threatens to Scale Back Corporate Tax Cuts," CNBC, July 27, 2020, https://www.cnbc.com/2020/07/27/top-ceos-give-big-to-gop-as-biden-threatens-to-scale-back-corp-tax-cuts.html (January 25, 2021).

360 *Trump listened and said he wanted the competition to be fair*: Jennifer Jacobs, "Oracle's Safra Catz Raises Amazon Contract Fight with Trump," *Bloomberg*, April 4, 2018, https://www.bloomberg.com/news/articles/2018-04-04/oracle-s-catz-is-said-to-raise-amazon-contract-fight-with-trump?sref=dJuchiL5 (January 25, 2021).

360 *Alphabet dropped out of the competition*: Naomi Nix, "Google Drops Out of Pentagon's $10 Billion Cloud Competition," *Bloomberg*, October 8, 2018, https://www.bloomberg.com/news/articles/2018-10-08/google-drops-out-of-pentagon-s-10-billion-cloud-competition?sref=dJuchiL5 (January 25, 2021).

361 *"If big tech companies are going to turn their back"*: Mike Stone, "Jeff Bezos Says Amazon Wants to Work More with the Pentagon," Reuters, December 7, 2019, https://www.reuters.com/article/us-usa-pentagon-amazon/amazon-ceo-says-wants-to-work-more-with-pentagon-idUSKBN1YB0JL (January 25, 2021).

361 *"Which one is that, the Amazon?"*: "President Trump Meeting with Prime Minister of the Netherlands," C-SpAN, July 18, 2019, https://www.c-span.org/video

/?462777-1/president-trump-meets-dutch-prime-minister-mark-rutte (January 25, 2021).

361 *"Looks like the shady and potentially corrupt practices"*: Donald Trump Jr., Tweet, July 18, 2019, https://twitter.com/DonaldJTrumpJr/status/1151905489 472630785 (January 25, 2021).

362 *suspended the process*: Billy Mitchell, "JEDI Complaints Under Review by New Defense Secretary," *FedScoop*, August 1, 2019, https://www.fedscoop.com/jedi -mark-esper-review-congress-complaints/ (January 25, 2021).

362 *Esper recused himself*: Frank Konkel and Heather Kuldell, "Esper Recuses Himself from JEDI Cloud Contract Review," NextGov.com, October 22, 2019, https://www.nextgov.com/it-modernization/2019/10/esper-recuses-himself -jedi-cloud-contract-review/160782/ (January 25, 2021).

362 *"To me, it goes back to, if anything, Microsoft staying out of politics"*: Monica Nickelsburg and Todd Bishop, "Satya Nadella: Staying Out of Politics, Focusing on Tech, Helped Microsoft Win Pentagon Cloud Contract," *GeekWire*, November 1, 2019, https://www.geekwire.com/2019/satya-nadella-staying-politics-focusing -tech-helped-microsoft-win-pentagon-cloud-contract/ (January 26, 2021).

363 *competing retailers Walmart and Target avoided AWS*: Jay Greene and Laura Stevens, "Wal-Mart to Vendors: Get Off Amazon's Cloud," *Wall Street Journal*, June 21, 2017, https://www.wsj.com/articles/wal-mart-to-vendors-get-off -amazons-cloud-1498037402?mod=e2tw (January 26, 2021).

364 *a ninety-three-page article in the* Yale Law Journal: Lina Khan, "Amazon's Antitrust Paradox," *Yale Law Journal* 126, no. 3 (2017): 710–805.

364 *Khan was an unlikely figure*: Davis Streitfeld, "Amazon's Antitrust Antagonist Has a Breakthrough Idea," *New York Times*, September 7, 2018, https://www .nytimes.com/2018/09/07/technology/monopoly-antitrust-lina-khan-amazon .html (January 26, 2021).

365 *Politicians started referencing it in interviews*: Alexis C. Madrigal, "A Silicon Valley Congressman Takes On Amazon," *Atlantic*, June 19, 2017, https://www .theatlantic.com/technology/archive/2017/06/ro-khanna-amazon-whole-foods /530805/ (January 26, 2021).

365 *"hipster antitrust"*: Kostya Medvedovsky, Tweet, June 19, 2017, https://twitter .com/kmedved/status/876869328934711296 (January 26, 2021).

366 *In a sign that regulators were yet to be swayed*: Brent Kendall and Heather Haddon, "FTC Approves Whole Foods-Amazon," *Wall Street Journal*, August 23, 2017, https://www.wsj.com/articles/whole-foods-shareholders-approve-merger -with-amazon-1503498623 (January 26, 2021).

366 *Margrethe Vestager . . . opened an investigation*: Adam Satariano, "Amazon Dominates as a Merchant and Platform. Europe Sees Reason to Worry," *New York Times*, September 19, 2018, https://www.nytimes.com/2018/09/19 /technology/amazon-europe-margrethe-vestager.html (January 26, 2021).

366 *DOJ would examine Google and Apple . . . Facebook and Amazon*: David Mc-Laughlin, Naomi Nix, and Daniel Stoller, "Trump's Trustbusters Bring Microsoft Lessons to Big Tech Fight," *Bloomberg*, June 11, 2019, https://www.bloomberg.com/news/articles/2019-06-11/trump-s-trustbusters-bring-microsoft-lessons-to-big-tech-fight?sref=dJuchiL5 (January 26, 2021).

367 *"hold big tech companies accountable"*: "Cicilline to Chair Antitrust Subcommittee," January 23, 2019, https://cicilline.house.gov/press-release/cicilline-chair-antitrust-subcommittee (January 26, 2021).

368 *"We remain prepared . . . important issues"*: Kim Lyons, "Nadler Calls Amazon Letter to Judiciary Committee 'Unacceptable,'" *The Verge*, May 16, 2020, https://www.theverge.com/2020/5/16/21260981/nadler-amazon-bezos-seller-judiciary (January 26, 2021).

368 *previously vowed under oath*: Lauren Feiner, "Amazon Exec Tells Lawmakers the Company Doesn't Favor Own Brands over Products Sold by Third-Party Merchants," CNBC, July 16, 2019, https://www.cnbc.com/2019/07/16/amazon-tells-house-it-doesnt-favor-own-brands-in-antitrust-hearing.html (January 26, 2021).

370 *technical glitch with Congress's video conferencing software*: Laura Hautala, "Tech Titans Face Video Glitches in Congressional Testimony, *CNET*, July 29, 2020, https://www.cnet.com/news/tech-titans-face-video-glitches-in-congressional-testimony/ (January 26, 2021).

370 *revelations from* The Everything Store: Brad Stone, *The Everything Store* (Boston: Little, Brown and Company, 2013), 294–300; 241–246.

370 *Pramila Jayapal . . . avowed Amazon critic*: David McCabe, "One of Amazon's Most Powerful Critics Lives in Its Backyard," *New York Times*, May 3, 2020, https://www.nytimes.com/2020/05/03/technology/amazon-pramila-jayapal.html (January 26, 2021).

370 All quotes from the July 29, 2020, big tech antitrust hearing verified against the official transcript at https://www.rev.com/blog/transcripts/big-tech-antitrust-hearing-full-transcript-july-29 (February 27, 2021).

376 *The solution was "no surprises"*: Karen Weise, "Prime Power: How Amazon Squeezes the Businesses Behind Its Store," *New York Times*, December 20, 2019, https://www.nytimes.com/2019/12/19/technology/amazon-sellers.html (January 26, 2021).

377 *A TV commercial that flooded U.S. airwaves*: "Supporting Small Businesses," YouTube video, 0:30, "amazon," October 5, 2020, https://www.youtube.com/watch?v=4qwk2T8-SRA&ab_channel=amazon (January 26, 2021).

377 *The final report from the antitrust subcommittee*: House Committee on the Judiciary, "Judiciary Antitrust Subcommittee Investigation Reveals Digital Economy Highly Concentrated, Impacted by Monopoly Power," October 6, 2020, https://judiciary.house.gov/news/documentsingle.aspx?DocumentID=3429 (January 26, 2021).

377 *"Our investigation leaves no doubt"*: Ibid.

378 *eMarketer, put Amazon's share of U.S. ecommerce sales at 40 percent*: "Amazon Remains the Undisputed No. 1," *eMarket*, March 11, 2020, https://www.emarketer.com/content/amazon-remains-the-undisputed-no-1 (January 26, 2021).

378 *utter dominance in the U.S. in books and e-books*: Matt Day and Jackie Gu, "The Enormous Numbers Behind Amazon's Market Reach," *Bloomberg*, March 27, 2019, https://www.bloomberg.com/graphics/2019-amazon-reach-across-markets/?sref=dJuchiL5 (January 26, 2021).

379 *"failed to produce the financial data"*: Subcommittee on Antitrust, Commercial and Administrative Law of the Committee of the Judiciary, "Investigation of Competition in Digital Markets," October 2020, p. 318.

379 *waived a separate $15 a month charge*: "Ultrafast Grocery Delivery Is Now FREE with Prime," AboutAmazon.com, October 29, 2019, https://www.aboutamazon.com/news/retail/ultrafast-grocery-delivery-is-now-free-with-prime (January 26, 2021).

380 *competition chief Margrethe Vestager charged Amazon*: Foo Yun Chee, "Europe Charges Amazon with Using Dominance and Data to Squeeze Rivals," Reuters, November 10, 2020, https://www.reuters.com/article/eu-amazon-com-antitrust/europe-charges-amazon-with-using-its-dominance-and-data-to-squeeze-rivals-idUSKBN27Q21T (January 26, 2021).

380 *"One of the unintended consequences"*: Döpfner, "Jeff Bezos Reveals."

CHAPTER 15: PANDEMIC

384 *150 million Prime members worldwide*: Spencer Soper, "Amazon Results Show New Spending Splurge Paying Off; Shares Jump," *Bloomberg*, January 30, 2020, https://www.bloomberg.com/news/articles/2020-01-30/amazon-holiday-results-crush-wall-street-estimates-shares-surge (January 26, 2021).

386 *Amazon stopped all nonessential employee travel*: Jeffrey Dastin, "Amazon Defers 'Non-essential' Moves Even in U.S. as Corporate Travel Bans Spread," Reuters, February 28, 2020, https://www.reuters.com/article/us-china-health-amazon-com/amazon-defers-non-essential-moves-even-in-u-s-as-corporate-travel-bans-spread-idUSKCN20M2TZ (January 26, 2021).

386 *work from home for two weeks*: Taylor Soper, "Amazon Changes Coronavirus Plan, Tells Seattle Area Employees to Work from Home until March 31," *GeekWire*, March 4, 2020, https://www.geekwire.com/2020/amazon-changes-coronavirus-plan-tells-seattle-area-employees-work-home-march-31/ (January 26, 2021).

386 *for the rest of the year*: Monica Nickelsburg, "Amazon Extends Work from Home Policy to January 2021, Opens Offices with New Safety Measures," *GeekWire*,

July 15, 2020, https://www.geekwire.com/2020/amazon-extends-work-home -policy-january-2021-opens-offices-new-safety-measures/ (January 26, 2021).

386 *canceled all in-person interviews*: Roy Maurer, "Job Interviews Go Virtual in Response to COVID-19," *SHRM*, March 17, 2020, https://www.shrm.org /resourcesandtools/hr-topics/talent-acquisition/pages/job-interviews-go -virtual-response-covid-19-coronavirus.aspx (January 26, 2021).

387 *"This isn't business as usual . . . best play its role"*: Jeff Bezos, "A Message from Our CEO and Founder," Amazon, March 21, 2020, https://www.aboutamazon.com /news/company-news/a-message-from-our-ceo-and-founder (January 26, 2021).

387 *video chatting with Tedros Adhanom Ghebreyesus*: Jeff Bezos, Instagram post, March 26, 2020, https://www.instagram.com/p/B-NbzviHy5B/ (January 26, 2021).

387 *talking with Washington governor Jay Inslee*: Jeff Bezos, Instagram post, March 27, 2020, https://www.instagram.com/p/B-QSpVsHQcq/?hl=en (January 26, 2021).

387 *walking through a fulfillment center and Whole Foods*: Amazon News, Twitter video, April 8, 2020, https://twitter.com/amazonnews/status/124809282807030 1697?s=20 (January 26, 2021).

388 *30 percent of Amazon workers*: Karen Weise and Kate Conger, "Gaps in Amazon's Response as Virus Spreads to More Than 50 Warehouses," *New York Times*, April 5, 2020, https://www.nytimes.com/2020/04/05/technology/coronavirus -amazon-workers.html (January 26, 2021).

388 *fearing that they might be next*: Benjamin Romano, "Amazon Confirms COVID-Positive Employee in One of Its Seattle-Area Warehouses," *Seattle Times*, March 28, 2020, https://www.seattletimes.com/business/amazon/amazon -confirms-covid-positive-employee-in-one-of-its-seattle-area-warehouses/ (January 26, 2021).

388 *half of all Amazon deliveries globally*: Matt Day, "Amazon Is Its Own Biggest Mailman, Shipping 3.5 Billion Parcels," *Bloomberg*, December 19, 2019, https://www.bloomberg.com/news/articles/2019-12-19/amazon-is-its-own -biggest-mailman-delivering-3-5-billion-orders (January 26, 2021).

388 *two-thirds in the U.S.*: "Amazon Posts Self-Delivery Record in July, Consultancy Says," *Benzinga*, August 14, 2020, https://www.benzinga.com/news/earnings /20/08/17085321/amazon-posts-self-delivery-record-in-july-consultancy-says (January 26, 2021).

388 *make plastic face shields*: Eugene Kim, "Leaked Emails Show Amazon's Drone Delivery Team Is Manufacturing Face Shields for COVID-19 and Crowd-sourcing Employee Ideas to Improve Warehouse Safety," *Business Insider*, May 6, 2020, https://www.businessinsider.com/amazon-drone-delivery-team -is-manufacturing-covid-19-face-shields-2020-5 (January 26, 2021).

389 *millions of masks to employees and was donating N-95 masks*: "Getting Millions

of Masks to Our Employees," Amazon, April 5, 2020, https://www.aboutamazon
.com/news/company-news/getting-millions-of-masks-to-our-employees (January 26, 2021).

389 *withdrew Mother's and Father's Day promotions*: Dana Mattioli, "Amazon Retools with Unusual Goal: Get Shoppers to Buy Less Amid Coronavirus Pandemic," *Wall Street Journal*, April 16, 2020, https://www.wsj.com/articles/amazon-retools-with-unusual-goal-get-shoppers-to-buy-less-amid-coronavirus-pandemic-11587034800 (January 26, 2021).

389 *"household staples, medical supplies and other high-demand products"*: "Temporarily Prioritizing Products Coming into Our Fulfillment Centers," *Amazon Services Seller Forums*, March 2020, https://sellercentral.amazon.com/forums/t/temporarily-prioritizing-products-coming-into-our-fulfillment-centers/592213 (January 26, 2021).

389 *selling those items was a mistake*: "Investigation of Competition in Digital Markets," pg. 270, https://www.documentcloud.org/documents/7222836-Investigation-of-Competition-in-Digital-Markets.html#text/p270 (January 26, 2021); Adi Robertson and Russel Brandom, "Congress Releases Blockbuster Tech Antitrust Report," *The Verge*, October 6, 2020, https://www.theverge.com/2020/10/6/21504814/congress-antitrust-report-house-judiciary-committee-apple-google-amazon-facebook (January 26, 2021).

389 *another seventy-five thousand workers*: Dana Mattioli, "Amazon to Expand Shipments of Nonessential Items, Continue Adding Staff," *Wall Street Journal*, April 13, 2020, https://www.wsj.com/articles/amazon-seeks-to-hire-another-75-000-workers-11586789365 (January 26, 2021).

389 *Distance Assistant*: Brad Porter, "Amazon Introduces 'Distance Assistant,'" Amazon, June 16, 2020, https://www.aboutamazon.com/news/operations/amazon-introduces-distance-assistant (January 26, 2021).

390 *track the location of employees inside warehouses*: Mark Di Stefano, "Amazon Drops Pandemic Test to Track Warehouse Workers Through Wi-Fi," *The Information*, November 30, 2020, https://www.theinformation.com/articles/amazon-drops-pandemic-test-to-track-warehouse-workers-through-wi-fi (January 26, 2021).

390 *in twenty-three states*: Paris Martineau, "Amazon Quietly Expands Large-Scale Covid Testing Program for Warehouses," *The Information*, September 24, 2020, https://www.theinformation.com/articles/amazon-quietly-expands-large-scale-covid-testing-program-for-warehouses (January 26, 2021).

390 *thousands of tests a day across 650 sites*: "Update on COVID-19 Testing," Amazon, October 1, 2020, https://www.aboutamazon.com/news/operations/update-on-covid-19-testing (January 26, 2021).

391 *"injecting Amazon with a growth hormone"*: Matthew Fox, "'COVID-19 Has Been Like Injecting Amazon with a Growth Hormone': Here's What 4 Analysts Had to Say About Amazon's Earnings Report as $4,000 Price Targets Start to Roll

In," *Business Insider*, July 31, 2020, https://markets.businessinsider.com/news
/stocks/amazon-earnings-wall-street-reacts-blockbuster-report-analysts-stock
-price-2020-7-1029456482 (January 26, 2021).

392 *at least five Amazon workers in Italy and Spain*: Matt Day, Daniele Lepido,
Helen Fouquet, and Macarena Munoz Montijano, "Coronavirus Strikes at Amazon's Operational Heart: Its Delivery Machine," *Bloomberg*, March 16, 2020,
https://www.bloomberg.com/news/articles/2020-03-16/coronavirus-strikes-at
-amazon-s-operational-heart-its-delivery-machine?sref=dJuchiL5 (January 26,
2021).

392 *French FCs would stay closed for a month*: Matthew Dalton, "Amazon Shuts
French Warehouses After Court Orders Coronavirus Restrictions," *Wall
Street Journal*, April 16, 2020, https://www.wsj.com/articles/amazon-shuts
-warehouses-in-france-11587036614 (January 26, 2021); Mathieu Rosemain,
"Amazon's French Warehouses to Reopen with 30% Staff—Unions," Reuters,
May 18, 2020, https://www.reuters.com/article/health-coronavirus-amazon
-france/amazons-french-warehouses-to-reopen-with-30-staff-unions-idINK
BN22U27G?edition-redirect=in (January 26, 2021).

392 *"Amazon is gorging itself"*: Pierre-Paul Bermingham, "Amazon Under Fire in
France as Coronavirus Restrictions Hit Rivals," *Politico Europe*, November
5, 2020, https://www.politico.eu/article/spotlight-falls-on-amazon-as-french
-businesses-are-restricted-by-lockdown-rules/ (January 26, 2021).

393 *hand sanitizer dispensers were often empty*: Sam Dean, "Fearful of COVID-19,
Amazon Workers Ask for State Probe of Working Conditions," *Los Angeles Times*,
April 9, 2020, https://www.latimes.com/business/technology/story/2020-04
-09/fearful-of-covid-19-amazon-workers-ask-for-state-probe-of-working
-conditions (January 26, 2021).

393 *a single disinfectant wipe*: Sebastian Herrera, "Fired Amazon Warehouse Workers Accuse Company of Retaliation, Which It Denies," *Wall Street Journal*,
April 14, 2020, https://www.wsj.com/articles/fired-amazon-warehouse-workers
-accuse-company-of-retaliation-which-it-denies-11586891334 (January 26,
2021); Spencer Soper and Matt Day, "Amazon Drivers Received Single Wipe to
Clean Vans Before Shifts," *Bloomberg*, March 18, 2020, https://www.bloomberg
.com/news/articles/2020-03-18/amazon-drivers-received-single-wipe-to-clean
-vans-before-shifts?sref=dJuchiL5 (January 26, 2021).

394 *workers were initially told to keep only three feet apart*: Benjamin Romano, "Amazon Confirms Seattle-Area Warehouse Employee Has Coronavirus," *Seattle Times*, March 28, 2020, https://www.seattletimes.com/business
/amazon/amazon-confirms-covid-positive-employee-in-one-of-its-seattle-area
-warehouses/ (January 26, 2021).

395 *"to stand up for something that's right"*: Josh Eidelson and Luke Kawa, "Firing
of Amazon Strike Leader Draws State and City Scrutiny," *Bloomberg*, March 30,

2020, https://www.bloomberg.com/news/articles/2020-03-30/amazon-worker -who-led-strike-over-virus-says-company-fired-him (January 26, 2021; "Interview with Chris Smalls," Emily Chang, Bloomberg TV, March 30, 2020, https:// www.bloomberg.com/news/videos/2020-03-30/striking-amazon-employee -accuses-company-of-retaliation-video (February 28, 2021).

395 *Compounding the unfolding public relations problem*: Paul Blest, "Leaked Amazon Memo Details Plan to Smear Fired Warehouse Organizer: 'He's Not Smart or Articulate,'" *Vice News*, April 2, 2020, https://www.vice.com/en/article/5dm8bx /leaked-amazon-memo-details-plan-to-smear-fired-warehouse-organizer -hes-not-smart-or-articulate, (February 28, 2020).

396 *Amazon job listings for intelligence analysts*: Hayley Peterson, "Amazon-Owned Whole Foods Is Quietly Tracking Its Employees with a Heat Map Tool That Ranks Which Stores Are Most At Risk of Unionizing," *Business Insider*, April 20, 2020, https://www.businessinsider.com/whole-foods-tracks -unionization-risk-with-heat-map-2020-1?r=US&IR=T (January 26, 2021); Nick Statt, "Amazon Deletes Job Listings Detailing Effort to Monitor 'Labor Organizing Threats,'" *The Verge*, September 1, 2020, https://www.theverge .com/2020/9/1/21417401/amazon-job-listing-delete-labor-organizing-threat -union (January 26, 2021).

397 *Jumpp gave an interview to CBS's* 60 Minutes: "Amazon worker: At least 600 Amazon employees stricken by coronavirus," CBS, May 10, 2020, https://www .cbsnews.com/news/amazon-workers-with-coronavirus-60-minutes-2020-05 -10/ (February 16, 2021).

397 *around twenty thousand*: Amazon's "Update on COVID-19 Testing."

397 *Amazon also dismissed Katie Doan, a Whole Foods employee*: Lauren Kaori Gurley, "Whole Foods Just Fired an Employee Who Kept Track of Corona Virus Cases," *Motherboard*, March 29, 2020, https://www.vice.com/en/article /y3zd9g/whole-foods-just-fired-an-employee-who-kept-track-of-coronavirus -cases (February 28, 2021).

397 *Bashir Mohamed, a Somali FC worker*: Sarah Ashley O'Brien, "Fear and a firing inside an Amazon warehouse," CNN, April 22, 2020, https://www .cnn.com/2020/04/22/tech/amazon-warehouse-bashir-mohamed/index.html (February 28, 2021).

397 *Courtney Bowden, a Pennsylvania worker*: Caroline O'Donovan, "This Fired Worker Says Amazon Retaliated Against Her. Now the Company is Facing Charges," *BuzzFeed News*, December 4, 2020, https://www.buzzfeednews.com /article/carolineodonovan/amazon-worker-retaliation-coronavirus (February 16, 2021).

397 *not a single competitor had released similar data*: Amazon's "Update on COVID-19 Testing."

398 *"Firing whistleblowers . . . drink that poison"*: Tim Bray, "Bye, Amazon," Ongoing

by Tim Bray, April 29, 2020, https://www.tbray.org/ongoing/When/202x/2020/04/29/Leaving-Amazon (January 26, 2021).

399 *Brad Porter*: Brad Porter, "Response to Tim Bray's Departure . . ." LinkedIn, May 5, 2020, https://www.linkedin.com/pulse/response-tim-brays-departure-brad-porter/ (January 26, 2021).

401 *Its most profitable year ever*: Spencer Soper, "Amazon Projects Revenue Signaling Strong E-Commerce Demand," *Bloomberg*, February 2, 2021, https://www.bloomberg.com/news/articles/2021-02-02/amazon-projects-revenue-signaling-strong-e-commerce-demand (February 28, 2021).

401 *Amazon employed one million full . . . for the first time*: Karen Weis, "Pushed by Pandemic, Amazon Goes on a Hiring Spree Without Equal," *New York Times*, November 27, 2020, https://www.nytimes.com/2020/11/27/technology/pushed-by-pandemic-amazon-goes-on-a-hiring-spree-without-equal.html (February 28, 2021).

402 *"Jeff's legacy . . . unrecognizable"*: Annie Palmer, "Jeff Wilke, Amazon's Consumer Boss and a Top Lieutenant to Bezos, Will Step Down in 2021," CNBC, August 21, 2020, https://www.cnbc.com/2020/08/21/amazons-consumer-boss-jeff-wilke-to-step-down-in-2021.html (January 26, 2021).

402 *Clark would write a letter . . . of Joe Biden*: Annie Palmer, "Read the full letter Amazon sent to Biden offering to help with Covid-19 vaccines," CNBC, January 20, 2021, https://www.cnbc.com/2021/01/20/amazon-sends-letter-to-biden-offering-to-help-with-covid-19-vaccines.html (February 28, 2021).

402 *Christine Beauchamp . . . Colleen Aubrey . . . Alicia Boler Davis from operations*: Jason Del Ray, "Jeff Bezos finally added 2 more women to Amazon's senior leadership team—joining 19 men," *Recode*, December 5, 2019, https://www.vox.com/recode/2019/12/5/20998013/amazon-s-team-leadership-women-jeff-bezos-tech-diversity (February 28, 2021); Taylor Soper, "Here are the three Amazon execs who just joined Jeff Bezos' elite 'S-team' leadership suite," *GeekWire*, August 21, 2020, https://www.geekwire.com/2020/three-amazon-execs-just-joined-jeff-bezos-elite-s-team-leadership-suite/ (February 28, 2021).

402 *MacKenzie Scott surprised the world*: Sophie Alexander and Ben Steverman, "MacKenzie Scott's Remarkable Giveaway Is Transforming the Bezos Fortune," *Bloomberg*, February 11, 2021, https://www.bloomberg.com/features/2021-bezos-scott-philanthropy (Feburary 28, 2021).

403 *"We will not tiptoe . . . climate change in the world"*: Nick Tilsen, "Shifting Power and Emboldening Indigenous-Led Climate Solutions: NDN Collective on Bezos Earth Fund Grant," NDN Collective, November 25, 2020, https://ndncollective.org/shifting-power-and-emboldening-indigenous-led-climate-solutions-ndn-collective-on-bezos-earth-fund-grant/ (January 26, 2021).

404 *Amazon Care*: Blake Dodge, "Amazon Wants to Provide Medical Care to Workers at Major Companies. Here's an Inside Look at Amazon Care," *Business In-*

sider, December 16, 2020, https://www.businessinsider.com/inside-amazon
-care-telehealth-employers-2020-12 (January 26, 2021).

405 *his job as CEO*: "Amazon.com Announces Financial Results and CEO Transition," Amazon, February 2, 2021, https://ir.aboutamazon.com/news-release
/news-release-details/2021/Amazon.com-Announces-Fourth-Quarter-Results
(February 17, 2021)

406 *Bezos wrote in an email to employees*: "Email from Jeff Bezos to Employees,"
Amazon.com, February 2, 2021, https://www.aboutamazon.com/news/company
-news/email-from-jeff-bezos-to-employees (March 10, 2021).

409 *"Out of this World," was the theme of the party*: Nick Maslow, "Lauren Sanchez
Plans Party Celebrating Billionaire Boyfriend Jeff Bezos' Space Flight, Source
Says," *People*, August 6, 2021. https://people.com/human-interest/lauren-san-
chez-throwing-jeff-bezos-party-to-celebrate-space-flight/ (December 5, 2021).

410 https://twitter.com/RepAdamSchiff/status/1417639459647115266

410 *"He looks like a mash-up" ... "douse Neil Armstrong with Gatorade"*: Katie Shep-
erd, "Late-night hosts mock Jeff Bezos's space 'joyride': He celebrated 'like it
was the end of a yacht race'," *The Washington Post*, July 21, 2021. https://www.
washingtonpost.com/nation/2021/07/21/stephen-colbert-bezos-space-cowboy/
(December 5, 2021).

413 *He gave $200 million to the Smithsonian's National Air and Space Museum*: Gra-
ham Bowley, "Jeff Bezos Gives $200 Million to National Air and Space Museum,"
The New York Times, July 14, 2021, https://www.nytimes.com/2021/07/14/arts/
design/jeff-bezos-200-million-national-air-and-space-museum.html (December 5, 2021).

413 *In September, he donated another billion to the Bezos Earth Fund*: Katherine
Anne Long, "Bezos pledges to spend $1B on conservation efforts in the Congo,
the Andes and the tropical Pacific Ocean", *The Seattle Times*, September 20, 2021,
https://www.seattletimes.com/business/amazon/bezos-pledges-to-spend-1b-on-
conservation-efforts-in-the-congo-the-andes-and-the-tropical-pacific-ocean/
(December 5, 2021)

413 "President Obama is strongly supportive of unions", Nicholas Kulish, "Jeff Bezos
gives $100 million to the Obama Foundation", *The New York Times*, November
22, 2021, https://www.nytimes.com/2021/11/22/business/bezos-obama-foun-
dation.html (December 5, 2021)

414 "In this effort, we are governed by a humbling belief . . .", MacKenzie Scott, "Seeding by Ceding", *Medium*, June 15, 2021, https://mackenzie-scott.medium.com/
seeding-by-ceding-ea6de642bf (December 5, 2021)

415 *In April, he paid $23 million to add a fourth condo . . .*, Avery Hartmans, "Jeff
Bezos reportedly now owns $119 million worth of real estate in a single building in
New York City", *Insider*, August 18, 2021, https://www.businessinsider.com/jeff-
bezos-buys-fifth-nyc-condo-212-fifth-avenue-report-2021-8 (December 5, 2021)

415 *In November, the couple paid $78 million for a 14-acre estate on the south shore of the Hawaiian island of Maui*, Mary K. Jacob, "As Jeff Bezos buys up Maui, Hawaiian locals hope for the best", *The New York Post*, November 4, 2021, https://nypost.com/2021/11/04/as-jeff-bezos-buys-up-maui-hawaiian-locals-hope-for-best/ (December 5, 2021).

415 https://twitter.com/elonmusk/status/1402689914836197376?lang=en

416 *"As Exec Chair I will stay engaged in important Amazon initiatives"*, Jeff Bezos, "Email from Jeff Bezos to employees", AboutAmazon.com, February 2, 2021, https://www.aboutamazon.com/news/company-news/email-from-jeff-bezos-to-employees (December 5, 2021).

417 *Amazon added to its sacred list of 14 leadership principles two new entries*, Taylor Soper, *"Amazon adds two new leadership principles just days before Jeff Bezos steps down as CEO"*, Geekwire, July 1, 2021, https://www.geekwire.com/2021/amazon-adds-two-new-leadership-principles-just-days-jeff-bezos-steps-ceo/ (December 5, 2021).

417 *They lived in a 10,000 square foot home*, Matt Day, *"Absolutely a Sprint': How Andy Jassy Raced to the Top of Amazon"*, July 2, 2021, *Bloomberg News*, https://www.bloomberg.com/news/articles/2021-07-02/after-bezos-new-ceo-inherits-amazon-on-a-roll-but-roiled-by-labor-unrest (December 5, 2021).

418 *The company had gone on a spending spree, doubling the size of its warehouse network . . .*, Sebastian Herrera, "Amazon Builds Out Network to Speed Delivery, Handle Holiday Crunch", The Wall Street Journal, November 29, 2021, https://www.wsj.com/articles/amazon-builds-out-network-to-speed-delivery-handle-holiday-crunch-11638181801 (December 5, 2021).

Index

About the Author

Brad Stone is senior executive editor of global technology at *Bloomberg News* and the author of the *New York Times* bestseller *The Everything Store: Jeff Bezos and the Age of Amazon*, and *The Upstarts: Uber, Airbnb, and the Battle for the New Silicon Valley*. He has covered Silicon Valley for more than twenty years and lives in the San Francisco Bay area.